Irony's Antics

Irony's Antics

Walser, Kafka, Roth, and the German Comic Tradition

✦

Erica Weitzman

NORTHWESTERN UNIVERSITY PRESS
EVANSTON, ILLINOIS

Northwestern University Press
www.nupress.northwestern.edu

Printed in the United States of America

10 9 8 7 6 5 4 3 2 1

ISBN 978-0-8101-3360-0

The Library of Congress has cataloged the original, hardcover edition as follows:

Weitzman, Erica, author.
Irony's antics : Walser, Kafka, Roth, and the German comic tradition / Erica Weitzman.
pages cm
Includes bibliographical references and index.
ISBN 978-0-8101-2983-2 (cloth : alk. paper)
1. German literature—20th century—History and criticism. 2. Walser, Robert, 1878–1956—Criticism and interpretation. 3. Kafka, Franz, 1883–1924—Criticism and interpretation. 4. Roth, Joseph, 1894–1939—Criticism and interpretation. 5. Irony in literature. 6. Comic, The, in literature. I. Title.
PT405.W35316 2014
830.9180904—dc23

2014005099

CONTENTS

ACKNOWLEDGMENTS

It is an irony of authorship that only the person whose name is printed on a book's cover truly knows how much others have had a hand in its making. I would first of all like to thank all those in the Departments of Comparative Literature and German at New York University whose guidance and encouragement has made this work possible. I am particularly indebted to Anselm Haverkamp for being an unfailing source of support, inspiration, and productive challenges over the years, and to Avital Ronell for her generosity as much as for her setting the example of a scholarship as rigorous as it is tonic. Paul Fleming not only provided invaluable suggestions throughout the writing of this book, but also helped with his own research to lay its foundations. Eckart Goebel and Jacques Lezra lent their talent, dedication, and unflagging enthusiasm to the project during its progress. I would also like to extend my thanks to Emily Apter, Jay Bernstein, Eliot Borenstein, Simon Critchley, Patrick Deer, Peter Goodrich, Werner Hamacher, John Hamilton, Martin Harries, Mikhail Iampolski, Jacques le Rider, Christoph Menke, Gerhard Neumann, Nancy Ruttenburg, Mark Sanders, Richard Sieburth, Elke Siegel, and Joseph Vogl, all of whom offered ideas, assistance, and advice at crucial junctures. Albrecht Koschorke and Juliane Vogel at the Universität Konstanz helped to provide a home base and a community of interlocutors during the final phases of this book's preparation.

The writing of this book was facilitated by a stipend from the Deutsche Forschungsgemeinschaft (German Research Foundation), which allowed me to spend three years as a doctoral fellow with the Graduiertenkolleg "Lebensformen und Lebenswissen" at the Europa-Universität Viadrina, Frankfurt (Oder) and the Universität Potsdam.

An especial debt of gratitude is owed to Henry Carrigan at Northwestern University Press for believing in this project from its early stages, and to Nathan MacBrien for seeing it through to its completion. I am also obliged to the two anonymous readers of the manuscript for their attentive readings and comments.

A section of chapter 3 of this book has appeared in modified form under the title "Almost Necessary: Kafka's Kantian Situation Comedy," *MLN* 126, no. 3 (April 2011). A section of chapter 4 has been published in modified form in German translation under the title "Momentausnahmen: Joseph Roths 'dokumentarische Komik,' " in *Joseph Roth als Stilist: Annäherung durch Theorie und Übersetzung* (Heidelberg: Winter 2013), edited by Nora Hoffmann and

Natalia Shchyhlevska of Johannes Guttenberg-Universität Mainz, who also organized the corresponding workshop. This book has additionally benefited from my being able to present other sections at conferences at the Katholieke Universiteit Leuven, the University of Virginia, and the City University of New York. My thanks also go to Susan Bernofsky and the editors at New Directions for allowing me to republish her translation of Walser's microscript "Usually I first put on a prose piece jacket," a feat of poetic transmogrification which I would not gladly have dared to attempt to outdo.

Finally, this book could never have been written without the care and support of my friends and colleagues, both within and outside the academy. I particularly would like to thank Yael Almog, Sage Anderson, Magali Armillas-Tiseyra, David Auerbach, Siarhei Biareishyk, Elizabeth Bonapfel, Jeffrey Champlin, Amy Cimini, Michael Gallope, Micaela Kramer, Julia Ng, Katharina Piechocki, William Rauscher, Suzanne Scala, Chadwick Smith, Phillip Usher, Alejandra Uslenghi, and my colleagues in "Lebensformen und Lebenswissen" for having all amply furnished the proof, many times over, that friendship is indeed as fun as it is serious. And most of all, I want to thank Thomas Dikant—for being almost always willing to read my drafts, for being there, and for helping me to laugh.

ABBREVIATIONS

Works cited frequently in the text and notes are referred to using the following abbreviations:

A	Hegel, G. W. F. *Hegel's Aesthetics: Lectures on Fine Art,* vols. 1 and 2. Translated by T. M. Knox. Oxford: Oxford University Press, 1975.
AI	Hegel, G. W. F. *Vorlesungen über die Ästhetik I.* Edited by Eva Moldenhauer and Karl Markus Michel. Frankfurt am Main: Suhrkamp, 1970.
AII	Hegel, G. W. F. *Vorlesungen über die Ästhetik II.* Edited by Eva Moldenhauer and Karl Markus Michel. Frankfurt am Main: Suhrkamp, 1970.
AIII	Hegel, G. W. F. *Vorlesungen über die Ästhetik III.* Edited by Eva Moldenhauer and Karl Markus Michel. Frankfurt am Main: Suhrkamp, 1970.
AB1	Walser, Robert. *Aus dem Bleistiftgebiet,* vol. 1: *Mikrogramme aus den Jahren 1924–1925.* Edited by Bernhard Echte and Werner Morlang. Frankfurt am Main: Suhrkamp, 1985.
ANTH	Kant, Immanuel. *Anthropology from a Pragmatic Point of View.* Translated by Robert B. Louden. Cambridge, Eng.: Cambridge University Press, 2006; *Anthropologie in pragmatischer Hinsicht.* Hamburg: Meiner, 2000.
CI	Kierkegaard, Søren. *The Concept of Irony, with Continual Reference to Socrates.* Translated by Howard V. Hong and Edna H. Hong. Princeton, N.J.: Princeton University Press, 1989.
CPJ	Kant, Immanuel. *Critique of the Power of Judgment.* Translated by Paul Guyer and Eric Matthews. Cambridge, Eng.: Cambridge University Press; *Kritik der Urteilskraft.* Hamburg: Meiner, 2006.
CPR	Kant, Immanuel. *Critique of Pure Reason.* Translated by J. M. D. Meiklejohn. Amherst, N.Y.: Prometheus, 1990; *Kritik der reinen Vernunft.* Hamburg: Meiner, 1998.
DL	Kafka, Franz. *Drucke zu Lebzeiten.* In *Kritische Ausgabe,* edited by Wolf Kittler, Hans-Gerd Koch, and Gerhard Neumann. Frankfurt am Main: Fischer, 2002.

F Schlegel, Friedrich. *Fragments*. In *Friedrich Schlegel's* Lucinde *and the Fragments,* translated by Peter Firchow, 143–240. Minneapolis: University of Minnesota Press, 1971; *Fragmente*. In *Kritische Friedrich-Schlegel-Ausgabe,* vol. 2: *Charakteristiken und Kritiken I (1796–1801),* edited by Hans Eichner, 147–272. Munich: Schöningh, 1967.

FKA Walser, Robert. *Fritz Kochers Aufsätze*. In *Das Gesamtwerk,* vol. 1, edited by Jochen Greven, 7–48. Geneva: Kossodo, 1972.

HDE Preisendanz, Wolfgang. *Humor als dichterische Einbildungskraft: Studien zur Erzählkunst des poetischen Realismus*. Munich: Eidos, 1963.

JRU Freud, Sigmund. *Jokes and Their Relation to the Unconscious*. In *The Standard Edition of the Complete Psychological Works of Sigmund Freud,* vol. 8, translated by James Strachey. London: Hogarth, 1960; *Der Witz und seine Beziehung zum Unbewussten*. In *Gesammelte Werke,* vol. 6, edited by Anna Freud. London: Imago, 1940.

JRW1 Roth, Joseph. *Werke 1. Das journalistische Werk 1915–1923*. Edited by Klaus Westermann. Cologne: Kiepenheuer & Witsch, 1989.

JRW2 Roth, Joseph. *Werke 2. Das journalistische Werk 1924–1928*. Edited by Klaus Westermann. Cologne: Kiepenheuer & Witsch, 1990.

JRW3 Roth, Joseph. *Werke 3. Das journalistische Werk 1929–1939*. Edited by Klaus Westermann. Cologne: Kiepenheuer & Witsch, 1991.

JRW4 Roth, Joseph. *Werke 4. Romane und Erzählungen 1916–1929*. Edited by Fritz Hackert. Cologne: Kiepenheuer & Witsch, 1989.

JRW5 Roth, Joseph. *Werke 5. Romane und Erzählungen 1930–1936*. Edited by Fritz Hackert. Cologne: Kiepenheuer & Witsch, 1990.

OI Schlegel, Friedrich. "On Incomprehensibility." In *Friedrich Schlegel's* Lucinde *and the Fragments,* translated by Peter Firchow, 257–71. Minneapolis: University of Minnesota Press, 1971; "Über die Unverständlichkeit." In *Kritische Friedrich-Schlegel-Ausgabe,* vol. 2: *Charakteristiken und Kritiken I (1796–1801),* edited by Hans Eichner, 363–72. Munich: Schöningh, 1967.

PR Hegel, G. W. F. *Elements of the Philosophy of Right*. Translated by Allen W. Wood. Cambridge, Eng.: Cambridge University Press, 1991; *Grundlinien der Philosophie des Rechts*. Edited by Eva Moldenhauer and Karl Markus Michel. Frankfurt am Main: Suhrkamp, 1970.

PS	Hegel, G. W. F. *The Phenomenology of Spirit.* Translated by A. V. Miller. Oxford: Oxford University Press, 1977; *Phänomenologie des Geistes.* Edited by Eva Moldenhauer and Karl Markus Michel. Frankfurt am Main: Suhrkamp, 1970.
T	Kafka, Franz. *Tagebücher.* In *Kritischer Ausgabe,* edited by Hans-Gerd Koch, Michael Müller, and Malcolm Pasley. Frankfurt am Main: Fischer, 2002.
UEK	Vischer, Friedrich Theodor. *Über das Erhabene und Komische.* Frankfurt am Main: Suhrkamp, 1967.
V	Kafka, Franz. *Der Verschollene.* In *Kritische Ausgabe,* edited by Jost Schillemeit. Frankfurt am Main: Fischer, 2002.
VA	Richter, Jean Paul. *Horn of Oberon: Jean Paul Richter's* School for Aesthetics. Translated by Margaret R. Hale. Detroit: Wayne State University Press, 1973; *Vorschule der Ästhetik.* Edited by Wolfhart Henckmann. Hamburg: Meiner, 1990.

All translations are my own unless otherwise noted. Where existing translations are cited alongside the original version, page numbers are separated by a semicolon and refer to the English and original-language texts, respectively.

Irony's Antics

Introduction

✦

The Comic Ethos

> Laughter in philosophy hasn't exactly been common in the European tradition, indeed precisely for philosophical reasons.
>
> —Hans Blumenberg, "Der Sturz des Protophilosophen"

> Wit's dignity humanity's charter.
>
> —Friedrich Schlegel, *Philosophical Fragments*

World Irony

In his 1921 short essay "The Irony of Things" (the first section of the three-part "Three Small Observations") Hugo von Hofmannsthal leaves no doubt: the era is one of irony.[1] More, even, the era is one of irony become *comic,* of an all-encompassing world-irony for which laughter is the only possible logical conclusion and appropriate ethical response. Glossing the spurious aphorism of Novalis (in fact an aphorism of Hofmannsthal's own making),[2] "After an unsuccessful war, comedies should be written [Nach einem unglücklichen Krieg müssen Komödien geschrieben werden]," Hofmannsthal comments, "Comedy's proper element is irony, and in fact, nothing is better suited to make the irony that rules over all the things of this world clear to us than a war that turns out badly" (40). In the same way that the joke was for Jean Paul a little over a century earlier, irony, for Hofmannsthal, is first and foremost a question of relation;[3] more precisely, "true comedy"—in contrast to both the solemnity of tragedy and the normative structures of bourgeois drama—"places its individuals in a thousand-times entwined relation to the world; it puts everything in relation to everything and thereby everything in a relation of irony" (40). Just as the traditional farce is a matter of destinies and understandings at cross-purposes, and just as wit has been famously defined as a matter of "similarities among dissimilar things [Ähnlichkeiten unter ungleichartigen Dingen]" (*ANTH* §55, 116; 130), here juxtaposition with the non-identical suffices to throw phenomena into an ironic, that is, an inherently non-identical light. The fact that something could be other—or thought otherwise—makes it already within itself not quite itself, a fundamental comedy of categorization that reigns throughout the world.

Hofmannsthal's description of comical irony thus recalls Schopenhauer's theory of the laughable (*das Lächerliche*) set down almost a century previous in *The World as Will and Representation,* which explains the source of laughter in typically post-Kantian terms as a contrast between concept and reality, ideal and real, will and representation.[4] However, Hofmannsthal's account differs from the philosopher's theories in one small but crucial point, thus signaling a change, if not in irony per se, then at least in the imagination of irony, as well as its relative position vis-à-vis the comic, in the post-fin-de-siècle, postwar age. In Schopenhauer's conception—which is indeed less irony than a kind of metaphysical satire—the ideal is effectively negated by the real (and vice versa), thus producing a laughter of philosophical contempt that in fact has its source in an unacknowledged but implicit higher ideal: namely, the *anti-ironic* ideal of the principle of *non*-contradiction. In contrast, the "mutual irony [wechselseitige Ironie]" (42) of Hofmannsthal's conception compares real with real with real in a chain of ironies *without* higher principle, with the ultimate result of bringing everything to a state of permanent incommensurability and instability. Hofmannsthal's examples are contemporary and concrete: the notion of the hero ("he who would stand up and attack") is ironized by the trench soldier ("who had a shovel and dug himself in"); the sovereign subject is ironized by the masses; the organized group is ironized by the formless mob, which is in turn ironized by the masses militant; these are ironized by nationalist emotions which are ironized by whoever momentarily steps forward to lead the nascent nation; the nation-state is ironized by the idea of class struggle, the notion of class struggle is ironized by the actual working conditions of the triumphant proletariat, and so on and so forth until all history is caught up in an ironic chain without end or point of reference (41). Yet Hofmannsthal reminds us too of the perennial ironizations effected by the conditions of the ontological itself, by the facts of physical materiality and concrete need, by the contingency of events, by the supposedly autonomous subject made a tool of the objects that he handles. And perhaps foremost in Hofmannsthal's catalog of irony—a practical and basically unironic list that ironically ironizes Schlegel's ironic taxonomy in his seminal essay "Über die Unverständlichkeit" ("On Incomprehensibility")[5]—stands the epistemological ur-irony of the "thousands of details based in reality against the premature and consciously untrue synthesis" (42). Whereas Schopenhauer derives laughter from a caustic mockery of the *lack* of synthesis—be that lack itself ever so real—for Hofmannsthal it is synthesis *itself* that is the highest irony of all, as something that attempts to end or even pause the unending ironies that the circumstances of the contemporary world only serve to consistently highlight. Thus "we find ourselves thoroughly within the element of comedy—or rather within an element of an all-around irony such as no comedy in the world possesses" (43). Comedy emerges as a product or mode of irony when the volatility of all contexts pulls on the tragic-heroic paradigm "like the rays of sun on a snowman" (40),[6] paradoxically, at a point in time where there is no longer any stable place in the world from which to laugh.

Hofmannsthal ends his remarks on contemporary society with a brief analysis of the previous great age of irony, the age of romanticism. If irony after the First World War is the inescapable form of all relation, the very element, as it were, in which the world exists and moves, the poets of the romantic era—which Hofmannsthal repeatedly and explicitly characterizes as a similar age of war and its aftereffects—consciously undertook to make the irony they experienced into "a fundamental element of their attitude to life and art [ein Grundelement ihrer Lebens- und Kunstgesinnung]" (Hofmannsthal 43), thereby to turn it into a potential medium of freedom and individual transcendence. In this assessment, however, Hofmannsthal shows that despite all his canny appreciation for his own times, he nevertheless remains to a large degree a child of an earlier era. Given the implacability of his preceding paragraphs, the conclusion to Hofmannsthal's text is of a surprising sentimentality, ending in swelling cadences with a humanist *détournement* of a verse from the Luther Bible's translation of Second Corinthians: "Now the Lord is the Spirit: but where the Spirit is Lord, there is liberty [Denn der Herr ist der Geist. Wo aber der Geist der Herr ist, da ist die Freiheit]" (Hofmannsthal 44).[7] This enthusiastic valuation of—a no longer, or rather not yet, comic—romantic irony as that which unleashes imagination and the freedom of the spirit in defiance of empirical reality, rationalist dogma, and Lutheran anti-humanism alike, although perhaps in line with certain aspects of the romantics' own conception of their project,[8] ignores the ironies inherent to *it*. Hofmannsthal's plea for a life of ironic (self-)creation sets up the human subject alone of all things as the disposer of a domesticated and utilizable irony, the stable and ultimately non-ironic core of a world of infinite possibility. He thus posits irony as exactly what it never was: a way out of itself. In so doing, Hofmannsthal's investigation not only falls short of later critiques of romantic irony such as that of Kierkegaard, who observes that at a certain point in its development, "irony is no longer directed against this or that particular phenomenon, against a particular existing thing, but [. . .] the whole of existence has become alien to the ironic subject and the ironic subject in turn alien to existence, [. . .] as actuality has lost its validity for the ironic subject, he himself has to a certain degree become unactual" (*CI* 259), it also falls short of the understanding of romantic irony's earliest practitioners: not only the Hofmannsthal-commandeered Novalis but especially Friedrich Schlegel, who, speaking from the point of view of a post-*Athenäum* hindsight, wryly admits that in his project for creating a new kind of total ironic readership, "I meant it seriously enough and not without some of the old penchant for mysticism" (*OI* 260, translation modified; 363–364).[9]

Hofmannsthal's triumphal ending is all the more surprising because it actually forgets the insight with which the essay itself begins, namely the no longer able to be ignored connection between irony and the comic. Indeed, it is precisely the critique of romantic irony that returns irony to the comic, and the comic to irony: not because irony is some kind of laughable error, but because it must become irony to the ironic degree, the irony of irony itself, deprived of mystical tendencies and dialectical horizons. These mystical tendencies and dialectical horizons are of course intrinsic to the history of irony, and irony is not thinkable without them. However, as products of the very irony they would do away with, at a certain historical moment they lose both their currency and their credibility, possibly for good. Then a denuded irony comes out into the open, not just as the occasional enabler of subjective freedom but as the knowing performance of the contingency of all relation. And this coming out into the open of irony not only *can only be* comic, it *is* the comic.

The Turning Point of the Joke

Though Hofmannsthal focuses primarily on the situation after (the) war, the form of comedy towards which his essay gestures is already in development well before the catastrophic collapse of the European balance of powers. In his "joke book" of 1905, *Jokes and Their Relation to the Unconscious,* Sigmund Freud revisits the strangely canonical (since at least Aristotle) and yet perpetually marginal (since Aristotle's qualified depreciation) theme of laughter and the comic. Freud's aim in this book, of course, is less to elaborate a new theory of the comic than to use the joke as further evidence for the validity of his new science of psychoanalysis. Like dreams and slips of the tongue (the respective subjects of Freud's two previous major works), the joke's seeming negligibility makes it an apt object for corroborating the truth of the psychoanalytic method, one of whose main principles is the hidden centrality of the apparently marginal. Reciprocally, psychoanalysis seems to present a particularly fitting methodology for an examination of the comic, which not only has traditionally been considered a "lower" form than that of more "serious" modes of representation, but is also often assumed to inhere precisely *in* the contrast between lowness and sublimity, triviality and matters of consequence. Thus, as with the other apparent cast-offs of experience granted new dignity within the psychoanalytic repertoire, Freud's examination of the apparently negligible subject of the joke—in a way similar to that of Hofmannsthal's essay—refigures the conception of the comic from the exception to the rule. At the same time, Freud's focus on the joke folds within the comic the question of representation and of language that is inseparable from any discussion of irony, be it in its early career as rhetorical figure or in its later expansion as epistemological-ontological inevitability. And perhaps most significantly of all, the analysis of the joke returns the "concept" of irony[10] to the domain of the comic, forcing a reconsideration of the definitions as well as the implications of both.

Jokes, of course, are not quite the same thing as comedy or the comic, and indeed are so specific and generically constrained that it hardly seems justified to make any great claims for them at all. Nevertheless, jokes have a tendency to make themselves heard in every discussion on the comic (often literally, in their retelling), serving as a kind of controlled testing situation for what the comic is and how it functions. The comic is not reducible to jokes, but jokes are the comic genre par excellence; the achieving of comic effect is their raison d'être and only explicit claim. Nevertheless, Freud himself appears to reject a direct correlation between jokes and the comic as he understands both categories. It is impossible not to hear the circumspection—familiar to anyone acquainted with Freud's rhetoric of scientific scrupulousness—in the subjunctive of the sentence on the first page of the book's introduction: "The first impression one derives from the literature is that it is quite impracticable to deal with jokes otherwise than in connection with the comic [Man gewinnt aus der Literatur zunächst den Eindruck, als sei es völlig untunlich, den Witz anders als in Zusammenhange mit dem Komischen zu behandeln]" (*JRU* 9; 5). Indeed, by the third page of his introduction, Freud will have already called this initial assumption into question, designating the joke alone as the specific—and alone psychoanalytically relevant—object of his study. Yet not only does the question of the comic remain throughout Freud's examination, even reappearing in a later chapter, but also Freud's theory of what he terms "joke-work [Witzarbeit]" (in direct analogy to his idea of "Traumarbeit" formulated a mere four years earlier) cannot fail to redound to—and act upon—the history of comic theory up to his time, and Freud's rejection of the relationship between jokes and the comic will turn out to be less an advance in terminological precision than an early signal of what may be termed an epochal shift, a turn to a new *ethos of the comic* that simultaneously turns the comic along with it.

In initially setting apart the joke and the comic, Freud is, as so often (and like Hofmannsthal), clearly influenced by Schopenhauer, who posits the binary wit/folly (*Witz/Narrheit*) as the main division within the field of the laughable.[11] Schopenhauer's description of *Narrheit* in fact bears similarities to Bergson's later influential theory of laughter in his essay of the same name,[12] an essay which Freud explicitly references as the model of what he, for his part, terms "the comic [das Komische]" (see *JRU* 208–9 and 222–23; 238–39 and 253–54). Freud himself, meanwhile, clearly takes from Schopenhauer—here unacknowledged—the notion of "double entendre [Zweideutigkeit]" (on which more below), as well as an emphasis on the obscene joke and the question of intention.[13] But unlike Schopenhauer, whose fairly neutral classification ultimately holds *Witz* and *Narrheit* to be merely two complimentary modes of the same faulty conjunction of concept and object, Freud wants to prove that the joke, in contrast to comic "foolishness," bears within it a qualitatively different, repressed and decipherable, "serious" significance corresponding precisely to the significance of the dream in *The Interpretation of Dreams*. As a mini-narrative meant above all to be *told*, the joke functions vis-à-vis instances of social repression—the sexual, racial, and moral taboos of polite society—in the same way that the essentially private medium of the dream functions vis-à-vis instances of personal repressions, desires, and traumata, and the telling of a joke involves a triangulation of repression/narrator/listener in a way precisely analogous to the triangulation repression/analysand/analyst of clinical psychoanalysis. Thus, whereas the comic is located merely in the preconscious of childish pleasure and play, in the polymorphous perversity of nonsense, the joke is situated in the "intellectual sources" (*JRU* 208; 237) of the Oedipal subject; it is a psychic repression-machine that can also be made to work the other way, revealing to analysis the unconscious sources of the laughter that is its primary symptom.[14]

But though Freud insists that "in most cases [. . .] a clear distinction is to be made between jokes and the comic" (*JRU* 207; 236), more often than not he himself blurs the boundary between the two. Really or seemingly in debt to his predecessors in the field of comic studies (in particular Kant, Jean Paul, and Bergson), Freud usually appears to consider those forms of the comic that are not jokes proper either naive and unwilled versions of jokes, stagings of the joke in expanded form, or particularly apt metaphors, in that sense of *Witz* that in English can be separated out through the word "wit." The moral of Freud's own story, in any case, remains the one he formulates at the end of the section, emphasized in spaced type: "*the joke is, so to speak, the contribution made to the comic from the realm of the unconscious* [*der Witz ist sozusagen der Beitrag zur Komik aus dem Bereich des Unbewußten*]" (*JRU* 208, translation modified; 237). Freud's metaphor here is, *so to speak*, itself a witty one, evoking an image of what the book indeed already performs: the unconscious—or perhaps its envoy psychoanalysis—offers to the comic the gift of the joke as both token of esteem and proprietorial act, as the sovereign of a land rich in gold might present a ring to the neighboring monarch. Yet this schema, however well it may encapsulate what Freud intended with his book, does not in fact hold up in terms of Freud's own theories. For if the joke is a comic manifestation of the unconscious, or rather a manifestation of the workings of the unconscious through comic methods, then the joke would in fact be the contribution to the *unconscious* out of the realm of the *comic*. But even this does not make much sense, given that for Freud, there can hardly be an aspect of psychic or cultural life—and that includes the comic—in which the unconscious did *not* have a role, indeed of which it was not the very origin and basis.[15] The argument is ultimately a circular one: for if, as Freud elsewhere claims, "one of the functions of jokes is to make hidden sources of pleasure accessible once more" (*JRU* 202; 230), then the comic affect to which the joke supposedly "contributes" comes from nothing less than the not yet accessible "sources of pleasure" of the comic itself. It is not the case, in other words, that comic pleasure allows the ordinarily repressed themes of the joke to find expression by "bribing" the listener's inner censor into quiescence (see *JRU* 103; 113); rather, the *joke* is an expression of the repression of the *comic*, in which repression does not lead to the comic's disappearance but, much like the dream, to its reappearance in altered form.[16] The conclusion to be drawn from this is less that Freud is in error with his classificatory system than that the joke, in its capacity as both verbal act and model for the unconscious, also highlights what is actually at stake in the comic for the subject and its knowledge, beyond the guilty pleasures of social transgression or the mere derision of the cognitively dissonant. Effectively, the ambivalent semantics of the joke *becomes* the comic—or the comic becomes *it*.

The question of whether the Freudian joke or the Bergsonian banana peel should provide the prototype for the comic as a whole may at first seem a matter of indifference. To see why this is not so, it is necessary to turn to some of the more implicit implications of Freud's claims and statements. In the conclusion of his introduction, Freud presents an initial justification, or rather apologia, for his enterprise, in the form of an appeal to authority of the most *großbürgerliche* kind possible. Though jokes may indeed traditionally be regarded as frivolous by science and art alike, it is nevertheless the case that "even men of eminence who have thought it worth while to tell the story of their origins, of the cities and countries they have visited, and of the important people with whom they have associated, are not ashamed in their autobiographies to report their having heard some excellent joke" (*JRU* 15; 13). As the footnote to these lines discretely indicates, Freud is referring to the *Lebenserinnerungen* of the art and culture critic Jacob von Falke, who describes in proper Bildungsroman style his life from his idyllic childhood in northern Germany to his apotheosis as world traveler and director of the k. k. Österreichische Museum für Kunst und Industrie.[17] The passage in which Falke devotes the most sustained attention to jokes that he has heard along his way in fact occurs in the brief chapter devoted to his travels in Ireland, in which "humor and wit [Humor und Witz]" are cited as the Irishman's "national inheritance":

> Despite poverty, despite the vexed political and social relations that have excited the mood to the point of hatred and murder, the Irishman has not been forsaken by his national inheritance, humor and wit. *Irish fun* [in English in original] is still at home everywhere and is what makes life in Ireland so pleasant. You can find merriment on the street with the cabman, among the common women, with the lowliest man of the people. (Falke, *Lebenserinnerungen* 270–71)

Here a sense for the comic appears as an exotic detail, the native ornament of Irishmen and -women in lieu of a proper national costume—which, Falke moreover recounts in the paragraph just preceding this one, they lack due to the very same poverty for which their humor provides a balm. Humor is the applied art of the Irish, out of the only "material" they have to work with. It is thus not surprising at all that Falke might have thought these jokes worthy of note in his memoirs, for "Irish fun" is like a Chinese vase or a rug from Samarkand: local handicraft an enterprising German must go abroad to find.[18]

In view of this colonialistic exoticization of humor, Freud's bid to claim jokes as an essential manifestation of the psychic apparatus appears in a somewhat different light. At first, of course, it may seem that Freud is working on a similarly exoticizing model as Falke, insofar as it is above all Jewish jokes, as many critics have observed and as Freud himself makes no bones about, that provide the examples for Freud's study.[19] Freud comments, "I do not know whether there are many other instances of a people making fun to such a degree of its own character [daß sich ein Volk in solchem Ausmaß über sein eigenes Wesen lustig macht]" (*JRU* 112; 123).[20] While Freud thus indeed posits a particular ethnic-national group—not incidentally, the one to which he himself belongs—as the preeminent purveyors (as well as objects) of jokes, unlike Falke, who bids a final farewell to Ireland in a sentimental and humor-*less* rhetorical flourish (see Falke 272), Freud incorporates the "Jewish joke" as the paradigm of joking per se—and thus, according to the logic of his own argument, as the paradigm of the workings of the unconscious itself. Jews are not, as the Irish are for Falke, the producers of wit as exotic cultural heritage; rather, their humor—all too easily perceived as deviation, curiosity, or mere neurotic symptom—is *exemplary.* The joke may indeed be a cultural product, an example of folk art—which, far from having its source in a rarified aesthetics of genius, "acts almost like an event of universal interest; it is passed from one person to another like the news of the latest victory" (*JRU* 15; 13)—but it is also one that no household, no "psychical economy" (see *JRU* 156; 175) is without.

Language Games

Wittgenstein, according to the notes of his 1932–33 Cambridge Lectures, takes Freud to task for essentially confusing analytical and descriptive—in other words, *scientific* and *aesthetic*—modes of investigation. "The question, 'What is the nature of a joke?' " says Wittgenstein, "is like the question, 'What is the nature of a lyric poem?' [. . .] What Freud says about the subconscious [*sic*] sounds like science, but in fact it is just *a means of representation.*"[21] Wittgenstein means this as critique—or at least as a reminder not to subscribe too literally to a dogmatic orthodoxy of psychoanalysis—but it may in fact be a charge that Freud himself would not have rejected.[22] Indeed, rather than providing the refutation of Freud's observations on jokes, Wittgenstein's remark lays bare, better than any sympathetic commenter could, what is actually at stake in Freud's book and what binds it, not merely to histories of political and social marginalization or the multivalent question of Spirit vs. psyche, but also to the question of what it means to represent and what it means to claim and what it means to mean: in other words, to the rhetorical/aesthetic phenomenon of *irony* as epistemological problem.[23]

Freud in fact emphasizes the linguistic or hermeneutic aspect of his inquiry on jokes from the very first, beginning with a discussion of the wordplay—"double entendre [Zweideutigkeit]" (*JRU* 40; 41), "double meaning [Doppelsinn]" (36; 36), "multiple use of the same material [mehrfacher Verwendung des gleichen Materials]" (33; 33)—on which so many jokes are based. Freud himself largely attributes the significance of linguistic ambiguity to the joke's economical or energy-saving function, its "tendency to economy [Ersparnis]" (44; 45), even going so far at one point as to draw parallels between the phenomenon of the comic and notions of technological progress (see *JRU* 195; 222–23). In one of the many examples in this book of a seemingly unconscious stutter or effect of contagion, Freud appends to his discussion of double entendre a footnote in which he takes issue with Kuno Fischer's use of the term "Zweideutigkeit" ("double entendre," but also "ambiguity" or "double significance"). Whereas Fischer, says Freud, wants to signify with "Zweideutigkeit" the idea that of the two possible meanings of a joke, one will always be privileged as the dominant one, Freud himself understands the term to indicate that both of the meanings present in the joke do equal work, adding, in an ostensible attempt at conciliation, "Nomenclature of this kind is a matter of convention; linguistic usage has arrived at no firm decision" (*JRU* 41; 41). In other words: "Zweideutigkeit" is *zweideutig*—and moreover in Freud's sense of the term. At the same time, this sly establishing of dominance over Fischer in this instance paradoxically and just as slyly acts as evidence for Fischer's own, more hierarchical hermeneutic practice, whereby Freud's implicit ceding of the dominance he has just established shifts the balance now in his direction, finally bringing the debate over the term "Zweideutigkeit"—again, according to Freud, the essential aspect of the joke—into a state of permanent, performative, and above all *constitutive* oscillation and exposing Freud's text as itself a kind of *double entendre,* not just a book on the latent meaning of jokes but also and especially a performative claim about the latent joke of meaning.[24]

Wittgenstein's pique seems to stem in part from just this consideration, that Freud failed to realize the radical *linguistic* and *logical* implications of his jokes theory, assimilating it instead within a—despite everything actually less troubling—schema of sexuality and repression. And insofar as language and logic determine perception and understanding, the joke—as Shoshana Felman has emphasized in her analysis of the humor of Austinian speech-act theory—exemplifies the "general problematization of the presumption of 'knowing' "; like Austin's droll equivocations, the joke "is directed at subverting the *cognitive evidence* inherent in the constative."[25] As will become evident, this subversion of the constative function of language that the joke in every case performs is what links it categorically to irony and its perpetual undermining of conceptual foundations, to its status as, in Kierkegaard's words, "a nothing that devours everything, and a something one can never grab hold of, something that is and is not at the same time" (*CI* 131). Likewise, irony's central role in the functioning of the joke helps to elucidate why this same all-devouring irony is—again, in Kierkegaard's words—"something that at rock bottom is comic" (*CI* 131). Jokes are verbal units but jokes are also jokes on verbal units, differentiated from the performatives of Austin's concern only (but crucially) in the sense that not just their internal structure but also their explicit theme, content, and the very source of their effectiveness is the putting of their own premises on display and into question.[26] The joke is, so to speak, an "allegory of reading" in its most compressed form: not just one more illustration of hermeneutic or epistemological instability, but this instability's festival and consummate *mise á l'acte*.[27]

The Law of Nonsense

Another rhetorically curious passage in Freud's rhetorically curious book occurs in the context of what one might term its first true breakthrough moment. Freud cites an urbane witticism of Heinrich Heine as an excellent example for the study of the technique of jokes, only to interrupt the analysis rather suddenly, saying, "It is a pity that this fine example involves such complicated technical conditions. We can arrive at no clarification of it" (*JRU* 48; 50). Freud subsequently opts instead for one of the low, *Ostjude*-themed "bath jokes" as an object simpler—"For we do not insist upon a patent of nobility from our examples [Wir verlangen nämlich keinen Adelsbrief von unseren Beispielen]" (*JRU* 49; 50)—and hence more conducive to scientific analysis. But this evaluation, it turns out, is in fact not precisely true: for no sooner is the joke introduced than Freud breaks off again, this time for a wholly different reason: "If one laughs at a joke really heartily, one is not in precisely the best mood for investigating its technique" (*JRU* 49; 50). If Heine's joke is ostensibly too complex to be analyzed, the difficulty presented by the example of folk humor is that it is simply too funny. The uncontrollable laughter it inevitably gives rise to impedes scientific thinking. Naturally, such an excuse, like the whole of Freud's simulation of essayistic spontaneity, is a put-on and patent absurdity: if Freud is writing the joke down (all the more so if he is dictating), he can no longer be literally laughing, certainly not "really heartily." If one thinks of laughter as the physical sign of affect, mood, or "disposition"—indeed, "humor," in the older sense of the term—then Freud's point is really less that he is physically incapable of the task of analysis, but rather that he is too libidinally attached to engage in objective inquiry. Cathexis and analysis are opposite terms; a truly good joke entails cathexis a priori (this is the famous automatism of laughter), thus is no fit object for analysis, and yet anything *other* than a truly good joke would not be a fitting object of analysis for an analysis of good jokes. The wordplay that occurs in this same paragraph drives home Freud's point about the difficulties of scientific objectivity in the case of the joke (all the more so if the pun is as unintended as it seems to be).[28] In the course of the analysis of a joke that is, despite what Freud says, in fact less about physical uncleanliness ("Have you taken a bath?") than its moral counterpart ("What? Is there one missing?"), Freud comments, "And this answer cannot be robbed of being a joke by any extension or modification, so long as its sense is not interfered with" (*JRU* 49; 50). The possible robbery of the bath is thus compounded by the impossible robbery of the joke, through the very punning mechanism that makes the first robbery possible and the latter impossible to begin with.[29]

Herein lies the problem to which Samuel Weber alludes when he comments (in regard to an early letter of Freud to Fliess on his psychoanalytic method) that "the authority of a scientific discourse that treats of distortion, deception, and deformation depends on its keeping itself free of the phenomena it seeks to comprehend."[30] Hans Blumenberg alludes to a similar problem in his study of the philosophical reception of the story of Thales of Miletus, the astronomer and "proto-philosopher" who fell into a well because he was too busy looking at the stars.[31] For Blumenberg, the laughter of the Thracian maid at the hapless Thales comes from the confrontation between theory and world, speculative logic and empirical data—or, in variants after Plato, insight and received ideas—that all subsequent philosophy has had in one way or another to negotiate. If the original Thracian maid's mocking laughter once again has something distinctly Schopenhauerian about it, however, measuring Thales's claims to theoretical knowledge against his lack of practical know-how, a somewhat different problematic is introduced in the study of precisely that which gives rise to laughter itself. Theory becomes laughable for Freud, not because of too much distance from its object of study, but because of a too close identification with it, to the extent that this object functions according to the very thing that puts the authority of the theory that would comprehend it into question.

Sarah Kofman has likewise observed the methodological tension between (general) theory and (particular) anecdote in Freud's joke book, which presents itself as an effort to piece together the "*disjecta membra*" of previous works on jokes and unify them under the coherent master discourse of psychoanalysis.[32] Kofman goes on to remark that one of the traditional definitions of *wit,* too, is the joining together of disparate elements analogous to the reconciliation of forces within the Hegelian dialectic (although contrary to Kofman, this is not a theory particular to Hegel), thus making Freud's methodology witty insofar as it is Hegelian and Hegelian insofar as it is witty. Freud himself rejects the traditional notion of the joke as a matter of binary contrast, describing it, in direct analogy to his theories of the dream-work, as a multiple-stage process of "condensation [Verdichtung]," "displacement [Verschiebung]," and "representation by nonsense [Darstellung durch Widersinn]" (see *JRU* 159; 181). But if the joke does at all bear similarities to the dialectic as an essentially synthetic structure—whose disparate images are ultimately brought together in the *Pointe,* the punch line—it is as a linking together of concepts or images not on the basis of their necessary complementarity, but rather, on the basis of their *resistance* to cognitive or narrative assimilation, Hofmannsthal's previously cited irony of the "thousands of details founded in reality against the premature and consciously untrue synthesis" (42). Thus the joke acts as the "deformed mirror of Spirit, its caricature" (Kofman 70).[33] From its "dialectic" emerges no synthesis that could establish itself, only the temporary and gratuitous release of laughter,[34] which may well ask to be repeated,[35] but cannot be turned into a genuine synthetic concept or stage in a linear process.[36]

In this context, it is tempting to say that the joke (or more precisely, the joke work) is a joke on the pretensions of speculative logic itself. But such an interpretation, however attractive, is also misleading; for if the joke were merely a joke on speculative logic, it would mean that there was another, better form of logic or thinking able to judge and mock from a privileged position. If this were the case, the Freudian joke would simply replicate the two opposite but complimentary poles that inevitably come up in all discussions of the comic: on the one side, the comic of subversion, on the other, the comic of conservation. The comic of subversion, at least as commonly conceived, is a comic of mockery, which exposes contradictions in the status quo from a higher perspective of non-contradiction and logical coherence.[37] Its characteristic form is satire; its aim is often (though not always) to challenge the status quo for progressive political aims.[38] The comic of conservation, on the other hand, intentionally stages deviations or aberrations from the norm in order to laugh at them from the perspective of the norm, which is itself taken for granted as the standard against which what is comical will be measured. Its characteristic form is farce;[39] its aim is to reestablish normative values while at the same time allowing for temporary release and relief.[40]

Both of these—formally similar, if ideologically opposed—modes, genres, or uses clearly have their place in the history of the comic. Yet what Freud ultimately effects in *Jokes and Their Relation to the Unconscious,* even if it is not always fully clear to him, is something different, not merely an application of existing theories of the comic but rather a radical rethinking of the comic and its consequences. Such a rethinking is enabled, precisely, by Freud's implicit inclusion of the always associated but never fully elaborated corresponding problem of irony. For if irony is ultimately the troubling of all knowing—at least, insofar as knowing is dependent on representation, that is, *non*-mystical—then the joke, with its mechanisms of ambiguity, deferral, and hermeneutic dissonance, is one of its paradigmatic manifestations. In a discussion of the role of nonsense and faulty logic in both the comic and the joke, Freud asks the question, "In what instances, then, will a joke appear before criticism as nonsense? Particularly when it makes use of those modes of thought which are usual in the unconscious but in conscious thought are proscribed as logical errors [in welchem Falle wird nun der Witz vor der Kritik als Unsinn erscheinen? Besonders dann, wenn er sich jener Denkweisen bedient, die im Unbewußten üblich, im bewußten Denken verpönt sind, als der Denkfehler]" (*JRU* 204; 233). Nonsense and faulty logic are, Freud states, hallmarks of the unconscious, critique and criteria of logic products of consciousness. But Freud's line of reasoning in this crucial passage significantly begs the question; indeed, in yet another uncanny doubling of his object of investigation, the passage displays almost the same form of logic as the famous joke of the broken kettle that Freud retells immediately thereafter (see *JRU* 205; 234). Freud defines nonsense as that which appears to conscious thought as faulty logic, but this is itself a tautology, since faulty logic *is* nothing other than logic that has been judged nonsensical by consciousness. Meanwhile, the unconscious, as Freud describes it, will not and cannot have a notion of sense; it is pre-logical, or rather, obeys a "logic" not recognized by consciousness as such, a "logic," moreover, out of which the conscious notion of sense must nevertheless emerge. This is not to say that the distinction between "sense" and "nonsense" thereby disappears, but that this distinction is already a product of nonsense itself, that the "usual" nonsense of the unconscious is that which makes the sensible critique of consciousness possible.[41]

This, however, is not yet sufficient for the production of comic affect, but merely its precondition. Comic affect emerges when nonsense and the sensible critique it sorts itself into—or in another discourse, irony and its "conclusion"[42]—meet once again, present to consciousness, that is, *to* critique and representation, which are themselves inseparable from nonsense. The joke is thus less to be understood as a collision of "heterogeneous representations that often, according to the law of the power of imagination (of association) lie far apart from one another" (*ANTH* §54, 115; 129) than as a "compromise [. . .] between the demands of rational criticism and the drive not to renounce the old pleasure in words and nonsense [zwischen den Anforderungen der vernünftigen Kritik und dem Trieb, auf die alte Wort- und Unsinnslust nicht zu verzichten]" (*JRU* 203–4, translation modified; 232), in the understanding, however, that critique and pleasure in nonsense are not opposed to but rather the supplements of one another. Thus if the comic emerges from, in Alenka Zupančič's words, "the joint articulation" of competing logics, "which is never visible in the given reality, yet is constitutive of it" (*The Odd One In* 59), the most basic of all such articulations is that which takes place between the "logic" of non-logic and the critical logic that is at once produced out of and set against it. This is also precisely the legacy of irony, insofar as irony poses the initial questions of identity (in the sphere of the ontological) and representation as adequation (in that of the aesthetic).[43] And if irony (or contradiction and non-identity) *is* "constitutive" of reality, it can no longer be subject to approbation and ridicule, not even approbation and ridicule of the highest metaphysical order such as Schopenhauer's critique of the phenomenal per se from the point of view of the concept and the concept per se from the point of view of the phenomenal. Similarly, it is also no longer possible to take flight into the supposed freedoms of romantic irony, as Hofmannsthal still makes a somewhat halfhearted attempt to do, for irony comprises not only the phenomenal and normative world but also the subject who would escape it and the ideas—including that of the "absolute will [unbedingte Willkür]" of irony itself (*F* 193; 202)—that would provide the means of that escape.

What remains as a possibility is the *recognition* of the paradoxical pervasiveness of irony and the play of nonsense as ironically conscious representation. That is, what remains is *the comedy of irony,* irony *as* comic. In the joke, Freud shows how irony—that which can so easily tip over into the tragic on the one hand, or the mystical or utopian on the other—gets turned into something potentially evocative of laughter. The way that it does so—as paradigmatically in the joke—is *by staging itself,* by ironically performing itself and thereby leading itself to a conclusion that it can by its own nature not sustain. This staging of irony, and the ensuing making-comic of that staging, is paradoxical insofar as it relies on a form of judgment that irony precludes a priori, which in turn is staged as comic, ad infinitum. This is the structure of the post-judgmental and non-dialectical comic that, as I will argue, in the early decades of the twentieth century develops out of romantic irony as its simultaneous continuation and critique. Thus Freud's theory of the joke, similar to but in a far more rigorous manner than Hofmannsthal's expository essay, announces the advent of what one might call the ethos of the comic, or rather *the ethos of comic irony,* in which the understanding of irony as the ultimate basis of that which is comical coincides with the understanding of irony as something that can only be taken comically. After the end of art, after the joke of the psyche, after unsuccessful wars, irony has nowhere to go but—comically—through itself.

Outline of the Work

The first chapter of this book traces the development of this comic irony from the special attention paid in the Enlightenment and especially the romantic eras not only to irony, but also to wit, humor, comedy, and play. The thinkers of the romantic period take up the Enlightenment's interest in wit as both analogue of and counterpoint to reason, and its interest in play as medium of human freedom, and transform these into a notion of irony that maps structures of play onto reason and representation themselves. While *comedy* as a genre quarantines this play with logic and sets it aside as risible error, with irony's eventual encroachment into realms beyond generic borders—exemplarily so in the *Athenäum* project and the writings of Friedrich Schlegel—the tenuousness of this quarantine becomes apparent. Hegel remains the one to have seen the consequences of this most clearly, and his *Lectures on Aesthetics* may well be read as a monumental attempt to protect against the spread of irony and its consequences for art and ethics alike. If irony is the metastasizing of subjectivity and the giving up of objective points of reference, the art of irony, or in Hegel's words, "subjective humor," is art's irresponsible abandonment of real-world reference in favor of mannerist play and wit, the abandonment of art's task of mediating between symbol and idea and thus "das Allerunkünstlerischste"—the absolutely inaesthetic thing (see *A* 68; *AI* 98). Hegel's alternate proposal, which he terms "objective humor," is an attempt to stabilize the loss of ontological and hermeneutic stability for which romantic irony is the cipher. By the twentieth century, however, irony will regain its prominence, and in the disappearance of romantic irony's utopian function, this irony becomes itself ironized and objectified, replacing subjective humor's whimsy with a "comic irony" that takes irony as its object while never ceasing to be *of* the irony that enables the comic in the first place.

The chapter "The Playgrounds of Literature: Robert Walser" begins with a reading of Walser's earliest prose work, *Fritz Kochers Aufsätze* (*Fritz Kocher's Essays*), a collection of fake school exercises supposedly written by the slightly dim titular character (who also happens to bear the name of a real former classmate of Walser's). Through an analysis of the particular temporality of the novel's setting and of the self-referentiality, citationality, and performed ineptitude of Fritz's language, this chapter argues that Walser's writing represents both a parodic answer to Schiller's notion of the "play-drive [Spieltrieb]" in *On the Aesthetic Education of Man,* as well as a revival of the "subjective humor" that adapts Schiller's relation of play and freedom into a program of unlimited artistic license. Yet Walser does not merely reprise subjective humor's reworking of the ideologies of *Bildung* and human freedom; looking back after the turn of the century from the other side of the decadent lament for the artist's inconsequence, he also ironizes the very license that subjective humor celebrates, at the same time demonstrating that an ironic self-referentiality is nothing other than the personalized realism that is the ostensible aim of "objective humor" itself. This meeting of subjective and objective humor is pushed to its logically absurd extreme in the posthumously published short pieces (most of them written during Walser's long residency at the mental clinic in Waldau) which Walser baptized with the name of the *Bleistiftgebiet,* or "pencil zone." In the *Bleistiftgebiet* works in particular, Walser stages the irony of representation and reference as an unending source of self-amusement, exposing Hegel's opposite of art as the disavowed essence of art itself.

The third chapter looks at the first of Kafka's three novel fragments, *Der Verschollene* (*Amerika/The Man Who Disappeared*). While *Der Verschollene* has often been dismissed as a minor work or indeed an exception within the Kafkan canon, I argue that the novel already contains the basic structural elements—which are, precisely, *comic* elements—of much if not all of Kafka's subsequent writing. The chapter first discusses the question of representation versus performance in Kafka, and Kafka's shift of focus, similar to that of Walser, from a nineteenth-century emphasis on naturalistic representation to text as self-producing process. Second, the chapter takes a look at the famous physical comedy in Kafka's work to show how Kafka, quoting from and adapting the slapstick repertoire of vaudeville and silent film, reinterprets (*against* a Bergsonian vitalism) the relationship between matter and spirit for the age of mechanization. Finally, the chapter examines Kafka's situation comedy or comedy of plot, showing how Kafka deploys the pseudo-category of the "almost necessary," formulated in an early letter to the future wife of Max Brod, in order to expose the inherent comedy of Kant's analysis of causality in the First Critique, a comedy which bears decisively on the post-metaphysical implications of Kafka's professional duties while also establishing the fundamental principles of his characteristic narrative structures.

The final chapter, "Bearing Wit to History: Joseph Roth," focuses on the feuilletons that Roth wrote in the hundreds for a variety of newspapers from the years 1917 to 1939. While many of Roth's feuilletons seem to approach the genre of political and social satire practiced with unflagging zeal by fellow Austrians such as Karl Kraus and Elias Canetti, Roth in fact refuses the elevated authoritative position that such traditional satire demands, and his journalism reflects an understanding of the impossibility of such a position as well as the ethical dubiousness of presuming to occupy it. This is in part a reflection of the subgenre of the feuilleton itself, a hybrid form characterized by the combination of occasional observation and personal musings: like Walser's writings—albeit in a radically different tonality—the unhappy composite of Hegel's "objective" and "subjective" humors. The chapter first analyzes how the particular generic conditions of the feuilleton and Roth's special practice of juxtaposition allow him to put the notion of a "true" representation into question, while at the same time claiming truth for a wit traditionally seen as the opposite of rational analysis. This complication of the relationship between wit and facticity is also bound up with Roth's interest in the question of authority, in both the political and the literary sense. Roth stages political theology—understood as the transcendent legitimation of worldly authority—as immanent comedy, going beyond ideology critique to hold its paradoxes in ironic suspension. Likewise, Roth ironizes the function of the author, bringing to light the performative dimensions of the writing subject and the relationship between text and world.

✦

Shift in terminology [. . .] German irony
—Franz Kafka, *Octavo Notebook F*

Finally, a brief note on the choice of terminology. Novalis speaks truer than he knows when he writes (this time in actual fact), "What Fr. Schlegel characterizes as irony is, to my mind, nothing more than the consequence or character of sobriety [Besonnenheit], the true presence of spirit. Schlegel's irony seems to me to be true humor. For an idea to have several names is to its advantage."[44] Not only problems of translation but also semantic drift and the convoluted history of reception have made anything more than a pragmatic and provisional distinction among terms relating to the comic all but impossible. Irony itself can be variously Socratic, Schlegelian, Kierkegaardian, narrative à la Thomas Mann, deconstructive à la Paul de Man, dramatic, rhetorical, "postmodern," etc., and hardly has to imply the specifically *comic* irony that will be at issue in the following chapters.[45] "Wit," while unquestionably related to the comic, is nevertheless too specific, and although it is indeed the closest cognate of the German *Witz,* like irony it has undergone numerous semantic shifts over the years and, at least in English, now carries unshakeable overtones of the salon and the bon mot. I have also tried to avoid using the term "comedy" as a catch-all term, considering this to be rather a technical designation for a particular literary/dramatic genre with a certain set of fixed conventions. Comedy is intrinsically comic (or at least aims to be), but not all that is comic is a comedy. The term *Lustspiel,* which will also appear from time to time, perhaps better suits my meaning, insofar as it describes a kind of "pleasure play" not necessarily bound to generic constraints. But besides the potential unwieldiness of foreign terminology, "Lustspiel," like "comedy," is too strongly determined by the weight of literary tradition, and thus also too technical to be of use here.

I have opted against the term "humor" for several reasons. Foremost among them is to be able to retain the difference between Hegel's "objective humor" and "subjective humor," which function as the opposite poles of a post–"end of art" art in his aesthetic philosophy and which provide the source—although not the substance—of the eventual turn to comic irony. I also wished to distinguish the subject of this study from that of Wolfgang Preisendanz in his book *Humor als dichterische Einbildungskraft* (*Humor as Poetic Imagination*), which has provided an essential point of departure for the present work. Despite the great catholicity of his analysis, Preisendanz's "humor" essentially falls on the side of Hegel's "objective humor," describing a particular form of realist narrative tempered by inner feeling. Even if that were not the case, Preisendanz himself is emphatic on the point that his term "humor" should not be conflated with the comic or with that which is funny or amusing. The term "humor" has also been given too strong of an affective valence by Freud, who in his essay of the same name defines it above all as a wry forbearance in regard to personal suffering.[46] Certainly, the term "the comic" contains its own difficulties (not least of which is the fact that adjective nominalization sits uncomfortably with the English language). I have nonetheless chosen it as what seems to me the most neutral and comprehensive of all the unsatisfactory possibilities at hand. What I am then calling "comic irony" announces the reappearance of irony as celebrated by the romantics and excoriated by Hegel in a way that now performs this irony, beyond all earlier incarnations, in specifically comic mode, at the same time as this irony, with all of its implications, is recognized to make up the structure of the comic. Irony returns to laugh at its own antics, which were—funnily enough—the point of laughter all along.

Chapter One

✦

Senses of Humor: The Origins of Comic Irony

> Let them prattle ever more
> On what they'll never comprehend.
> Some will wander without end.
> Artists will crack up in scores.
> —Friedrich Schlegel, "On Incomprehensibility"

The Setup: Irony and the Comic

There is hardly an examination of the phenomenon of irony that does not eventually find itself having to pay heed to the question of the comic, and, by the same token, there is almost no discussion of the comic, comedy, humor, or the joke that manages to avoid using the word "irony." And yet the affiliation between irony and the comic, so seemingly self-evident, is still largely unexplained in the critical literature. The empirical obviousness of this connection—the fact that one often laughs, say, at remarks deemed ironic—serves to mask the fact that the relationship between these two phenomena, not to mention their respective definitions, does not necessarily go without saying. There are, at least, *theories* of comedy, the comic, or laughter that seem to have little to do with (certain conceptions of) irony, and irony, for all its frequent association with the comic, is just as often spoken of as a traumatic, tragic, or at least not exactly funny matter. Jean Paul, while he too slots irony in with his discussion of wit and humor, nevertheless maintains that irony "as pure representative of the ridiculous object must always appear eulogistic and serious [als reiner Repräsentant des lächerlichen Objekts, immer lobend und ernst erscheinen muß]" (*VA* §36, 107; 148). Hegel and Kierkegaard similarly (although naturally with crucial points of difference) describe irony as "the nullity of everything objective and valid in and for itself" (*A* 66; *AI* 96), the "infinite nothing" (*CI* 26) which forms "the first and most abstract qualification of subjectivity" (*CI* 264).[1] For Lukács, who applies the Hegelian conception of irony to questions of genre, irony is the "objectivity of the novel," the name for the tragic alienation of the novelistic hero within a world of contingency.[2] Paul de Man, while also associating irony with the comic, describes irony in hardly comic terms as "a consciousness of madness, itself the end of all consciousness [. . .] a consciousness of a non-consciousness, a reflection on madness from the inside of madness itself."[3] Nor do theories of laughter or funniness necessarily partake of the discourse of irony. Hobbes infamously describes laughter simply as "sudden glory" in the vanquishing of an enemy,[4] but even in less bellicose and more strictly comic interpretations of the phenomenon of laughter, such as that of Bergson, the emphasis falls on social normativity and the correction of error; or, as in the theories of both Bakhtin and Freud, on libidinal release in opposition to societal, institutional, or psychological repression;[5] or, as in Jean Paul's and Friedrich Schlegel's theories of wit, on the geniality of the creative thinker and the synthesizing or analogical power of imagination; or, as in Baudelaire, on human beings' essentially "satanic" condition in their positioning at the midpoint between infinite divine spirit and finite material nature.[6]

Despite the above examples, however, an almost axiomatic notion of the correlation between irony and the comic persists, and thus also persists the problem of determining the specific nature of this correlation. On the one hand, as I have argued in the introduction to this book, irony is a matter of the making and the determination of sense, and more particularly, of the troubling of the distinction between sense and nonsense. On the other hand—in an interpretation typified by, but hardly limited to, de Man's above-cited (and Baudelaire-derived) definition—irony is a matter of the doubled consciousness of self, the self watching itself watch itself ad infinitum until world and external reference fall away entirely. These two definitions are not as far apart as they perhaps seem, for the self-conscious self, at least in Hegel's analysis, is conscious above all of the contingency of his or her own actions and perceptions; and the very way in which sense is constituted, the act of making sense itself is, as de Man too observes, a matter of the belatedness and difference, rather than the presence and correspondence of sign and world or indeed sign and meaning—and thus a matter of nonsense itself, if nonsense is understood as precisely this non-correspondence. If sense-making thus corresponds to what Benjamin calls "the will to symbolic totality,"[7] then irony corresponds to the disappointment of—or, as we shall see, the playful disregard for—such a will, as well as to the allegory of which, in Benjamin's assessment, irony is also a "variant [Umbildung]" (*Origin* 188; *Ursprung* 166).

The following chapter will therefore argue that irony, as a mode—intimately related not only to allegory but also, significantly, to the joke—in which "the relationship between sign and meaning" in the broadest sense of both terms "is discontinuous" (de Man, "Temporality," 208–9), is precisely that which constitutes the basis of the comic, even if, as Benjamin's analysis of the baroque *Trauerspiel* indicates, it is certainly not always necessarily taken as such. As unlikely as it may initially seem for a study of the comic, the basis of this argument will be an examination of Hegel's *Lectures on Aesthetics,* which may claim the honor of being the first and greatest attempt to keep irony and the comic definitively apart. This is of course not to say that others have not insisted on the distinction between the two modes (or forms, structures, even "concepts"), as the selection of opinions about irony listed above already make plain. But Hegel is the one to have seen most perceptively the consequences of a coming together of the aspect of irony with that of the comic, and to have developed a systematic theory of art and an interpretation of art's history designed precisely to protect against such a fusion. It is then an irony of the history of philosophy that this same theory will turn out to be dependent for its logic on the very affinity of irony and the comic that it is meant to forestall. If Hegel's *Aesthetics* thus ends up being the comedy of itself, however, it also reveals—along with Schlegel's pivotal work on irony, "Über die Unverständlichkeit" ("On Incomprehensibility")—a new form of irony, an irony that not only forms the basis of the comic, but has also become *itself* potentially comic, and whose avowal or disavowal will become one of the most salient questions of aesthetics after aesthetics' supposed closure.

Subjective Humor, or the Unseriousness of Representation

Hegel begins the second part of his *Lectures on Aesthetics*—and his history of art proper—with a contemplation of the symbol. The symbol is, strictly speaking, not quite yet art; it is rather "the threshold of art [Vorkunst: literally, pre-art]" (*A* 303; *AI* 393), but *as* this pre-art, it also constitutes "the beginning of art in terms of both its concept and its historical appearance" (*A* 303, translation modified; *AI* 393). If "art as such consists precisely in the kinship, relation, and concrete interpenetration of meaning and shape" (*A* 304; *AI* 395), the symbol, overcoming the true arbitrariness of the sign of which it is nevertheless a subset, constitutes the first tentative step toward bringing material form and abstract idea together in one. Such a perfect correspondence is of course not as heuristic a notion as it might sometimes seem: it does indeed take place, says Hegel, in the golden age of classical art as exemplified by classical Greek sculpture, in which form and idea exist in perfect balance and complementarity. Such an equilibrium, however, is only possible insofar as the "idea" to which the "form" of Greek statuary corresponds is, as it were, literally superficial: the idea of the absolute as the very idea of form itself. The earlier period of "symbolic" art, on the other hand (which Hegel more or less equates with ancient Egyptian, Near Eastern, and Indian art), is characterized by an essential division between an unpracticed form and a content or notion that far exceeds it. Cruder but in a way more profound than classical art, "symbolic art" attempts to incarnate (a primitive conception of) the idea in impoverished earthly forms, while nevertheless remaining unconscious of the very impoverishment of these forms vis-à-vis the idea. In the primitive stages of art, then, the symbol still constitutes a "defective unification [mangelhaften Vereinigung]," "a *battle* between the content which still resists true art and the form which is just as little homogenous with that content"; thus "the whole of symbolic art may be understood as a continuing struggle for compatibility and incompatibility of meaning and shape (*A* 317–18, translation modified; *AI* 411–12).

In this way, the symbol sets the stage for the drama of forms that will be played out in the *Aesthetics*. Indeed, insofar as art is ultimately to aim for a perfect correspondence between the idea and the sensuous form in which the idea is expressed, the symbol in Hegel's conception becomes no less than the symbol for art *as such*. But the "separation of Idea and shape" (*A* 81; *AI* 114) that Hegel sees as the fundamental characteristic of art at its inception is in danger of reappearing at every moment. This separation, and the need to overcome it, is what motivates art in the first place, but it is also the threat inherent to art, the threat that will arguably be art's undoing. For at the same time as it lies at the bottom of all aesthetic manifestation, "the symbol by its very nature remains essentially ambiguous [das Symbol seinem eigenen Begriff nach wesentlich *zweideutig* bleibt]" (*A* 306; *AI* 397). The symbol is essentially ambiguous or equivocal, first, because one can never say with certainty whether something is meant *as* symbol (as opposed to a literal or factual presentation of the object), and second, because even *when* something is confirmed as a symbol, one can still never be sure what the idea symbolized by the symbol is to be (all the more so the more foreign the art is to one's own time and culture). This diagnosis of the symbol's dubiousness remains valid even before taking into account more sophisticated uses, in which it is no longer merely a matter of emblematic communication, but of even less translatable transferences between form and content. In general terms, then, the problem is the following: not only can no symbolic form successfully contain the content it is meant to express, but also any determinate content or conceptual meaning finds itself actually exceeded by its symbolic representation. And yet art emerges, for Hegel, precisely as the struggle to match form to content and to understand content through form. Thus the essential ambiguousness of the symbol is also the impossibility and the inevitability of art alike; art's lack of necessity—the essential arbitrariness of every determinate presentation vis-à-vis the ideal—is the very thing art must repress in order to *become* art, at the same time that art only comes to be at all *through* this repression.

The undoing of this repression, of course, can be a notion of the future alone: it is the dream of an art without art, that is, of an art devoid of both intention and determinate form. Such a dream is the substance of Hegel's famously contested "end of art" thesis: through the progressive revelation of the essential contingency of art's formal aspects, the concrete form of art will annihilate itself of its own necessity. Art will "realize" that it is ultimately nothing but a confused grasping after essential content with means that can never be adequate to it, after which will be left finally pure content without representation, "truth," in the form of religion, and, even more, philosophy. Eva Geulen has shown that this dream of the end of art is even more radical than Hegel himself suspects: the moment one begins to contemplate art as beautiful—which is as much to say, the moment of aesthetics itself—art (or at least, autonomous or "fine" art) has ceased to be, but at the same time the continual repetition of this cessation is, even in an orthodox interpretation of Hegel's dialectic, the very condition of art's *being* art. To think art, therefore, is already in some way to think art's end.[8]

However, even before this (perhaps not yet or never quite arrived at) moment, the dawning consciousness of the primitive symbol's ambiguity, the understanding of it not as something inherently filled with meaning but as mere convention, produces an increasing split between form and content "until only the arbitrariness of positing meaning remains" (Geulen 37). While later stages of art, in Hegel's schema, will correct and supplement this problematic, this splitting is nevertheless one that will repeat itself again and again throughout art's historical progression. Each time the crisis is that of art's internal necessity, that is, the very instability of the dominant form of representation, until, in "romantic" art, art enters its final crisis, the crisis of representation itself:

> The aspect of external existence is consigned to contingency and abandoned to the adventures devised by an imagination whose caprice can mirror what is present to it, *exactly as it is,* just as readily as it can jumble the shapes of the external world and distort them grotesquely [. . .]. Thereby the separation of Idea and shape, their indifference and inadequacy to each other, come to the fore again, as in symbolic art, but with this essential difference, that, in romantic art, the Idea, the deficiency of which in the symbol brought with it deficiency of shape, now has to appear *perfected* in itself as spirit and heart [als Geist und Gemüt in sich *vollendet*]. (*A* 81; *AI* 113–14)

If, in Hegel's analysis of the "symbolic form of art," "a complete reciprocal interpenetration [Ineinanderbilden] of meaning and expression" (*A* 421; *AI* 539) fails to be achieved, Hegel's assessment of romantic art is that it gives up on this "reciprocal interpenetration" entirely. And yet the contingency to which romantic art relinquishes both "external existence" and artistic representation is not a mere epiphenomenon, but something built into, indeed essential to Hegel's philosophical narrative in the *Aesthetics.* The fact that Hegel posits a form of truth which is to supersede art does not make it any less the case that art is a necessary element in the process of this truth's coming to be; indeed, this "truth" is no more and no less than this process of becoming within art's self-effacement, the consciousness of contingency itself and the distanced—that is, in the strong sense, the *aestheticizing*—contemplation of the forms that contingency takes.[9] Art is not art without the tension between representation and represented that keeps it from being a mere self-evident tautology; at the same time, this always latent tension is what prevents art from being identical to the necessary tautology of Spirit.

The point here is not simply to dismiss Hegel's schema on the grounds of a pragmatic connoisseurship (an objection to which Hegel himself already provides a correspondingly pragmatic answer). It is rather to argue that the contingency of meaning inherent to art—and not just to art—constitutes the anxious center *and* limit of Hegel's discourse on aesthetics, and that this discourse itself is a mechanism designed to obscure the paradoxically central liminality of this necessary contingency. And in "romantic" art, the art of modernity, the increasingly high stakes will force this necessary contingency out into the open, threatening the cohesion of the mechanism itself just as the mechanism gathers energy from this very threat.

Two moments in particular stand out in the *Lectures on Aesthetics* as flashpoints in this history of art's struggle with its own vulnerability. The first of these moments is *allegory*. This "frosty [frostig]" and "bleak [kahl]" (*A* 399, translation modified; *AI* 512) figure, corresponding essentially (if not exclusively) to art's first symbolic phase, is a kind of over-thought intensification of the inherent non-reconciliation of form and content, a perpetually insufficient form of signification whose lack must always be filled by an explicative supplement that renders the allegorical figure superfluous to begin with. Allegory stands as an amplification, if not indeed the parody, of the latent danger of the "separation of Idea and shape, their indifference and inadequacy to each other [die Gleichgültigkeit, Unangemessenheit und Trennung von Idee und Gestalt]" (*A* 81; *AI* 114) that even the most accomplished artwork holds within it. Here Hegel does not let the opportunity pass to take a swipe at his favorite sparring partner Friedrich Schlegel, whom he quotes as claiming that "every work of art must be an allegory" (*A* 400; *AI* 513). On one level, of course, Hegel's objection is simply an aficionado's argument against the rehabilitation of crude didacticism in art, of art become a mere rebus for abstract concepts and ideas that would not only result, in terms of form, in a potential reversion to primitivism, but, in terms of content, would also break philosophy's monopoly on the true expression of the universal. Art must embody ideas and concepts, of course, but it must not actually *be* ideas and concepts, not even in coded form. Of such a revival of allegory as Schlegel seems to recommend, only a non-aesthetic, intellectualized art and an impure, aestheticized philosophy (both of which indeed not so far from what the *Athenäum* project called "criticism") can be the results.[10]

And yet, despite Hegel's dire forebodings and the *Athenäum* group's own unorthodox methods, Schlegel's actual statement does not conflict with but rather corroborates the implied lessons of the *Lectures on Aesthetics*. What

Schlegel in fact says (as mediated through his character Ludoviko in the *Gespräch über die Poesie* [*Dialogue on Poetry*]) is: "all beauty is allegory. The highest can only be said allegorically, precisely because it is inexpressible."[11] As the line of dialogue that directly proceeds this statement makes clear—"All of the sacred play of art is only a distant copy of the infinite play of the world, the eternally self-creating artwork [Alle heiligen Spiele der Kunst sind nur ferne Nachbildungen von dem unendlichen Spiele der Welt, dem ewig sich selbst bildenden Kunstwerk]" (Schlegel 324)—for "beauty" one may here read "art" as such, or more precisely, art conceived as autonomous aesthetic creation differentiated from the world out of which it emerges. If Hegel would perhaps reject Schlegel's description of the world as "the eternally self-creating artwork," it is nevertheless the case that not only the developmental model suggested by this figure but also the figural ("In other words," says Ludoviko [Schlegel, *Gespräch* 324]), even typological relation of fine art to all other aspects of existence is very much in the Hegelian spirit. Both Hegel's own history of beautiful art and his parallel history of *Geist* are bracketed on the one side by the "defective unification" (*A* 317; *AI* 411) of the symbol, and on the other side by the "cancel[ing] of the difference between objectivity and content" (*PS* §804, 490; 588) in thought at the same time as art as mere representation is divested of this same task. Art, doomed by the particularity and the sensuousness that is its indispensable attribute to always fall short of more abstract forms of knowledge, must therefore rest in this defective or deficient unification of which allegory is, indeed, the exemplary figure.[12] If Hegel still insists that art make the effort to transcend its own deficiency—up to and including the point where it transcends itself into nonexistence—Schlegel, here at least, chooses to linger with allegory as the allegory for art's paradoxical but necessary failure to fulfill the lack that it itself constitutes.[13] "All beauty is allegory" is thus nothing more than an epigrammatic prefiguration of Hegel's own later implicit admission that art is, according to its very concept, always insufficient to the Idea.[14]

If allegory is art's immanent threat set out as a regression to its pre-aesthetic origins, the second major moment in the undermining of art's claim to necessity, which Hegel names "subjective humor," will be the carefree admission of art's failure, the luxuriating of art in its own late confusion. Although Hegel devotes comparatively little space to subjective humor within the *Lectures on Aesthetics,* the phenomenon nevertheless occupies a privileged place, and not just because of its contemporaneity. For it is here that art, at the end of its trajectory, finally meets its nemesis. Along with the seemingly opposed but actually complementary mode of imitative realism, "subjective humor" does not just constitute the "dissolution of the romantic form of art [Die Auflösung der romantischen Kunstform]" (*A* 593; *AII* 220)—something that could, at least theoretically, be a precursor to still newer art forms[15]—but signals no less than "the decay and dissolution of art itself" (*A* 576; *AII* 198).

Realism, for its part, portrays "the contents of ordinary daily life which is not apprehended in its substance (in which it has an element of the ethical and divine), but in its mutability and finite transitoriness" (*A* 595; *AII* 222). What results from such an art of "prosaic objectivity" (*A* 595; *AII* 222) is merely a dull, automatic reproduction of everydayness, "the contingency of immediate and in itself unbeautiful and prosaic existence [die Zufälligkeit des unmittelbaren, für sich genommen unschönen und prosaischen Daseins]" (*A* 596, translation modified; *AII* 223). The surprising and paradoxical result of this dynamic, however, is that it is not the objective world, but the personality and talent of the artist that is thereby highlighted. That which is represented in the realist artwork is of little importance; ultimately, the emphasis falls on the pure reproductive skill of the artist himself, and art, despite its apparent formal solidity, is reduced to the contingency of which it is always in danger (see *A* 600; *AII* 229).

If bare realism thus falls short of art's spiritual task, however, "subjective humor" poses an even greater and much more urgent threat. "Subjective humor," in Hegel's definition, is "the perversion and derangement of everything objective and real by means of wit and the play of a subjective outlook, and it ends with the artist's personal productive mastery over every content and form" (*A* 576; *AII* 198). Here no longer is anything like a reconciliation of subject and object through formal representation even attempted. Rather, assuming the privilege of individual freedom and ironic distance granted by the modern consciousness, the practitioner of subjective humor abandons the real world as referent entirely, favoring instead fantasy, imagination, embellishment, whimsicality, and wit as childish substitutes for real matter in the contemptuous negation of objective criteria for judgment.[16]

Naturally, the "humor" of "subjective humor" (as with the "humor" of "objective humor," to be discussed in detail below) should not be understood in the way the word is commonly used today.[17] As Hegel employs it, it clearly has far more to do with its older meanings of "mood," "disposition," at most something like "cheerfulness of temper." But Hegel's use of the term seems nevertheless to mark a shift toward its current meaning, in a way that should not be assumed to be self-evident. Far more, even, than in the case of comedy per se, Hegel instinctively allies subjective humor with that which is *funny*:[18]

> The natural error in this connection is to suppose that it is very easy to make jests and to be funny about oneself and everything available, and that this is why the form of the humorous is commonly snatched at; but it happens equally commonly that the humour becomes flat if the author lets himself go in the field of the contingency of his notions and pleasantries [Einfälle und Späße] which, strung loosely together, deviate into indefiniteness, and, often with deliberate bizarrerie, conjoin the most heterogeneous things. (*A* 601; *AII* 230)

Hegel's main point in this passage, that without an anchoring formal necessity art quickly turns to frivolousness, is, if not incontrovertible, clear enough. But Hegel's linguistic slippage between "subjective humor" as form, mode, or genre on the same level as Greek tragedy or medieval romance, and "the humorous" as an affect synonymous with "[making] jests and [being] funny," "notions and pleasantries," and attached to the egoism of subjective humor as if by default points to a larger problem of definition or derivation.[19] Moreover, the passage also raises the question of how the "form of the humorous" should be determined, if "subjective humor" is, in Hegel's definition, an art precisely without specific form. Curiously, wit and jokes appear here as at once the antithesis of art, and art's default position: both the "form" that art takes when it ceases to be art and the anti-form that causes art to cease to be in the first place.

The embarrassment in which Hegel finds himself in this passage is doubly crucial for both a reading of the *Aesthetics* and an understanding of the role of the comic (which, for all Hegel's discussion of "humor" and of comedy, is never broached *as such*) within it. For the question of wit, jokes, and nonsense is inscribed in the history of art and consciousness: not, indeed, as an act of so-called subversion, a cheeky tongue (or a tongue in cheek) stuck out at the "didactic and utilitarian spirit of the Enlighteners with their narrow and artificial optimism" (Bakhtin 37), but as an inevitable supplement to artistic creation and consciousness themselves. Kant already notes the structural similarity—but fundamental difference—between *wit* and *judgment* as models of cognition: "The activity of comparative wit is more like play; but that of judgment is more like business [Des vergleichenden Witzes Tun und Lassen ist mehr Spiel; das der Urteilskraft aber mehr Geschäfte]" (*ANTH* §55, 116; 130). From Shaftesbury to Jean Paul and beyond, wit or *Witz* has been described as a kind of pseudo- or anti-logic, a play ratiocination and parody of syllogistic thinking. In Jean Paul's famous formulation, *Witz*—not yet to be confused with the joke proper—is "the disguised priest who joins every couple [der verkleidete Priester, der jedes Paar kopuliert]" (*VA* §44, 123; 173). If the syllogism combines organically linked terms in the service of a valid conclusion, wit brings together terms linked only arbitrarily or indeed not at all (except, of course, within the witticism itself) in the service of what is at best a flash of momentary insight, at worst a willful imposition of fancy onto the very structure of thought.[20] At the same time, however, wit, etymologically related to the German *Wissen,* or knowing,[21] provides (at least in the Enlightenment formulation of the concept) a model for thought or intellectual invention itself and comprises the structural analogue, if not indeed the substance, of the "genius aesthetic," the idea of art as a product of the "exemplary originality of the natural endowment of a subject for the free use of his cognitive facilities [musterhafte Originalität der Naturgabe eines Subjekts im *freien* Gebrauche seiner Erkenntnisvermögen]" (*CPJ* §49, 195; 207–8).

Wit is thus a form—even if, in certain interpretations, a debased or minor form—of what poetic genius always does, that is, combine heretofore distinct elements into a new and unexpected but nevertheless perfectly fitting whole.[22] Kant significantly follows his analysis of wit in *Anthropology from a Pragmatic Point of View* with a discussion of the experimental method (*ANTH* §56, 118–19; 133–34), with the clear intention of juxtaposing the two as contrasting epistemological forms. Similarly, in the *Critique of Judgment* Kant stresses not only the originality of art but also, in contrast to the ephemerality and anti-normativity of wit, art's necessary *regulative* or *rule-making* character—"since there can also be original nonsense [da es auch originalen Unsinn geben kann]" (*CPJ* §46, 186; 194). But despite all examination of the question of judgment, it is still not entirely clear how that which sets a new standard may be rigorously distinguished from mere nonsense, and the very least that may be said is that in post-Kantian thought, wit and genius are *structurally* similar, perhaps only distinguishable after the fact by the consequentiality of their conclusions[23]—a conundrum, incidentally, that not a few of Schlegel's fragment-aphorisms attempt to think through. Schlegel's programmatic (and, in multiple senses, witty) statements such as "Wit is absolute social feeling [Geist], or fragmentary genius" (*F* 144; 148); "Wit is logical sociability" (*F* 149; 154); "Understanding is mechanical, wit is chemical, genius is organic spirit" (*F* 221; 232); and perhaps above all, "If wit in all its manifestations is the principle and the organ of universal philosophy, and if all philosophy is nothing but the spirit of universality, [. . .] then the value and importance of that absolute, enthusiastic, thoroughly material wit is infinite" (*F* 191–92; 200) are ultimately only part of an attempt to understand the nature of the difference—or lack thereof—between a genial freedom of thought and the production of mad nonsense. Even more explicit in this regard is Novalis, who in one of *Blütenstaub*'s aphorisms comments, "Wit emerges where imagination and judgment touch [Wo Fantasie und Urtheilskraft sich berühren, entsteht Witz]."[24] Thus wit (in Jean-Luc Nancy's formulation in specific reference to Novalis) is "the specific, modern outgrowth of the philosophical crisis of *judgment*," the concrete manifestation of the radical skepticism that the Kantian Copernican turn inevitably entails.[25]

It is on account of this increasing insecurity—perhaps the romantic problem par excellence—of the relative status of analysis and insight, genius and wit, *Geist* and *esprit*, that what in Kant still seems despite everything more qualitative than evaluative becomes in the *Aesthetics* both more pronounced and more pernicious. In the art form or mode of subjective humor, the assimilatory power that Hegel reflexively attributes to wit appears in a manner that clearly shows how this seemingly harmless party trick of cognition presents a decisive problem for Hegel's idea of art as such. For Hegel's historicization and teleolization of Kantian aesthetics means that even a norm-giving poetic genius shall always ultimately be subordinate to Spirit, the very binding power of the norm; thus even wit as an *analogue* of poetic creation falls under the suspicion of arbitrariness and non-necessity. In Hegel's model, the true artist is emphatically *not* the one with the cleverest and most original notions—such as the Jena romantics et al., carrying Kant's philosophy a few steps too far, seem to believe; the true artist is the one most in tune with and best able to concretize the spirit of the age: a talent that implies the avoidance of wit, not its cultivation.[26] Hence Hegel's fulgurations—as an uncharacteristic argument to opinion otherwise inexplicable—on modern art's lack of popular appeal.[27] Hence, too, wit's more than merely incidental role in romantic art, which, in Hegel's view, has mistaken virtuosity for greatness and the notion of genius for an artistic blank check.

More serious than the consequences of wit for the ideal of the artist, however, are the consequences that wit has for the work of art and, especially, for the history and the status of art itself. In terms of the appropriate pairing of object and representation that art must at least attempt to effect, wit is an invalid—one is almost tempted to say an *unaufhebbar*—form of thought and of expression, in which art degenerates from a patient search for appropriate forms to a mere chasing after effect. But just as wit may be separated from genius only with difficulty or willful distortion, here too wit is structurally analogous to, if not indeed identical with, the image-making that is for Hegel the very substrate of art itself. In *Vorschule der Ästhetik* (*Preschool of Aesthetics*), Jean Paul already names metaphor (here barely distinguished from allegory) "figurative wit [bildlicher Witz]," noting that "as there is no absolute sign—for each sign is also a thing—there is in the finite realm no absolute thing, but each thing means and signifies" (*VA* §49, 129–30, translation modified; 182–83). This potential arbitrariness of language, a commonplace since at least Aristotle,[28] is the reason why Hegel, for his part, holds the trope of metaphor comparatively at a distance: while acknowledging its part in poetic language, he also cautions that it is "always an interruption of the course of ideas and a constant dispersal of them, because it arouses and brings together images which do not immediately belong to the matter at hand and its meaning" (*A* 407–8; *AI* 523). If this is the case, however, then metaphor—elsewhere named by Jean Paul, in a performatively evocative figure, as "transubstantiations of the spirit [Brotverwandlungen des Geistes]" (*VA* §49, 131; 184)—is ultimately of the same ilk as the allegory that for Hegel must be overcome within art, and that for Benjamin is "beyond beauty [. . .] in the realm of thoughts, what ruins are in the realm of things."[29]

This constellation is one that Lacan will carry to its furthest and most far-reaching conclusions by returning *Witz* to its earlier affiliation with metaphor, and describing the former as the reverse motion of the latter "at the precise point at which sense emerges from non-sense [où le sens se produit dans le non-sens]."[30] That is to say, *Witz*—or here also the joke, in the Freudian sense—is located at the point where non-meaning is produced in meaning, where the signifying chain is decomposed into its pre-symptomatic, preconscious, pre-logical undecidablity. Thus wit, thematized in the Enlightenment and the early romantic era as at least a certain kind of thinking and knowing—even to the point of being deemed the transubstantiation or *transportation* (*meta-phora*) of Spirit itself—and subsequently disavowed as a mere intellectual ornament, a temporary holiday from social and logical constraints, or the undoing of spiritual progress, reemerges in Freud as a model of the psychic apparatus equivalent to that of the dream (see *JRU* 159–80; 181–205) and, in Lacan and subsequent thinkers, finally appears as the necessary corollary of the process of sense-making itself.[31] In Lacan's model, sense and nonsense are nothing but symptoms of the metaphorical or the joking process (and reciprocally, the symptom is the "sense"—or perhaps, in the case of neurosis and psychosis, the "nonsense"—that the psyche makes of data without inherent order or meaning).[32]

If wit/*Witz* thus emerges in the twentieth century as the dubious core of semiotics, the conditions of this emergence are already prepared by the romantic and pre-romantic question of how to separate original creation from simple inanity. Yet such an interpretation should not therefore be taken to mean that wit (not to speak of metaphor) is equivalent to the mere absence or negative of sense. Rather—as Lacan takes care to describe it—it is the moment of the passage *between* sense and nonsense, in which the determinations of both sense and nonsense are not only held in suspension, but indeed created as a result of this passage. Lacan plays on the phrase "mot d'esprit"—joke, *Witz,* but also "the word that in French is *the* word *par excellence,* the word whose patronage is none other than the signifier of spirit" (Lacan, "Agency of the Letter," 175, translation modified; "L'instance de la lettre," 508)—in order to (re-)make Jean Paul's point that the Hegelian *Geist* and the Freudian *Witz* are ultimately different functions of one and the same mechanism. And if here "we realize that it is his very destiny that man challenges when he derides the signifier [c'est sa destinée même que l'homme met au défi par la dérision du signifiant]" (Lacan, "Agency of the Letter," 175, translation modified; "L'instance de la lettre," 508), it is because this very possibility of deriding the signifier emerges out of the signifier's co-origin with the risible: the risible and the signifying determine *each other.* This mutual determination is precisely the inherent "ambiguity" of the symbol vis-à-vis the world that, for Hegel, is the symbol's simultaneous promise and threat. Indeed, *being* inherently ambiguous, the symbol casts doubt on the very possibility of art to adequately represent *anything*; given that the symbol is also the proto-form and immanent spiritual force of art, without which art is no longer art but reality or mere thing, what is at stake here is no less than the validity of aesthetics as such.

This productive yet problematic ambiguity of the symbol in Hegel is precisely what Freud will later take as consciousness's passkey to the unconscious layers of the psyche within the paired mechanisms of the dream and of the joke. In the latter in particular, the ambiguous or "multiple-use" symbol (here, word) is given ludic treatment as a function of a libidinal economy: wordplay and "pleasure in nonsense [Lust am Unsinn]" (*JRU* 125–27; 140–42) represent not just the lubricious pleasure of skirting social mores to which Freud unsurprisingly devotes the bulk of his attention, but also the "demonstrations against the compulsion of logic and reality [Auflehnung gegen den Denk- und Realitätszwang]" and release from the "pressure of critical reason [Drucke der kritischen Vernunft]" (*JRU* 126; 141). But given that sense and reason are products of the superegoic censorship that is inseparable from the unconscious, Freud's distinctions end up collapsing into one another, and it is hard to say where sense begins and "pleasure in nonsense" ends.

What Lacan in the above passage calls "derision" may then, without great distortion to his meaning, be retroactively translated in Freudian terms as *play*. Play—which, for Hegel, again, effects the "perversion and derangement of everything objective and real [Verkehren und Verrücken aller Gegenständlichkeit und Realität]" (*A* 576; *AII* 198)—is the literal derision of the signifier insofar as it suspends the passage from wit to reason or spirit (and vice versa), maintaining them in a state of pleasurable tension instead of forcing a resolution.[33] Hegel's two catastrophes of art—a slavishly mimetic replication and the anti-mimesis of "subjective humor"—may be reinterpreted along Lacanian lines as, respectively, an excess of meaningfulness or its deficiency: "more matter with less art," to borrow a phrase—or more art with less matter. If this is indeed the case, then despite Hegel's own disinclinations, play's capacity to suspend the process of meaning-making would in fact be the only thing that preserves art as functioning mechanism. But it would also be the reason that all art remains essentially suspect for Hegel, in terms of philosophy's task at best a necessary evil, since art, according to its very nature, would then be incapable of "making sense" in the first place.[34] Tellingly, what Hegel finds most objectionable in the new artistic trends is a kind of self-serving pleasure in the act of art-making itself: as he puts it, the "business of joking merely for the sake of joking [Geschäft des Spaßes nur des Spaßes wegen]" (*A* 296; *AI* 382). Far from Schiller's pedagogically motivated idea of play as something allied to beauty and set precisely *between* objectivity and subjectivity, "law [Gesetz]" and "physical exigency [Bedürfnis],"[35] here play is the abandonment of art's proper task of reconciling particular and universal, sensuous form and universal Idea, in favor of mere aleatory connection—and thereby is also the dramatization of the potential contingency of representation as a whole, carried to its self-indulgent extreme.

Of course, the dynamic of wit and spirit whose stakes Lacan allusively but clearly lays out is not necessarily one exclusive to art. But art—as the domain of "Spirit" in which not only representation per se, but also, correspondingly, the contingency of representation vis-à-vis signification, or even "Spirit" itself, is not just foregrounded but *inherent*—drives the bidirectionality of signification to the point of intolerability. And the (for Hegel) pseudo-synthetic art of subjective humor, which rejects notions of artistic objectivity in order to exploit the presumably more easily available resources of an arbitrarily inclined wit, is the mode of art that makes a literal mockery of the notion of a necessary connection between reality and representation, between referents in the world and forms on the canvas or words on the page, and thus constitutes, at least so long as art retains some sort of claim on truth, the wholesale mockery of the progress of Spirit. In the art "form" of subjective humor, the two elemental dangers of wit—the unchecked play of genius and the linguistic self-referentiality of metaphor—are finally brought together, with disastrous results:

> In thus drawing together and concatenating material raked up from the four corners of the earth and every sphere of reality, humour turns back, as it were, to symbolism where meaning and shape likewise lie apart from one another, except that now it is the mere subjective activity of the poet which commands material and meaning alike and strings them together in an order alien to them. (*A* 601; *AII* 230)

In forcing apart the bonds between form and content whose reconciliation has been *the* task of the history of aesthetic development, subjective humor brings us right back to the beginning of civilization, to the primitive chaos of signification. The intolerable difference from "primitive" stages of art, however, is that this chaos is no longer the result of a naïveté, a latency or not-yetness of form vis-à-vis understanding. Its dismemberment of meaningfulness takes place under the sign of subjective sovereignty, the artist who holds himself in contempt of the universal in order to make violent, intentionally incongruous connections. Thus art as a carrier for Spirit is rendered null and void, its former expressive potential halted in regressive play. Subjective humor, the style of "mediocrity and what is partly wishy-washy, partly characterless [Gemeinheit und das zum Teil Läppische, zum Teil Charakterlose]" (*A* 68; *AI* 98) is thus no less than the end of art before the end of art, the paradoxical anti-aesthetic art form par excellence. From this point onwards, philosophy will take over the responsibility for substantial truth and the production of meaningful meaning. Meanwhile art—if it is to be *this* kind of art—can be left to the jokers who ruined it.

Wit's End: Irony

This absolute threat to objectivity and objective representation posed by the witty and whimsical subject is the reason why "subjective humor" is time and again twinned with irony in the *Lectures on Aesthetics*.[36] "Irony," as the term is used by Friedrich Schlegel and his associates in the *Athenäum* group, variously designates a certain notion of the self-creating, self-reflecting subject; the "continuous self-parody of Plato's Socrates" (*F* 156; 160; compare

OI 265; 368); the "form of the paradoxical" that is "everything that is simultaneously good and great" (*F* 149, translation modified; 153; compare *OI* 266; 368); "logical beauty" (*F* 148; 152); "the clear consciousness of eternal agility, of an infinitely teeming chaos" (*F* 247; 263); and, in one of Schlegel's more epigrammatic and enigmatic formulations, "a permanent *parekbasis.*"[37] In terms of the first of these definitions, at least, which is the one Hegel most picks up on, it is easy to see how "subjective humor" may arise out of irony as the almost all-too-literal application in the work of art of personal creative freedom taken to its outer limit. At one point, Hegel explicitly describes subjective humor as irony "made into a form of art [zur Kunstform gemacht worden]" (*A* 67; *AI* 96), and even if he did not, his constant ascription of subjective humor's failure to the mania of the unchecked ego, "for which all bonds are snapped and which can live only in the bliss of self-enjoyment" (*A* 66; *AI* 95), does the same work.

But irony is not just that which supposedly gets put on display as illegitimately limitless freedom in the work of subjective humor; irony is also *itself* a question of representation and adequation. Cicero's oft-cited definition of irony as "saying one thing and meaning another,"[38] while clearly referring to the far more restricted phenomenon of verbal or rhetorical irony, fixes irony not just as the trope of linguistic reversal but as, in Paul de Man's words, the "trope of tropes" ("Irony" 165), the figure that points to figuration—the possibility of saying things differently—as such.[39] This possibility of saying things differently that verbal irony explicitly invokes, moreover, involves not only those forms of expression that would be more than merely denotative, but also, as in the case of metaphor, the very volatility of the "merely denotative" itself. De Man's subsequent definition of irony—which sees Schlegel's aphorism and raises it—as "the permanent parabasis of the allegory of tropes" ("Irony," 179) derives in part from this aspect: irony is the dropping of the mask, the whispered aside to the audience, the breaking of the fourth wall in a history of representation ordinarily so committed to its verisimilitude.

This throwing into question of the premises of representation is why Hegel finally names irony "das Allerunkünstlerischste" (*AI* 98): the absolutely inaesthetic thing. If irony, even in the simplest of its potential manifestations, is a mode in which "the sign points to something that differs from its literal meaning and has for its function the thematization of this difference" (de Man, "Temporality," 209), then it can not *but* pose a problem to a theory of art that considers art's fundamental task that of reconciling sign and meaning. What Hegel is unable, or rather unwilling to think through at this point is how an art which is *of* mimesis or representation (even in the strong sense of both terms) could also "represent" the ambiguity of representation as such. For while those moments in the *Aesthetics* where a particular form "dissolves [*sich auflöst*]" are as numerous as they are crucial to Hegel's narrative of development, here it is not this or that form, but the very function of art itself, art's internal necessity, that is in question. Just as a private idiom is no language, ironic art is anti-art; it breaks all organicist connections of the artwork and turns it into a formless nothing of random idiosyncrasies.

Presumably, if when verbal irony thus already troubles the premises of idealist aesthetics, it may still always be reined in by taking recourse to notions of intention and a commonsensical, or at least a consensual, hermeneutics.[40] But as de Man also points out, such a delimitation of irony is in fact problematic, in that once the problem of hermeneutics is opened up by irony, it quickly becomes clear that even the most seemingly uncontroversial and obvious of interpretations can only ever be provisional and without rigorously logical certainty.[41] The event of this infinite spiral of irony—perhaps, in Schlegel's words, when "irony runs wild and can't be controlled any longer" (*OI* 267; 369)—is also the source of irony's definitional confusion: irony, which initially refers to rhetorical moments of reversed meaning or ambiguity of utterance, comes to stand for the ambiguity of utterance per se, thus for the fraught nature of all interpretation and rules and finally for a hermeneutic and moral relativism in which the criteria for judgment are exclusively the jurisdiction of the individual *subject,* a subject whose jurisdiction—last but not least—itself falls under the same ironic processes that have already thrown language and world alike into confusion. This is as much to say that "irony" in the romantic sense goes well beyond the still ultimately restricted phenomenon of rhetorical irony, while nevertheless deriving distantly from it. Hegel, starting from the moment when irony takes on its wider epistemological import, describes it in terms of Fichte's "*ego* that remains throughout abstract and formal [durchaus abstrakt und formell bleibende Ich]" (*A* 64; *AI* 93), which simultaneously posits its own world and negates it through a solipsistic subjectivity: "Consequently everything that exists in and for itself becomes only a *show* [*Schein*] not true and genuine on its own account or through itself, but a mere *appearance* due to the I in whose power and caprice and at whose free disposal it remains" (A 64–65; *AI* 94). At this crucial point in the *Aesthetics,* the hierarchy of appearance and reality is overturned: no longer is reality something *to be* represented; representation (by the self to the self) is taken as the sole substance of reality. If Hegel's aim in the *Aesthetics* is to show how art emerges out of historical states of being, this is clearly in part as a countermeasure to irony, in which aesthetics posits itself as *prior to* ontology.

Such a philosophical *hysteron proteron* not only eliminates the mimetic function of art that Hegel takes for granted; it also, and indeed as a corollary to this elimination, makes objective truth a matter of precisely that which should be its opposite: that is, a matter of *poeisis.* Not just art, but through art truth itself becomes subject to the bad originality of romantic dilettantism. Thus it is that in the *Philosophy of Right*—where irony is condemned in even stronger terms, if possible, than in the *Lectures on Aesthetics*—"irony" appears as the "evil that is universal within itself [das in sich ganz allgemeine

Böse]" (*PR* §140, 121; 279), and Hegel describes an ironic stance towards morality as that which

> knows indeed what is ethically objective, but rather than forgetting and renouncing itself in order to immerse itself in its earnestness and to act according to it, holds itself apart from it even while relating to it in order to know *itself* as that which *wills* and *decides as it wishes* and which could *just as well* will and decide otherwise [. . .]. It is not the thing that is admirable; instead, I am what is admirable, I am master over the law and the object, with which, according to my whims, I *merely play*, and within this ironical consciousness, wherein I allow the highest to perish, I *merely enjoy myself*. (*PR* §140, 120, translation modified; 279)

I leave aside the specifically political and social implications of Hegel's thought here[42] to remark simply that the notion of onanistic play that Hegel sets out in this passage precisely repeats the condemnation of his discussion of subjective humor. Just as subjective humor's aesthetic play signals the negation of art's mimetic meaningfulness, play shows up in the ethical-political realm as the original sin of *pleasuring oneself*, a narcissistic and sterile *jouissance* whose object of desire is itself and whose means are its own ends.[43] In both art and the political sphere, the ironist breaks free from the objectivity of content, refuses to recognize the triviality of his particular will in the face of the universal, and creates, in short, his own rules (and then breaks even *them*). The consequence of this is not only an "inartistic" art, but also a morality that proclaims "the vanity of all the ethical content of rights, duties, and laws" (*PR* §140, 139; §140, 279).

Schlegel's aforementioned association of irony and parabasis, with all its corresponding promises of literal and metaphorical revelation, should indicate that, paradoxically or not, irony is not innocent of its own claims to truth. Kierkegaard remains the one to have appreciated this fact most keenly, noting, with his typical sensitivity to paradox, that irony "is earnestness about nothing—insofar as it is not earnestness about something" (*CI* 270). Thus, or nevertheless, whatever "irony" is—and even irony's "inventor" (see *A* 66; *AI* 95) cannot be called consistent on this score—it is not simply the nihilistic self-reflexivity that Hegel and his disciples claim it to be. In the opening paragraphs of Schlegel's "On Incomprehensibility," his ironic apologia for his own role in the promotion of irony, he speaks (in an oft-commented passage) of the wish for "a real language, so that we can stop rummaging about for words and pay attention to the power and source of all activity [eine reelle Sprache, daß wir aufhören möchten, mit Worten zu kramen, und schauen alles Wirkens Kraft und Samen]" (*OI* 260; 364). Schlegel's gesturing to the "great frenzy of such a Cabala" (*OI* 260; 364) of linguistic utopianism, while itself clearly (and, as we will see, significantly) ironic, nevertheless indicates that for Schlegel there can be neither irony nor non-understanding without a corresponding idea of understanding, a time to come of a Hermeneutic Revolution (to match the other revolutions of the era) in which "humanity will at last rise up in a mass and learn to read" (*OI* 261; 365). Indeed, Schlegel's stated desire for a "real language" bears a decided affinity with Hegel's description of art as the precarious representational counterpart to a representation-free philosophy. As with the ostensible clarity of a post-aesthetic thought, the transparency of a "real language" means not only that the effort of interpretation (and the corresponding potential for mis- or non-understanding) is at an end, but also that the conflict between the representational nature of language and the truth claims of philosophy—which both Hegel and the *Athenäum* group struggled, in their different ways, to resolve—is finally decided. A language without hermeneutic resistance is a language that has canceled itself; truth shines out unmediated, freed from the prospect of linguistic refraction.

Hegel naturally recognizes that this condition is not yet the case, yet expresses faith in its imminence within the domain of philosophy. For Schlegel, however—and this the crucial point of divergence—such a condition is not only not yet fact, but also will never be fact, and if Schlegel's previous writings gestured toward a utopian horizon not so dissimilar to that of Hegel, here such a horizon only exists any longer as an object of wry self-parody—"I break off at this point so as not to profane prematurely the worship of the highest divinity" (*OI* 269; 371)—and the approach to the "mystery" (*OI* 261; 364) of human being is not only not simple but irremediably crossed with all sorts of taboos and prohibitions. Schlegel brings his essay to its rhetorical climax in praise of a point of human knowledge "that must be left in the dark, but in return shores up and supports the whole thing and would lose all of its power the moment one tried to break it down into reason [in Verstand auflösen]" (*OI* 268, translation modified; 370). Indeed, even the aforementioned invocation of a "real language" is a profoundly ironic act—in fact, an act of parody, which distorts the famous lines from Faust's opening monologue in Goethe's (in 1800 still uncompleted) drama into a cheekily sincere-insincere admission of failure.[44] Schlegel stages himself as a failed—because all too successful—version of Goethe's demonically bound scholar-magician, one who alienated his public "out of the thoughtlessness of youth" by presenting truth "naively" and "nakedly" in "an eternal hieroglyph" in his *Lucinde* (*OI* 261; 364)[45] and who was subsequently obliged to cook up a more "popular medium" "to bond chemically the holy, delicate, fleeting, airy, fragrant, and, as it were, imponderable thought" (*OI* 261; 364). If, as Friedrich Kittler has argued, Goethe's *Faust* marks the simultaneous beginning of German literature and hermeneutics in the tragedy of magical decryption, the failed "Faustian experiment of trying to insert Man into the empty slots of an obsolete discourse network,"[46] then Schlegel's Goethian parody marks the beginnings of the comedy of this tragedy, not only in the ironization of the latter's subjective pathos but also in the abandonment of both the melancholic search for an original past of signification and the utopian search for a stable future meaning.[47]

Far from the modes of linguistic mourning or linguistic utopianism, then, Schlegel's essay is inscribed in a network of decontextualized citations and transmuted figures, making the seemingly messianic "project of a 'real language' not only the idea of a work *with* words, but also and precisely the work *in* language, between words, a work *on* language that permanently alters and shifts standards of denomination."[48] Here irony is no longer a regrettable source of non-understanding or a facetious and self-indulgent style of obfuscation; it is the condition of a non-understanding that is not a problem but rather something salubrious and generative, if not indeed constitutive of, or possibly even synonymous with, language as such—thus making any unmediated relation between language and object not only a definitional paradox but also an epistemological falsehood.[49] It is no doubt for this reason that for Schlegel it is not *Spirit* (or its equivalent) that is named as the eventual goal of progress, but understanding or reading itself: "readers who will know how to read" (*OI* 269; 371). Given, however, that Schlegel prefaces his hope with the exclamation "Welche Katastrophe!"—in mock horror (and francophone echo) marking the literally down-turning or mis-troping (*kata-strophe*) consequences of a totalized readership—it is not entirely clear that what Schlegel means here is not in fact readers who will know how to read *ironically,* who will abandon altogether a belief in hermeneutic consensus, much less in objective truth or mystical immediacy. As Hegel had anticipated, the interpretive power of the subject is now indeed privileged over the objectivity of the world. However, far more salient is the self-generating force of language itself, which supersedes any notion of subjectivity or linguistic-hermeneutic *adaequatio*. Thus just as the originally split nature of art confirms the fundamentality of the irony that Hegel so disdains, the irony of positing oneself, legacy of the Kantian-Fichtean heritage, becomes the underlying condition, not just of all art, but also of all that from which art should have been kept rigorously separate.[50]

And yet, partially for this reason, Schlegel's belated self-evaluation, far from being simply a further building block in the project of romantic irony, also represents a sea change in irony's career. For "On Incomprehensibility" is in fact not the mea culpa for a demolished objectivity or the semi-despairing plea for a mystic hermeneutics to come that it is so often claimed to be, but rather the preeminent and performative instance of "the irony of irony" (*OI* 267; 369) that Schlegel himself names as the last phase of the development of irony, indeed quite in the same manner as Hegel posits a "comic consciousness" as the ante-penultimate moment of Spirit.[51] Irony remains, of course, but now stripped of its last vestiges of utopian ambition. As the ironic citationality of the essay already shows, the championing of the "progressive universal poetry" (*F* 175; 182) of romantic art that characterized Schlegel's earlier work in the *Athenäum* project has been transformed into a self-implicating and skeptical stance, which hardly reinstates the rationality of reason or the dominion of positive truth, but also sees neither resting place nor true horizon in the creative power of the individual or the collective. And even if the "prospect of a limitlessly increasing classicism" (*F* 175, translation modified; 183) still remains to a degree open and available, this is itself in the form of non-understanding and obscurity, whereas full understanding is nothing but the "catastrophe" of a universalized triviality at the point where a perfectly transparent hermeneutics and a total irony at last join hands.

In short, Schlegelian irony has led Schlegel to the point at which this irony is itself recognized under the sign of irony, and that irony which had previously, if inconsistently, functioned as a way out of the ironic predicament of non-reconciliation—namely, as the carefree disregard for reconciliation that constitutes the primary target of Hegel's ire—is now folded into the very predicament to which it gives its name. Schlegel's accomplishment here is not to be underestimated. For if it is often difficult to discern what actually separates irony from the self-conscious subject that appears at the end of Hegel's *Phenomenology of Spirit,* it is just as difficult to differentiate this irony from the negative hermeneutics that makes not only the self-conscious subject but also any true meaningfulness, uncompromised historiography, or non-self-annihilating narrative strictly impossible. What seems at first a glaring contradiction here is in fact none at all. For both of these notions of the subject—the perfect sanity of self-identicalness and the madness of non-identity—are two sides of the same coin.[52] They are opposing interpretations of the same problem of what happens when not only the necessary connection of interpretation to phenomena is broken, but this brokenness is also recognized: in other words, when irony breaks out of its classically rhetorical quarantine and emerges as explicit relational/perceptional mode, the consciousness of the (self-)represented nature of the phenomenal world. If Hegel's proposed solution is to attempt to capture irony as one moment within the dialectic of consciousness, which will ultimately be able to shake off a broken sensual representationality in favor of a greater holistic (abstract) whole, de Man, for example, insists in contrast on the continued presence of such a brokenness *within* the purportedly whole as the latter's bad conscience and, eventually, undoing.[53]

Schlegel, for his part, in "On Incomprehensibility," both recognizes and ultimately repudiates both of these conclusions to the ironic predicament. Such a repudiation is particularly trenchant, but also particularly humorous, because what is ostensibly to be "concluded" in the essay is above all Schlegel's own ideas, philosophy, and life's work. In this context, it is telling that de Man, in "The Concept of Irony," fully elides the tonal difference between "On Incomprehensibility" and Schlegel's earlier writings. De Man's atypical *in*attention to literary texture here is especially noticeable in his reading of the passage from "On Incomprehensibility" that he quotes at the conclusion to his own talk:

> But is incomprehensibility really something so unmitigatedly contemptible and evil? Methinks the salvation of families and nations rests upon it. If I am not wholly deceived, then states and systems, the most artificial productions of man, are often so artificial that one simply can't admire the wisdom of their creator long enough. Only an incredibly minute quantity of it suffices: as long as its truth and purity remain inviolate and no blasphemous rationality dares approach its sacred confines. Yes, even man's most precious possession, his own inner happiness, depends in the last analysis, as anybody can easily verify, on some such point of strength that must be left in the dark, but that nonetheless shores up and supports the whole burden and would crumble the moment one subjected it to rational analysis. Verily, it would fare badly with you if, as you demand, the whole world were ever to become wholly comprehensible in earnest. (*OI* 268; 370)

To this de Man comments sarcastically, "That sounds very nice" ("Irony" 184). Yet even a cursory reading of this passage in its original context reveals that Schlegel hardly means the "niceness" that de Man is apparently at such pains to deconstruct.[54] In its overblown phraseology, in its continued provocation of allying a reverence for governmental institutions and philosophical systems with the dazzlement of aesthetic creation, in its counterintuitive suggestion that irony remains "true and pure" by being protected from a disruptive rationality, and in its perverse praise of artificiality couched within the linguistic commonplaces of the discourse of natural genius, it is difficult not to recognize that here, at least, Schlegel is no longer (if ever he truly was) earnestly promoting an idealistic program of collective genial creativity and revolution through aesthetic formalization. To the contrary: in "On Incomprehensibility," Schlegel directs the last act of the *Athenäum* group, in which he unrepentantly continues to praise provocation in support of normativity, call clarity equivocalness, and insist on standards of truth that are paradoxically dependent on their own disruption. The decisive difference from his previous writings, however, is that now Schlegel—playing both Socrates *and* his interlocutors—no longer excludes irony itself (as well as all that came under its purview) from these same paradoxes.[55]

Schlegel comes to see what Hegel, in his very disdain for irony, could not: that also the willful subjectivity of irony itself, with its promises of a "constant fluctuation between self-creation and self-annihilation" (*F* 167, translation modified; 172) does not escape the ironic dilemma: the playing self is also played with, to the point of not having anything it could call a "self" any longer. In Hegel's words (not quite on irony but on that comedy that contains irony within it): "The pretensions of universal essentiality are betrayed in the self; it shows itself to be entangled in an actual existence and drops the mask, precisely insofar as it wants to be something genuine" (*PS*

§744, 450, translation modified; 542). But such a "genuineness," letting go of irony's play, itself turns out to be only an emptiness and "comic spectacle [komische(s) Schauspiel]" (*PS* §746, 452; 544). What for Hegel is the foundation of the situation of the unhappy consciousness is for Schlegel then indeed a kind of fulfillment, if perhaps not quite the one he had wished for. In the folding of romantic irony within irony itself, the enthusiastic irony of the *Athenäum* group meets its end.[56] In its place, however, emerges the "irony of irony" as an irony *conscious* of itself as irony and yet whose consciousness is always *of* irony: an irony, in other words, which has become *comic*.

This is not meant in the sense of the "comedy of the comic [Komik der Komik]," the "comic judgment on the comic" with which Adorno would have modern art damn itself.[57] Such a judgment merely mocks mockery in support of a still higher principle, be it that of the ethical impossibility of all previous forms of artistic pleasure. Comic irony, on the other hand, is that which Hegel himself predicts with his assertion that irony "as the individuality of the genius [. . .] implies that not only is there to be no seriousness about law, morals, and truth, but that there is nothing in what is lofty and best, since, in its appearance in individuals, characters, and actions, it contradicts and destroys itself and so is ironical about itself" (*A* 67; *AI* 97). For Hegel, this self-ironizing—and thus also irony-ironizing—form "almost brushes up against the principle of the comic" (*A* 67, translation modified; *AI* 97). As will be shown below, however, such a form does not merely brush up against the comic, but overtakes it, becoming an irony with which one simply cannot play games [ist durchaus nicht zu scherzen]" (*OI*; 208) because now it too is in on the joke.

Objective Humor, or The Stabilization of Irony

Such a second-degree irony, however, is not immediately to come to fruition. With Schlegel's infamous turn to Catholicism and the subsequent transformation and reactivation of his own concept of irony—leaving aside for the moment the myriad other factors in the changing mood of the times—the insights he achieved in "On Incomprehensibility" enter a period of latency.[58] As for Hegel, it is no doubt due to an intimation of the fundamental inherence of irony within representation, not to mention the potentially disastrous consequences of this inherence for all other aspects of his philosophy, that he, for his part, announces the end—not of art, exactly, but of art as the valid attempt at the representation of essential truths in concrete form. And yet here too Hegel resists fully drawing the conclusions of his own argument, seeking instead to carve out what could be called a future for art after its "end": in Hegel's words, "the standpoint from which art can pursue its activity even in these days" (*A* 595; *AII* 222). What is required is a form that will guarantee that Idea and form can still hang together within art, even as art itself loses its world-historical relevance. "Objective humor"—the conspicuous terminological antidote to a dangerous and anti-aesthetic "subjective humor"—is the name with which Hegel baptizes this fragile correspondence, a modern (but decidedly non-"ironic") spiritualization of art that will provide an opportunity for *artworks* even in the era of art's "self-transcendence" (*A* 607; *AII* 237).

Despite the crucial saving function that "objective humor" is to perform, however, what Hegel actually means by his term is left somewhat vague. From the few remarks on the subject in the *Aesthetics,* it appears that what he has in mind is what one might today term psychological realism or sentimental fiction, in any case a form of art or (as the stress seems to fall) literature aimed at presenting human life in all its variety and complexity: as Hegel puts it, the "withdrawal of man into himself, a descent into his own breast, whereby art strips away from itself all fixed restriction to a specific range of content and treatment, and makes *Humanus* its new holy of holies: i.e., the depths and heights of the human heart as such" (*A* 607; *AII* 237). In his study *Humor als dichterische Einbildungskraft,* Wolfgang Preisendanz has systematized Hegel's objective humor as a response to a series of three problems or oppositions that art faces at the end of the *Lectures on Aesthetics.* These oppositions, which should by now have a familiar ring, may be summarized thus: first, the idea of the creative originality of the artist as the "true objectivity," confronted with the necessary non-correspondence between the infiniteness of interiority/subjectivity and the concrete appearance of the work of art itself; second, the demand for realism or verisimilitude in art, faced with the interdiction against *mere* realism (which, again, is on the one hand inadequately "spiritual," and on the other hand, ends up being nothing but a showcase for the artist's personal and subjective skill); and third, perhaps most significantly, the necessity of reconnecting objective reality with inner experience or "imagination [Phantasie]" faced with the inherent arbitrariness of any such connection (see *HDE,* esp. 133). The two catastrophic outcomes to this situation—the two ways in which the above oppositions may *fail* to be resolved—are, again, the pure prosaic mimicry of realism and the anarchic poetasting of "subjective humor." Objective humor is then the solution to this seeming impasse, a "coalescence of these extremes" (*A* 608; *AII* 239) of contingent objectivity and absolute subjectivity, emerging out of their very apogee and crisis.

Thus Preisendanz—himself an eminent thinker of the comic, the joke, and the laughable—here also takes care to distinguish Hegel's concept of objective humor from that which might fall within the realm of the comical or the funny. To the contrary:

> That which [. . .] makes itself felt as humor is nothing but the (apparent) inadequacy of the event and its execution [die (scheinbare) Unangemessenheit von Vorgang und Vortrag], the tension between the

> occurrence as such and the form of its narration. Epic humor [. . .] can here be defined as the subjective illumination of an objective occurrence, *that in itself neither has any comical quality whatsoever, nor should be made comical* [die als solche keinerlei komische Qualität hat, die auch nicht "komisiert" werden soll] but which is nevertheless "enveloped" by a certain humor [von einem gewissen Humor "umwittert"] through its formation within subjective reflection. (*HDE* 15, emphasis added)

The word "umwittert" (enveloped, shrouded, surrounded) in this passage is in fact a quotation from Thomas Mann, from his own claim for humor in his novel *Joseph and His Brothers.* Preisendanz comments directly on his borrowing of Mann's word:

> I have emphasized the word "enveloped," because it indicates so well the humorous polarity of the object and its mediation; this metaphor corresponds precisely to the compatibility of humorous structure with a represented reality that is in itself thoroughly neither comical nor made comic, and thereby bears witness to the fact that epic humor is fundamentally unrelated to the specific qualities of the things to be represented [. . .], but rather, that it should first of all be seen solely as a type of narrative structure which constantly produces and manifests a tension between presentation and situation. (*HDE* 12–13)

As both this passage and Preisendanz's own examples of "objective humor" make clear, the humor that "envelops" the narration of the event is itself neither comic nor particularly available for comedy. The subtitle to Preisendanz's book, *Studien zur Erzählkunst des poetischen Realismus,* already indicates the degree to which Preisendanz's concern here is not with comic modes of expression at all,[59] but rather with a certain literary style more or less assimilable to the German realist novel from the nineteenth century to the present day. This form has as little in common with the comic as objective humor has to subjective humor. Indeed, it is precisely the difference *between* these forms that will be at stake here.

Hegel himself offers as possible models of "objective humor" the examples of Greek epigram, Persian lyric poetry, and Goethe's *West-Eastern Divan.* This is not the place to wonder why Hegel's recommended art forms for Western culture in its historical and spiritual maturity should be respectively obsolete, non-Western, or in conscious mimicry of non-Western modes, although given Hegel's concern with art as the concrete manifestation of the culture and ethos of its time, such temporally or geographically foreign examples do indicate a certain future marginalization of art as a whole. More important, however, is the question of how Hegel's "pure delight in the topics, an inexhaustible self-yielding of imagination, a harmless play" (*A* 611; *AII* 242) differs, exactly, from the apparently *harmful* play and excessive freedom of subjective humor.[60] For "objective humor" cannot simply be equated with the sentimental arabesques of modern lyric poetry or the wry epiphanies of modern prose, however much Hegel's description seems to anticipate them both. In fact, much like "subjective humor," objective humor—bespeaking Hegel's dearth of specifics—seems to be less a genre or even a set of formal requirements than a kind of mood or mode of art, less a form of art than an attitude toward art's appropriate role in and relationship to the world.

Preisendanz himself locates the specificity of objective humor in Hegel's concept of "Verinnigung in dem Gegenstande" (*AII* 240). This phrase, translated by Knox as "a growing intimacy with the object" (*A* 609), is in fact an untranslatable multiple pun, compacting together at least the words "innig" (tender, heartfelt, ardent), "Innigkeit" (intimacy, depth—of feeling, friendship, etc.), "Vereinigung" (reunification), "Erinnerung" (remembrance), and "Verinnerlichung" (internalization, spiritualization). Here should also be pointed out the oft-noted resonance of the German for "objects," literally "those which stand against" or "counter-situations" (similar to the Latin etymology of "ob-ject," or "thrown against") which makes Hegel's call for "an inexhaustible self-yielding of imagination [ein unerschöpfliches Sich-Ergehen der Phantasie]" (*A* 6II; *AII* 242) within them all the more provocative. Indeed, "Verinnigung in dem Gegenstande" is not (as the English translation might seem to indicate) a simple sentimental melting of the subject into a welcoming world. Hegel's phrase, not without its own curious dash of wit, maintains the hard resistance of the objective world vis-à-vis the artist's self, but *in this resistance* is the self preserved, and that as something more than mere arbitrary will: perhaps even as "the reconciled return out of his other into his self" (*A* 539, translation modified; *AII* 155) in the form of artistic expression. Preisendanz associates such a dynamic with Hegel's notion of the "Concept of the Absolute as Love" (*HDE* 127; see *A* 539; *AII* 155), but one could just as easily call it the master/slave dialectic of aesthetic realism: the artist has free jurisdiction over his objects (in a way that is nothing if not socioeconomic in its implications) and yet at the same time needs these objects to constitute himself as artist and as self. Art and subject exist alike as the reflection of objects in the self and of the self in objects: "for art does not need any longer to represent only what is absolutely at home at one of its specific stages, but everything in which man as such is capable of being at home" (*A* 607; *AII* 238). If the "exterior reality with which modern poetry is concerned is characterized by the 'perfectly developed universal mediations of civil society,' in which the human being everywhere has to do not with what is his own, but rather 'with alienated objects lying outside his own sphere wherein he is master' " (*HDE* 129; quotations are from *A* 260–61; *AI* 337–38), then art is now to provide a solution to this alienation by synthesizing and overcoming this alienation within itself, thus making possible a "Heroic Age" (*A* 260; *AI* 337) for a brave new materialist world.

It is through this process—and *only* through this process—that art has the possibility of a future for Hegel. Subjective humor is simultaneously the mode of an "alienation or diremption between poetry and empiricism, feeling and experience, inner and outer reality" (*HDE* 136–37) and the attempt to transcend this same alienation through acts of fantasy and witty creation. But the arbitrariness and willfulness of fantasy as a tentative solution to a generalized "alienation or diremption" is art's death knell according to the Hegelian schema—and thus precisely what Hegel seeks with "objective humor" to historicize, to limit, and to overcome: not by the exercise of fantasy over and above diremption, but as the transformation of diremption into dialectic and the ostensible incorporation and neutralization of division within the relation of subject to world itself.

Thus, although Hegel naturally does not say so, objective humor, like subjective humor, also partakes of a kind of irony. In this case, however, the irony in question is essentially that of the "stable irony" defined by Wayne C. Booth as a specifically literary technique that "delimits a world of discourse in which we can say with great security certain things that are violated by the overt words of the discourse,"[61] or that of the "ironic mood" described by Beda Allemann that "requires a particular insight into secret ongoing connections and 'backgrounds,' "[62] and perhaps especially, that of the novelistic irony theorized by Georg Lukács as the mutually determining constellation of the "contingent world and the problematic individual."[63] Such forms of irony, which achieve the status of artistic form with Hegel's "objective humor," are maybe not even structurally all that different from the irony of *Athenäum* romanticism, but for the fact that they begin from the assumption of irony's *limit*, a point at which all irony is finally absorbed and reflected back from the non-irony of the conscious subject. The merely "apparent [scheinbare]" quality of the "the tension between the event as such and the manner of narration" (*HDE* 15) that Preisendanz circumspectly inserts within parentheses is in fact the decisive factor in objective humor's self-definition. For despite all of objective humor's ostentatious narrative contradictions and wistfully lit contingencies, there nevertheless must come the moment when these apparently tense relations come to an agreement, when "humor" stops and "objectivity" begins. In other words: objective humor solves the problem of the representation of irony that subjective humor (as the limitless representation of irony per se) was unable to do, through the simple and ingenious device of *narrative distance*. Beyond fixed determinations of topic and form, narrative and the subject of narration themselves now come to provide the solid ground to which even the loose chains of contemporary art may be firmly anchored.

In this way, objective humor plays with, but, even more importantly, also displays and *thematizes* the relationship of subject to object, form to content, saying to said. In this thematization of the subject/object relationship, the alienation inherent to it—the slash in subject/object—is *reconciled*, albeit in a particular and limited way. The thematization of the gap between representation and reality ends alienation through the aestheticization—and hence, the (aesthetic) mastery—of that gap. This thematization or formalization of the relationship between subject and object then becomes *the* subject matter, and indeed *the only* subject matter, proper to a future art. The choice of object is of course free, but the relationship between the two—and by extension, the relationship between self and world in toto—is fixed in a kind of unequal interdependence. Such interdependence is in turn not too difficult to conflate with the calmly consuming gaze of the upstanding bourgeois citizen, whose possessions satisfy him because he feels that they are not alien objects—mere "Gegen-stände"—but rather constitutive parts of his own being. Even if the novelistic hero himself remains alienated from his fate and his world, the controlled irony of "objective humor" avoids such alienation precisely in claiming it, in establishing the "freedom of the writer in his relationship to God, the transcendental condition of the objectivity of form-giving" (Lukács, *Novel,* 92).

It is a curious fact of the *Lectures on Aesthetics* that Hegel twice references "that familiar saying" (*A* 46; *AI* 70) from the Terentian comedy *Heauton Timorumenos* (*The Self-Tormentor*), "Nihil humani a me alienum puto," "I count nothing human alien to me."[64] The first time Hegel quotes this, within the introduction to the *Aesthetics,* he does so admonishingly, as a criticism of the idea that the aim of art would be simply to display the gamut of human emotions and experience in its variety. While Hegel states that this is indeed a formal aspect of art, this is so precisely in a negative sense, in which art "without any explicitly fixed aim would thus provide only the empty form for every possible kind of content and worth" (*A* 47; *AI* 72). Hegel reinforces his point here with a political analogy. Art cannot be the mere presentation of human variety any more than the state can be a mere collection of people: in order to properly *be* art or state, there must be a guiding idea and a consensus of purpose. The artwork or state without a necessary connection to "a higher *substantial* end" is a contradiction in terms, in fact not art or state at all but merely aesthetic or political anarchy (see *A* 48; *AI* 73).

The second time that Hegel refers to Terence's maxim, however, in the section "The End of the Romantic Form of Art," it is in an *affirmative* sense, to recommend the study of human nature in its variety as art's current and culminating task (see *A* 607; *AII* 237–38). Hegel's naturalized, German, paraphrastic citation of Terence in this section—in contrast to the directly quoted Latin of the introduction—only serves to further emphasize the difference between the two moments. No longer is "everything human" a matter of sheer cumulative multifariousness; at this later stage of both art and the *Lectures on Aesthetics* itself, this multifariousness has been subsumed under the category of "*Humanus*" (*A* 607; *AII* 237), of human being *as such,* which now forms the "higher substantial end" of art that a merely superficially anthropocentric art had lacked. If before the representation of human beings had constituted merely a chaotic proliferation of disparate instances, now these instances add up to a real conceptual whole.[65]

And yet this subsumption of anthropocentric subject matter under an anthropological concept actually only evades the problem that Hegel has previously posed, as he himself admits in the paragraphs directly following (see *A* 604–6; *AII* 238–40). For despite its elevation to conceptual dignity, human experience remains a weak basis for a weak art, an art out of which no new classics, but only pleasantly ephemeral reflections of contemporary experience will henceforth emerge. Hegel merely reverses the formerly condemned gathering of indiscriminate content within an essentially empty form into a tolerance for this empty form *as* content: that is, the "empty form" of human being as such.[66] And the preeminent expression of this is no less than the very romantic irony—as the contingency of aesthetic form and the blankness of the abstract subject—that both "objective humor" and the philosophical consideration of art itself were supposed to guard against.[67]

Thus irony reenters through the back door of Hegel's philosophy of art. The controlled irony of objective humor is intended to accept the contingency of form while restricting it to a merely formal problematic, to acknowledge the relativity of representation in safety by containing it within the "harmless play" cited above, the "depth of feeling and a cheerfulness of the inwardly self-moving heart which [. . .] lift the soul high above all painful entanglement in the restrictions of the real world [eine Innigkeit und Froheit des sich in sich selber bewegenden Gemütes, welche (. . .) über alle peinliche Verflechtung in die Beschränkung der Wirklichkeit hinausheben]" (*A* 611; *AII* 242).[68] But this cheerful intimacy or interiority of feeling, which should—Hegel's word choice here could hardly be more charged—effect the soul's "Hinaushebung" from reality, differs from irony only in that very *Hinaushebung*. For the real difference between the "inwardly self-moving heart" of the objective humorist and the "bad, useless" (*A* 67; *AI* 97) ironist bent on "living as an artist and forming one's life artistically" (*A* 65; *AI* 94) is that the latter insists on form/representation as a problem, not just within the protected *Spielraum* of autonomous art, but also *within* painful reality itself.

Hegel's prescription for art as *comédie humaine* thus appears precisely as a homeopathic remedy against irony, a defusing of irony's explosive potential by confining it to the "harmless play" of the always-already superannuated mode of objective humor. But the attempt to defuse irony through the "harmless play" of objective humor is a patent if touching absurdity, for the very notion of play as the free but uncommitted manipulation of objects and concepts *implies* irony as its foundational gesture, as in the previously quoted passage from the *Philosophy of Right,* in which Hegel describes the "evil that is universal within itself" of ironic consciousness as that which "merely play[s]" (*PR* §140, 121; 279) with laws and morals. Objective humor's ironizing subject can be separated from subjective humor's irony *of* the subject only through the ruse of the "end of art"—a ruse which not even Hegel himself was willing to carry to its full conclusion.[69] Objective humor thus contains latently what the school of romantic irony had always made explicit: the generality of the essential contingency of form and the resultant blurring both of the supposedly safe borders of the aesthetic and the subject/object distinction upon which the category of the aesthetic rests. The neutralization of irony within the frame of a capacious humanism and a museumized art only succeeds on the one hand in calling up the specter of kitsch and sentimentality that will henceforth haunt European art as its bad conscience,[70] and on the other, in making irony into precisely the negating force Hegel always feared it would become.[71] Humor's lack of end turns out to be a dead end. It is, to say the least, a laughable predicament.

The Art of Irony: Comedy and the Comic

Where, then, is the comic in this story? If "objective humor" is the tenuous perpetuity of art as a curio shop of intimate reflection, and irony or subjective humor is the permanent play of non-coincidence between representation and represented, what has happened to that which might be a source of humor in the colloquial sense, a source of laughter? We have already seen how Hegel assumes the affinity between "subjective humor" and the amusing incongruities of wit, as well as how wit joins with irony to trouble both the Hegelian vision of art and the integrity of speculative dialectics as a whole. But further investigation is still required to see how the comic, as form, breaks out of its customary restriction to the satirical, the droll, the frivolous, and the happily ended, and takes on wider significance as a genuine aesthetic and epistemological mode: indeed, one whose "structural categories [. . .] constitutively coincide with the world as it is today" (Lukács, *Novel,* 93) in a way perhaps more fundamental than those of objective humor ever did.

To do this, however, we must return to Hegel, this time in regard to his sparse but decisive passages on comedy. Comedy shows up prominently, if briefly, twice in Hegel's work: first in the *Phenomenology of Spirit,* where it appears as the realization of the contingency of particular forms of ethical being, then later in the *Lectures on Aesthetics,* where it is treated almost solely as a literary category, that is, as comedic drama, with all of its generic conventions (stock characters, happy endings, etc.) intact.[72] Unlike either subjective humor or irony, both comedy as a genre and comedy as a principle are fully compatible with the principles of speculative dialectics, insofar as they both act as the force of the negative itself, that is, a force capable of revealing the emptiness of things previously taken for given in order to clear the ground for new forms of awareness and ways of being.[73] In the *Phenomenology,* comedy appears as the *phase* before that of the unhappy consciousness, which for its part constitutes "the counterpart and the completion of the comic consciousness that is perfectly happy within itself" (*PS* §752, 454–55; 547). If the unhappy consciousness is the "tragic fate of the self-certainty that should have been able to be in and for itself [. . .] the pain that expresses itself in the hard word that God is dead" (*PS* §752, 455, translation modified; 547), comedy is the childlike carefree moment before this grief has sunk in, the innocent taunting of the dead God without an awareness yet of the direness of the consequences.

In the *Aesthetics,* however, while Hegel's definition of comedy is perhaps simpler than that of the *Phenomenology,* its relative value becomes somewhat more complicated. On the one hand, the *Aesthetics* ends where the *Phenomenology*'s unhappy consciousness begins, with a lawless irony threatening to sink ethics and art together (see *PS* §748–53, 453–56; 546–48). On the other hand, insofar as art itself is a basically ossified mode that must be, if not done away with, at least relativized and secularized—declared as "dead" as God is, so to speak—comedy is necessary as the genre of art which laughs at—and thereby negates—art itself. Thus comedy, although it is clearly less noble than tragedy, is in a way even more significant, insofar as it constitutes the happy performance of the annihilation of the inessential that is both the goal of art and the reason for its apparent self-abolishment.[74] This criterion of the annihilation of the *inessential,* however, is the crucial qualification for comedy as a *genre,* as well as what distinguishes it from the all-devouring irresponsibility of the irony that it nonetheless resembles. The comic, writes Hegel, "must be restricted to showing that what destroys itself is something inherently null, a false and contradictory phenomenon, a whim, e.g., an oddity, a particular caprice in comparison with a mighty passion, or even a *supposedly* tenable principle and firm maxim" (*A* 67; *AI* 97). With this, Hegel is adhering to the classical Aristotelian idea of comedy, according to which laughter derives from "an error or disgrace that does not involve pain or destruction."[75] For Hegel, this "error or disgrace" may be applied to the structure of the dialectic both literally and analogically: on the comedic stage, the "negative"—now concretized and allegorized into foolishness, gracelessness, mishap, confusion, vulgarity, vice, and so on—is explicitly presented and performed; at the same time, it is the eventual disappearance of the negative under the withering effects of the laughter it elicits that constitutes not only the real happy end of the play, but also comedy's entire philosophical and moral usefulness.[76]

The view of comedy as the mockery of error is, of course, one of the most commonly propagated and tenacious definitions of the comic, whose advocates include such disparate figures as Hobbes (in his aforementioned passage on laughter as the sensation of "sudden glory"), Shaftesbury (who defends comedy on the grounds that it shames and exposes human folly), and Bergson, whose famous theory of laughter describes it essentially as a corrective mockery of rote behavior, of the "mechanical encrusted on the living [du mécanique plaqué sur du vivant]" (Bergson, "Laughter," 84; *Le Rire* 44). For obvious reasons, such theories often erroneously privilege a didactic and utilitarian *satire* as the form of the comic per se—and even when they do not do so explicitly, the punitive theory of comedy still always presumes that to laugh is to laugh *at*; its underlying idea is that to laugh is to despise. Beyond the rather unflattering picture of human nature that it paints, such an idea of comedy is problematic in that it posits laughter as at once a symptom of scorn for evil or error, the reaction to the difference between this error and the ideal from which it deviates, the expression of joy over this error's defeat, and the instrument of this defeat itself. Thus it is unclear, according to this interpretation, whether comedy should inhere in error as such—in which case it is difficult to see what constitutes the comic's particularity—or in the lampooning thereof—that is, in the making-comic of this error—in which case the theory simply begs the question.[77]

Hegel, for his part, takes pains to distinguish his own theory of comedy from "the laughter of derision, scorn, despair, etc." (*A* 1200; *AIII* 528), and his stress on the fundamental non-seriousness of the comedic protagonist's "absolutely reconciled and cheerful heart" (*A* 1220; *AIII* 552) and comedy's intrinsic "infinite light-heartedness and confidence" (*A* 1200; *AIII* 528) lack to a certain extent the didacticism of many other interpretations of comedy's function.[78] Nevertheless, his description of comedy as the negation of the inessential similarly assumes a laughter of derision, even if here the laughter has been elevated to the level of the ontological.[79] In this case comedy acts as no less than the *aufhebende* force of the dialectic itself, laughing away all "caprice, folly, and perversity" (*A* 1194; *AIII* 521). Like tragedy, comedy displays the overcoming of the particular and the inessential, and the gradual but inevitable triumph of the true and the actual. The fundamental difference between the two dramatic modes is that comedy—paradoxically, precisely as a function of its triviality or "lightness"—*also* effects its *own* dissolution, its dissolution *as form*. Whereas tragedy stages the untenability of particular forms of life, particular representations, particular subjectivities, comedy stages the inessentiality of life-forms, representation, and subjectivity as such. In other words: comedy, the representation of universal insubstantiality, has as ultimate result the universalization of the insubstantiality of representation.[80] If this disastrous predicament is not overcome, what emerges, once again, is the "allerunkünstlerischste" art of subjective humor. If it is overcome, art and its history of representing are overcome along with it.

It was Hegel's student Friedrich Theodor Vischer who most thoroughly saw and developed the critical function of comedy within speculative dialectics. Yet for all his championing of and reliance on Hegel's teachings, the somewhat idiosyncratic Vischer, who was also strongly influenced by the comic theories of Jean Paul, diverges in several crucial ways from his master. Vischer's system of aesthetics is a ternary system in which the beautiful constitutes a synthesis of the opposing polarities of comic and sublime. The consequence of this reorganization is that the negative force of the comic, already present in Hegel, is, unlike in Hegel, no longer the negation of the foolish, erroneous, or trivial, but instead of the great and profound, and laughter itself appears not as that which chases away the ontologically contingent, but as a belittling of ontological bombast, indeed as God's own sense of humor about himself:

> The God of theism must fear laughter in earnest: for he would maintain himself in permanent distance from the world, and does not admit to the interpenetration of the finite and the infinite [. . .]. Only the God of the speculative worldview brings the comic over to his side and thus has no need to avoid it, for it is within his own self alone that he is laughed at. Finitude, commonness, indeed, even evil, when they place themselves next to him and say, I too am here, they can go ahead and have their fun; the Lord grants it to them, for he harbors them within himself as moments whose necessity he recognizes, but only as something already vanquished and powerless. (*UEK* 166–67)

Despite Vischer's basic adherence to the premises of speculative dialectics, the shift in emphasis effected within the above passage is far from insignificant. Vischer's first move is to transform the comic from a purely negative or subversive force to the aspect of particularity and finitude within the dialectical process—a thought not so far from that of Hegel himself, even if Vischer, for his part, lays stress on the positive necessity of this very particularity. Yet the implications of this constitute a further turn of the comic away from a strictly Hegelian perspective: for if a speculative God must incorporate the comic in order not to be a brittle metaphysician who tolerates no contradiction, then the comic no longer exists as the logically necessary but ontologically contingent negation of the divine, but is instead a constitutive part of the divine itself. To overstate somewhat, only a comic God is not destroyed by comedy; the divine is dependent on precisely that which is supposedly its opposite.[81]

Disregarding for the moment the question of whether the good humor of such a relationship is as tenable as Vischer appears to believe, the essential thing to note at this point is that comic is no longer a matter of the negation of opposing binary terms, but of a suspended contradiction of phenomena nevertheless inextricable from one another. Similar to Jean Paul's definition of humor as "the inverted sublime" (*VA* §32, 88; 125), Vischer's comic is the inherent co-implication of the small within the great, in which the great is "sublime and yet not sublime": "This is a contradiction, a *contradictio in adjecto,* and this contradiction is precisely the comic" (*UEK* 176).[82] Vischer's aphoristic statement can be read literally here: the comic is not merely that which diminishes the sublime or the simple opposite of the serious at which it is so often left; rather, the comic constitutes the *aporia* of the sublime, a paradox within sublimity itself. Such a thesis also explicitly refutes Hegel's central conviction that the comic should negate only that which is *supposedly* serious, leaving true seriousness and value intact.[83] In contrast, Vischer argues that "the true jest must never attack that which is only apparently sublime; it must always attack a true sublime and may even take aim at the highest sublimity, and on the other hand it must be admitted that insofar as it reconciles itself to the comic [sich dem Komischen bequemt], every sublimity is deficient" (*UEK* 169). Here the sublime is not negated by the ridiculous; it *is* the ridiculous, insofar as it is sublime, and the comic is not the negation of the sublime but its paradoxical status as a totality continually cut through by its own "deficiency."

Although Vischer himself considers this to be simply one more scene in the dramaturgy of the dialectic, he also does not shy away from associating the supposedly controlled and corrective genre of the comic with the notoriously uncontrolled phenomenon of romantic irony. Indeed, for Vischer, the only difference between irony and the comic is that the comic is an aesthetic *category*, whereas *irony* has to do with the domain of aesthetics as a whole. And if the comic "wants nothing but contradiction" (*UEK* 181), irony applies this contradictoriness to the question of representation that lies at the core of the philosophy of art itself: "Frivolity declares common and Idea-denuded appearance to be the only real thing and repudiates the idea as such" (*UEK* 182). If the comic is the expression of the inner contradiction of the sublime and its ricochet back towards the non-sublime sublimity of the perceiving subject, irony is the force that reveals through this pseudo-sublime subjectivity the impossibility of a true representation beyond representation itself, that turns the possibility of a true image or an authentic language back to the uncertain ground of mere appearance.

Hegel himself allies Schlegelian irony explicitly with the comic at several points in the *Aesthetics*, taking care, of course, to distinguish the two modes. But despite Hegel's disdain for the former, the only real difference between irony and the comic for Hegel is "the content of what is destroyed" (*A* 67; *AI* 97). Yet just this criterion, which should be so decisive for the distinction between irony's bad nihilism and the purifying force of the comic is, in the context of the Hegelian dialectic, precisely the confirmation of their essential relation. For if irony, as Hegel seems at times to imply, is merely a comedy that doesn't know when to stop negating (see *A* 159–60; *AI* 210–11), and the history of art is a process of the perpetual becoming-contingent of forms once considered to be absolute, then there is no guarantee that *any* forms are absolute. Ultimately, there is no way to know what is "a *supposedly* tenable principle and firm maxim" (*A* 67; *AI* 97) and what is a real one. In this way, Vischer's insight into the inherent affinity between romantic irony and the comic becomes the finger on the raw nerve of Hegel's system.[84] For Hegel, "comedy" may, or indeed *must* be put into service as a tool of negation, but only insofar as this strengthens the Idea of dialectical becoming, which itself is not to be touched. In Vischer's interpretation, in contrast, the only thing *not* potentially subject to comedy, paradoxically enough, is irony itself (even if it is irony *as* the Idea of dialectical becoming); but that which is the very essence of seriousness (or the seriousness of essence) is the most comic thing of all.

Yet the comic in Vischer's analysis is not merely a localized version of a more universal irony; it also has a specific task: namely, to be the phenomenal manifestation of irony, irony's expression and performance. If irony is infinite negation, then the comic, in Vischer's words, is "*poetically presented* infinite negativity [*poetisch dargestellte* unendliche Negativität]" (*UEK* 182, emphasis added)—which is as much as to say, the comic is the *aestheticization of irony*. Thus the comic is no longer to be equated with *comedy* as the presumed sublation of the ironic negative; it is, rather, the ironic *performance* of that negative, which was in fact never a negative at all, but the very substructure of the system itself. That which for Hegel is the "Allerunkünstlerischste" —a mode of art that, if it is not strictly impossible (and is indeed "made into a form of art" [*A* 67; *AI* 96] in subjective humor), nevertheless destroys art's fundamental premises and hence exists as a pure contradiction in terms—is in Vischer turned on its head to become, *as* contradiction in terms, not only a valid artistic principle but *the* art form par excellence. Even if Vischer's aesthetic theory was not quite to have the lasting influence that Hegel's did, this reversal of Hegel's conclusions within a dialectical framework presages a positive future for irony in art and for art in irony that Hegel himself could not have foreseen. Having lain dormant in objective humor, irony returns once again to the fore, this time not to save art from its contradictions but in art to bear its contradictions out.[85]

Punch Line: Comic Irony

The question remains, of course, to know how irony, as the supposed antithesis of form, becomes concretized in aesthetic form in the first place. Hegel's apprehension of "subjective humor" as a mode of indiscriminate wittiness already provides a partial answer: insofar as irony makes a serious formal determinacy definitionally impossible, an undisciplined and merely ludic expression—"we see nothing develop, everything just fizzles out [man sieht nichts werden, alles nur verpuffen]" (*A* 602, translation modified; *AII* 230)—emerges as unstable default option and source of narcissistic pleasure. A slightly different idea of what an art of irony might look like is provided by Paul de Man in his critique of Peter Szondi's interpretation of romantic irony, which de Man argues is in fact not irony at all but "the aesthetic *Aufhebung* of irony by means of the notion of distance" ("Irony" 182). For Szondi, the Schlegelian project is one ultimately determined by a "will to the canceling of antitheses and the unification of separate terms [Der Wille zur Aufhebung der Gegensätze und zur Vereinigung des Getrennten]."[86] Irony is thus the name for both the "split" that makes up the "essence of modernity," and contradictorily (as de Man suspects), for the hope of this division's healing, the "cancellation," in other words, of what it itself is. The situation that irony creates, according to Szondi, is then a potentially "tragic" one: irony tears apart meaning in the hope of its reconstruction, thereby establishing a notion of transcendence which it itself already forecloses. Thus irony "tolerates perfection only in the past and the future; everything which confronts it out of its present is measured according to the standard of infinity and thereby annihilated" (Szondi 18).

It is only through the establishment of aesthetic distance (such as Szondi reads in the *Lustspiele* of Ludwig Tieck) that something like pleasure and presence can be recuperated from the tragic non-reconcilability of which "irony" signifies both the fact of and the fight against.[87] For de Man, however, this is thoroughly a false solution, as he comments: "That could indeed be said of the comic, and in a sense Szondi is not discussing irony but confusing the two [. . .]. Irony is not comedy, and theory of irony is not a theory of comedy. This could be said about a theory of comedy, but it is precisely what a theory of irony is not. It is disruption, disillusion" ("Irony" 182). The *Aufhebung* of irony by means of distance that de Man rejects here is indeed one of the most common topoi in discussions of the comic,[88] although it is perhaps more accurately attributed to the wry authorial consciousness and aesthetic *mastery* of irony of "objective humor." Objective humor's *Aufhebung* of irony is, however, not structurally much different from Hegel's notion of comedy, which offers a higher truth—a literal or metaphorical happy ending—after each one of irony's negations: so to speak effecting on the level of World Spirit what objective humor enacts merely as narratological triumph. The decisive factor in all these cases is once again that a stable moment of untouchable non-irony is posited from which irony can be safely contemplated and kept in check—even if such a moment only exists "tragically," as a past that never was or a future that never will be.

But despite de Man's differentiation between a true, "disruptive" irony and an irony dishonestly stabilized into either objective humor or classical comedy, such "distance"—that is, aestheticization, "poetic presentation" (see *UEK* 182)—is, as de Man himself surely knows, itself inherently ironic: and in a sense de Man is not discussing the comic but confusing it with Szondi's limited conception thereof. For if aesthetics is haunted from the beginning by the ambiguity of the sign and the discontinuity of language, subject, and world (exemplified but not exhausted in both allegory and the joke), than *any* so-called aesthetic distance beyond irony can only compound, as was indeed the case in objective humor, the irony which was intended to be bracketed and defused. The "aesthetic *Aufhebung* of irony by means of distance" that de Man criticizes is thus no facile escape hatch into subjective certitude, but *already* the very "disruption, disillusion" he charges Szondi with ignoring. If irony is "the self of art," then art cannot save the self from irony.[89] This means that there can be no legitimate *Aufhebung* of irony into the presumed safety of a mimetically and semiotically stable comedy or humor; but it also means that there can be no legitimate tragedy of irony, since whatever could be posited counter to irony, turning it into loss of *something*, is itself already a fiction.

Just as Hegel's depiction of subjective humor as the art of irony under the sign of infinite subjective freedom is problematic in that, as Hegel himself states, irony ultimately also undermines the possibility of the autonomous subject of which irony is supposedly the apotheosis, any aestheticizing perspective that might be posited counter to irony is already cut through with the irony that all aesthetic representation always implies.[90] The self-referential, self-implicating, doubly ironic turn given to the ironic explosion of wittiness described as "subjective humor" and exemplified—but far from concluded—in Schlegel's "On Incomprehensibility" does not result in the stabilization of irony within the perceiving consciousness of the narrating subject, but rather realizes a new form of irony that truly broaches no fixed point, neither in the subject nor the objective world, neither in a messianic future nor an original past. This is just the ludic irresponsibility and sterile hall of mirrors Hegel feared, perhaps, or the "madness" upon which de Man insists (see "Temporality" 216), and yet it avoids the pathos of both of these figures by continually undermining even those standpoints from which a form of pathos might emerge. As in the redoubling Freudian mechanism of the joke, the ironic moment of critique—or, if one will, "distance"—breaks in within irony to annul pathos; but this moment, far from being something from which one could reconstitute a stable worldview, only confirms the epistemological contingency and availability for play of everything that it regards, including and especially itself. This specifically comic form of irony, a *late* irony, is one recognized and deployed with particular implacability by the authors discussed in the following chapters—who all, in their various ways, understood that in a world that has entered the phase of a properly comic ethos, in a world to which irony has returned, nothing, including irony, is to be taken very seriously.

Chapter Two

✦

The Playgrounds of Literature: Robert Walser

> And as soon as the play-drive begins to stir, with its pleasure in semblance, it will be followed by the shaping spirit of imitation, which treats semblance as something autonomous. Once man has got to the point of distinguishing semblance from reality, form from body, he is also in a position to abstract the one from the other, and has indeed already done so by the very fact of distinguishing between them.
>
> —Friedrich Schiller, *On the Aesthetic Education of Man, in a Series of Letters*

> The opposite of play is not seriousness, but—reality.
>
> —Sigmund Freud, "Creative Writers and Day-Dreaming"

> Laughter just means life.
>
> —Robert Walser, "Wie sie sich so selber fallen ließ"

The Twilight of the Idylls

Few authors have thematized the humoristic or comic nature of their own writing more than Robert Walser. Several critics have drawn attention to the phrases from the composition "Profession" in *Fritz Kochers Aufsätze,* "It would be fun to be a juggler [Gaukler sein wäre schön]" and "Clown? Yes, I think I have a talent for jesting [Clown? Ja, ich fühle, ich habe zum Spaßmachen Talent]" (*FKA* 30) as evidence—albeit ventriloquized—of Walser's comic tendencies.[1] Perhaps more illuminating, however, are the following lines, written some twenty years later in one of the many posthumously deciphered and published prose sketches that Walser sometimes referred to as his "Pencil Zone," the "Bleistiftgebiet": "I am absolutely my own educator [Erzieher]; maybe this is the reason why I long to be educated. How amusing that would be for me. What a comedy [Lustspiel]. Sometimes nonsensicalities are just beautiful [Manchmal sind Unsinnigkeiten wunderschön]."[2] This comedy of the autodidact, so to speak, of the self who splits himself into pupil and educator at once, less to develop himself than because such a short circuit of ignorance and knowledge would be "amusing," is exemplary for Walser's work. The *Lustspiel* that ensues from this process—a *Lustspiel* that is indeed no less than the body of Walser's work itself—is one that undermines the notion of education in all its forms and applications, through the irony of a farcical solipsism transforming learning and development into that very childish pleasure in nonsense whose channeling into more productive activities is precisely education's aim.

It should thus come as no surprise that such a pedagogical *Lustspiel* as Walser describes, particularly when performed within literature, is one that not only undoes the premises of *Bildung,* but also puts into question the *bildende* functions of classical and romantic aesthetics: in particular, the Schillerian notion that the function of art is to advance human freedom through the balance of the sensuous and the rational within the "play-drive [Spieltrieb]," whose object, says Schiller, "may therefore be called *living form:* a concept serving to designate all the aesthetic qualities of phenomena and, in a word, what in the widest sense of the term we call *beauty.*"[3] Walser, it is clear, early on takes Schiller's idea of the *Spieltrieb* and its connection to both beauty and "living form" as a personal summons and lifelong vocation. It goes without saying, however, that this will be a *Spieltrieb* with a difference. For Walser—living long after Schiller's liberationist fervor has settled into a Biedermeier *Gemütlichkeit* and excluded by both birth and temperament from the canons of "great" literature[4]—the beautiful no longer consists in the balance of sensuous appearance and rational idea, nor of perception and affect, but in the staging of sheer nonsense and absurdity in the abandonment of a guiding principle. And yet to long to be one's own educator is, in Schillerian terms at least, already a logical impossibility or vicious circle, requiring one to produce the ideal beauty that would teach oneself to recognize the ideal beauty that one is already producing.

Philosophically speaking, then, Walser is rigorously correct: the beauty that emerges from such a play-drive is nonsense indeed, in the most literal way possible. Nevertheless, the fact that such nonsensicalities, too, can "sometimes" be beautiful indicates that Schiller's optimism regarding the aesthetic disposition's ability to reconcile sense and idea (a pair which reappears in Hegel as objectivity and subjectivity) is fundamentally misplaced. However close Walser's educational yearning is to Schiller's notion of play as the mediator between individual drives and the lawfulness of the ideal, his corresponding self-development, out of which arise only the beautiful amusements of *Lustspiel,* is also a form of "mere play [bloßes Spiel]" (Schiller, *Aesthetic Education,* 105; *Ästhetische Erziehung* 235) which Schiller dismisses with the words "Of course, we must not think here of the forms of play which are operative in actual life [Freilich dürfen wir uns hier nicht an die Spiele erinnern, die in dem wirklichen Leben im Gange sind]" (*Aesthetic Education* 107, translation modified; *Ästhetische Erziehung* 237). In contrast, not only is Walser's play with himself very much operative in real life, but also wholly, even excessively "directed to very material objects" (*Aesthetic Education* 107), the precise ground for Schiller's disqualification. As the lines right before Walser's stated wish for self-education explain: "I have resources of a constant war with myself, I go off to war and make peace with myself again and thus am uninterruptedly in the most pleasant exertion [unausgesetzt in angenehmster Anspannung]" (*AB1* 72). Insofar as its end is nothing but itself, nothing but the perpetuation of its own mock battles and enjoyable strain, Walser's play is truly "mere." This so characteristic mereness, however, *as* mereness, will also prove much more than merely significant for Walser's interventions in the history of German letters and his contribution to the development of comic form within it.

A complete list of direct mentions of nonsense, laughter, joking, being comical, and the like in Walser's texts would be a tediously lengthy one. Particularly but not exclusively in the short prose of his later period, self-referential statements of a comic nature or intention are such a regular feature of Walser's writing they could almost be said to be its main connecting element. Of course, the fact that someone speaks of laughter and joking hardly means one can assume this someone has the power to elicit laughter himself—and indeed much of the early critical literature on Walser, even when acknowledging parodic or playful strains in Walser's prose, has tended to view his work under the sign of alienation and mental instability, or at best a childlike nonchalance and regional-pastoral naïveté.[5] Such interpretations are certainly facilitated by the biographical details of Walser's life: his failure to achieve substantial recognition for his writing in his own lifetime; his feelings of inferiority as a Swiss German and younger son of a struggling lower-middle-class family; his solitary, impecunious, and transient lifestyle; his family history of depression, suicide, and mental illness; and his own nearly unbroken internment in sanatoria during the last several decades of his life. Beyond merely the temptations of the biographical, however, such interpretations appear to be made possible by the critical prejudice that the comic, at least when it is not an instrument of polemical social critique, is not to be taken seriously. For such a view, the comic can be but the failure of seriousness, a tragic incapacity to activate the norms that would provide the stability of real meaningfulness and the potential for real decisive action.

In Walser's case, this belief, always questionable, is doubly misleading, given that it is precisely the premises and appurtenances of this seriousness that Walser places in doubt. However, the other dominant critical tendency—to read Walser as the simple inheritor of the romantic ironic tradition or, indeed, as the holy fool of German literature, who through a kind of natural insouciance is able to "playfully claim his aesthetic freedom in an increasingly administrated world"[6]—is just as misleading. The crucial aspect that both these portrayals—the pathological and the happy-go-lucky—fail to convey is the very radicality of Walser's ironic auto-didacticism, the post-romantic comedy of irony that forecloses (even while maintaining in suspension) unrestrained play and the solemnity of beauty alike.[7] Such an irony is indeed *not* a mere lingering within Hegelian "comic consciousness" as the perfectly plastic—and exemplarily "cheerful"—relation both to one's own self-identity and to subjective conditions of knowledge. Nor, however, is it exactly de Man's directly corresponding "unrelieved *vertige,* dizziness to the point of madness" ("Temporality" 215). For Walser's irony is not *only* irony; it is also the canny staging of the ironic predicament, a literal "making fun" of irony's "madness" itself.

"So, for example, once I said to my childhood friend Firmiani," writes Walser in a text from 1924, "'Hey, I'm insane.' I said it to him on a whim. It was just an idea. But he took it seriously. With such worried eyes he looked at me. And thus he spoke: 'I trust you're just talking crazy' [Wohl sprach er: 'Du wirst dich hoffentlich irren']."[8] This unintentional joke that Walser places in the mouth of the boyhood friend is also the joke played on readers who attribute the aleatory and occasional quality of Walser's writings—"It was just an idea" [Es war lediglich ein Einfall]—to personal incapacity, simple-mindedness, an agenda of subversion or a gesture of withdrawal. Rather, as Walser writes in the same piece: "I amused myself, quite simply, as they say, like crazy [Ich amüsierte mich, ganz einfach, wie man sagt, wahnsinnig]" (*AB1* 33). Walser's writing is "subjective humor" taken to the point where it doubles back on itself to become a crazy form of impromptu self-amusement that knows itself to be mad, without, however, thereby removing itself to a safe distance from the nonsense it professes. That is to say, Walser feeds the liberationist project of aesthetic education through the Fichtean and romantic notion of the "absolute subject," revealing an aesthetics whose movement is utterly circular and folded in upon itself, of which one can say with Benjamin that it is a matter "*not* of the cognition of an object through intuition, but of the self-cognition of a method, of something formal."[9] When this self-knowledge itself becomes contingent, however, when the "radical, mystical formalism" (Benjamin, *Concept of Criticism* 123) that pervades the early romantic theories of reflection turns into mere "whim" and "idea," when educator and student, poet and world collapse in one—then an irony is activated for which neither de Man's mournful temporality nor the futuricity of the early Schlegel can hold valid: as I would once again like to claim, another name for a romantic irony that has outlived the romanticism that created it may well be the comic.

"Anyone Who Is Naturally Witty Has to Especially Watch Out"

Even leaving aside the fact that Walser chose for his first major published work, *Fritz Kochers Aufsätze* (*Fritz Kocher's Essays*), the conventional and literally puerile genre of the (mock) school composition, it is difficult not to be aware of the complicated identity of writing and playing that forms the primary leitmotif of the text. The "essays" themselves (after the "editor's introduction")[10] open with a painfully multilayered reference to this identity. In the opening lines of the first of the *Aufsätze,* the portentously titled "Man [Der Mensch]," the pupil Fritz Kocher writes with characteristic earnestness: "You could compare man to a well-arrayed pleasure garden, if our teacher would permit such allusions. Sometimes man writes poetry, and in this highest, noblest state he's called a poet [Man könnte den Menschen mit einem wohlangelegten Lustgarten vergleichen, wenn unser Lehrer dergleichen Anspielungen erlaubte. Der Mensch dichtet zuweilen, und in diesem höchsten edelsten Zustand nennt man ihn einen Dichter]" (*FKA* 8). If the first sentence's strained and stale metaphor, expressly marked as a cliché at the very moment of its saying, points to a form of lyrical language that is already well exhausted by the time Walser begins his literary career,[11] the cliché hidden in the second sentence of this passage is of a well-nigh emblematic significance for Walser's poetic concerns. The beginning of Fritz's second sentence is an echo of the maxim "Der Mensch dichtet, Gott schlichtet [approximately: Man creates; God arbitrates]."[12] Fritz, recalling the words of the proverb without remembering their context or conclusion, opts for a strategy of redundancy, making what had once been a conventionally edifying thought about the humbleness of human effort before an omnipotent God into a pure tautology and pastiche, debasing human being's "highest, noblest state" into a mere mechanical repetition of commonplaces and bringing the very ideology of *homo faber* that the proverb assumes into question.

At the same time, however, Fritz's image of human being as a "well-arrayed pleasure garden," however much a stale quotation from the archive of German popular literature, can be taken seriously insofar as it gestures towards a particular Walserian topology of play that will be carried through this text, granting the staleness of old metaphors a new significance in their very staleness. Play is here precisely the result of the repetition of edifying clichés that, *as* clichés, have lost their access to reference and can thus no longer serve their original edifying purpose. But this loss of edifying purpose is also, at the same time, the text's occasion and a priori. The very first sentence of the book—"The young man who wrote these essays died shortly after his exit from school" (*FKA* 7)—not only potentially evokes the farcically literal image of Fritz suffering a fatal accident immediately upon stepping across the school's threshold, it also indicates that what is most prominently and significantly absent in this work is any notion of cause and effect, continuation, or aftermath, indeed of temporality whatsoever, that would provide some sort of end point to the repetition of lessons and grant Fritz's education meaning.

Fritz Kocher, in other words, has no future. The mediocre but dutiful pupil, so concerned with the conventions of the grown-up world, so willing to immerse himself in society's clichés, or rather quite sincerely (if unsuccessfully) taking these clichés to heart as his own, will never get a chance to put his education to use, to translate his indoctrination into the actions of the good citizen he evidently would apparently like very much to be.[13] It is an indication of the closed temporality of the work, for example, that when Fritz finally settles on a theme in the composition "Free Topic [Freithema]" (*FKA* 24–26), it is that of a description of his classroom. Meanwhile, in "School," Fritz writes, with unwilled double entendre, "How would one pass the time, if not with homework assignments!" (*FKA* 20). What at first appears as yet another bit of Kocherian flattery takes on a fully ontological significance: for there is in fact no objective world of consequences outside the schoolroom for Fritz Kocher; there is no time outside the time of homework, which is, in turn, the time of the book itself. In this way, the figure Fritz Kocher does not constitute a critique of *Bildung* so much as its *ad absurdum* inflation: the pure pupil with neither past nor future, eternally sitting at his desk in "the waiting room of life" (*FKA* 19), he is all *Bildung, Bildung* for its own sake, whose only tangible results are the school compositions which were to have been its means, not its ends. If play is to be distinguished from seriousness by its gratuitousness, its freedom with respect to real ends, this aspect of the *Aufsätze* already places the text under the sign of play and the rejection of the educational ideology of Walser's time. But it also makes claim that, contrary to Hegel's edifying program of objective humor as an attempt to bring the subjective destiny of the individual in line with his world, and even contrary to Schiller's idea of aesthetic play itself as the proper training for the full unfolding of human potential, a specifically non-teleological, indeed *pointless* constellation of play, wit, and a meaning-emptying practice of citation delineates the space of the "classroom"—the space, that is, in which writing happens.[14]

While the text's central conceit thus annuls the ideology of development on a characterological and narratological level, it abrogates development even more boldly on the level of style. Exemplary here is the pandering address to the teacher, already cited, that follows directly upon the garden metaphor: "if our teacher would permit such allusions [wenn unser Lehrer dergleichen Anspielungen erlaubte]" (*FKA* 8). The aside, of course, is nothing but a bit of schoolboyish obsequiousness, if not a sheer absurdity: for the metaphor, bad as it is, has already been set down, and whether the teacher would allow it or not is clearly no longer really relevant. It is precisely in light of this irrelevance, however, that it becomes clear that what is alluded to or played on (*an-gespielt*) in Fritz's pleasure garden of the human is, above all, *language*: specifically, language's capacity for producing apparent sense out of mere word and sound association (both within a text itself and between texts and paratexts), borne out already in the same sentence with the rhyming words "vergleichen [. . .] dergleichen." It may moreover be supposed that this awkward slant rhyme, appearing already in the context of an apparently casual and context-motivated reference to language, is in part what calls forth the image of the poet in the next sentence, the one who tautologically incarnates the "highest, noblest state" of humanity insofar as he is poetizing. As in the case of the unconscious quotation contained in the sentence's beginning, the stream of thoughts driven by word association shows the ennobled human condition of the creative writer to be in fact mere mindless sonic automatism. In the place of the poet as vatic "legislator of the world"[15] is the pupil who demonstrates despite himself that sense is nothing more than the persistence of nonsense.

Such a move is not the first and certainly not the last in *Fritz Kochers Aufsätze*. In general, Fritz's language is characterized by an awkward mix of naive observations, forced metaphors, non sequiturs, and badly managed quotations from society's storehouse of clichés; indeed, Fritz's style often seems to be a textbook illustration of rhetorical "don'ts," to the point where the sentences of the compositions end up annihilating themselves in a flagrant performance of stylistic ineptitude. One particularly egregious instance of such stylistic ineptitude occurs at the beginning of the composition "School": "I maintain that school is useful. It keeps me for six to eight hours every day in its iron or wooden claws (school desks)" (*FKA* 18). The infelicity of the metaphor is clear: the threatening image of being held in the school's claws is patently in ludicrous contrast with the professed aim of praising. (Fritz's subsequent words of tribute, "[School] is there and I love and admire facts. I like going to school and I like leaving it" [*FKA* 18] may similarly be said to fall somewhat short of their laudatory aspirations.) If the metaphor is not poor enough as is, it is made all the more so through the parenthetical clarification appended to it, which deprives it of the last shred of natural or symbolic character it might have had and makes language appear instead as pure artificial institution. The pupil Fritz writes at the crossing of persuasion and its self-deconstruction (or simply its disintegration), the very image of conventional language at the threshold of its inculcation.[16] The spectacular half-failure of this inculcation that is evinced in his compositions not only confirms Fritz as a dim bulb, but also and more importantly demonstrates the very magnitude of the pedagogical efforts that must be made merely in order to *be* linguistically conventional. As a result, though Walser's style here has nothing that immediately marks it as being particularly experimental (for all of Fritz's infelicities, his language is still well within the bounds of the normal and the colloquial), it is in a way more radical than many works that would aspire to that label. Walser does not attempt, like the practitioners of the heroic avant-garde, to transform language or test its outermost limits. His strategy, in contrast, is to bring language and its forming within the sphere of the comic. First forced to reveal its artificiality, arbitrariness, and plasticity—a thing already accomplished in shorthand by having the work be comprised of school compositions, that is, as *exercises* in writing[17]—it is then compelled nonetheless to go through the farce of trying to mean something, a state of affairs that reveals the poet's condition, once again, to be something distinctly less than "noble."

Thus, despite the intentional/unintentional comic double entendres of some of Fritz's statements, they should not be assumed to hide a secret and hence more "real" meaning behind their énoncés. Rather, in the "boundless positivity"[18] of *Fritz Kochers Aufsätze,* the real action takes place profoundly on the surface. In a reading influenced by Walter Benjamin's assessment of Walser's characters as partaking of a "heartrending, [. . .] completely inhuman, imperturbable superficiality,"[19] Massimo Cacciari points to a general lack of hermeneutic depth within the compositions, speaking of the language of one passage in *Fritz Kochers Aufsätze* as one of "extreme discretion [. . .]. It is the irony of the awakened, of those who know that the idea of their waking is a perfect no-place in the *Abendland*" (*Posthumous People* 168). However, a closer reading of the passage with which Cacciari is concerned makes it clear that Walser's language in fact has far more in common with the discordant "song of many voices singing in the highest tones" (*FKA* 11) of which Fritz supposedly disapproves than with the minimalist clarity Cacciari attributes to it,[20] and it is plain that whatever "special ironic tonality" Fritz possesses (see *Posthumous People* 143) , it is emphatically *not* that of a judicious subject awakened to the knowledge of his displacement, as Cacciari suggests, but rather of a confusion that fails even to recognize itself:

> If I were a painter, and it isn't out of the question that I might become one, since obviously no one knows their destination in life, I would most ardently like to be an autumn painter. I'm only afraid that then my colors wouldn't be up to the mark. Maybe I still don't understand it enough yet. And why should I worry anyway about something that hasn't even happened? I ought and need only to concentrate on the moment. Where have I heard these words before? I must have heard them somewhere, maybe from my older brother, who's a student at the university. Soon it will be winter, snow will swirl, oh, I can hardly wait! When everything's so white, one knows things better in class. Colors fill up the memory with all kinds of weird stuff. Colors are just a too-sweet muddle. I like things that are one color, one tone. Snow is like a song entirely in one note. Why shouldn't color be able to give the impression of singing? White is like a murmuring, whispering, praying. Fiery colors, for example autumn colors, are a shouting. Green in midsummer is a song of many voices singing in the highest tones. Is that right? I don't know if that's a good description. Well, the teacher will be so kind as to correct it. (*FKA* 11)

These conditional musings on becoming a painter so as to be able to paint autumn genre scenes are followed by a bromide that is no less than the vulgarized echo of Hegel's "Verinnigung in dem Gegenstande" (*AII* 240), the call for the artist to observe and know the world around him in the service of a humanist and realist art in which "the poetic dimension is no longer contained in the relationship between poetic feeling and the reality of experience that becomes visible only within the explicit formation of this relation, but rather is to be found in the innermost being of the externally existent itself" (*HDE* 132). While Fritz's statement "I ought and need only to concentrate on the moment [Mich soll und muß doch nur der Augenblick innig beschäftigen]" may at first seem, however banal, at least to be a heartfelt personal observation, it is exposed in the sentences that follow as nothing but another quotation, this time on Fritz's own admission: "Where have I heard these words before? I must have heard them somewhere, maybe from my older brother" (*FKA* 11). Thus a passage whose subject is precisely aesthetic and personal authenticity turns out to be nothing but secondhand wisdom, a wisdom, moreover, whose authority is derived from its coming from Fritz's older brother, "who's a student at the university" (*FKA* 11), that is, whose own knowledge is itself doubtless a citation from his professors and schoolbooks. What at first appears as a genuine reflection on consciousness and individual experience turns out to be nothing more than a quotation of a quotation of a quotation.

Similarly, Fritz's professions of love for the monotone in this essay, not necessarily absurd in themselves, become so when contrasted with his earlier statement that "it makes you sad to think that these colors are a sign of a general colorlessness [man wird traurig, wenn man denkt, daß diese Farben das Zeichen zu einer allgemeinen Farblosigkeit geben]" (*FKA* 10) and his expression of his wish to be an autumn genre-painter because of the beauty of autumn colors. Once again, it is clear that Fritz is not developing a logical thought or deeply felt intuition at all, but simply following a chain of arbitrary and almost purely linguistic associations. The sentences that announce this new and contradictory wish for the wintertime are particularly noteworthy for their sonic qualities: the sudden, awkward w-alliteration and internal rhyme of "Soon it will be winter, snow will swirl, oh, I can hardly wait! [Es wird bald Winter werden, Schnee wird wirbeln, ach, wie ich mich darauf freue!]" (*FKA* 11), one of Fritz's many misplaced attempts at lyrical language, or the line that follows, "When everything's so white, one knows things better in class [Wenn alles so weiß ist, weiß man alles viel besser in der Stunde]" (*FKA* 11), in which the repetition of "weiß" in two semantically unrelated senses produces a dissonant pseudo-pun with undesired meanings and implications. Fritz's unintended wordplay combines educational instruction with the blankness of a snow-covered landscape (a combination made all the more noticeable in Walser's/Fritz's avoidance of the usual verb in this context, namely, "lernen"): the denotative meaning of the sentence may be that the winter landscape's lack of stimulus is conducive to intellectual endeavor, but the connotation is that "knowing" in the school is actually a matter of emptying out one's mind.

Or as Fritz himself dutifully notes: "the indolence of a schoolboy thinks that words just produce themselves out of words. This, however, is nothing but a vain and dangerous notion" (*FKA* 45), continuing, "joking is permitted in school compositions, but only as light, delicate ornaments. Anyone who is naturally witty has to especially watch out. Jokes that sound nice when they come out of your mouth rarely come out well on paper [Witz darf in Aufsätzen vorkommen, aber nur als leichte, feine Zierde. Ein von Natur Witziger muß sich besonders in acht nehmen. Die Witze, die hübsch klingen, wenn sie aus dem Munde kommen, nehmen sich nur selten auch auf dem Papiere gut aus]" (*FKA* 46). Unsurprisingly, it is the very rules that Fritz obediently parrots that are most frequently violated in his essay book. Not merely explicit remarks such as "I've really babbled well [ich habe eigentlich gut schwatzen]" (*FKA* 26), but also and especially the frequent tautological expressions, redundancies, and associative series of words (e.g., "every day I shall and want to be stronger, freer, nobler, richer, more illustrious, hardier and foolhardier [von Tag zu Tag stärker (. . .) freier, edler, reicher, berühmter, kühner und tollkühner]" [*FKA* 9]) amply demonstrate that one of the salient principles of Fritz's style is indeed words producing themselves merely from other words, a principle of homonymy over semantic sense or indeed a wit so "natural" that it does not even intend its own wittiness: the naive-comic of the child, who, in Freud's words "can produce nonsense [. . .] directly and without compromise" (*JRU* 185; 211).

Verena Ehrich-Haefeli has characterized the language of *Fritz Kochers Aufsätze* as one that turns conformity to linguistic norms into play precisely through these norms' "exaggeration" (341), thus effecting a "fundamental rejection of instrumentalizing, goal-oriented thought" (Ehrich-Haefeli, "'Gaukler sein wäre schön,'" 343). If grammatical structures are mental structures, and right speech is right thinking, Fritz Kocher's paratactic poetry of incorrectness undermines the pedagogical goal of conformity and shows up grammatical and stylistic correctness as the tools of domination that they in fact are.[21] Thus, "insofar as *Fritz Kochers Aufsätze* radically puts the consensus upon which bourgeois reality depends into question, it can be included as one of the essential texts that inaugurate modernism at the beginning of the [twentieth] century" (Ehrich-Haefeli 344). Such an interpretation is given credence by Walser's frequent parodying of the commonplaces of pedagogic socialization, such as in the self-referential school composition "The School Composition [Der Schulaufsatz]" where Fritz, declaring, "style is a sense for order [Stil ist Ordnungssinn]," manages nonetheless to demonstrate only the great *lack* of a sense for order in his poor brain. But while *Fritz Kochers Aufsätze* is indeed one of Walser's most directly satiric and, so to speak, social works, its comic aspects should not be handed over so quickly to a directly politicized or thematic reading.[22] Nor should its status as a foundational text of modernism (as I would also like to claim) be assumed to be just because it acts as a critique of the consensus-making force of normal logic and speech.[23] A more significant reason why *Fritz Kochers Aufsätze* can be counted as a foundational text of modernism is that this very play with logic and language disrupts the rhetoric proper to literary mimesis—not only in its naive forms but also in its most complex manifestations. Or more precisely still, Walser's early text makes mimesis into what mimesis had always seemed to resist becoming: a thing of comedy.

"Objective humor" was supposed to be the solution to the crisis of art after the age of spontaneous natural genius gives way to an overly self-conscious preciosity, a lasting art form which would bring together the twin tendencies of a skilled but slavish realism and an expressive but arbitrary imagination.[24] This mode is one that indeed determines the development of the bourgeois novel in the decades after Hegel. "I wanted to begin straightaway," writes Walser's fellow-Swiss Gottfried Keller in his semi-autobiographical Bildungsroman *Der Grüne Heinrich*,[25] "to treat things with love and attentiveness and to stick close to nature, to do nothing excessive or irrelevant and to be completely clear with every brushstroke."[26] The chapter in which these words appear ends with Keller's character in a state of profound artistic block, which is temporarily mitigated only to later return conclusively as the mature narrator realizes with disappointment that he lacks the talent as a painter to achieve the goals he has set for himself. Keller's novel thus ends in the consciousness of creative inadequacy, of a personal inability to represent the world whose implications are nevertheless general and exemplary.

If Keller's Heinrich must give up his desire to capture reality in painted images (a renunciation, of course, for which the novel itself partially compensates), later artists and writers in general, and Walser in particular, will find these goals already foreclosed from the beginning, less from a lack of faith in one's own talent than through a lack of faith in the goals themselves. And yet it is also not the case that Walser is able to gain access to the "profane illumination" that Benjamin identifies, for example, in the aesthetic premises of surrealism: a "materialistic, anthropological inspiration, to which hashish, opium or whatever else can give an introductory lesson."[27] Walser's own writing lacks the belief in the "flashing moment of mimetic connection"[28] that grants a surplus value to objects to the point of positing a fully mystical relation between self and world. Indeed, such a form of mystical relation, however apparently different in both affect and ideology, may be considered the hypertrophic intensification of objective humor, pushing Hegel's mutually constituting dynamic of psychological interiority and thingly exteriority to its utmost limit.[29] In contrast, Walser's prose is neither mystical nor exactly mimetic in the traditional use of the word, positing a real mediation of the word between self and thing; it is not even humorous, in the sense in which Preisendanz attributes the term to Keller.[30] Rather, it is *playful*. There is no magical kingdom of words in Walser's writing, but a sandbox, in which castles are built and knocked down with the same gleeful or distracted ease.

It might therefore seem possible to consider Walser's work the proper heir to the "subjective humor" of the romantics. And yet this, too, though tempting, would be just as misleading. For despite all clear affinity with and debt to the romantics, Walser is just as clearly uninterested in repeating their program. Or rather, his texts bear witness to the fact that this program, with its hyperbolization of the Enlightenment's genius aesthetic and its undercurrents of progressive utopianism, is no longer available to the writer in the twentieth century; indeed, this has itself become a watered-down cliché every bit on the level of (and fully compatible with) the bourgeois ideologies of *Bildung* and self-development. If Walser's writing is to be taken as a form of subjective humor at all, therefore, it must be seen as a late form, if not indeed a posthumous one, and while Walser's writing resists the temptations of mimesis—be it a mimesis of "objective humor" or of "profane illumination"—it recognizes just as much the arbitrariness of arbitrariness and the dubiousness of the more extravagant claims made on behalf of the power of imagination.[31]

Still more significant than this recognition, however, is that Walser's rejection of both of these modes of writing reveals a blind spot at the center of the mimesis debate as such. For in spite of all objective humor's pretensions to realist representation, the one thing that was never allowed to enter the text was paradoxically the thing most actually present in the writer's mind: the act of writing itself. Walser's work answers the question of what happens when this last taboo of realism is broken, when the process of the writing of the work *itself* becomes the "object" of the writing. Walser's writing in fact takes Hegel at his word—specifically, his complaint that in modern times, "no content, no form, is any longer immediately identical with the inwardness, the nature, the unconscious substantial essence of the artist" (*A* 605; *AII* 235)—turning "objective humor" into "subjective humor" and vice versa as a consequence of their own respective internal logics. In this way, Walser's writing is not the simple (or tragic) breakdown of mimesis that so many critics claim it to be, nor an avant-gardistic rejection of same, but the carrying through of the logic of mimesis to its ultimate, comical conclusion.

Far more than merely providing the occasion for another good laugh at society's expense, therefore, *Fritz Kochers Aufsätze* inaugurates the comedy of post-realist fiction in all its guises. Walser's doubly ironic play with representation marks the abyssal moment when writing takes writing—more, the present moment of writing—as its topic, when the objective world simply is the world of the thinking, writing self, toward which the writer cannot *but* feel intimacy. Such a situation helps to explain Walser's love of the banal and the workaday, and at the same time clarifies why the proliferation of workaday details in his writing somehow fails to create a coherent and as it were tangible picture. Once the task of sensitive, anthropocentric representation becomes structurally indistinguishable from subjective fantasy, everything is permitted. As Fritz famously writes: "I like to write about everything just the same. It's not looking for a particular topic that excites me, but rather picking out fine, beautiful words to write about it [Ich schreibe über alles gleich gern. Mich reizt nicht das Suchen eines bestimmten Stoffes, sondern das Aussuchen feiner, schöner Worte]" (*FKA* 24). The catch, perhaps, is that the one thing that is *not* permitted is the forgetting of this very permissibility vis-à-vis the discarded or at least deemphasized idea of meaning-making as such. Such a tension, between the pleasure in seeking out "fine, beautiful words" and the consciousness of its emptiness, finally makes Walser's unsentimental education a *Lustspiel* that almost writes itself.

The Objectivity of Irony

Corresponding to this problem of representation in language is Walser's long-lasting interest in ekphrasis and synesthesia, or rather in the possibilities and limitations of various media for art.[32] Annette Fuchs has argued that Walser's Biel-era picture-descriptions effect a "subversion of the realist imperative," adding that Walser's "descriptions no longer function as the pictorial analogue of knowledge, but rather as the analogue of a subjectively experienced imaginary, which only becomes representable through them" (Fuchs, *Dramaturgie des Narrentums,* 88–89). The presentation of the "realistic imperative" as a form of knowledge already lies in the background of *Fritz Kochers Aufsätze,* even if most of the assigned topics—"Man," "Poverty," "Politeness," and so forth—do not particularly lend themselves to realist or illustrative reproduction.[33] Indeed, Fritz frequently displays a vivid anxiety about the obligation to approach such abstract themes through a purely verbal medium, complaining for example in the composition "Nature," "it's hard to write about nature, especially for a student in the second A-class. About people it's okay: there, there are fixed features. But nature is so indistinct, so fine, so ungraspable, so infinite" (*FKA* 22). Elsewhere he makes an attempt at synesthetic description: "How should I put it? Music is a weeping in melodies, a remembering in tones, a painting in sounds. I'm putting it badly" (*FKA* 44).[34] In the short piece *A Painter* (*Ein Maler*), published in the same volume as *Fritz Kochers Aufsätze* and not incidentally illustrated by Walser's older brother Karl, Walser writes, "I could never be a poet, because I love nature too impetuously [. . .]. In the depiction of nature, [the poet] will always fall short of the painter, it can't be otherwise. The paintbrush will always put even the finest word exercises to shame, and it's good that this is how it is."[35] In light of these sentences, Fritz's synesthesia appears as a kind of lame amateur expressionism, in which a floridly metaphoric and ornamental style steps in to compensate for the unreliability of linguistic adequation. The very lameness of this expressionism, however, also means that the doubt about language's capacities also extends to the expressive potential of figurative and poetic language, as well as Fritz's denigration of his own metaphors—"I'm putting it badly [Ich kann es schlecht sagen]"—not only constitutes what is probably the truest statement in his compositions; it also lays down the law against fine style as a solution to the problems of literary representation.

Despite the imperative to clarity and accuracy of representation, however, the abstractness of many of the assigned topics upon which Fritz is made to write is also an indication that more than just a dogmatically objective realism—be it only in the form of its "subversion"—is at stake. For what is wanted in the compositions is in fact not exactly mere replication but rather a kind of individual and affective meditation on the assigned topics, the mutual constitution of subject and world, or, indeed, the "appearance and activity of imperishable humanity in its many-sided significance" (*A* 608; *AII* 239). For this reason, the opposition of writing as the "analogue of knowledge" to writing as the "analogue of a subjectively experienced imaginary" (Fuchs 89) can be said to perpetuate a certain romantic fallacy: for in the end, the attempt at the psychologically faithful representation of subjectivity, even in its most whimsical moments, is no less mimetic in its impulses than the attempts at faithful representation of the objective and exterior world.[36] The examination of the subject as object in psychological realism effectively fuses the terms "objective" and "subjective"; while the turn inwards indeed indicates a change of focus whose importance must not be underestimated, it is, nevertheless, not yet a change of form.

Thus it is clear that the presentation of the workings of the "subjectively experienced imaginary" is hardly the opposite of art as the imitation of reality, but, to the contrary, complements it and extends its reach.[37] And although this (romantic) extension of the mimetic is indeed a factor in Walser's writing, this is so only as a secondary process. The subject does not come to itself and its authenticity through the gathering of external perceptions and knowledge, nor in the free expression of its inner *Einbildungskraft*. As Fritz's compositions demonstrate over and over again, not only are *Einbildungskraft* and knowledge *already* clichés, already the citations of citations in regard to which authenticity is a near total illusion, but also whatever spontaneity that does exist in Fritz's expression is (at least in terms of the pedagogical demands of its setting) semi-nonsense and error, at best battered into the appearance of sense and at worst the betrayal of linguistic sense by itself.

Thus—rather than celebrating the subjective imagination in a carnivalesque trampling of "objective" norms, engaging in a praxis of existential lassitude, or withdrawing into hermeticism and "autism" as a protest against social alienation[38]—Walser is, in his first long work, already tentatively demonstrating the fundamental irony of representation. Such a move sets Walser in a playful-antagonistic relation not only to the realist tradition, but also to the romantic tradition.[39] What these modes of literature have in common, broadly speaking, is the attempt to convey in verbal form a "real" and to a certain degree unmediated reality of images, actions, or emotions—whether this reality is one of the material world and existing social relations, or of the apparently borderless realms of the imagination. However, Walser's work neither rejects such mimetic impulses in a proto-avant-garde gesture, nor plays out the contradictions of the mimetic on a stage of violence or pathos.[40]

One is tempted once again to redeploy Marx's immortal phrase: the first time, mimesis occurs as tragedy; with Walser, as farce.

Of course, as noted above, Walser's texts do not abandon the notion of representational "content"; while the qualities of his prose clearly diverge from those of conventional realism (with the possible exceptions of *Geschwister Tanner* and *Der Gehülfe*), even the most meandering of Walser's pieces are neither pure mechanical language nor dadaist (quasi-)nonsense. Walser's work is not anti-mimetic so much as hyper-mimetic: it is the overbid of realism, in which realism loses its claim to verisimilitude in its own excess of reference. It is thus the tension between this exaggeratedly referential aspect of Walser's writing and the simultaneous exposure of the irony of reference's premises that brings his work into the realm of the comic.[41] Significant here is the fact that—as the frequency of Walser's fractured picture-descriptions and literary retellings attest to in particular—Walser's engagement with the question of mimesis and reference is, again, usually a secondary or even a tertiary engagement.[42] For Walser is not simply struggling with the idea or process of literary representation, as has so often been claimed, but rather—according to the logic of the "irony of irony"—making this struggle itself the theme and the object of the joke.

In Preisendanz's discussion of Friedrich Schlegel, he defines the latter's concept of "poetic humor [dichterische Humor]" as the product of

> the fear of a literature that would be nothing more than literal and naively conceived mimesis of pre-given empirical or factual reality, in which "base reality is presented merely for its own sake (ergo unpoetically)." Ever since the ancient world's identity between poetry and life ceased to be and writing came to stand under the sign of the dualism of inner and outer reality, two dangers have threatened literature: the one, of the aporia of every utterance whatsoever insofar as it is dependent on the setting-down of inherently finite things, the other, of art's self-given task of the mere copying of the world of appearances, in which imagination lets itself be overpowered by the movement, the laws, and the systems of the subject matter and all that exists; "art as such is annihilated and sinks down into empirical materialism." (*HDE* 28)[43]

"Humor," similar to its position in Hegel's *Aesthetics,* thus functions for Preisendanz as the solution to the naive mimesis of art as soulless replication of the phenomenal world. Humor performs the "relation of tension between the consistency of that which is narrated and the manner of narration" (*HDE* 11); it maintains the lost relationship between art and life while nevertheless keeping a critical distance between the two, thereby preserving the balance between them that otherwise threatens to tip over into either mere imitation on the one hand, or ever more rarified flights of imagination on the other.

And yet the balance of this mimetic-affective mode, which rests already on a contradiction or distance that is properly ironic in nature, ultimately remains a precarious one. Humor's "latency of form"[44] can thus be attributed not only to its mutability, its ability to contain not just all of a life but indeed even all other possible genres (as its characteristic genre, the novel, makes clear); it also refers to the very tenuousness with which it holds its own contradictions and mutability in check. The very lability of the realist novel allows the literary problematic that creates it to lie dormant; the form that can absorb everything broaches no contradiction. There is, however, one thing that the novel of objective humor may not, strictly speaking, contain, *the* thing that not only raises up once again the specter of arbitrariness but also threatens to dismantle the novel's dramatic illusionism. Although the friction between poetry and life, representation and reality—in short, the irony inherent to mimesis—suffuses the novel of objective humor, this friction is nonetheless never allowed to become the novel's subject. When it *does* becomes the novel's subject—in other words, when the contradictions implied or latent in humor are thematized, or, as they are in Walser's most radical works, self-reflectively dramatized—then it becomes something else; then the "humor" of the realist novel becomes comic, or rather, becomes the comedy of the irony of humor as form.

It is in this shift that Walser's curious prose finds its place. The oft-quoted remark from *Fritz Kochers Aufsätze,* "What do I know, I write because I think it's neat to fill up the lines with such pretty little letters. I couldn't care less about the 'what' [Was weiß ich, ich schreibe, weil ich es hübsch finde, so die Zeilen mit zierlichen Buchstaben auszufüllen. Das 'Was' ist mir vollständig gleichgültig]" (*FKA* 24), is an indication of how Walser's writing early on abandons a notion of realist representation and its obligation to reflect upon the given and anthropocentric world. And while Walser's first impulse is clearly to turn to the "subjective humor" of irresolute or whimsical play with identities and forms, with language and logic, for instance along the lines of his literary master Jean Paul,[45] his play is not merely a reflection—as subjective humor was in Hegel's account—of the historical divorce between art and necessity that provides the opportunity for apparently anarchic excesses of literary self-enjoyment. Nor, however, can Walser's writing quite be named the true fulfillment of Friedrich Schlegel's desire for a form of literature that would "make poetry lively and sociable, and life and society poetical; poeticize wit and fill and saturate the forms of art with every kind of good, solid matter for instruction, and animate them with the pulsations of humor" (*F* 175; 182). For Schlegel and his associates, the decoupling of art from social and cultural necessity was simultaneously an opening up of art to its possibility of an "infinitely increasing classicism" that "recognizes as its first commandment that the will of the poet [die Willkür des Dichters] can tolerate no law above itself" (*F* 175; 183).[46] By the time Walser begins writing, however, not only has the discourse in general shifted to other concerns for art's function, but also the freedom of the poet, practitioner of that "universal art of the spirit which has become free in itself and which is not tied down for its realization to external sensuous material" (*A* 89; *AI* 123) has proven all too easy to attain, for no law needs to govern that which "is and remains [. . .] a thing of the past" (*A* 11; *AI* 25).

In his study *Portrait de l'artiste en saltimbanque* (*Portrait of the Artist as Circus Acrobat*), Jean Starobinski has shown how the clown, that quintessential figure of comedy, functions for artists of the late nineteenth and early twentieth centuries as a "disguised self-portrait [autoportrait travesti]."[47] The clown as motif is a means for artists to vaunt their creative prowess and freedom, but it is also a means by which to mock this same freedom, since the freedom of the artist only exists by virtue of the very inconsequentiality of the prowess on which the artists so pride themselves and which that freedom permits. This constellation of freedom and irrelevance validates Hegel's warnings about romanticism and spans the gap between the initial optimism of Schlegelian irony and the jaded style of late romanticism:

> The leap of [the] clown, his vertical escape from a deceptive real, constitute one of the best possible emblems of the exhilaration proper to *romantic irony:* they are the hijinks of a spirit who affirms his freedom through the violent refusal of an imperfect contingency. Hegel's harsh verdict can be applied here: in imagining that it can raise itself above the spectacle of human vanity, ironic freedom renders itself hollow and futile. The flight towards the regions of pure ideality gets lost in an abstraction without content. (Starobinski, *Portrait,* 40)

The clown—here specifically the clown/acrobat of Théodore de Banville—is the sign of pure virtuoso skill, without aim, without message, seemingly even without submission to the laws of physics, much less to aesthetic or ethical norms. In this sense, it is fully comprehensible that the figure of the clown comes to act as a parodic or "low" stand-in for the figure of the artist, the parody of art's exalted task and standing in the world (all the more so after the cultural and political hopes of romanticism fail to materialize or are neutralized in the political turmoil and conservative backlash of mid-nineteenth-century Europe). Art's aesthetic autonomy turns into its social and political isolation, resulting in the artist's own loss of faith in a creative freedom that comes increasingly to seem besides the point.[48]

It is therefore hardly surprising that Walser, like so many of his contemporaries, should make use in his writing of the clown or fool figure as the symbol par excellence of the simultaneous liberty and marginality of the artist's task.[49] But Walser's writing displays a crucial difference from both the "transcendental buffoonery" (*F* 148; 152) of early romantic subjective humor and the melancholy arabesques of late romanticism, even if it clearly also bears the marks of both. Artistic freedom and its discontents is a perpetual theme in both Walser's literary work and his letters and recorded statements; and yet the ideological pathos of artistic freedom, in its utopian as well as its tragic versions, is absent.[50] Or rather, it is present, indeed nearly omnipresent—but itself only in comic or parodic form. For Walser, the essential limitlessness of the artist in regard not only to object and treatment, but also to language and style—indeed, eventually even to the size and legibility of the script itself—no longer holds the utopian potential of the great collective artwork and the achievement of the absolute as aesthetic creation. Yet this loss is no longer, if indeed it ever was, something fatal to be mourned. Nor is it the shame of a guilty society that rejects genius for mediocrity and conformism and reduces the role of the artist to that of sideshow master. For the always present flip side of the late romantic clown is (in Schopenhauer's words) "not only suffering, the essential martyrdom of genius as such, but also its constant transition into madness."[51] Artistic freedom under the pressure of the world's constraints induces not merely a frivolous, self-involved art, as Hegel had feared, but indeed the total marginalization of imaginative life and, finally, the very disintegration of the artist as subject.[52]

This cul-de-sac of romantic irony is not where Walser ends up, however, but precisely the place from which he begins. "Anyone who is naturally witty has to especially watch out" (*FKA* 46), not just for reasons of schoolhouse conventions of seriousness, but also because too much free rein given to wit leads to the disintegration of writing and language into mere nonsense. At the same time, however, given that the ostensible sanity of aesthetics has nonsense at its very core, even the Schopenhauerian pathos of the mad artist and the tragic harlequin is as foolish as any other bad joke. Clownish though it is and announces itself to be, Walser's writing strategy is thus not exactly a continuation of the ambiguous fashionableness of the clown in late romanticism that Starobinski thematizes—much less a revival of the carnival fool of the middle ages à la Bakhtin—but rather a parodic exemplum of Lacoue-Labarthe and Nancy's assertion that "the most radical irony would consist in the way that a mathematization of literature, building on an impossible Mathesis, would result in the futile and grotesque multiplication of all books, books by everyone and about everything, a multiplication of insignificance at the very locus of the operation" (*The Literary Absolute* 127). If the clown is the symbol of romantic irony's vision of an aesthetic absolute, then Walser is the last clown, who recognizes more than anyone both the essential inconsequence of the acrobatic, norm-defying artistic gesture and the impossibility of confining such gestures to a restricted space of aesthetic play cordoned off from the life in which it is inscribed. But he is also the clown of clowns, in that he neither laments this inconsequence, nor treats the simultaneous generality and triviality of the aesthetic as a form of social or cultural decadence.[53] Instead he makes himself, his writing, the ultimate gesture and playground of inconsequence and freedom, folding irony into irony and creating, out of the death of the clown, the birth of the (ironic) comic.

Vita Puerilia

If *Fritz Kochers Aufsätze* begins with a mask, it seems to end with a parabasis:

> We have a head class clown in the class. He provides us with more laughs in a quarter of an hour than ten others in a whole year [. . .]. His jokes, which are inexhaustible, make the air shake with our laughter [. . .]. He is also a handsome, clever boy, a good athlete, intelligent, but shockingly careless [. . .]. He'll come to a bad end one day, when he gets caught in one of his wild, foolhardy pranks [. . .]. In a way, he's an aristocrat. All thoughtless, unmindful people are. They play by playing tricks on people. [Sie spielen, indem sie übeltun]. It's their passion, and to be wholly gripped by a passion may not be very smart, but it's lovely. He's like a sort of king with us. We gladly obey him, because each one of us secretly feels sorry for his mischievousness. That's our little world. (*FKA* 47–48)

More than Fritz's tentative boast of his own "talent for jesting" (*FKA* 30), the lines on the "head class clown [Haupthalunke]" which make up more than half of the final composition, "Die Schulklasse [Our Class]," appear as Walser's clearest statement in this text of his own adopted role of humorist. Given that Fritz Kocher was in fact the name of an actual classmate of Walser's,[54] one can easily interpret the "Haupthalunke" of the above passage as being no less than the self-revealing of Walser himself, emerging from the wings, so to speak, of the stage of Fritz Kocher's small world where he has been latently present this whole time. Such a configuration would be the clearest and indeed quite literal example of what Fuchs has called, with reference to Helmuth Plessner's theory of laughter, Walser's "eccentric subjectivity":[55] Walser presents himself as autobiographical subject within his own text, not as first-person narrator or subject of narration but as marginal character described in an offhand but consequential manner by the narrative voice and whose appearance closes the circle of the compositions introduced by the anonymous "editor" who is the "real" Walser and, not impossibly, also the "Haupthalunke." The appearance of the author from behind his author function stops the performance in its tracks, "killing" the character Fritz Kocher in the literal (that is, the literary) sense and bringing out the truth of its own performativity as the truth of the text, much in the same way that Hegel's comic consciousness eventually sets aside its many masks and prepares the way for the conversion of consciousness within revealed religion.

In this light, it would not even be too outrageous to expect the death of Fritz Kocher, like the sacrifice of Jesus on the cross, to provide the necessary passage out of the comic and its limitless play with contingency into the harmonized consciousness of post-tragic, post-comic Christian universalized subjectivity, which is to say, modern self-knowing.[56] But Walser's clownish parabasis is in fact not as simple or as unidirectional an unmasking as it may at first seem, and one would be hard pressed to say that at the end of *Fritz Kochers Aufsätze* one actually achieves the satisfaction of a revelation, illumination, or resolution. If there is indeed an unmasking at the end of *Fritz Kochers Aufsätze,* it is less an illustration of the epistemological teleology marked out by Hegel's comic consciousness than its wholesale parody, and it seems more likely that Fritz Kocher meets his untimely end *not* so that Walser as *persona* could take off the mask and be "something actual [etwas Rechtes]" (*PS* §744, 450; 542), but merely because Walser as *author* ran out of ideas for school composition themes. For it is not just that the class clown is identical with Walser, who then gives fictional voice to Fritz, who then describes Walser. Rather, Fritz's voice itself is thoroughly saturated with an ambivalent, both conscious and unconscious, class-clownery—not least in Fritz's many admonitions against the comic mood, which from the perspective of the last essay may indeed be read as Walser's projection onto his character and "classmate" of a properly Hegelian fear of the wit and subjective humor that constantly threaten to break out and contaminate the controlled space of objective realism.

In this sense, the parabasis of *Fritz Kochers Aufsätze* once again bears a far greater similarity, not to Hegel's description of absolute knowledge, but to the complementary and inverted notion of de Man's "absolute irony," "a consciousness of a non-consciousness, a reflection on madness from the inside of madness itself" ("Temporality" 216). This absolute irony, whose infinitely regressing reflection gives the lie to the infinitely *progressing* reflection of Hegelian absolute knowledge, is for de Man primarily the result of the "double structure of ironic language: the ironist invents a form of himself that is 'mad' but that does not know its own madness; he then proceeds to reflect on his madness thus objectified" ("Temporality" 216).[57] Such an "objectification" or rationalization of madness—which is for de Man above all a result of the fact that even consciousness is never direct, but always filtered through and formed in a language that must itself constitutionally miscarry—is at the least highly paradoxical, for madness is just that which by definition cannot be objectively or rationally known, a fortiori that which cannot possess objective or rational knowledge of itself.

While for de Man this situation applies to *all* language regardless of the respective speaker's temperament or presentation, there is indeed also a kind of more evident doubleness to Walser's language, a language which on the one hand exploits the comic possibilities of naïveté too cannily to be understood as naive in any real sense, but on the other hand is too genuinely, giddily "naive" to be taken as a pure satire on naïveté. At this point, we can raise the question that de Man backs off from: "Could we think of certain texts [. . .] as being truly meta-ironical, as having transcended irony without falling into the myth of an organic totality or bypassing the temporality of all language?" ("Temporality" 223). Unsurprisingly, de Man appears to remain skeptical of such a possibility. However, in Walser's case, at least, the question is not so much answerable in the affirmative as simply wrongly posed. Walser does not succumb to irony; nor, however, does he transcend it: *he makes it the point.* The paradox involved in the objectification of madness and nonsense is for Walser *the* comic object of his writing, the "irony of irony" immanent to the (inseparable) processes of writing and living alike. "Laughter just means life [Lachen bedeutet eben Leben]" (*AB1* 33) is thus for Walser no tossed-off bromide, but a shrewd judgment—after both the disappearance of "the ancient world's identity between poetry and life" (*HDE* 28) and realism's spectacular failure to compensate for this loss—on the *ironic* fusion of art and life within his own artistic production.

This identity of art, life, and laughter becomes increasingly pronounced, of course, in Walser's later career. It is manifest above all in the posthumously published pieces known as Walser's "microscripts," the hundreds of short prose pieces (and one novel) written mainly on scrap paper in a microscopic, barely legible but scrupulously aligned Sütterlin script made even more difficult to read by Walser's idiosyncratic use of abbreviations and his seeming indifference to the relative sharpness of his pencil point.[58] If *Fritz Kochers Aufsätze* thematizes language's potential for nonsense and self-contradiction (particularly when measured against the implacable norms of grade school pedagogy), the microscripts constitute a far more internalized repetition of this problematic. The microscripts resemble the occasional prose of Fritz Kocher's compositions, but now the frame story that both literally and figuratively authorized the *Aufsätze*—and to a degree indeed allowed the work to conform to standard narrative convention—has been done away with, the personae that populate its "little world" flattened into one sustained narrative voice. In this way, the comic undermining of conventional realism, which in the *Aufsätze* was still filtered through a certain authorial consciousness enough to constitute a gentle satire, has now lost whatever stabilizing remove to which the earlier text might have been able to lay claim. As if seen through binoculars, the problem of representation—of the representation of representation—comes right up to the surface of vision. One should nonetheless be wary of falling into the interpretive pathos of certain critics, who stress in Walser's late prose the deferral of standard narrative reference and the narrator's lack of obvious agency in relation to his environment. For what is of the essence in the microscripts is in point of fact *not* the problematic mediation between self and world, but precisely the hints and references *to* these problems of mediation. And while it is doubtless true that Walser's texts flout conventional notions of narrative logic, value, and self, it seems at least worth considering that in his later work, rather than having descended into a genuinely tragic crisis of representation, Walser has refined his comic timing.

Certain at any rate is that this flouting of narrative convention comes not as the crisis of but as the *solution to* Walser's struggles with writing. The conditions under which what would come posthumously to be known as the "pencil zone [Bleistiftgebiet]" (Walser's term) or the "microscripts [Mikrogramme]" (Greven's appellation) are described by Walser in a 1927 letter to Max Rychner:

> Such exactitude in the composition of an essay probably seems ridiculous to you. But for me all this penciling about [Bleistifterei] has a significance. Namely, for the writer of these lines, there came a period when he hated the pen dreadfully, terribly, when he was weary of it in a way that I can hardly describe to you, where he became utterly dumb as soon as he started to use it even a little bit, and so in order to free himself from this writing-pen-fatigue, he began to pencil around, to doodle, to scribble. With the help of the pencil it became easier for me to play, to write again [wieder besser spielen, dichten]; it seemed to me as if through it my old pleasure in writing came back to life.[59]

The reasons for Walser's writer's block are no doubt various, but one cause must certainly be the very thing Hegel warned against: that an art without sufficient necessity easily goes astray in its own freedom.[60] The impossibility of continuing the project of a "progressive universal poetry" (*F* 175; 182) and a complementary suspicion of anything resembling engaged literature[61] means that Walser could easily have served as the exemplary fulfillment of not just one, but both of Hegel's baleful prophecies for art: on the one hand, the "deliberate nearing of the contingency of immediate and in itself unbeautiful and prosaic existence" (*A* 596, translation modified; *AII* 223) of realism, and on the other, the "baroque juxtaposition of that which is objectively furthest apart and the most motley jumbling together of random objects" (*A* 601, translation modified; *AII* 230).

Trapped in the seeming inevitability of having to allow these two options to define the experience of literature, and faced with the lack of success of his own previous literary ventures, Walser experiences a span of creative paralysis. The *Bleistiftsystem* that allows him a passage out of his "writing-pen-fatigue [Schreibfederüberdruß]" is one that will shift the ordinary relation of freedom and necessity in literature that irony and objective humor both still maintain, if perhaps from opposite sides of the equation. For while objective humor privileges the phenomenal world as it manifests itself to human perception, and irony privileges the freedom of the creative act as such, in both cases the physical method of composition, the banal actual act of writing itself, is arbitrary and of no interest. Within the *Bleistiftgebiet,* on the other hand, the rules governing the act of writing are *the* indispensable condition of the artwork, whereas the content becomes thoroughly trivial and occasional, a dominance of the merely present that reciprocally holds in check any remnant of the ideology of creative genius.

It is also a significant fact of Walser's letter about the tentative beginnings of what is perhaps his masterwork that its occasion is the sending back of corrected proofs, that most mundane and un-genial task of an author who desires a readership in the age of commercial presses. In his early correspondence with his publishers, Walser reveals himself as careful, even finicky with regard to his books as material product, as in a 1912 letter to Rowohlt/Wolff: "The page proofs that you were kind enough to send me are quite good. However, they seem a bit too heavy and big to me. I'd like to have the letters smaller and lighter, and I respectfully ask you to send me *Brandstetter's* type book for review" (*Briefe* 56). Walser proves himself in a way just as finicky with the formal conditions of his current pencil manuscripts in the letter to Rychner, not only making gentle fun of the exactitude with which he follows his own arbitrarily created rules, but also designating his writing practice as an inflexible, impersonal "system": "I am indebted to the pencil system, which is combined with a consistent, office-like system of transcribing, true torments, but this torment teaches me patience, in such a way that I have become an artist in patience-having [Ich verdanke dem Bleistiftsystem, das mit einem folgerichtigen, büreauhaften Abschreibesystem verquickt ist, wahre Qualen, aber diese Qual lehrte mich Geduld, derart, daß ich im Geduldhaben ein Künstler geworden bin]" (*Briefe* 300). Such self-conscious and half-serious (but nevertheless serious) dedication to the rules of the game is precisely the point: with the *Bleistiftsystem,* Walser artificially establishes the literary version of what Susan Bernstein has called, in relation to *musical* performance, the "persistent resistance of the instrument," the physical constraints that necessarily temper art's autonomy even in the absence of all other social and aesthetic checks.[62] Abandoned to personal freedom and public neglect, Walser's solution is "to pencil around, to doodle, to scribble [zu bleistifteln, zu zeichneln, zu gfätterlen]," to rediscover the pleasure of writing *as* play and to play according to rigid laws of his own making.

First, however, Walser experiences an artistic autonomy *without* material resistance, one which induces a creative agoraphobia, a resistance that is total because it is of the creative impulse itself. This situation is what leads Walser to take recourse to the ruse of a self-imposed subjection and humility, the appearance of constraint even if within the most absolute freedom possible.[63] Walser's metaphor of the "Büreauhaftigkeit" of his writing system is key here: Walser rediscovers the figure of the clerk or "Commis," whom he had once contrasted favorably to those "immodest writers and scholars," who, "with each scrap of language they set down, hope to become famous and recompensed."[64] In the clerk's "silent writing existence [stilles Schreibdasein]" (Walser, "Commis," 52), virtuosity *itself* is transformed from a sign of freedom into a sign of submission; even his "sudden flashes of ideas [Blitzidee(n)]" ("Commis," 52) are not expressions of his being, but merely the perfect products of another's will. In this sense, with the *Bleistiftgebiet,* Walser becomes, not just his own absolute educator, but also his own absolute boss, from whom he—the clerk *in perpetuum*—is permanently obliged to take dictation.

The grounds for the peculiar treatment of the dynamic of freedom and constraint that will play out—and play—in Walser's late short prose, as well as the implications of this dynamic for the writing subject and the objects of representation, are already being readied in Walser's more conventional prose works. The characteristically Walserian figure of the servant or menial, to which much critical attention has justly been paid, functions in particular as thematic parallel to Walser's aesthetic concerns. The aforementioned sudden demise of the young Fritz Kocher is already a harbinger of this motif: the ripe potential of the student on the threshold of maturity—"How I long to step out of this dull youth into big public life" (*FKA* 31)—will turn out to be, as the reader knows from the very first pages, no potential at all. The dramatic irony that runs through the *Aufsätze* is an explicit parody of the novel of development with its pedagogical demands and ideology of free will. A similar parody of the freedom of individual will appears in the novels *Der Gehülfe, Geschwister Tanner, Der Räuber,* and perhaps most strikingly, in *Jakob von Gunten,* in which—in structural equivalence to Fritz's premature physical death—the narrator proclaims his premature *social* death, announcing in the very first paragraph, with precocious frankness: "But one thing I know for certain. In my later life I will be a lovely, round-as-a-ball zero."[65]

Rüdiger Campe has contrasted the model of the "institutional novel," of which *Jakob von Gunten* is a premier example, to previous models of the novel such as the picaresque, the novel of conversion, and especially the novel of education or Bildungsroman.[66] The identification of *Jakob von Gunten* as an "Institutionsroman" means that, for Campe, the answer to the question posed by the title of the single textbook the students in *Jakob von Gunten* possess, "What is the goal of the Benjamenta boys' school?" (Walser, *Jakob von Gunten,* 8) can be nothing other than: the book itself. The textbook is the school, which is the text: a co-implication or identity whose telos, such as it is, can only be the mutual undoing of both.[67] In the same way that Fritz Kocher "dies" once he is removed from the milieu that defines him, the adored schoolmistress Fräulein Benjamenta perishes—and the school and the book along with her—once Jakob is allowed to penetrate the mysterious "inner chambers" that form the one object of desire of an otherwise explicitly desire-less plot. "It's not much, and we keep repeating it," remarks Jakob at the beginning of his studies, "but maybe there is a secret hidden behind all these nothingnesses and ridiculousnesses [Nichtigkeiten und Lächerlichkeiten]" (9). This esoteric secret of the school, however, turns out to be itself nothing but a placeholder and a void: "Anyway, now I've finally been inside the real inner chambers," announces Jakob, "and I have to say, they don't exist [und ich muß sagen, es existieren gar keine]" (130–31). The inner chambers of the institution are indeed every bit as much a "Null" as that which Jakob announces on the first page he is growing up to be; once they are revealed, the only possible option is the collapse of the school and Jakob's flight with the school's director Herr Benjamenta for the empty signifier (or signifier of emptiness) of the desert.[68]

Jochen Greven has explicitly connected the motif of the servant with the present tense (or present-tense effect) of most of Walser's narratives. "What is not to be found in Walser," he writes,

> is future: no hope, worries, projects, plans, actions for the next day—if such things do chance to be mentioned, it is only in a negative light [. . .]. To serve, to be subservient somewhere, is the paradoxical way out of the dilemma of being simultaneously obliged and unable to act [der paradoxe Ausweg aus dem Dilemma des Handelnmüssens und Nichthandelndürfens]. Thus the servant remains innocent, conserves himself, and insofar as he evaluates nothing, decides nothing, he knows nothing but the moment of the here-and-now. (Greven, *Figur am Rande,* 91)

This absolute present of servitude is intimately associated with the comic nature of Walser's prose, and not just in terms of the Aristotelian commonplace that comedy, unlike tragedy, has to do with "low" characters. Or rather, it touches on a neglected reason for this commonplace. Most often, the distribution of the common and the noble to comedy and to tragedy, respectively, has been explained as comedy's basis in error and distance from the ideal, "the laughable," in Aristotle's words, being but "a species of what is disgraceful."[69] But perhaps the more decisive factor in the suitability of the poor and humble for the purposes of comedy is that however wise or foolish, virtuous or vicious, perfect or peculiar they may be, they are universally—at least in terms of traditional public life and the collective destiny of peoples—*without consequence.*[70] The slave or the private person is unfree by definition, and therefore not able to act upon the world, certainly not in the way the heroes of tragedy and epic are obliged to do. With the rise of the bourgeois novel, however, the destiny of individuals without obvious world-historical significance also becomes a proper topic for serious literature; Walser therefore raises the stakes, making his characters not only unimportant private individuals, but servants, clerks, and assistants whose wills are professionally and *definitionally* dependent on the wills of others—as Jakob explains: "The education that we enjoy consists mainly of impressing upon us patience and obedience" (*Jakob von Gunten* 7)—and who, moreover, explicitly and emphatically state their *lack* of interest in making their mark on the world, individuals to whom the *vita activa* is as strange as it is unavailable.

Structurally similar to the servant's lack of access—or lack of desire for access—to the *vita activa* is the, for Walser, equally characteristic motif of the child. Here the connection to the comic is more intuitive, for the child is the exemplary locus of the play-drive (the very thing by which Schiller had, however paradoxically, hoped to bring mankind to its maturity). "Youth counts for a lot," writes Walser in one prose piece from around 1924, "nearly everything, and the younger an appearance in the world of people is, the higher one automatically values it [. . .]. Splendid and invaluable are all those who are still lying in baby carriages, who have to be carried around and who have [not] yet gained the power of speech at all, they are the very, very highest."[71] The child not yet able to speak is the sign of the suspension of becoming, a fantastical or utopian suspension of which language is, precisely, the limit. If infancy is "the transcendental experience of the difference between language and speech, which first opens the space of history,"[72] Walser's work can be seen as an attempt (although significantly, one whose impossibility is also known in advance) to get away from the historicity of discourse and back to, in the words of Giorgio Agamben, "an experience of language as such, in its pure self-reference" (*Infancy and History* 6).

It is no coincidence that, in the letter to Rychner, Walser compares his works of the past ten years to school compositions and remarks that with the *Bleistiftsystem* he learned "boyishly—to write again [knabenhaft wieder—schreiben]" (*Briefe* 301). The *Bleistiftgebiet* texts represent Walser's return to the writing of his ironically self-given *Lehrjahre.* Not only does much of Walser's late prose stylistically resemble the claustrophobic mock compositions of *Fritz Kochers Aufsätze,* it also rejects the narrative temporality in which the other novels do sometimes dabble and of which Fritz Kocher is swiftly deprived with comic violence. Taken as a whole, then, one might say that Walser's *Bleistiftgebiet* is a Bildungsroman in reverse; or rather it is a Bildungsroman without the *Bildung,* with neither the teleology of the subject nor the corresponding idea of *Vollkommenheit* that constitute the Bildungsroman's guiding principles.[73] Walser's rejection of the formal demands of the Bildungsroman contains within it the refusal to grow up, to relinquish uninstrumentalized action for duty and proper socialization.[74] Like the figure of the servant, the figure of the child serves as a counter-image to the social, philosophical, and narratological models of progress. In place of a notion of dialectical development under pressure from the outside world is substituted an occasional, autodidactic, and seemingly merely desultory mode of biographical as well as narratological presentation, in which "the infinitely light playing with nothing that is not terrified by it but even rises to the surface on occasion" (*CI* 270) that constitutes irony is taken as the fundamental principle of an art whose only object is its own diverting contingency.

"Should It Be Forbidden, for Instance, to Amuse Oneself Innocently?"[75]

The ironic withdrawal or holding in abeyance of the world of action—in the narratological as much as the social sense—thus also means that despite their ostensibly servile or powerless status, Walser's characters move through a space, like that of the virtuoso and the clown, in which everything is permitted: indeed, the perfect "state of spiritual well-being and repose" of comic consciousness (*PS* §747, 453; 544). This absolute spiritual well-being "such as is not to be found anywhere outside of this Comedy" (*PS* §747, 453; 544) is what Walter Benjamin means with his statement that Walser's characters "are figures who have left madness behind them,"[76] or what Giorgio Agamben, following in Benjamin's footsteps, calls Walser's "neutrality with respect to salvation."[77] Yet, as we have already seen, this image of Walser as permanent child and happy-go-lucky *Taugenichts,* or even as Bartleby-like figure of ontological suspension,[78] to which his novels seem to lend themselves on the level of content, is indeed only half of the picture. For it must be emphasized that it is in fact only in the *restricted* freedom of the *Bleistiftgebiet* that Walser rediscovers his "Schriftstellerlust," and what is at issue in Walser's writings is not simply the blissful lassitude of infinite play, but the way in which this infinite play is given definite form: in other words, the process by which "comic consciousness" actually becomes *comic.*

An early note of Walser's from April 1901 serves to demonstrate this process, in what could be taken as both a prototype of *Bleistiftgebiet* prose and a prophetic commentary on Walser's late comic style:

> I'm at a loss as to what I should write here. The girl is laughing, I see it, and it doesn't bestow any volubility upon my wit [es traut meinem Geist keine Geläufigkeit zu]. Does nothing. Really? Nothing at all? Ah, so then I'll write:
>
> To be witty means to be happy. [Geistreich sein heißt glücklich sein.] Be glad and you are full of wit. Rich in joy is rich in jokes. The happy person is never at a loss for ideas. I am glad that I am allowed to be here in the girl's presence, so I must be full of jokes. Adieu, gladness, you've done your job well.
>
> Farewell, jokes. This in memorandum. (Walser, *Briefe,* 11)

The elegiac tone of this note should not distract from the fact that it is wittiness or jokiness that is set out, at the very beginning of Walser's writing career, as the thing that overcomes longing, apathy, and above all, the embarrassment of not knowing what to write about. The piece begins with not one but two voids: the void of language, and the void of all that one might use language to describe. Even the brief image of the girl, seemingly the one peg on which to hang a descriptive poetics, acts as a barrier rather than a gateway to the fullness of representation, and her image is as elusive here as her laughter is apparently unmotivated. As in the *Aesthetics,* where a gratuitous funniness comes in to fill up the vacuum of narrative reference, what follows just as inevitably from Walser's narrative double void is the idea of wit itself, together with a not unwitty meditation on the relation of happiness to wit in which happiness somewhat tautologically appears as the original source of witty ideas that produce happiness. In the note, of course, Walser bids farewell to wit in light of its failure to make good on its promises. But wit—and especially the *thematization* of wit that this note also exemplifies—in fact never ceases to be the central reference point of Walser's writing; and after the great embarrassment of "dumbness" to which Walser attests in the letter to Rychner, it becomes the foundation of Walser's entire work, at once the source from which his ideas flow and the content of these ideas themselves.

Or as Walser himself writes in one of the microscripts' many self-referential lines: "On the high peaks stand giant remembrance-forms [Erinnerungsgestalten], though I can't really say what I actually mean by that, but really, doesn't it sound nice, and my words could perhaps be compared with dancers who present the tattering of everything ideal in a maybe slightly grotesque manner [die die Verlumpung alles Ideellen zur vielleicht etwas grotesken Darstellung bringen]."[79] This passage is not only one of the thousands of examples of Walser's enactment of an ironic self-referentiality; it is also a live performance, as it were, of the way in which irony itself—the "tattering of everything ideal"—becomes comic precisely through the play with this "tattering." The characteristically Walserian false start of the passage alludes to the two literary genres to which Walser is ostensibly temperamentally closest—the pastoral and the autobiographical—only to immediately veer away from them into what is not only a parabasic breaking of the fourth wall, but also a statement neutralizing the very premise of the sense of what has come before (not to mention challenging the notion of authorial intention) in the bald admission that he does not even understand what he himself is saying. Rather than conveying the meaning originally attributed to them, words are "dancers" (or rather, "dancing girls [Tänzerinnen]"),[80] chosen purely according to the criterion of how they sound. Reference is thus rejected in favor of an aesthetic form which is itself purely contingent and ornamental, a matter of self-entertainment; in turn, however, through this very self-entertainment, the contingency of form becomes not just its own object but also its own form of reference.

Another microscript of the same period declares this even more bluntly: "So listen, this is how it is: since the story comes from a book, I have to try to season it with jokes, to embellish it with laughabilitiness [Also hört, es ist so: Weil die Geschichte eine angelesene ist, muß ich sie mit Witz zu würzen, mit Lachhaftigkeit zu verschönern suchen]."[81] Against Hegel's sneer that the "natural error" of subjective humor "is to suppose that it is very easy to make jests and to be funny about oneself and everything available" (*A* 601; *AII* 230), here wit and funniness are *the* decisive factors for a successful piece of writing. And yet the self- and audience-admonishing insistence with which Walser introduces his writing strategy also suggests that Walser does not simply dismiss Hegel's criticism, but takes it as a specific challenge and problem to be explored. For in the above passage (among countless other examples) Walser is in fact not just being ironic "about oneself and everything available"; he is also being ironic about the irony that is the most "available [vorhanden]" of all: that is, about the possibility and permissibility of being ironic at all and in the first place, of joking and playing within an art that has abandoned its representative function but not its representative form.

To get a clearer idea of how Walser implements such an irony of aesthetic irony, it will be useful at this point to examine a piece from the *Bleistiftgebiet* in detail and as a discrete unit. The following integral short text, dated March–April 1925, may be considered exemplary for the dynamic that takes place in Walser's late prose of the "growing intimacy" in the "object" of irony itself:

> Usually I first put on a prose piece jacket, a sort of writer's smock, before venturing to begin with composition, but I'm in a rush right now, and besides, this is just a tiny little piece, a silly trifle featuring beer coasters as round as plates. Children were playing with them, and I watched them play. This game was unfolding in front of one of our restaurants, and a little dog had been enlisted in the little game. Oh, how his tail stood erect with pride as he found himself accorded equal rights. The dog appeared to be beside himself with joy, and the children noticed this too, and this silly doggish joy made them laugh. Then I too was made to laugh by the laughter of the children, and the little plates, these silly beer-glass mats, were filled with radiant joyousness at seeing themselves employed to playful end. Even these little mats could scarcely help thinking themselves in possession of equal rights when they went rolling across the ground with the same self-determination as the dog and children who ran to catch them, which was precisely what produced this happiness. Were these children by any chance unhappy? Not at all. Was the dog? The dog was silly, and being a silly dog, he was overjoyed, and it was nothing but happiness making his tail stick up like that, and as my own peculiar spirit witnessed this, it was so filled with glee I can't even express it, and the little mats, that rivaled the dog in silliness, oh how happy they were! I can't properly put it into words, and now the woman in the white blouse gazing down attentively from the silly, happy window at the little dog, the children, and the game with the little mats: a certain loneliness sank down majestically about her. All majesty must quite naturally have lonelinesses wafting about it. And now once more this foolishly happy tail with all its irresponsibilities. Gazing upon this sum of insouciance, misgivings arose in me as though these misgivennesses were the tails of dogs soaring up victoriously in pride, which by no means bears witness to a highly developed intelligence but nonetheless might apparently be proof of a certain innocuousness. Whenever this little dog snapped up one of the little rolling mats, it was taken from him at once, and the dog always expressed his gratitude at being

relieved of his burden. And for an entire year I watched this game. An entire year? For a fib like this I shall have to beg forgiveness for an entire year, and this I shall do joyfully and with precision, even if I were to lose in this way an entire little yearlet of my life, after all I do possess a sufficient wealth of strength, prospects, sillinesses, and, I hope, clevernesses as well. And now these shoes on the delicate, voluptuously delectable feet of that, as it is surely permitted to say, genteel young lady decked out with maximal tastefulness who came trembling along at—let's be so clever as to say—an unsupervised age, swaying as she softly, softly walked. I gazed after this beautiful woman, this ideal of a lady, for perhaps four long years, and now because of this untruth I shall have to ramble about in exquisitely beautiful apologies for the next four years, a stroll I am certainly looking forward to, should this pleasure not be begrudged me. To contemplate a little foot for four years on end. What a great achievement! And these little feet appeared to be smiling at me, that is, perhaps it's more like this: It appeared to me that the little shoes were smiling, for how happy it must have made them to cling to the feet of so enchanting a creature. The children's game was dragging on endlessly, but "endlessness," you are lying, and now I shall have to spend an eternity begging and stammering for the indulgent granting of comprehensive comprehension on account of this lie, which I am only too glad to do, although it shall take rather a long time indeed, but I am patient and happy to suffer having all my snapped-up-nesses taken away from me again. The little mats were behaving in such a charmingly silly way as they trundled off. A little dog and children and respectabilities, and what shall I now receive in exchange for all these things? Please do respond at once. Might I add also that he—while she was sitting there reading newspapers—was obliged to tidy up the rooms she rented out? How awful it was, the way she kept waving him about, and he at once by no means misinterpreted each of her barely visible gestures, but rather seized and grasped them quite correctly, and for this, to add insult to injury, she hated him. I could write you a thirteen-hundred page, that is to say, a very fat book about this if I wanted, but at least for the time being I don't want to. Maybe later. Look forward to what might be coming, my friend, and until then, farewell. To conclude, however, let me quickly add one last thing. It would be such a shame if I were to fail to mention, at the last minute as it were, the fact that each time he had completed his work she doled out to him nothing more than a piece of dry bread. Her name was Rosalinde. He, however, was nameless. It would not have been fitting for him to have a name—this namelessness made him happy and thus he was provided for. The piece of bread always tasted fabulous to him, and when he was eating it, Amazonian rivers of faithfulness flooded through him.

> What a devotion that must have been! I know that you are namelessly grateful to me for these few lines. Oh these slice-of-bread affairs! God-ful! I feel as if I could continue this report on into all incredulity . . . What else does the infinite consist of other than the incalculability of little dots? When she was handing him a piece of bread like that, she didn't even look at him but rather continued reading her newspaper undisturbed. She gave it to him utterly mechanically. That's what was so wonderful about it, the part that cannot be surpassed, the way she gave him the bread utterly, utterly mechanically. The mechanicalness of the gesture is what was so beautiful about it. I have also written this prose piece, I must confess, utterly mechanically, and I hope it will please you for this reason. I wish it pleases you so much it will make you tremble, that it will be, for you, in certain respects, a horrific piece of writing. I did not even groom myself properly in order to write it. This alone should suffice to prevent its being anything other than a masterpiece or, as we would no doubt rather say with forbearance, masterworklet. We wish to give forbearance the upper hand, and isn't it true that you were glad about the late addition of the piece of bread? I most certainly was. I would presuppose the greatest joyfulness on this score, for this is the most important thing, and you must consider it the best. You must without fail be satisfied with me, do you hear? Without fail. And then that little mat. This reality. This treasure trove of in-fact-having-occurred-nesses. This car drove off, and he and she were sitting in the back. How do you like my "trove" and "drove"? Make a note of these words! They're not my invention. How could such delicate expressions have originated with me? I just snapped them up and am now putting them to use. Don't you think my "trove" is *ben trovato*? Please do be so good as to think so. Accept my heartfelt greetings and do not forget the pride of that silly little dog. He was adorable.[82]

Walser begins the piece straightaway with a winking evocation of the idea of great art, the conditions of whose creation are so sacrosanct that its adepts require special articles of clothing—or at least, in proper romantic style, a sartorial mark of distinction to put one in the creative mood.[83] And yet, while the narrator claims to normally take part in this Parnassian practice, he also declares that for the present text this is unnecessary, insofar as it will be only "a tiny little piece, a silly trifle [ein ganz kleines Stück, ein ganz dummes]" whose content is nothing more lofty than the beer coasters of the restaurant in which the author sits. The very ailment that once befell Walser's pen, as recounted in the letter to Rychner, now fills the piece and the things described within it with such joy that the author's spirit is "so filled with glee I can't even express it, [. . .] I can't properly put it into words [so vergnügt, wie ich's gar nicht sagen kann, [. . .] Ich kann's gar nicht recht in Worten wiedergeben]."

In place of Walser's earlier lament for his literary muteness, then, emerges an enthusiastic *claiming* of literary muteness within the "silliness [Dummheit]" of the piece itself. In this connection, it is also worth noting the root "Wort [word]" buried in the German "Unverantwortlichkeiten [irresponsibilities]" that according to Walser fills the "foolishly happy tail [dieser dummglückliche Hundeschwanz]," making abdication of language implicitly abdication of duty and abdication of duty abdication of language, the giving up, not merely of one's writer's smock, but of one's very status as acting subject and *zoon logikon*. And yet it is also only through the giving up of this status that something like happiness, in the sense of a mute, animalistic self-enjoyment, can emerge; indeed, paradoxically, it is only in the context of this mute happiness—once again, "I can't properly put it into words"—that writing becomes at all possible.

It is in this context of the professed dumbness of the piece that the ambiguous antecedent of the second sentence—"Children were playing with them, and I watched them play [Kinder spielen damit, und ich schaute zu]"—provides the crucial thematic center not just of this piece but of the *Bleistiftgebiet* as a whole. For while in the sentence after that it quickly becomes clear that the "real" object of reference, that is, what the children are playing with, is in fact simply the beer coasters, the sentence could also be read as saying that it is the "tiny little piece" itself that constitutes the object of their play.[84] If irony is associated with play in the assumption that ludic randomness is the first default option for the subject possessed of neither principle nor identity, then Walser's double entendre literalizes this ontological metaphor, placing a pre- or non-rational play on the same level as genial creative force. Indeed, Walser's designation of these objects of play as "Spielzwecken [playful end(s)]" is no less than a travestying of Kant's famous "purposiveness without purpose [Zweckmäßigkeit ohne Zweck]" (see *CPJ* §10, 105; 71), self-reflexively marking the function of play within art *in distinction* from Kantian aesthetics. For Kant, of course, play has too much of self-interest and mere pleasure to be properly aesthetic, standing at the opposite pole from the ethical instrumentalization that similarly precludes aesthetic contemplation. From the elimination of both the immediately pleasurable and the practically good comes Kant's notion of *Zweckmäßigkeit*, the appearance of a telos without telos as the result of the internally lawful play of the faculties. Yet, as Walser's word "Spielzwecken" indicates, Kant's "purposiveness without purpose" is still all too purposeful, hiding within it the higher and indeed absolutely teleological goal of the establishment of an orderly rational universe. In contrast, Walser, abandoning notions of rational order, recognizes the play of the faculties—and indeed of everything else—as an utterly present, self-gratifying end in itself.

Walser's description of the dog's play also bears an obvious similarity to Freud's famous *fort-da* game, the central case study for his analysis of play and the starting point for his investigation into the pleasure principle and its beyonds. Both Walser and Freud present the toss-and-retrieve games of the dog and the little boy, respectively, not only as the paradigm of the play activity, but also (Freud explicitly, Walser implicitly) as compensations for loss, loneliness, and powerlessness. Walser even speaks in nearly Freudian terms of the dog's quasi-orgasmic "relief [Erleichterung]," consistent with the manifest phallic quality of its upright tail. Yet despite these evident similarities, there remains a crucial difference in the two authors' interpretations. For in Freud's analysis, play is bound up, not just with the experience of loss and compensation, but, even more intimately and significantly, with the mimetic impulse. While Freud rejects the need for a "special imitative instinct [Nachahmungstrieb]" to explain play's mechanism,[85] such rejection in fact only serves to strengthen play's imitative function, as play is described neither as mere imitation for the sake of imitation nor as happy distraction from experienced suffering, but rather as the imitation *of* experienced suffering as a way to effect that suffering's overcoming: "Initially [the child] was passive in relation to the experience [of the mother's departure], he was affected *by* it; now he brings himself into an active role by repeating this experience, unpleasurable though it was, as play" (Freud, *Beyond the Pleasure Principle,* 16, translation modified). In Freud's account, the toy that the child throws away is the mother who has gone away; the child's ability to repeatedly discard and retrieve the toy is his way of establishing control over a situation that is initially only painful, and in which he is initially powerless. The critical point here, however, is less the specific affective valences of Freud's model than the aesthetic assumptions that shape his theory. Representation—*aesthetic mastery*—offers the subject the possibility of sovereignty that real life refuses.[86] For Freud, play is never something primary, but always and in every case a substitute or secondary phenomenon (the "real" or primary experience being that of mother-loss); it is thus always already a semiotic and rational process, a metonymic substitution for and repetition of a reality which is itself not any fun.

This metonymic substitution, of course, leads Freud ultimately to his notions of the death drive and of repetition compulsion as the secret automatized core of an ostensibly libidinal and goal-directed psychology—situating psychoanalysis not just beyond the pleasure principle, but also, indeed, beyond the phenomenology of spirit. In this sense, it is both curious and telling that Freud's mimetic-traumatic account of the origins of play is also in part a radicalization of his earlier 1908 essay, "Creative Writers and Day-Dreaming": as the title indicates, a comparison of the writer's *Schreibtrieb* to the psychic mechanisms involved in play and fantasizing. Here, in contrast to *Beyond the Pleasure Principle,* children's play is conceived not as the imitation of traumatic past events for the sake of present control, but as an imitation of future control in an attempt to speed its coming; in other words, children's play is always a play at being adult, a mimicry of adult life in premature, miniature form.[87] Freud is here perhaps at his most anti-romantic, assimilating the creative potential of fantasy and imagination to a notion of egoistic self-development within empirical world-relatedness. Play has not just a wish-fulfilling but also an utterly pedagogical function:[88] through play as copying, the child learns that which he or she will later become. Play is thus, counterintuitively, the child's attempt to accelerate the attainment of maturity, to conjure away the fact of one's deprivation via the negative and indeed unreal pleasure of the simulation of what one wishes to have.

Walser, unsurprisingly, has other ideas about where such a pedagogical mode must lead. It is an indication of Walser's divergence from the Freudian model, for example, that the dog's aforementioned "relief" comes not from the *da* of the fort-da game—that is, from the coasters' successful repossession—but from the *fort* of the coasters being *taken away* so as to start all over again: and if play offers a diversion from loneliness and doubt for Walser, it is not as compensation, symbolic substitution, or wish projection, but as a kind of repetition *non*-compulsion: the permanently happy resolution of a self-imposed frustration, which, moreover, "by no means bears witness to a highly developed intelligence [(zeugt) durchaus nicht von hochentwickeltem Verstand]." Such a game may well be onanistic, but it is *not* mimetic, certainly not as a second-degree metaphor for a reality more really real. If anything, the contrary is true. Walser makes play the archetype of which everything else is the iteration.

This is the case in the above piece, for example, in the subplot of the white-blouse-clad woman ("Her name was Rosalinde," the narrator belatedly interrupts the narrative to tell us):

> I gazed after this beautiful woman, this ideal of a lady, for perhaps four long years, and now because of this untruth I shall have to ramble about in exquisitely beautiful apologies for the next four years, a stroll I am certainly looking forward to, should this pleasure not be begrudged me. To contemplate a little foot for four years on end. What a great achievement!

It would be easy to mistake this subplot or leitmotif for a conventional story of desire and the "true" subject of the piece, whereby the narrator's perambulations around Rosalinde and her foot would be the symbolic core formally reflected in the piece's own rhetorical peripateticism, which would, in turn, be the symptom of the sublimation of repressed or frustrated desire. Yet the very explicitness of this parallel in the piece serves to negate the mimetic relation between text and (ostensible) object that a conventional interpretation would suggest. More precisely, it *reverses* this relation, for here form is not the natural symbolic expression of a state of affairs; rather, *the narrated "state of affairs" is a commentary on form after the fact.* That is to say, even the minimal subject matters of this piece—the woman and the game with the beer coasters—function as excuses for the taking-place of writing and not the other way round, that is, writing as (transparent or incidental) medium for the description of (significant) subject matter.[89] Narrative verisimilitude is further undercut through the narrator's immediate declaration that the stated four-year duration of the narrator's longing is an "untruth"—an untruth, however, that is just as soon reasserted in the following sentence, as if the narrator's admission of mendacity was of no consequence. And in fact, the admission *is* of no consequence: for it is ultimately neither the love relationship nor its dreamt-of consummation that is of significance; what provides both content and pleasure alike is rather the anticipation of "exquisitely beautiful apologies" itself: the anticipation of the further delay and nonfulfillment that is moreover a direct result of the narrator's untrustworthiness in the first place. Similarly, the classic fetishism of the narrator's attention to the woman's feet should be seen as the sign, not of a failure of proper (heterosexual, generative) consummation, but of a *prolongation* of pleasure, a resistance to goal-orientedness and the normative demand to come to the point in either erotic or narratological matters.[90]

As the narrator continues: "I could write you a thirteen-hundred page, that is to say, a very fat book about this if I wanted, but at least for the time being I don't want to. Maybe later. Look forward to what might be coming, my friend, and until then, farewell." In typical Walserian fashion, in lieu of a real story, the reader (who with the unannounced shift from *Sie* to *du* is transformed from passive reader to confidant and co-conspirator) is given only the potential of a story. But this potential of a story—or rather the announcement of said potential with the clear intimation that even the potential for a story sometime in the future is a fiction—is also no less than the subject of the narrative itself, which the reader is peremptorily ordered to be content with, in the same way that, a few lines later, the "nameless" "he" (presumably but not unambiguously the narrator himself) contents himself with the crust of bread administered to him by the (presumably) aforementioned woman. The connection between the reader and the "he" is reinforced a few sentences later as the narrator interrupts himself to announce to the reader, "I know that you are namelessly grateful to me for these few lines [Ich weiß, daß du mir für diese paar Zeilen namenlos dankbar bist]." Here the narrator exchanges roles with the woman, and the reader is slotted into the place of the similarly grateful and anonymous "he," while the "tiny little piece [ganz kleines Stück]" of the narrator becomes—in a sort of transubstantiation in reverse—the "piece of dry bread [Stück trockenes Brot]." Thus the narrator's subsequent rapturous cry, "Oh these slice-of-bread affairs! [O solche Brotverabreichungsbeziehungen! literally: O, such bread-dispensation-relationships!]" refers not just to the relationship between the "he" and the bread-distributing Rosalinde, but also to the relationship between the narrator and the reader, who should similarly experience the humble piece—which, like most of the microscripts and like the "endless" beer coaster game, consists indeed of little else but an "incalculability of little dots [Unabsehbarkeit von Pünktchen]"—as an experience of utmost delectation.

For as the narrator subsequently orders, with sudden imperiousness: "You must without fail be satisfied with me, do you hear? Without fail. And then that little mat. This reality. This treasure trove of in-fact-having-occurred-nesses. [Du mußt unbedingt zufrieden mit mir sein, hörst du? Unbedingt. Und dann jenes Tellerchen. Diese Wirklichkeit. Dieser Fond von Tatsächlich-vorgekommenheiten]." But what can "this reality" mean in such a work, in which the things described are so clearly fungible, if not indeed wholly negligible? First, it should be noted that the fungibility and negligibility of narrative objects in Walser's prose pieces are not necessarily in contradiction with the aforementioned overbid of mimesis. What is lacking is not quite reality, and certainly not concrete detail, but rather the ordinary ordering and hierarchizing of reality that stands in for normal thinking and is thereby fundamental to any "reality effect." In the same way that the dog and the beer coasters are "accorded equal rights [gleichberechtigt]" with the children, all the objects of Walser's prose—from the most trivial to the most seemingly significant, from the clearly citational to the supposedly directly experienced, from empirical phenomena to stream-of-consciousness chatter—are placed on one and the same plane, the even plane of the text itself. In this way, the question of reference, that is, the dialectical relation between author and object, becomes moot. Everything is just as real as anything else, up to and including the words whose interaction operates quite independent of their representative function.

Such an independence is reinforced with the narrator's claim that his composition has been written "mechanically." This adverb first makes its appearance in the immediately preceding description of Rosalinde's philanthropy: "That's what was so wonderful about it, the part that cannot be surpassed, the way she gave him the bread utterly, utterly mechanically. The mechanicalness of the gesture is what was so beautiful about it." Other than this, the narrator does not comment explicitly on his use of this word. He does do so, however, obliquely and as it were performatively in the penultimate sentences, the punch line of the piece's internal joke:

> This reality. This treasure trove [Fond] of in-fact-having-occurred-nesses. This car drove off, and he and she were sitting in the back [im Fond]. How do you like my "trove" and "drove"? [Wie findest du mich mit meinem "Fond"?] Make a note of these words! They're not my invention. How could such delicate expressions have originated with me? I just snapped them up and am now putting them to use. Don't you think my "trove" is *ben trovato*? [Hältst du "Fond" nicht gleichsam für einen Fund?] Please do be so good as to think so.

Walser's piece thus also functions as an extended adverbial pun or delayed-action Tom Swifty: it has been written "mechanically"—because at the end there is an automobile in it. But mechanical too is the particular kind of wordplay that, present throughout the piece, in these sentences is brought decisively into the foreground. The word "Fond" that appears in the first sentence of the above passage in the sense of "trove, store, reserve" is used again in the next sentence with the equally current meaning of "back seat." The word is then metamorphosed into the word "Fund," which itself refers to the word "Fond" as linguistic unit. Language is thus allowed to proliferate automatically—or indeed, mechanically—via a chain of associative homonymic puns and phonetic modifications. Meaning is not expressed through language; it is *produced* through a verbal play in which words' haphazard discovery, semantic flexibility, and the sheer allure of their fanciness provide the ground rules for their implementations.

Thus the narrator admits, "I just snapped [the word] up and am now putting it to use." This apparently inconspicuous sentence in fact provides the means by which to understand the full significance of this "masterpiece or [. . .] masterworklet [Meisterstück oder -werkchen]." The word "Fond" is "snapped up [aufgeschnappt]" by the narrator just as the beer coasters are "snapped up" over and over by the dog, just as the woman's gestures are "seized and grasped" by the narrator, just as the narrator's recounted pseudo-facts are snapped up and then taken away again by himself, in a play that is organized not around a recuperative imitation- or wish-fulfillment mechanism, but according to a logic—opposed to mourning and development alike—of infinite or circular (perhaps even beer coaster-shaped) progression, for which the "endlessness" of the children's play is indeed the most accurate figure. Children, dog, and narrator all alike are caught up in a mechanically repeating "ganz dumm," but for this very reason gratifying game or writing practice. And it is precisely this very "dumbness," this lack of sense, objective, or protocol—"I did not even groom myself properly in order to write it"—that constitutes the indispensable condition of game and writing alike.

The *opposite* of dumbness might be what neither the dog nor the narrator nor the prose piece can properly lay claim to, namely responsibility, purpose, order, a real goal instead of a "Spielzweck." But a real goal in this sense is a false goal, the joyless goal of a great literature that Walser already mocks with the very first lines of the piece. Or even if the goal of great literature is not to be described as entirely joyless, the narrator declares himself content with the humble pleasures of picking up bits and pieces here and there, just as the dog is each time grateful when he has caught a coaster in his mouth, just as the taste of the dry crust of bread causes "Amazonian rivers of faithfulness [Amazonasströme von Treue]" to flow through the narrator. When the reader is commanded at the end of the piece not to "forget the pride of that silly little dog [den Stolz des dummen Hundchens nicht (vergessen)]" it is a reminder that the ultimate compositional rule of this "silly trifle featuring beer coasters [ein ganz dummes (Stück) mit Biergläseruntersätzen]," this excuse for and product of mute animalistic play, is *pleasure* as its own justification:

> I would presuppose the greatest joyfulness on this score, for this is the most important thing, and you must consider it the best. You must without fail be satisfied with me, do you hear? Without fail. And then that little mat. This reality.

Unlike in Freud, play is not *opposed* to reality, its mere simulation or suspension;[91] play *is* reality, and all things that take part in the real, objective world are "enlisted in the little game [in's Spielchen verwickelt]." Similarly, the highest criterion for art has become no more and no less than the "joyfulness" derived from this play—and indeed not just any joyfulness, but the egoistic joyfulness of the writer, who dictatorially commands that the reader follow his taste. This, too, is a pure parody of Kantian aesthetics, specifically Kant's caution that "cognitions and judgments must, together with the conviction that accompanies them, be able to be universally communicated, for otherwise they would have no correspondence with the object: they would all be a merely subjective play of the powers of representation [ein bloß subjektives Spiel der Vorstellungskräfte]" (*CPJ* §21, 122; 96). Instead of convincing, Walser simply *demands* consensus from the reader, demonstrating the flimsiness of judgments of taste and opening the door again to the mere play of the imagination. The art that is the goal of play and the art that has play as its goal answer the question of what can become of art when neither the pedagogical rewards of taste nor the self-discovery of the subject in the world seem anymore to be available.

And yet it must also be emphasized once again that despite a seemingly aleatory and ludic compositional method, Walser's "Spielzweck" refers not just to play *as end,* but also to a *play end,* a play with ends—including and especially that of play itself. This does not mean, of course, that his writing simply reverts to the status of a "free play that is nevertheless also suitable for the understanding [ein freies und zugleich dem Verstand angemessenes Spiel]" (*CPJ* §53, 206; 224) in which the imagination is gently reined in by notions of proportion and *sensus communis.* Rather, Walser's prose quivers ("I wish it pleases you so much it will make you tremble") between not one but two opposing ironies: the anarchic irony of play vis-à-vis reason, in which reason's claims are shown to be shored up by the aleatoriness that reason purports to reject, and the "irony of irony" of play's own constitutional deficiency. Play, in other words, is all that is left to art in the loss of its self-evidence, but play—Walser grants this concession—is also not able to return self-evidence to art. However, rather than seeking refuge from this lack of self-evidence in a reaffirmation of aesthetic norms or a turn to psychological expressivity, Walser takes the vicious circle one step further, transforming it into a game in which he is no less enmeshed for being able to write about it. Walser's bid to take the superannuated idea of the "identity of poetry and life" (*HDE* 28) at its literal word thus not only makes comedy out of the idea of representation, but also explodes the "constant and fundamental polarity between [. . .] narrated world and subjective reflex" (*HDE* 151), particularly as it is expressed in the bourgeois novel as the sentimental destiny of the individual in the world. For despite the proliferation of everyday objects and phenomena, what Walser's work (especially the microscripts) ultimately represents is itself; its mode is not narrative but performative, and what it performs is the scene of its creating and the literally senseless amusements derived from it. No longer is the "sense-drive [sinnlicher Trieb]" of life (see Schiller, *Aesthetic Education* 101; *Ästhetische Erziehung* 236) tempered through form to become beauty; instead, life is created *out* of form as a function of the play with it.

This is the final joke Walser's writing plays on the twin legacies of irony and objectivity: to reveal their ultimate identity in what is simultaneously the most rigorously logical and the most literally nonsensical of conclusions. With this joke, Walser proves himself to be resolutely an artist of his time: one who holds to the early romantic legacy of wit and humor, but with the consciousness of having passed through the failure of its utopian schemes; one who can meet the exhaustion of cultural and aesthetic objectivity only by raising its latent humor to the infinite—that is, to the ironic—power, and from there reclaiming in the minuscule script of the *Bleistiftgebiet* the purposeless hilarity that a "great" literature necessarily had to mute. But here Walser himself may have the last word: "Whether you believe me or not: once Bruno Cassirer tried to suggest to me that I should write novellas like Gottfried Keller. I burst out roaring with laughter."[92]

Chapter Three

✦

Slap Happy: Comic Kafka

> More and more, the essential thing in Kafka seems to me to be humor. He was of course no humorist. Rather, he was a man whose fate was to keep running into people who made a profession out of humor: into clowns. Especially "Amerika" is a great piece of clownery [. . .]. Be that as it may, I think the key to Kafka would fall to him who could *reclaim for Jewish theology its comical side*. Has there ever been such a man? or would you be man enough to be that man?
>
> —Walter Benjamin, letter to Gershom Scholem, February 4, 1939

> Above all no jokes Franz.
>
> —Franz Kafka, "Die städtische Welt"

The Comic and Its Doubles

Franz Kafka's *The Castle* reaches a climax—insofar as the novel can be said to reach a climax—in a scene of the crudest sort of situation comedy. Having just gone through the ordeal of breaking with his fiancée, Frieda, K. stumbles by accident into the room of the Castle Secretary Bürgel. While the sleep-deprived K. drowses on his feet, Bürgel—in a passage similar to the more famous "Before the Law" parable of *The Trial*—opines on the only way to gain legal access to the Castle:

> "There remains, however," said Bürgel, [. . .] "in spite of all precautions, one possibility for the parties in question to use these nightly weaknesses of the secretaries, always assuming that it *is* a weakness, to their advantage. Admittedly a very rarely or, to put it better, almost never occurring possibility. It consists in this, that the party in question comes unannounced in the middle of the night [. . .]. The party in question, never seen, always expected, truly thirstily expected but

> for good reasons always considered unreachable, sits right there. His mere silent presence alone makes one want to enter into his poor life, to wander about there as if in one's own property and commiserate among his vain demands [. . .]. One must [. . .] show how the party in question, in all his helplessness, of the sort that no other being but just such a party in question is capable of, has indeed stumbled upon this opportunity, in which he now can, if he wants to, Mr. Land Surveyor [wie sie aber jetzt, wenn sie will, Herr Landvermesser], dominate the whole situation by doing nothing more than in some way bringing forward his claim, whose fulfillment is even now at the ready, which is, indeed, stretching out towards him" [. . .]. K. heard no more, he was asleep, sealed off [abgeschlossen] from everything that was happening.[1]

K.'s succumbing to the most common of physical incapacities at the very moment that the conditions for his salvation are being explained to him—conditions, moreover, which he is at that very moment already fulfilling—is a blatant joke played on K.'s fate and the reader's expectations alike. The representatives of the Castle, thirsting vainly for their applicant, can only receive him when they cease to expect him, just as the applicant can only be received when he ceases to want to be received. That the rarely occurring, exceptional, "or, to put it better, almost never occurring possibility" for achieving access to the Castle comes for K. only at the moment when he is incapable of acting upon it—literally the moment of unconsciousness or (in a particularly glaring pun) "Abgeschlossenheit"[2]—is not merely an instance of dramatic irony on Kafka's part and dumb unluck on the part of his protagonist. Rather, it is one among the many examples of how Kafka uses the principles of comic irony to structure his plots, principles that moreover—as this chapter will argue—constitute no less than the guiding idea of Kafka's work as a whole.

The connection between Kafka and the comic is hardly new, beginning already with Max Brod's comment in his 1937 biography that the student Kafka "could be enthusiastic and enraptured, then there was no end to jokes and laughter; indeed, he laughed easily and heartily and equally knew how to make his friends laugh."[3] Another of Kafka's friends and early critics, Felix Weltsch, declares that Kafka's humor is "not humor in the sense of witty merriment and light entertainment; it is a serious humor and precisely thereby can be linked in Kafka's writings to religion,"[4] as a means "that permits the writer to advance towards pure form and the higher 'sphere' [zur reinen Gestalt und zur höheren 'Sphäre' vorzudringen]" (*Religion und Humor* 90). Though Weltsch's juxtaposition of comedy and religion may at first glance seem provocative, it is essentially identical to the traditional dialectical notion of comedy as the negation of the finite, in which humor serves as a vehicle into the "higher sphere" insofar as it enables one to laugh at the world from the non-humorous perspective of eternity. Thus, even though Weltsch insists on the difference between Kafka's humor and the comic of mere trivial entertainment, his own notion of comedy—which continues to prove influential in Kafka reception—is in fact just as trivial, for it already marks as negligible or absurd all that which its laughter touches.

Such a version of the comic is in the ontological domain what the classical paradox—in which one term is turned into its opposite in order to produce unusual insight or striking effect—is in the logical one: mechanisms by which conventional and accepted modes of thought are shored up by holding up their opposites to ridicule. Kafka, however, wants more. As he himself writes on the subject of the paradox in a diary entry from November 1912:

> Certain is my aversion to antitheses. They may come unannounced, but they never surprise, for they were always already ready to hand; if they were unconscious, then they were unconscious only at the unconscious's outermost edge. They may generate thoroughness, depth, consistency, but only like a figure in a wheel of life; we've chased our little idea around in a circle. For all that they can be varied, they are completely without nuance, as if swollen with water they grow large under your hand, with their initial prospect out onto endlessness and with a finite and middling always identical size. They curl up, can't be stretched out, have no point of reference, are holes in wood, are an immobile assault, draw, as I have shown, antitheses down to themselves. May they pull all of them down to themselves once and for all. (*T* 259–60)

Unlike Kant, Kafka does not dismiss traditional wit on the grounds that it is a frivolous and untrustworthy form of thought in comparison to rational logic, suitable only for light diversion; to the contrary, he dismisses it on the grounds that such diversion is in fact not diverting *enough*. The fundamental problem for reason is not insoluble contradiction and non-identity, which can be presented in order to be laughed at, but rather *soluble* contradiction and *too much* identity, and just as "religious humor" only serves to condemn humor to the trivial and the profane, the comedic paradox's reversal of "normal" logic only confirms this logic in its very normalcy. Against both of these, then, Kafka demands a form of the comic which does not corroborate but disassembles conventional thinking, a *total comic,* for which there is no consoling reversal and from which there is no route back.

The strategy of this chapter, however, will be to attempt to sidestep the debate on Kafka's comedy to some degree by focusing on what is by common consensus considered to be the "lightest" of Kafka's major works, the early novel fragment *Der Verschollene* (*Amerika*).[5] Walter Sokel, in the course of making the widely accepted claim that "The Judgment" provides the "basic structure [Grundstruktur]" for Kafka's subsequent work, remarks within parentheses that "AMERIKA is antithesis," for good measure adding, "and AMERIKA was also started before THE JUDGMENT."[6] There are of course good reasons why *Der Verschollene,* for all the humiliations and horrors that befall its hapless protagonist Karl Roßmann, still appears as a sunnier counterpart to the other two novels, although the ones generally given—the novel's uncharacteristically optimistic ending or the eager-to-please naïveté of its main character[7]—are problematic and misleading. And while *Der Verschollene* is chronologically an early work, it is less accurate to say that Kafka becomes more "serious" in his later years than that the operations of the comic, which in *Der Verschollene* are still at their most exaggerated and thus most easily recognizable, become more and more integrated into his writing: not as diegetic content, but as structural principle.[8] One of the claims of this chapter will thus be that *Der Verschollene* is neither antithesis nor anomaly, but provides its own kind of "Grundstruktur," indeed an even more fundamental one than that of "The Judgment": and this not along the lines of the more familiar tragic-grotesque or ethico-political (not to speak of the sentimental-psychoanalytical)[9] models of reading Kafka, but in terms of precisely those qualities that seem to make the novel exceptional in Kafka's oeuvre.

A frequent point of focus for the analysis of Kafka's comic sense—one observed not least by Kafka himself—has been the comparison between his work and the writings of Charles Dickens, perhaps the most influential of all literary humorists.[10] Dickens's stamp is unmistakable, for example, in Therese's tale of her mother's death in the "Hotel occidental" chapter of *Der Verschollene,* a tale both naturalistic and pathetic in a way unusual for Kafka and indeed anomalous in the novel itself. But it is in fact the *contrast* with Dickens's methods, far more than the similarities, that is most useful for an understanding of the comic within Kafka's work.[11] The third-to-last sentence in Therese's tale of woe reads:

> Then her mother came to a little pile of bricks, before which the railing and probably also the path came to an end, but she didn't stop there, she kept going towards the pile, her agility seemed to have abandoned her, she knocked over the pile of bricks and toppled with it down into the depths [sie stieß den Ziegelhaufen um und fiel über ihn hinweg in die Tiefe]. (*V* 202)

Genuinely (and atypically) moving though this is in Kafka's novel, it finds what can only be called a parodic echo a mere several pages later, within the scene of Karl's unlucky reunion with Robinson at the Hotel occidental:

> Thereupon Robinson waved him over and whispered to him through lurching movements whose meaning was soon clear: "Roßmann, I feel sick." "Damn it," blurted out Karl and dragged him with both

> hands to the railing. And immediately out of Robinson's mouth vomit disgorged into the depths [Und schon ergoß es sich aus Robinsons Mund in die Tiefe]. (*V* 212)

The vomit of the staggering Robinson lost in the vertical depths of the hotel repeats the body of Therese's mother, lost in the vertical depths of New York's industrial architecture.[12] This is not merely a kind of imitation of Dickensian tragicomedy, in which the sentimental is lightened with the grotesque and the grotesque deepened with the sentimental, but a manifestation of Kafka's implacable and utterly *unsentimental* form of the comic that recognizes no ground—not even the abyssal one under the construction sites of New York—for pathos.[13]

The echo between the two passages quoted above also represents a form of that specifically textual irony, already seen—to different ends and with somewhat different premises—in Walser, of the divaricating production of words from words and images from images.[14] To an even greater extent than in Walser, if possible, in Kafka such literary parthenogenesis is a direct provocation of the bourgeois novel's bond between readerly affect and object of representation, and its foreclosing of the claims to reference—in particular, psychological reference—which the traditional novel can by no means do without.[15] This fact, that Kafka's work derives from a different source than that of the mimetic or the didactic, means that Kafka's writings are not even so much comedies of *something*, but rather somethings of *comedy*: examples of a pitiless ironic logic for which the comic can provide no relief, because it is itself what it would "relieve" itself from. In this sense, *Der Verschollene*'s satyr-play without a tragedy[16] and the young Karl Roßmann's exile from the pathos of the European family to the land of the happy end is no less than Kafka's own early self-sending into a new form of literature, whose seriousness lies precisely in its willingness to be in on the joke.

Inexplicable Dumb-Shows and Noise

The anti-realist character of Kafka's works may be partly attributed to the fact that Kafka begins his literary career as a movie- and, especially, a theatergoer. Kafka's frequenting of cinema houses[17] and his deep interest in the Yiddish theater of his day is by now well known; indeed, his encounter with the Yiddish theater in general and his friendship with the actor Jizchak Löwy in particular has been presented as the decisive factor in the "breakthrough" that led not only to the writing of "The Judgment" but also to his entire future stylistic development.[18] More significant than the specific details of the Yiddish theater of Kafka's day, however, seems to have been the encounter with theatricality and theatrical performance *as such*.[19] This is particularly so to the extent that theatricality and theatrical process come into conflict with the supposedly scriptural and specifically *non*-performative practice of writing. Kafka gives evidence of an awareness of the tension between *staging* and *describing* in a diary entry from October 1911:

> To my horror, the actors convince me time and again through their presence that the majority of what I have written about them up to now is false. It is false because I write about them with a consistent love (as soon as I write this down, this is also false) but varying strength and this varying strength does not strike loud and true at the real actors but instead loses itself with a thud in this love, which for its part can never be happy with power and therefore thinks to protect the actors by checking its force. (*T* 98–99)

Kafka understands the will to write—more specifically, to *represent*—as something essentially agonistic, even antagonistic. This antagonistic, representational will fails, however, as soon as it is mixed with love—itself paradoxically the impetus for writing in the first place—and thus the writing also fails to hit its object of representation. One possible solution to such a dilemma would be to then interiorize this failure, to transform it into a literature of affective subjectivity in which, for example, the writer would write about his *love for* the object as (knowable, verifiable) substitute for an impossible depiction of the beloved object itself. This, however, is not what happens in the above passage. In the above passage, a personified love rejects the weakened will to write on account of its initial adversarial stance toward the object, a stance for which love had nevertheless provided the incitation.

Crucial in this context is the fact that this inner melodrama of the writing life and the consequent impossibility of writing is set off by the actors' *presence*. Their performative presence and their presencing performance have a self-sufficiency and an immediacy that writing, for Kafka, here lacks: theater ostensibly bypasses the violence of writing's mediation through the physical incarnation of what is to be represented, whereas a merely descriptive, linguistic, and above all *scriptural* writing, in contrast, will always fail its object. Thus it becomes clear that if the theater (and to a lesser degree, the cinema) is an influence on Kafka's early work, this is so less in the repetition/adaptation of particular plot elements or the negotiation of a Jewish identity between orthodoxy and secular nationalism,[20] and far more in the aspects of theatricality, staging, and presence themselves, as a tentative solution to a crisis of writing brought on by the exhaustion of subjective pathos and appropriative mimesis alike.

Clearly, the theater is not always necessarily a space of the comic; *theatricality*, on the other hand, may be, insofar as the performative nature of the work of art means that the artwork's own contingency, in terms of both form and content, comes to the fore. In the extreme case, this gives way, again, to Hegel's "perverse originality [schiefen Originalität]" that "treats nothing seriously and carries on the business of joking merely for the sake of joking" (*A* 296; *AI* 383). Stanley Corngold remarks of "In the Penal Colony" that the events narrated therein "comprise a theatrical play, with the chief spectator—the explorer—seated in a cane chair in the orchestra, the whole a kind of amphitheater, with palisades. And [. . .] if this is a theater, then any amount of stage business is permissible."[21] But it is not just stage business that is going on in "In the Penal Colony" and other works of Kafka. It is also and above all *backstage* business, the mechanics of performance and the special effects that should lend verisimilitude to the narrative but, once revealed, reverse the normal order of function and themselves take center stage. This reverse in the order of function is then also potentially a *mal*function; the whole of "In the Penal Colony," for example, can be read as a cautionary fable about what happens when process overshadows performance.[22]

Here, then, is another way of reading that most troubling of happy endings, the chapter fragment in *Der Verschollene* describing Karl's entry into the "Teater von Oklahama." Most readings of this chapter tend to choose between one of two interpretive possibilities: either it represents a true salvation for his hero after his long wanderings in exile, a pleasantly ramshackle operation and heaven-analogue under whose aegis friends are reunited, the authorities are benevolent rather than hostile, and, most importantly, "All are welcome [Jeder ist willkommen]" (*V* 387),[23] or else it is simply more of the same under friendlier—and thus even more sinister—guise, a bureaucracy so monstrous it swallows the whole of society and in which Karl, officially accepting the appellation of "Negro," definitively confirms his status as subaltern.[24] Yet—and without necessarily contradicting either of these options—there is also a third interpretation, one which does not so much deliver a mimetic/ethical judgment as comment on the composition of the book itself: that is, to note that Kafka's first novel ends up in—or *as*—theater.[25]

Granted, this theater is also a theater in which no performance is ever staged, in which the only artistry on display is the art*less* cacophony of the female angels' trumpets (which Karl, apparently no longer a pianist, as earlier in the novel, but now a bugler, immediately masters with virtuoso ease), for which, moreover, "There wasn't much of an audience [Es gab nicht viele Zuhörer]" (*V* 390). One thing *is* performed in this theater, however, and that thing is *the theater itself*. Even the poster that announces the theater's general casting call is staged as performance, if also one whose carnival-barker-like words, given in direct speech, "didn't seem to find much approval [schien nicht viel Beifall zu finden]" (*V* 387). With this word "Beifall"—"approval," but also "applause"—Kafka explicitly announces that what follows is not truly about a theater, but is rather the *theater of theater*; in other words, it is about an organization whose interest and occupation, ostensibly the production of performance, is in fact *the performance of production*.

Such emphasis on process over product is to be found in the vast majority of Kafka's works (and is arguably one of the primary reasons for the incompletion of all of the novels). But it is here, in Kafka's first attempt at a novel, that this singular fascination—"For Karl, however, the poster indeed held a great enticement [Für Karl stand aber doch in dem Plakat eine große Verlockung]" (*V* 388)—is first called by its proper name. Kafka's inverting of the usual relation between work and *art*work is clearly reflected in the identity Karl is finally assigned by the theater authorities:

> "What kind of position do you feel you would be suited for?" This question potentially contained a trap, for why would anyone ask it, since Karl had in fact already been hired as an actor; nevertheless, though he recognized this, he still couldn't bring himself to give the answer that he felt particularly suited for an acting career. (*V* 407)

> But the gentleman took this seriously, as he took everything seriously. "Well now, an engineer," he said, "you can't become right now, but maybe for the time being it would be acceptable to you to do some menial technical work." "Certainly," said Karl, he was quite satisfied, even though if he accepted the offer it would be a demotion from the status of actor to that of technical worker, he thought in fact that he could be of more value with such employment. Anyway, he kept saying to himself, it wasn't so much about the kind of work, but about being able to stick around at all somewhere long-term. (*V* 408)

Even if it appears to represent a step down in the social hierarchy, Karl's demotion from "actor" to "technical worker" is, in fact, no disadvantage at all. For as "technical worker," he is far more in sync with the actual workings of the theater, made up of such innovations as the "machinery" (*V* 404) borrowed from the racetrack that announces the names of each new theater member to the administration.[26] Indeed, in point of fact there *are* no actors in the universally inclusive Theater of Oklahama. (Though Karl assumes he has been hired as an actor, this is never actually stated; nor is it specifically written that anyone else has been assigned to an acting role.) But there can also *be* no actors in the Theater of Oklahama, for the precise reason that everyone is *already* an actor—or rather because the workings of the theater administration and their employees' behind-the-scenes functioning *is* the play being staged here in a kind of eternal repertoire.

For the same reason, the Theater of Oklahama also lacks the other thing that would otherwise be required for a theater: namely, an audience. The description of the photograph of the President's private theater box begins, "At first glance you would think that it wasn't a loge, but a stage, to such an extent did the balustrades curve out into the open space" (*V* 412), ending, "It was impossible to imagine people sitting in this loge, it looked so splendidly self-contained [so selbstherrlich sah alles aus]. Karl did not forget his food, but he kept looking at the image that he had laid next to his plate" (*V* 413).

Thus Karl, viewing the picture, turns out to be the spectator of the empty place of the spectator and the witness of the vacant seat of authority which is itself a stage presented for viewing (upon which, however, nothing happens). *Spectacle* becomes *speculum:* no longer the mimetic presentation of being but instead a self-reflexive theatricality empty of all content.

The self-reflecting theatricality performed in the *theatrum mundi* of the Theater of Oklahoma[27] can moreover be said to expand well beyond the confines of the novel *Der Verschollene,* forming no less than the inverted stage on which Kafka's subsequent longer works, *The Trial* and *The Castle,* take place.[28] For what are the plots of both of these novels but the constant backstage preparations for a performance that never happens? The court eagerly exhibits to Josef K. its agents, auxiliaries, and underlings, all the while constantly withholding the desired scene of practiced law; the castle is all bureaucracy and backdoor dealings from which no statement of authority, no decision ever issues. In this sense, the mistake that Joseph K. and K. both make is to expect the performance at all (or to not realize that they are already performing). In contrast, Karl truly contents himself—"he was quite satisfied [er war sehr zufrieden]" (*V* 408)—with his status as technical worker, that is to say as stagehand, and with the process of the theater troupe *as,* precisely, process without foreseeable result. Whether one considers it to be sinister irony or sincere promise, the auspicious language of the last sentences of the chapter is unmistakable:

> Karl managed to get a window seat and drew Giacomo next to him. Thus they sat pressed against one another and for the most part looked forward to the journey, never before in America had they traveled so carefree. As the train began to move they waved with their hands out the window, while the fellows sitting across from them nudged one another and found the whole thing funny [lächerlich]. (*V* 416–17)

An earlier version of the manuscript has Karl and Giacomo waving out the window, "even though in America only children do such things [trotzdem das in Amerika nur Kinder machen]."[29] Even the image of the laughing youths can be read in light of the idea of theatricality and play: Karl and Giacomo clownishly *perform* the childish naïveté that causes their travel companions to chuckle.

To speak of the comic and theatrical elements of *Der Verschollene*'s fragmentary last chapters, however, is not quite the same thing as taking a side in the debate on whether or not these chapters constitute a genuine "happy ending" to the novel. To call the Theater of Oklahoma fragment an "ending" at all—in other words, that which would pronounce a retrospective and teleological judgment on the rest of the novel—is, while philologically debatable, nevertheless demanded to a certain degree by its explicit (if of course also parodic) religious imagery, and it is reasonable to think that Kafka the movie-lover might have associated the *ex machina* happy ending (here in any case equally in the form of parody) with American popular films and thus with America per se.[30] But to speak of an ending is also clearly misleading, and not just because *Der Verschollene,* like all of Kafka's novels, remained unfinished by its author. For the Theater of Oklahama chapter is far less about Karl's fate on the mimetic level and far more about the fate of that level (which the novel has up to this point held in suspension) as such. Thus Kafka's penultimate chapter is a "revelation" in another sense than that of the narratological or eschatological: it is a revelation of *method.* What is at stake in Kafka's novels (perhaps most of all in the novels) is a laying bare—and occasionally, as in the extreme case of "In the Penal Colony," a dismantling—of the machinery of theatricality/ritual itself.[31] If Kafka's writing career begins in the impossibility of writing faced with the "love" and "horror" caused by the unrepresentable presentness of actors acting themselves, then the only way to start writing is to strip off the mask of presentness itself and expose the emptiness—or the mere process and performativity—that lies behind.

In this sense, Kafka's Theater of Oklahama would seem to anticipate Derrida's description of Artaud's theater of cruelty as a "nontheological space," a space of pure performativity in the rejection of theater's classical mimetic function. The "theological" stage as defined by Derrida is essentially that of the European bourgeois theater attacked by Artaud, one characterized by the respect of authorial texts and the lack of agency on the parts of directors and actors who "faithfully" present these texts to an equally passive audience. It is the scene of representation as "voyeurism," whose "general structure" is one "in which each agency is linked to all the others by representation, in which the irrepresentability of the living present is dissimulated or dissolved, suppressed or deported within the infinite chain of representations."[32]

Precisely this is what Kafka's diary entry on his actor friends registers "horror" over—less of course in regard to the actors themselves than in his own attempt to represent them. Unlike the "horrific" proscenium stage of theological or realistic-mimetic literature, then, the contrastingly "cruel" Theater of Oklahama has no text, no director (the highest authority in evidence is the "Leader of the tenth Publicity Troupe" [*V* 411], who moreover doesn't seem to be paying much attention to the goings-on around him), no set but that of a temporary "racetrack," no stage, and, once again, no audience; it is almost literally Artaud's vision of "a revolving spectacle, which, instead of making the stage and auditorium two closed worlds, without possible communication, spreads its visible and sonorous outbursts over the entire mass of the spectators."[33] Representation in such a theater thus turns into "the autopresentation of pure visibility and even pure sensibility" (Derrida, "Theater," 238) or, rather, into the *means* (already comic on another level from its exaggeratedly baroque precision) through which representation is to be accomplished, which then becomes, going beyond Artaud, a kind of pure *in*visibility and *in*sensibility.

This emptying out of representation of the Theater of Oklahoma is already foreshadowed several times within the action of *Der Verschollene*. First—or rather last—is the negative example of Brunelda, the non-singing singer who nonetheless requires a constant contemplation and elaborate maintenance of her massive, potentially singing body. It might even be said that Brunelda functions as negative example not in the fact that her art remains unaccomplished—again, there is no art and almost no procedure in Kafka that is truly accomplished[34]—but rather because the maintenance that keeps her in this state of potentiality is too sloppy, too much not quite yet a process. That Delamarche is fully in her spell and that Robinson describes her as a "splendid singer [herrliche Sängerin]" (*V* 211), and "a great singer [eine große Sängerin]" (*V* 304), praising her with the words, "What a dame! [So ein Frauenzimmer!]" (*V* 303),[35] means merely that the two have—as one might well expect—bad taste in art.

Still more significant in terms of Kafka's anti-mimetic processuality is the oft remarked-upon description of the "American writing-desk" encountered during Karl's stay with his uncle. The rapt fascination and childish "pleasure [Vergnügen]" (*V* 57) that Karl manifests for the desk and its accouterments stand in direct contrast to the plain fact that Karl is in fact forbidden to use them. This prohibition—"The uncle, in contrast to Karl, did not approve of the desk [Der Onkel war zum Unterschied von Karl mit diesem Schreibtisch nicht einverstanden]" (*V* 58)—is moreover what marks the first and in many ways decisive moment of the tension between Karl and his uncle that ultimately results in the former's banishment and exile:

> It was one of the very latest inventions, nevertheless it reminded Karl vividly of the nativity scene at the Christmas market back home that had been exhibited to the amazed children; Karl, too, packed in his winter clothes, had often stood before it and incessantly compared the motion of the crank handle that an elderly man would turn with its effects on the figures [. . .]. Naturally, the desk was not built to remind one of such things, but in the history of inventions there was no doubt a similar hazy connection as that of Karl's memories. (*V* 57–58)

The uncle's interdiction on the use of the writing desk's mechanisms for the specious reason of their fragility is clearly at odds with Karl's childish desire to turn the crank simply to make it *go*, to set things in motion for the mere sake of motion, for the sake of a "pleasure without productivity, without identification, without the simulation or formation of the self" (Vogl, *Ort der Gewalt* 25). The blockage here is in fact a double one.[36] The uncle's ban stops Karl from playing with the desk, and thus prevents the desk from fulfilling its *mechanical* functions, but Karl's playful attitude toward the desk's gadgets and mechanisms already stops the desk from fulfilling its *ordinary* function, that is, of being a tool (of a kind) for producing writing. Of course, in another sense the writing desk *is* a tool for producing writing, and indeed of a far more significant kind; for if this is in fact the moment where Karl's desires and his uncle's demands come inexorably into conflict, with the ultimate consequence being Karl's luckless anabasis in America, then the desk and its interdiction is the mechanism that produces the book which is being read, that in turn describes the writing desk that is the very motive force of its own existence. Thus the writing desk description is both an initial example of the allure of process over product and a multivalent allegory for the scene of writing, which is, in turn, *precisely* the scene of play as process over product itself.[37]

The description of the American writing desk is not only the first hint of the eventual break between Karl and his patron; it is also, curiously, the moment in which the President of the United States makes the first of his two (non-)appearances in the novel, the pendent to his non-appearance in the photograph of the stage/loge of the Theater of Oklahama. The desk "had for example in its upper part a hundred compartments of varying sizes, and even the President of the Union himself would have been able to find a fitting place for every one of his files" (*V* 57). Each file of the hypothetical president has its own individual cubbyhole to contain it, just as each employee of the Theater of Oklahama has his or her specifically assigned place in the workings of the theater, down to the absurd specificity of the "Bureau for European High-School Students [Kanzlei für europäische Mittelschüler]" (*V* 401) into which *der Fall Roßmann* is ultimately sorted. As has frequently been noted, both of these images form a kind of allegory of democracy, or rather its Taylorist parody, in which, under an authority both absent and omnipresent, everyone has their station on the assembly line, in which *system* replaces *sovereignty.* Such a vision of streamlined biopower as the corollary to an equally streamlined industrial production leads Joseph Vogl, for one, to posit the Theater of Oklahama chapter as the logical continuation of the novel's plot rather than its idiosyncratic redemption, arguing that even in the half-paradise of the Theater of Oklahama Kafka is already cranking up the sinister machine of bureaucracy (see Vogl, *Ort der Gewalt* 31). The replacement of sovereignty with system—or of product with process—unquestionably mirrors the transformation from a genuinely *kaiserlich und königlich* form of government to the bureaucratic biopolitics of which Kafka was judged to be, long before Foucault, the first witness and most farsighted prophet. As Vogl expresses it: "It is not about the source, truth, and origin of the law, but about its modes of operation [Funktionsweise]" (*Ort der Gewalt* 3). But the several correspondences between the wind-up writing desk and the universal Theater of Oklahama already show that this movement from foundationalism to functionality is anything but unambiguous, and while the omnipresent force of unending system/process will indeed later weigh heavily on the protagonists Joseph K. and K.,[38] it must equally be noted that this same force is *also* that which Karl opposes to his uncle's anti-ludic instrumentalism and which the Theater of Oklahama puts on stage as the flip side to conventional authorship and vulgar mimesis.

This double bill of spectacle and power is performed yet a third time in *Der Verschollene,* in the scene of the political rally viewed from Brunelda's balcony. Here the breakdown of the system of participatory democracy into chaos and free-for-all—just that which has threatened participatory democracy since its invention—is a kind of reflection of the chaos of Brunelda's apartment, the songless singer both metaphor for and portent of the governor similarly unable to govern.[39] Motifs of sound strongly dominate in this scene, but these, like Brunelda's toneless shrieks, consist only of either indistinct noises or a cacophony in which no single tone can be discerned. Here is perhaps the clearest combination in *Der Verschollene* of the empty place of political sovereignty proliferating into sheer spectacle, a mass of sensory data without discernible focal point. (It is of course noteworthy that the election in question in the scene is not for a politician but for a *judge,* that most typical of absent authority figures in Kafka.) There is a further complication here, however. For the claim that the Theater of Oklahama chapter, the rally scene, and other moments of co-implicated spectacle in *Der Verschollene* provide an authentically nontheological space of theater as life and life as theater is, in fact, not quite the case. What the Theater of Oklahama chapter and other similar moments in *Der Verschollene* provide, rather, is the *representation of* this space. Banal as this statement might initially seem, this representation of non-representation, like the *photograph* of the president's empty theater box, destroys the claim to transcendence or *epiphaneia* that the nontheological theater of cruelty paradoxically but ultimately nevertheless tends towards. Just as Kafka admits the frustrated desire to "write down" the actors with whom he keeps company, he recognizes the yearning for the theological within the nontheological, the desire for the representation to be real, for the medial event, just for once, to occur without mediation.

Thus not just a cacophony of sound but also the blurriness of a frustrated scopophilia enters onto the scene. In the episode of the political rally Kafka stages the painfully mediated nature of representation with parodic violence, as the bosomy Brunelda literally puts the screws to Karl's powers of perception:

> "Don't you want to look through the opera glasses [Gucker]?" Brunelda asked and tapped on Karl's chest to show that she was talking to him.
>
> "I can see fine," said Karl.
>
> "Just try it," she said, "you'll see better."
>
> "I have good eyes," responded Karl, "I can see everything." [. . .] And now Karl already had the glasses against his eyes and could in fact see nothing [sah nun tatsächlich nichts].

> "I can't see anything," he said and wanted to push the glasses away, but she held them tight against his face and with his head buried deep in her chest he could move neither backwards nor sideways.
>
> "Now you can see," she said and adjusted the glasses' screws.
>
> "No, I still can't see anything," said Karl and thought about how, without wanting to, he had indeed [tatsächlich] relieved Robison of his duties, for Brunelda's insufferable moods were now let out on him.
>
> "When will you finally see?" she said and turned—now Karl had his whole face in her heavy breathing—the screws again. "Now?" she asked.
>
> "No, no, no!" cried Karl, although he could now in fact, if only very dimly, make out everything [trotzdem er nun tatsächlich, wenn auch nur sehr undeutlich, alles unterscheiden konnte]. (*V* 327–28)

Here optic technology comes in not to help but to hinder a natural good vision, an unavailable authenticity of perception whose status as normative ideal is betrayed by the repeated use—here a kind of magical thinking—of the word "tatsächlich."[40] And even when Karl eventually breaks free from Brunelda's double framing to get an unobstructed view of the street, what is there to be seen is itself a mediated spectacle that devolves into a melee as unfocused as the vision through the opera glasses already was. Kafka thus poses the problem of representation as an infinite optical regression, in which the tension between mediated and unmediated perception—the former painful or dubious, the latter utopian and vague—leads only to a generalized breakdown of perspective.

Kafka's partial answer to this breakdown is the aforementioned dramatization of the backstage, of, so to speak, the obverse of representation. In other words, it is *play.* As Derrida remarks on the self-implicating nature of the Artauldian dream:

> Because it has always begun, representation therefore has no end. But one can conceive of the closure of that which is without end. Closure is the circular limit within which the repetition of difference infinitely repeats itself. That is to say, closure is its *playing* space. This movement is the movement of the world as play. ("Theater" 250)

Without reference, without spectators or actors, the theater is allowed, provisionally, to turn in on itself. Kafka's work, like Walser's, thus demonstrates both the persistence of mimesis within anti-mimesis and that repetition within difference that is the ground structure for play.[41] And while Derrida will draw the lesson of "the tragic" from representation's "gratuitous and baseless necessity" ("Theater" 250), the tragedy of representation and the mourning that ensues can also be considered the last steps before representation's corresponding *Lustspiel.* In Benjamin's words, "Comedy—or more precisely: the pure joke [der reine Spaß]—is the essential inner side of mourning which from time to time, like the lining of a dress at the hem or the lapel, makes its presence felt" (*Origin* 125–26; *Ursprung* 106). Kafka's post-mourning world theater, the backstage theater of its own performance, plays the inversion of representation's tragedy at the same time as it sets the stage for the unrelenting amusements to come.

Humor, Risk[42]

Due to the theatrical, pantomimic, and two-dimensional nature of his texts as much as to their representation of mechanical process and comical calamity, Kafka has time and again been compared with comedians of the silent screen such as Buster Keaton, Harold Lloyd, and, in particular, Charlie Chaplin. Kafka's own opinion on Chaplin's work, meanwhile, is recorded in an anecdote in Gustav Janouch's biographical memoir, *Gespräche mit Kafka* (*Conversations with Kafka*). Upon being invited by his young admirer to attend a showing of Chaplin's films, Kafka gives his qualified approval to the comedian, calling him "no sentimental Pierrot, but also no scathing critic. Chaplin is a technician [Techniker]." "Like a dentist [Zahntechniker] makes false teeth," states Kafka, "Chaplin constructs imagination-prostheses [Phantasieprothesen]."[43] Some critics have taken this passage as evidence for the affinity between the actor and the writer; others, noting that Kafka in fact *rebuffs* Janouch's offer to attend the cinema, consider it proof positive of Kafka's disdain for such popular entertainment. Few, however, have remarked upon the heavy irony of the actual words with which Kafka declines his friend's eager invitation:

> "Thank you, no. Better not," said Kafka, shaking his head. "Joking is a much too serious matter for me. I could very easily end up standing there like a clown without his makeup [Ich könnte da sehr leicht wie ein total abgeschminkter Clown dastehen]." (Janouch 177)

It is in fact plain to see that Kafka's statement is neither enthusiastic approval nor scornful rejection, but a far more complicated admission of kinship, sympathy, condescension, and envy. Kafka fears that at the film screening he will appear, in contrast to Chaplin's own chiaroscuro greasepaint, as a clown *without* makeup, in other words a clown without alibi or alter ego, whose "real" identity and identity as a comedian cannot be kept separate by means of a mere costume change. Chaplin, therefore, is only *playing* the role of the comedian that Kafka always *is.* The actor as "Techniker" puts on his uniform and goes to work, but for Kafka, in a way similar to the distinction he makes between his office reports and his nighttime writing,[44] clowning is not a job; it is a *vocation.*

One can moreover take Kafka at his literal word when he calls Chaplin a maker of "Phantasieprothesen." With this comment, Kafka separates himself from Chaplin's public, who have lost their "necessary tools for feeling and thinking that would allow them to really take possession of the life that has been granted to them" (Janouch 177). Kafka's own imagination is active and powerful enough for him not to require such supplements. Nevertheless, Kafka the denuded clown recognizes both the craft that goes into the making of such prostheses and their potential usefulness, and is not adverse to borrowing the tools of Chaplin (or rather, of his predecessors)[45] for the fabrication of his own "machine-world" (Janouch 177). For the techniques of slapstick and physical comedy that Chaplin made as synonymous with his name as the dark side of bureaucracy was to become with Kafka's own are in fact heir to a long tradition of thinking about the body—and from there, about human being in general—that Kafka recognizes and plays with long before Chaplin's films ever make their way to the cinema houses of Prague.

It is in any case neither Chaplin nor Kafka, but Schiller who makes one of the earliest contributions to the discipline of slapstick studies, with his description of grace as "moveable beauty [bewegliche Schönheit]."[46] As Schiller specifies, grace is not simply beauty set into motion, but rather a motion that is beautiful precisely *as* motion. As opposed to static beauty, which, while certainly a property of the beautiful object, is also something wholly unwilled by this object and may only be truly experienced by a human observer,[47] the category of gracefulness inheres in human being and can apply only *to* it. Not merely reducible to the objectification of the material and sensual, gracefulness contains a moral or spiritual element: though it must be just as unwilled as static beauty (lest it become awkwardness and affectation), it requires the anthropological to be inscribed *within* it, and not, as it were, supplemented from outside. Thus grace "is a beauty not granted by nature, but brought forth by the subject itself" (Schiller, "Grace," 127). If beauty is the appearance of matter (in space) as idea, grace is the expressive manifestation (in time) of the beautiful soul.

Schiller's humanistic theories of grace find their continuation—and cheekily pessimistic reversal—in Kleist's "Über das Marionettentheater" ("On the Marionette Theater"). In this piece, grace, no longer the expression of the beautiful soul in the material body, now appears most perfectly in the body without soul, in the purely mechanical movements of the marionette. Lack of grace, on the other hand (in a way not so dissimilar to Schiller), consists in the error of taking oneself as thing in a deliberate attempt to *be* beautiful—something inanimate objects, by definition, can never do. In this way human being alone is vulnerable to gracelessness and, even more, to ridiculousness, as Kleist's interlocutor says of the suddenly self-conscious movements of the once graceful boy, which "had such a comical element that I had difficulty to contain my laughter."[48] The human consciousness that, for Schiller, enables grace, is for Kleist also what transforms grace into its laughable opposite.

But it is truly with Bergson's famous definition of the comic as the "mechanical encrusted on the living"[49] that the concept of the comic is brought to bear on the questions of human movement that Schiller and Kleist pose. While Bergson's dictum, early on in his book, that "the comic does not exist outside the pale of what is strictly *human*" ("Laughter" 62) is a long-standing commonplace of thinking on the comic,[50] it also clearly resonates with both Schiller's definition of grace and with Kleist's claim (through the mouth of Herr C.) that grace inheres "in that human physical form [. . .] that has either no consciousness at all, or an infinite one" (Kleist, "Marionettentheater," 345). For Kleist, the fallen condition of mankind—perpetually caught between the inanimate, the animal, and the divine—dictates that the human being is effectively doomed to a constitutional inadequacy and awkwardness. Although *unlike* Kleist (and like Schiller), Bergson locates grace exclusively in living, animate beings,[51] he nevertheless echoes Kleist's analysis in the admission that only the potentially graceful being is also potentially ungraceful, that is, can be ripped out of grace by self-consciousness and inflexibility: the "soul imparts a portion of its winged lightness to the body it animates: the immateriality which thus passes into matter is what is called gracefulness. Matter, however, is obstinate and resists" (Bergson, "Laughter," 78). But where Kleist's rethinking of grace, in its insistence on the non-human as the only entity *not* vulnerable to excesses of self-consciousness and thus to gracelessness, brings Schiller's theory to its radical and parodic extreme, Bergson takes a different and indeed more conservative tack, *extracting* Kleist's ironic post-humanism as the specifically laughable element of human behavior and motion. The always potential resistance of matter to the spiritual immateriality that "passes into" it is precisely Bergson's definition of the comic, which in Bergson's thoroughly corrective and moralistic analysis—"every rigidness of character, of mind, even of body will be suspect to society" ("Laughter" 73, translation modified)—bears the same purely negative relation to grace as ugliness does to beauty.

The publication date of Bergson's book on laughter alone would make his theories of interest for the consideration of the comic in Kafka's works. More than just this temporal coincidence, however, Kafka's comic sensibilities often play out in the selfsame borderland between the automated and the anthropomorphic, for example in the deservedly oft-quoted passage from a 1909 letter to Max Brod:

> For what I have to do! In my four district divisions—not even including my other work—the people fall as if drunk from the scaffolding into the machines below, all the beams topple over, all the embankments become loose, all the ladders slide out, whatever is placed on top falls down, whatever is placed on the ground is tripped over. And

> one gets headaches from all these young girls in porcelain factories who keep throwing themselves off of staircases holding towers of crockery.[52]

This passage may be easily read as an example of Bergsonian burlesque, as Kafka's unfortunate workers, in ignorance of the flexibility and alertness that for Bergson constitutes the essence of living life, toss themselves to their doom with mechanical regularity. But, as a closer look at this passage quickly reveals, Kafka's slapstick in fact constitutes less the illustration of Bergson's theory of laughter than the critique thereof. First, as Joseph Vogl has pointed out, in Kafka as well as in early slapstick the passage between the inanimate and the animate moves in not just one but in two opposing directions. Not only do human beings elicit laughter by turning into pseudo-objects, as in Bergson's model; objects also take on a life of their own, offering up as it were a resistance to their own objectification and becoming, in Siegfried Kracauer's words, "the shock troops of unconquered nature."[53] Building elements collapse apparently out of malice, ladders run away from their climbers, the world turns topsy-turvy and things take a perverse pleasure in the trouble thus created, as if rescinding their normal polite willingness to be of use for human subjects. Thereby are the seemingly essential categories of human and thing, subject and object dissolved into "a comic methodology that tracks, slackens, destabilizes, and finally tilts or topples principles and systems of judgment, or at least places them in an unseemly limbo."[54] In this destabilizing of systems of judgment, Bergson's definition of the human implied in his theory of laughter particularly suffers a blow. Laughter is no longer the social corrective for a badly managed vitality,[55] but rather a participatory response to the uncertainty of ontological borders, including and especially the ontological borders of the human being itself.

Yet more to the point than this image of a mad world that alienates what is most familiar and blurs even the most seemingly clear distinctions is the fact that—in Kafka as in most slapstick—this chaos of objects in motion *itself* maintains a kind of integrity. For what takes place in a slapstick scene is in fact not mere mechanistic lack of agility as the contrary to a regulative ideal of the gracious, ensouled human being,[56] nor merely the insurrection of the inanimate as a challenge to human exceptionalism. As anyone who has witnessed the intricate kinetics of a Keaton or a Chaplin short can attest, what takes place in slapstick is rather the staged *performance* of the fall, the *choreography* of accident; in other words, the *paradoxical gracefulness of clumsiness* as a factor of its representation. In slapstick, therefore, the loss of control—or, in Schillerian terms, of a proper equilibrium between materiality and will—that characterizes both daily ungainliness and the Bergsonian comic of the body no longer acts as the mere negation of grace, but becomes its own positive principle; indeed, in slapstick, a nimble ungainliness is staged as the very essence of human movement.

Such staging provides a further turn to Kleist's already paradoxical notion that, contrary to the idea of grace as the perfectly ensouled body, only in the totally mechanical or the totally ethereal body—"that is, in the marionette, or in God" ("Marionettentheater" 345)—is grace actually possible; among fallen human beings, on the other hand, gracefulness is something infinitely unavailable. In the performance of slapstick, then, something like a temporary respite from earthly clumsiness is achieved: a foretaste of paradise, if one will, yet—unlike, for example, in the illusion of airy disembodiment attempted by classical ballet—it is still a this-worldly paradise, in which the recalcitrance of the body remains present as a condition of its own redemption. Here grace happens as both product of and exception to the rule of unpredictability; that is, it is no longer a matter of orderly yet effortless action, but of the dumb-luck avoidance of catastrophic accident. Siegfried Kracauer comments on silent film's "inherent affinity" for coincidence:

> Unlike most circus productions, film comedy did not highlight the performer's proficiency in braving death and surmounting impossible difficulties; rather, it minimized his accomplishments in a constant effort to present successful rescues as the outcome of sheer chance. Accidents superseded destiny; unpredictable circumstances now foreshadowed doom, now jelled into propitious constellations for no visible reason. Take Harold Lloyd on the skyscraper: what protected him from falling to death was not his prowess but a random combination of external and completely incoherent events which, without being intended to come to his help, dovetailed so perfectly that he could not have fallen even had he wanted to.[57]

In other words, in slapstick, it is not the *accident* which is amusing, but the accidental *lack* of accident: movements that may well be mechanical, but are also far more graceful—or at least more propitious—than those which skill or presence of mind could provide for. In the context of Schiller's and Bergson's theories, Kracauer's subsequent dictum, "Accidents were the very soul of slapstick" (Kracauer, *Theory of Film,* 62) can be understood rigorously as grace is the "soul" in the body of human perfectibility to which the comic would be the corrective, happy accidents are the soul of a non-teleological slapstick in which things falling out right is just one more coincidence.

The elegant presentation of inelegant motion has a long and significant history, of course, and one that predates Kafka by many centuries. But in addition to its finding a fresh audience through the dissemination of modern vaudeville performances and especially of early silent film, the representation of accident was also propagated through the genuinely new medium of displays, exhibitions, films, and museums for the purpose of bringing attention to industrial safety and worker hygiene. In his study of the phenomenon of the work safety museum in the late nineteenth and early twentieth centuries, Stefan Poser speaks of the "staging of technology" of such pedagogical spectacles, noting that technological advancements were portrayed not only as "problem-solving techniques" but also as "impressive human accomplishments," and objects of "cultural value"[58]—that is to say, as aesthetic ends in themselves. At the same time, however, the concomitant *dangers* of technology were presented in a way aimed at arousing a no longer cathartic but rather didactic fear and pity, whereby the spectator would be given an impression of "an as it were automatic punishment-mechanism" (Poser, *Museum der Gefahren,* 126): the very image of an anthropomorphic or, indeed, quasi-divine technology that knows how to penalize those who fail to use it properly. In either case, the prevailing dramaturgy of these installations and films was one of direct emotional manipulation and clear, easy-to-understand visual presentation, optimally presented "in a playfully light and amusing form"[59] to keep the audience attentive and engaged.

Kafka, for his part, was well versed in these amusing and educational tools of industrialized biopolitical society, and refers to them in knowledgeable detail in several of his professional briefs. In one 1914 report, he praises the "cinematographic presentations [kinematographischen Vorführungen]" (Kafka, *Amtliche Schriften,* 184) of work safety films (loaned out by the Museum für Arbeiterwohlfahrt in Charlottenburg and the Berlin Allgemeine Elektrizitätsgesellschaft) in Prague and elsewhere. And in a report on "Accident Prevention and First Aid" from the year following, Kafka concludes dryly of an exhibition of "diagrams and graphic representations," "It was not observed that this object attracted particular interest. The press remained silent, the topic may well have been rather remote and difficult for them to understand" (*Amtliche Schriften* 275), comparing it negatively to another, more hands-on exhibition of machinery with "the safety features painted in bright red, so that they immediately caught the eye" (277). The first thing to be remarked here is Kafka's—in this case pragmatic—privileging of the concretely visual and exemplary over the discursive and general, and his attention, once again, to the importance of staging and presentation: indeed, one might go so far as to say, to the notion that things may be apprehended *only insofar as* they are staged. Secondly, while Kafka clearly appears to have found worker safety to be a serious and worthy aim, the letter to Brod at least makes clear that he was also able to regard even his work data and case studies as if they were comic performances. However, the comedy of these performances no longer has to do solely with the staging of the accident itself (whose details and real economic and psychological consequences must have been all too familiar to Kafka); it also has to do with a profound uncertainty in regard to the boundary between accident and intention, automatism and will, agility and ineptitude, in which the humanist and vitalist ideals of grace are not so much undone as remodeled on the assembly line.

The action of *Der Verschollene* is suffused with such ironic choreography of mishap. The first chapter, "Der Heizer" ("The Stoker"), could be mapped out in graphic fashion as a network of crossed vectors, whose apparatus is set in motion from the very second paragraph: "'So high,' he said to himself and, completely forgetting about disembarking, was gradually shoved up against the deck railing by the swelling crowds of baggage porters pushing past" (*V* 7). At first swept along by the wave of people, in the next paragraph Karl remembers that he has left his umbrella behind and moves against the onrushing motion of the crowd back into the bowels of the ship (whose multiple passages are, moreover, themselves blocked, shunting him finally into the Stoker's tiny room). This image of Karl as a single point in space set against the teeming masses is repeated almost exactly at the end of the chapter in the opposite direction, as the head machinist Schubal's supporters crowd the ship administration's office just as Karl is spirited away by his uncle:

> The two gentlemen shook hands. Karl was able only to silently and fleetingly offer his hand to the captain, for the latter was already being claimed by the crowd of around fifteen people who were filing in, under Schubal's direction a bit more subdued but still quite loud. The sailor asked the senator to permit him to go ahead and then parted the crowd for him and Karl, who passed easily through the bowing people. (*V* 51–52)

The sailor's parting of the machinist's mob to lead Karl into the Promised Land is immediately recognizable as a parodic version of the Exodus narrative—especially since Karl will only end up back at "Ramses," both the improbable name of the town in which the Hotel Occidental is located and the name of the sovereign who once reigned over the Jews' Egyptian Captivity.[60] This pattern of a single line of motion through an undifferentiated crowd can in fact be said to structure the whole book: from the initial failure to disembark to the abortive attempt to flee the heap of things and people in Brunelda's apartment, Karl is always, so to speak, going against the current. In this sense, if nothing else, the Theater of Oklahama does indeed represent a relaxation of the novel's trajectory. The very last sentence of the novel (as given in the *Kritische Ausgabe*) is a vision of the train to Oklahama speeding easily through and over obstacles, no longer being buffeted against them, in a long compound sentence whose very propulsion mimics the forward-rushing movement of the train's body.[61] Although like Moses, Karl will never actually reach the Holy Land, for the first time since his arrival on the continent, he is going, at least, in the same direction as everyone else.

In his analysis of what he terms Kafka's "poetics of accident," Benno Wagner quotes from a 1909 letter from Kafka to Ernst Eisner, the director of the Trieste-based insurance firm Assicurazioni Generali with which Kafka found his first professional employment. Wagner reads the letter, along with the humorous passage in the letter to Brod quoted above, as contrasting dramatizations of "an epistemological bipolarity"[62] between a subjective and individualized—that is to say, a humanist—account of accident on the one hand, and on the other hand, its quantitative and statistical treatment in the insurance profession in which Kafka played a not insignificant role. According to Wagner, the ironizing of individual perspective in light of probability calculation and institutional protocol creates the characteristic tension of Kafka's plots from *Der Verschollene* onwards, in what might be described as the post-technocratic problematization of Aristotle's attribution, in the *Poetics,* of comedy to the domain of probability as opposed to tragedy's concern with an individual fate.[63]

Yet there is also a further and more immediate connection between this letter's motifs and those of the contemporaneously written *Der Verschollene.* For a closer look at the letter reveals it to be, not just a multi-perspectival description of accident, but also a complex allegory for Kafka's own writing process and an implicit but clear statement of literary intent:

> One could say that there are people who have emerged out of the previous generation a little bit slower than the rest, one cannot demand that everyone follows with the same regular leaps of the time. But it goes without saying that once someone falls out of step while marching he can never again catch up; and yet the missed step also comes to appear in such a way that you might place bets on its being no human step, but you would lose. Just think of the look of a racehorse on the track, if you can hold its eyes; surely the mere look of a horse as it leaps over the hurdle shows the utmost, present, completely true essence of racing. The totality of the stands, the totality of the live audience, the totality of the surrounding area in a particular season, etc., even the orchestra's last waltz and the way one likes to play it nowadays. But if my horse happens to turn back and doesn't want to jump and goes around the hurdle or breaks out and runs wild in the middle of the track or even throws me off, then the overall view is apparently greatly enhanced. There are gaps in the audience, some fly up, some fall down, hands wave to and fro as if blown about by some wind, a shower of fleeting relations rains down on me and [it is] entirely possible that some of the audience members feel it too and empathize with me while I am lying there on the grass like a worm. Is that supposed to prove anything? (Kafka, *Briefe 1900–1912,* 115–16)

The image of the racetrack in this passage can right away be paired with its double in Clayton where the Theater of Oklahama's casting call occurs, and where Kafka's highly ironically named *Roß-mann* finally finds his way in the world (see *V* 387). To be added to this, however, is the hardly incidental fact that, even if the passage eventually ends up literally and figuratively running away with itself, it begins as an explicit meditation on none other than the young author Robert Walser (perhaps also suggesting the "orchestra's last waltz [letzten Walzer des Orchesters]" later in the letter). That is: this letter, which ends so unluckily and so exemplarily, opens with Kafka's reproach to his former boss and fellow literary enthusiast for not having purchased a copy of Walser's *Geschwister Tanner.*[64] Kafka continues in free-association mode by commenting on the character Simon (and implicitly, on the author Walser himself):

> Does he not wander about everywhere, happy to the tips of his ears, and in the end nothing will become of him except the reader's pleasure? That's a rather sorry career, but only a sorry career brings that light to the world that a not perfect but pretty good writer is able to produce [. . .]. Certainly, seen from the outside, people like that are also walking around all the time [. . .], but they are not differentiated in the least except through the lighting effects in fairly good novels. (*Briefe 1900–1912* 115–16)

Here it becomes clear not only to what extent Walser's influence lingers in the background of Kafka's first novel, but also how Kafka's horse/man Karl functions as fantasy doppelgänger and antagonist to Walser's Simon Tanner (whose story, however, Kafka admits or at least claims not to have read). Karl, too, is one of those unexceptional and slightly slow characters, of whose similarly "sorry career [schlechte Karriere]"[65] one should need no convincing.

But whereas Simon Tanner goes (or at least, is imagined by Kafka to go) through life without resistance or consequence—much as Walser, in Kafka's (mis-)evaluation, goes around as a talented but also still immature and undisciplined writer—Kafka, no doubt wanting to write more than merely "fairly good novels [ziemlich gute Romane]," is far stricter with both himself and his developing protagonist. And indeed, by the end of the letter, the image of the ambulatory outsider and *Taugenichts* that Kafka paints of Walser has been subtly transformed into something quite different: no longer a mere carefree circuit around the world (or the racetrack), but a risky, progress-blocking stumble of great significance. The too-slow and the too-fast alike experience only the homogenous mass, the event as "totality [Einheit]." But—as in the prose piece "Auf der Galerie," where not the bad circus act but the perfect virtuoso performance causes the spectator to weep in despair (see *DL* 262–63)—in the spectacle of the racetrack, it is only resistance and mishap that creates the series of differentiated actions. Of course, this—as Kafka says, breaking off the letter in frustration—hardly proves anything. But it is within this interplay of expected uniformity and unexpected discrepancy—or, following Wagner, of statistical norm and deviation (see Wagner, "Poetik des Unfalls," 440–42)—that Kafka attempts to make a "good career" for himself in his writing, as opposed to what he perceives as the temptation of happy-go-lucky wandering. While such conflictless wandering may still be preferable to the teleological self-actualization of the realist novel, Kafka opts against the one as well as the other, and looks instead to the simultaneous *anti*-teleology and *anti*-easygoingness of accident, fall, and misdirection to provide a new prototype for his creation of novelistic tension.

The complement to this obstacle course are those moments in which a streamlined and industrialized movement is exaggerated to the point of approaching the level of *ballet mécanique*. This is in evidence above all in the final scenes at the Hotel Occidental, in which Karl, fired in disgrace from his job as lift-boy, is led in a sort of farewell tour through the inner workings of the hotel, the hyperbolic efficiency of which is matched only by its outsized magnitude. "See, this is how we work here [Siehst Du, so wird hier gearbeitet]" (*V* 259), the Head Porter reprimands Karl as he drags him past the porters' lodge where the under-porters perpetually zigzag past one another on their miscellaneous errands. This exaggeration of assembly-line alacrity reaches its comic climax as Karl is finally propelled out onto the hotel's entrance and driveway, where, in a passage similar to the one in the letter to Brod, a super-rationalized organization reveals itself to be the alibi for a new kind of carnival:

> The organization of the security guards must not have been all that exemplary after all, there were bells being rung on all sides, but God only knows to what end, hotel employees went this way and that way through the doors in such numbers that one might have thought they wanted to inconspicuously make exit impossible, for there was not much other logic to be detected in such to-and-froing—anyway Karl was soon outside, but he still had to walk along the sidewalk of the hotel, for the street was unreachable due to the unbroken line of automobiles edging hesitantly along in front of the main entrance. The automobiles, so as to get to their masters as soon as possible, had been practically driven on top of one another, each one pushed forward by the one behind. Those pedestrians who were particularly eager to reach the street even climbed here and there through the individual automobiles as if these were public throughways, and it was all the same to them if in the automobile was sitting merely the chauffeur and the servants or the most elegant people. (*V* 266–67)[66]

Such descriptions of the hotel's functioning and the similarly factory-like character—as if merely an extension of its operations—of the hotel's vicinity are clear parodies of an America seen as the site of a new, ultra-efficient and ultra-modern culture, typified by what Arthur Holitscher in *Amerika Heute und Morgen* (whose importance as source text for Kafka's novel can hardly be overestimated) calls "the American pace, this pace set by modern

America's efficiency and sense of power, which fills the European with such wonder and awe" (384). Holitscher's phrase occurs in the course of a double polemic: on the one hand, against the modern American's willful ignorance of (European) tradition and high culture (see 382–83); and on the other hand, the American contempt for what Holitscher terms the "slow people"—that is, Native Americans and blacks—a point of connection which incidentally provides perhaps the most pertinent clue for an understanding of Karl's odd name-change in the Theater of Oklahama.[67]

In contrast to these latter peoples, who find themselves disdained and left behind by a society racing ever faster towards the finish line, Holitscher speaks—in a passage to which Kafka was clearly not insensitive—of the creation of no less than a new type of human being from that epitome of urban technology, the elevator:

> It is unthinkable that this eternal, unprecedented up-and-down-going [diese ewige, unerhörte Auf- und Nieder-Fahrerei] should not, in the length of time, alter the structure of the human body, of the human being who travels in such a fashion. The heart, the brain can't but undergo alteration, the good Lord made no provision in the animal kingdom for such a condition of upwards and downwards travel. A new type of human being will come along to be added to the other kinds of American beings, the skyscraper-man [der Wolkenkratzertypus], this will be the national cretin. (60–61)

There can be no doubt that it is partially in recollection of this passage that Kafka chooses lift-boy as profession for his young protagonist. Karl, formerly a normal, healthy, ground-floor-dwelling European, under the influence of the constant rapid vertical motion demanded by his job, runs the risk of becoming an example of "the national cretin [der nationale Kretin]."[68] Such a new kind of human being, whose heart and brain are deformed by the body's assimilation to unnatural mechanical motion, is a kind of machine-age analogue of the unsouled doll-body of Kleist's marionette theater, pulled likewise by strings directed by unseen hands up above: in the empty heads of the puppet and of the American cretin alike, the progress of European reason reaches a dead end.

Holitscher's description of the unnatural rising and falling motion of the elevators and its physical and psychical effect on the human being must have also struck a professional chord in Kafka, coming so near as it does to the documenting of the physical and psychical effects of work technology that comprised such a large part of his work for the Workmen's Accident Insurance Institute for the Kingdom of Bohemia in Prague. This is not so much to restate the point already made elsewhere that Kafka's work gave him a deep insight into and concern for both the human cost of modern technology and the biopolitical implications of securing the citizen's body,[69] than to emphasize that Kafka's work also represents a thinking of the possibility that such technologies could actually affect the very nature of human being—indeed, to the point of changing it entirely. The construction of the "Durchschnittsmensch" or "average man"—an anthropological novelty borne of the crossing of statistical tables with biopolitical exigencies—has been productively applied to Kafka's work, as the allegorical incarnation of statistical average in the form of the individual. To the *Durchschnittsmensch*'s inhabitance within the "order of comedy and social statistics"[70] and the Chaplinian sentimentality of the little man versus the Machine, however, should be added the anthropological novelty represented by Holitscher's "Wolkenkratzertypus," the American national cretin and presumptive Man of the Future.

It is in this context of no small importance that Holitscher's book briefly mentions Bergson as one of the dominant philosophical influences in America at the time of his travels. Bergson's influence can be particularly felt, according to Holitscher, in the masses of popular journal articles by "eugenicists, utopians, dietary reformers, back-to-nature-enthusiasts, civilization-destroyers, breath-fanatics" (404) promoting a diluted new-age vitalism as alternative to the mechanized lifestyle to which Holitscher more often turns his eye. The vegetarian, cure-taking, and somewhat neurasthenic Kafka was not foreign to such trends, which in any case found as much approval in European circles as they did in the New World.[71] Nevertheless, it is clear that Kafka finds the pseudo-pastoral utopias to which such self-care regimens implicitly allude to be essentially unviable, recognizing that in a rapidly industrializing world, the vertically oriented cretin and the horizontally oriented man of the land (who will himself later achieve parodic apotheosis in the form of *The Castle*'s immobilized *Landvermesser*) are no longer to be kept strictly apart.

But the hotel driveway passage quoted above only truly achieves the level of the comic with its final sentence, in the manifestly unrealistic image of the pedestrians cutting pathways through the cars' doors and windows: a behavior which Kafka has Karl describe, in droll understatement, as "exaggerated [übertrieben]" (*V* 267). This movement too can be analyzed in Bergsonian terms, as the pedestrians climb through the row of cars seemingly programmed to cross the street but not aware enough to take account of unforeseen obstacles. But while for Bergson, "If [. . .] we wish to define the comic by comparing it with its contrary, we should have to contrast it with gracefulness even more than with beauty" ("Laughter" 79), it must be admitted that this synchronized mechanicity, whatever its comical exaggeration and incongruity, has more in common with Kleist's lissome marionettes than with Bergson's robotic pratfalls, and one laughs at the image *not* because it is imperfect, but because it is so perfect in its imperfection, just as the joke of Kafka's factory girls lies not in their accidental falling from the staircases, but in Kafka's portraying their fall as choreographed chorus routine. Clearly, the conception of the human that Kafka's slapstick comedy implies is one that no longer has room for the Schillerian conviction that increased spiritual development will manifest itself as kinetic beauty. Yet nor does it countenance Bergson's similar—if in this case negatively expressed—notion that lack of proper spiritual development will manifest itself in a thing-like physical or mental clumsiness, indeed one so laughable that people will be graceful out of the sheer fear of ridicule. In contrast to both thinkers, Kafka reaches back to Kleist's notion of graceful spirit*less*ness, then takes it one step further by portraying not the inanimate object, but the human-become-object—precisely that which to Bergson is so anathema—as the source of grace itself.

In this way, Kafka presents a kind of parodic illustration of the cynical Herr C.'s suggestion that the "last chapter of the history of the world" will occur when human beings finally "eat again from the Tree of Knowledge, in order to fall back into the state of innocence" (Kleist, "Marionettentheater," 345). Paradoxically enough, it is only by means of a totally rationalized systematicity—in other words, through the final victory of human reason and spirit over corporeality and randomness—that the human being is able to emerge in its materiality and effective *absence* of spirit. Such an anthropological paradox recalls that to which Kracauer points in his discussion of that apotheosis of system within aesthetics, the "mass ornament":

> Because this Ratio [of the mass ornament] flees from reason and takes refuge in the abstract, uncontrolled nature proliferates under the guise of rational expression and uses abstract signs to display itself. It can no longer transform itself into powerful symbolic forms, as it could among primitive peoples and in the era of religious cults. This power of a language of signs has withdrawn from the mass ornament under the influence of the same rationality that keeps its muteness from bursting open. Thus, bare nature manifests itself in the mass ornament—the very nature that also resists the expression and apprehension of its own meaning.[72]

In the last chapter of the history of the world, mankind once again achieves the gracefulness of innocence by putting its excess rationalism in the service of the mechanical production of movement that, in its very regularity, ironically evokes the repetitive forms of raw nature. In the assembly line and the mass ornament, mankind comes full circle. This is the secret not just of Kracauer's Tiller Girls and Kafka's hotel employees, but also of physical comedians like Chaplin, who play with moments of lapse in this streamlined system without ever quite falling out of it. In a similar sense, Karl—as the tramp,[73] the Negro, the always-already exile, the one perpetually going against the flow of traffic—is the one who fails to assimilate himself quite fully to this new human order. (In view of Holitscher's aforementioned association of African Americans with "slowness" and the agricultural South, the mere phrase "Negro, technical worker" [*V* 409] must have already had, for Kafka, an inherently humorous oxymoronicness fortunately lost to the contemporary reader.) In this brave new world in which the vegetable/mechanical motion of physical bodies—the final identity of the organic and the inorganic—is the highest achievement of human reason, only real chance, real accident, the collapse of the faulty machinery of the new anthropology could have the power to break the indissoluble bond between system and individual.[74] No longer the mechanical, but the human is the laughable exception to the rule. And yet Kafka's work—informed by both the statistical protocols of his daytime writings and an intimation of the bankruptcy of humanist culture—also resists simply reinstating the human being as narrative focal point, depriving itself of the pathos of the individual for which Kracauer's essay, in contrast, still betrays a prickly nostalgia and to which Chaplin's films pay explicit homage. In Kafka's own staging of this situation, the saving accident is actually either that which paradoxically happens out of necessity, or that which only *almost* happens. As the chapter ending the unhappy "Robinson Case" concludes, "it seemed as though an accident was inevitable, but just at that moment, the all-enfolding traffic calmly received the straight path of this automobile, too, within itself" (*V* 270). That everything always functions like clockwork would be the final joke played on fallen human nature, which achieves grace by losing its soul.

The Euthanasia of Pure Reason

In a letter of December 28, 1908, to Elsa Taussig (later to become the wife of Max Brod), Kafka writes the following:

> Dear Fräulein,
>
> do not be alarmed, I only wish, as I have taken it upon myself to do, to remind you in good time (and as late as possible, so that you will no longer forget it) that you wanted to go with your sister this evening to the "Orient."
>
> Were I to write more, it would be superfluous and would even diminish the significance of the aforementioned, but I have always done that which is superfluous with more ease than that which is almost necessary. Namely, I confess, I have always allowed that which is almost necessary to suffer. I can confess this, because it is natural.
>
> For one is so glad that one has accomplished that which is wholly necessary (this of course must always happen right away, otherwise how could we keep ourselves alive for the cinematographs—don't forget about this evening—for gymnastics and painting, for living alone, for good apples, for sleeping in late, for being drunk, for things from the past, for a warm bath in winter when it's already dark out and for who knows what else) one is so glad, I mean, that one, just

> because one is so glad, does just that which is superfluous, and precisely neglects to do that which is almost necessary.
>
> I mention this in this way only because I knew, after that evening in your apartment, that it would be almost necessary for me to write to you. In the end, I failed to do this, for after the last cinematograph showing—take care to keep the two separate—such a letter was still almost necessary, but this incidental necessity was already fading into the past, although naturally according to another, formally more worthless tendency than the one in which that which is superfluous lies.
>
> But when of late you said to me that I should write you in order to show you my handwriting, then you put all the conditions for the necessary and thereby also for the superfluous into my hands.
>
> And yet that almost necessary letter wouldn't have been such a bad thing. You must consider that with me the necessary always happens, the superfluous usually, but the almost necessary, at least with me, happens only very rarely, whereby, robbed of all context, it can be slightly lamentable that is to say amusing.
>
> And so it is too bad about that letter, for it is too bad about your laughter over that letter, by which, however, I do not—you will surely believe me—mean to say anything against your remaining laughter, nor for example against that laughter that will be afforded to you this evening by the "Gallant Guardsman" or even the "Thirsty Gendarme." (Kafka, *Briefe 1900–1912,* 92–94)

These lines, flirtatiously tossed off to the future Mrs. Brod though they may be, provide no less than a description *in nuce* for Kafka's theory of comic plot. For whatever its frequency in real life may be, the "almost necessary" actually occurs not at all rarely in Kafka's work, but rather constantly provides the criteria for actions that are indeed just as lamentable as they are amusing. From the rhetorical shift that turns "The Judgment" from family romance to the tragedy of a failed Oedipus, to the hunger artist who would have been spared an otherwise inexorable anorexic oblivion had he merely been able to find a food he liked, to the previously cited scene from *The Castle* in which K. sleeps through the one possibility of his success, a spurious escape valve within seeming inevitability and logical circularity not only provides a certain comic tension, but furnishes the whole inner impetus and mechanism of the plot at large.

In the letter, Kafka already shows himself to be highly conscious of the peculiarity of this new ontological category. He graciously but pointedly notes the vast qualitative difference separating the laughter evoked by the "almost necessary [das fast Notwendige]" from the laughter evoked by the routine farces of the cinema of his day. The "remaining laughter [übriges Lachen]" that Kafka claims not to want to disparage is specifically the laughter of the movies that Kafka's letter is presently reminding Elsa Taussig to go and see, whose frivolousness Kafka gently mocks through his own parodically excessive formality, emphasized—if emphasis were necessary—with the humorous aside "you will surely believe me [Sie glauben mir bestimmt]."[75] If the laughter that accompanies such cinematic works is not quite "the superfluous [das Überflüssige]," it is as it were its dryer distillate, "übrig," something by the way, a residue of or pale substitute for the first superfluous (auto-)erotic gushing forth, perhaps even what is left over when the river (*Fluß*) of simple, natural pleasures has dried up. So Kafka does clearly mean something against this kind of laughter, which, itself a remnant, like Chaplin's fantasy-prostheses only fills in the idle spaces after the fulfillment of onerous duty.

It is precisely in speaking against this kind of laughter, however, that Kafka makes a bid for another, more fundamental, kind of laughter, a laughter which he must at the moment supposedly do without, but which, precisely in claiming to lack, he both characterizes and brings into being. This is as much as to say that the logic of the letter itself is an exemplary demonstration of the "almost necessary" that will appear again and again in Kafka's works as the characteristic model of his comedy of situation. It was "almost necessary," Kafka says, to write a letter to Elsa Taussig; therefore (or nevertheless) he did not do so. Her request for a handwriting sample—not incidentally the very symbol of personalized authorship—made a letter "necessary," however, and this necessity, once minimally fulfilled, opened up the opportunity for the superfluous action of writing still more that Kafka remarks in the second paragraph. In the process, the "almost necessary" is missed entirely—and yet what results is exactly the same as if the rare moment of the "almost necessary" had happened. For in point of fact, the "almost necessary" *does* happen, albeit as a kind of accident or misdirection, and the letter that Elsa Taussig receives is precisely the "almost necessary" letter that is "slightly lamentable that is to say amusing [leicht kläglich will sagen unterhaltsam]," even as Kafka laments, amusingly, the non-sending of the letter that he has in fact sent and the lack of ensuing laughter that—in fact—ensues.

Already in this early letter, the technique of the "sliding paradox" that Gerhard Neumann has distinguished in Kafka's late work—which adds to the traditional paradox of reversal (whose lack of appeal for Kafka has already been established) the further step of diversion or logical jump—is well in evidence, in this case unmistakably with comic intent.[76] The logical puzzle that Kafka sets up between the terms "necessity" and "superfluousness" does not effect a mere witty reversal of expected logic that could be re-reversed into its original "truth." (One could imagine an equally charming letter, for example, in which moviegoing and letter-writing were aspects of natural law, and office work was that which was extraneousness or accidental.) Rather, it shifts the paradox towards a third, contradictory, term, that of the "almost necessary." In Kant (and not just in Kant) the combination- and paradox-mechanisms of wit may, for all their inferiority vis-à-vis reason, still act as a "vehicle or garb for reason and its management of morally practical ideals" (*ANTH* §55, 117; 131–32). In Kafka, however, the deformation of traditional forms of wit—not through their elimination, but through their exponential overbid—comes to undermine such applicability to moral-practical ideas and indeed to place these ideas themselves under suspicion, creating a literary response to what, in an especially terse diary entry, Kafka formulates as the "horror of the merely schematic [Das Grauenhafte des bloß Schematischen]" (*T* 517). If, as Neumann writes, Kafka's sliding paradoxes "do not lead to a synthesis of contrarieties, as in the traditional paradox, but instead steer away from every expected coherence" ("Paradox" 706), then Kafka's delivery of certain metaphysical precepts to the operation of permanent paradox will prove to evoke a different sort of laughter than the merely by-the-way laughter of cinematic farce indeed.[77]

In the *Critique of Pure Reason,* Kant sets out to demonstrate the resolution of a fundamental manifestation of what he lists as the "third conflict of transcendental ideas" within the "antinomy of pure reason": namely, the classic problem of causality, the apparent contradiction between free will and necessity, or in Kantian terms, the seeming conflict between "freedom" and "nature" (see *CPR* 252–56; 548–55). Kant lets the "dogmatism of pure reason" (*CPR* 264; 568) speak against "empiricism" (*CPR* 265; 569): the first the espouser of a world in which every action is one link in a chain of causes and effects leading all the way back to one, singular and primal, cause; the second a principle in which everything that exists or happens is essentially random or contingent, did not have to be, and could well be otherwise. Kant gives shorter shrift to the latter, at the same time granting it a commonsensical truth as it applies to the world of sensuous phenomena (i.e.—as the label suggests—the empirical world) but *only* in this, limited sense. However, dogmatist determinism is no more true in Kant's reasoning, insofar as it falsely presumes a temporality that actually belongs to the phenomenal alone. Kant resolves the antinomy, therefore, by setting pure reason and the phenomenal as far apart as possible:

> As bounds were set to reason, to prevent it from leaving the guiding thread of empirical conditions and losing itself in *transcendent* theories which are incapable of *concrete* presentation; so it was my purpose, on the other hand, to set bounds to the law of the purely empirical understanding, and to protest against any attempts on its part at deciding on the possibility of things, or declaring the existence of the intelligible to be *impossible,* merely on the ground that it is not available for the explanation and exposition of phenomena. It has been shown, at the same time, that the contingency of all the phenomena of nature and their empirical conditions is quite consistent with the arbitrary hypothesis of a necessary, although purely intelligible condition, that no real contradiction exists between them and that, consequently, *both may be true.* (*CPR* 316; 644)

On the one hand, says Kant, the world is indeed made up of random and contingent—of superfluous—phenomena, and there is no ur-scene of temporal causality. On the other hand, however, pure reason, divorced from any obligation to appear as phenomena, allows for the somewhat tautological category of the "unconditionally necessary [unbedingt notwendig]," the "merely [. . .] transcendental and to us unknown ground of the possibility of sensuous phenomena" (*CPR* 317; 646). In fact, it can be said that Kant does not resolve the problem of freedom vs. determinism so much as set them together in opposition to his own, alternative proposition. "Contingency [Zufälligkeit]" and "dependence [Abhängigkeit]" are alike qualities of the sphere of "sensuous phenomena [Sinnenwelt]" (*CPR* 316; 645), but *true* necessity—as opposed to the dependent causal necessity attached to contingency—is the product of transcendental reason alone. This argument, as is well known, provides in turn the basis for Kant's dismissal of theological proofs of God's existence, together with his simultaneous insistence upon the existence of God as a transcendental or regulative idea, the gathering place for such concepts as "necessity, infinitude, unity, existence apart from the world (and not as world-soul), eternity without conditions of time, omnipresence without conditions of space, omnipotence, etc." (*CPR* 359, translation modified; 707–8), without which neither speculative thought nor the transition to practical reason is possible.

Such considerations would seem at first to have very little to do with the structures of situation comedy or the comedy of plot, in which, precisely, the chain of cause and effect, what Kant calls the "unlimited nature of the empirical regress [nirgend geendigten Regressus in der Reihe empirischer Bedingungen]" (*CPR* 316; 646), is placed squarely in the foreground: so to speak, put through its paces and made to demonstrate every occasion for possible mishap. The world of situation comedy, respecting the difference between pure and practical reason, is basically a world of immanence; it breaks only the laws that it itself establishes (and, more often than not, puts them back together again). Thus situation comedy tends perhaps more than any other form of the comic toward conservatism or in any case restoration, because its comedy only exists within a controlled situation. Where there is no more "situation," there is no more comedy. Corollary to this is that where there *is* situation, there is comedy, because the situation is designed to prepare precisely the kind of basis in which comedy likes to grow. Thus despite the fact that it may rely on clash, surprise, and the breaking of expectation, its comedy is "necessary." However unlikely the initial premises, and however extravagant the hijinks that might ensue within a particular plotline, the undergirding logic of most situation comedy is ultimately a conventional—indeed, a mechanical—one of cause and effect. Or rather, situation comedy forms a kind of parodic exaggeration of causal logic, in which accident and chance set off a series of rigidly determined actions until a second coincidence comes in to put an end to the chain of events. Thus such comedies are also "superfluous," insofar as the comic mechanism is only the result of an initial extrinsic misunderstanding, and could actually be stopped (as they ultimately always are stopped) with a simple message, a clarification, a judgment. The situation did not have to happen, and does—with a bit of luck, smarts, or outside intervention—eventually stop happening.[78]

In Kafka, on the other hand, the situation (almost) must happen, and never stops happening. This is not to suggest that Kafka's plots are illogical, something along the lines of the received wisdom that his stories are "dreamlike," "uncanny," or "surreal." To the contrary: just as Kafka borrows from clowning theatricality and slapstick for his images and descriptions, his plots—including but not exclusive to *Der Verschollene*—are carefully structured with tools borrowed from the subgenre of situation comedy. However, whereas in a standard situation comedy—or for that matter in any literary work making a bid for realism—the causal relationships are generally linear and narrative, in Kafka's plots these relationships are essentially static and circular, or indeed intrinsic, "almost necessary," to the point where the notion of causality actually ceases to be valid at all. Kafka's play with the conventions of situation comedy thus also resembles his handling of Dickensian tragicomedy as discussed above. Here, too, Kafka undertakes a conscious undermining of the naturalistic or quasi-naturalistic tradition by stripping its methods bare—"robbing them of all context" indeed—and at the same time pushing the logic of the genre to its breaking point.

The lamentable/amusing "almost necessary" structure of Kafka's plots differentiates his novels both from their naturalistic or psychological predecessors—above all, from the model of the Bildungsroman, which *Der Verschollene* explicitly references and parodies[79]—as well as from the tragic form so often attributed to his works. In the ideal or rather the schematic case, the Bildungsroman tells the story of a will increasingly in possession of itself and fulfilled in its original potentiality through the overcoming of exterior obstacles and inner uncertainties. Tragedy, meanwhile, can be schematized as the negative of this, a story in which a supposedly autonomous and perfectly realized will is undone by the rigid decrees of fate. Both of these models—the *bildungsromanhafte* and the tragic—require forms of sovereignty clearly not to be found in Kafka: in the former, the sovereignty of the individual and a society governed by common rational laws; in the latter, the sovereignty of God, gods, or monarch. These forms of sovereignty, however different from one another, provide a stable transcendent frame in which an earthly contingency may and indeed must play itself out as cause and effect.[80] For contingency is not opposed to action, but a necessary component thereof: in a world where all was determined in advance, where nothing could be other than how it is, choice and action would be impossible (at least as conceived in the terms of a modern, subjective agency).[81] However, the opposite is just as true: where there is *only* chance, that is, where the relations of cause and effect are utterly nugatory, there can be no action, because all actions are thoroughly irrelevant to what happens: *all* actions are superfluous. This antinomy is precisely what Kant attempts to resolve in his creation of a regulative ideal that would allow for the possibility of meaningful thought and action, removed from both ironclad causal determinism and total empirical randomness alike. The result of this, however, is that necessity ends up entirely on the side of the transcendent, and contingency entirely on the side of the empirical.[82] Thus the problem that so concerns Kant is not solved so much as displaced to a different realm, or rather to the impossible non-realm in which the transcendent and the immanent would—problematically—coexist.

This impossible non-realm of immanent transcendence is the theater in which Kafka stages his plots. The following piece, for example, one of the so-called "Zürau Aphorisms" from around 1918 (one of several originally sorted by Brod, injudiciously or no, under the title "Paradise"), dramatizes the structure of the Kantian antinomy as pseudo-Promethean slapstick and industrial-design joke:

> He is a free and secure citizen of the earth, for he is bound to a chain that is long enough for him to move freely throughout all earthly space, and yet only so long that nothing can pull him over the borders of the world. At the same time, however, he is also a free and secure citizen of heaven, for he is also bound to a similarly measured heavenly chain. If he wants to get to earth, he is choked by the heavenly neckband, if he wants to get to heaven, the earthly neckband chokes him. And yet he has every possibility and feels it, indeed he refuses to ascribe the whole thing to an error in the original fettering.[83]

The literal chains that bind Kafka's nameless "he" recall Kant's metaphoric "chain of causes [Kette von Ursachen]" (*CPR* 305; 629), disdained by the latter as an over-literalization of ideas of cause and effect. Here, however, Kafka refastens the chains that Kant imagines to have cast off, as a fetter so forgiving that one only feels it when one attempts to go between the spheres of heaven and earth, in the same way that Kant's ontology only hurts when one moves, that is, when the workability of the division between the transcendent and the empirical comes once again into question.

It is in this contradiction of the *grounds* for action, far more than the contradictions of actions themselves, that Kafka's meta-situation comedy takes place. The comic nature of Kafka's plots thus cannot be said to lie in the deliverance of human activity to mere chance in opposition to ideologies of necessity and the hierarchy of meaningfulness, the God's-eye view that Weltsch, among others, upholds.[84] The comedy lies rather in the compulsion to act within the almost total removal of possibilities for acting—the excising of *Handeln* from *Handlung*—when the categorical distinction between the transcendent and the empirical spheres can no longer be maintained.[85] Or, more to the point, the comedy lies in the demonstration that, in the collapse of the distinction between the transcendent and the empirical or in the doubting testing of the transcendent sphere, absolute necessity and absolute contingency effectively merge, reactivating Kant's antinomy of pure reason and confounding at least the *logical* possibility for rational action.

Thus Kafka's doctrine of the "almost necessary" first marks the suturing point or the moment just before the suture of these two apparent poles of the laws of causality, the by turns "amusing" and "lamentable," barely or indeed never really existing space of the acting subject.[86] The fact that the actions in Kafka's plots are "almost necessary" does not mean, of course, that Kafka's characters could somehow achieve a way out of their various predicaments, for example if they only tried harder or could find someone to help them. Precisely this assumption is what all three K-characters so tenaciously and mistakenly hold to—an assumption that, although it fails to do the protagonists any "real" good, also drives the novels' plots almost entirely. And even if an "out" exists—one thinks here, for example, of the "ostensible acquittal" held out to Joseph K. in *The Trial*[87]—Kafka's characters are usually unable to recognize, much less avail themselves of it; indeed they *may* not, for the "fault," such as it is, is not occasional, but constitutive—"an error in the original fettering"—to the point where it may not properly be considered a fault at all, but the condition for acting as such. Or more accurately: it is *both* a fault *and* the condition for acting as such. The "almost necessary" will thus prove to be the performative irony of Kafka's comedy of *Handlung*, the comic error *within* the error that is the only thing that makes errancy—in other words, action—possible.[88] In this way, the "almost necessary" functions as a reading both of the Judeo-Christian Fall and the Kantian teachings of moral law—and this not just as critique (which it also surely is) but as the eternal incontrovertible ground rules of the game.

This structure of the "almost necessary" stands out perhaps most clearly in the third chapter of *Der Verschollene*, the pivotal set piece "Ein Landhaus bei New York" ("A Country House Outside New York"). In this chapter, Karl is dismissed summarily from his uncle's good graces after a farcically miscarried stay at the country house of his uncle's associate Mr. Pollunder, an event that marks the break between his initial secure and promising conditions in America and his subsequent abandonment to the dangers of vagabond life. Arriving at Mr. Pollunder's house for what he imagines will be a pleasurable experience in his newly adopted land, Karl is dismayed to find Pollunder's fellow-associate and double Mr. Green at the door, and Green's presence indeed proves almost immediately to be a burden and a bother. The early dinner scene foreshadows the catastrophe to come in a (for Kafka) fairly plain use of authorial irony:

> The first words out of Mr. Green at dinner were expressions of surprise over the fact that Karl had gotten permission from his uncle for this visit. He raised one brimming soup spoon after another to his mouth and explained on his right to Klara, on his left to Mr. Pollunder why he was so surprised and how the uncle watched over Karl

> and how the uncle's love for Karl was so great that it could hardly be called the love of an uncle any more. "Not enough that he's meddling here unnecessarily, at the same time he has to go and meddle between me and my uncle," Karl thought and couldn't bring himself to swallow down any more of the golden soup. But then again he didn't want anyone to notice how upset he was and so began to shovel soup into himself in silence. The meal dragged on like a plague. (*V* 80)

Karl's judgment that this pleasure-killing "meddling [Einmischung]" between him and his uncle is "unnecessary [unnötig]" will of course prove to be grievously in error, insofar as Green's only purpose for coming to Pollunder's is the giving of the letter to Karl containing his uncle's marching orders—presumably the very "important business [großes Geschäft]" (*V* 78) mentioned upon Green's arrival that is to keep him at the country house the whole night through.[89] While the letter itself is apparently a consequence of Uncle Jakob's disapproval of Karl's acceptance of the invitation to the country house (an invitation, however, which was initially a suggestion of Uncle Jakob himself), it also seems in some vague way to be a consequence of the disaster of the visit itself and Karl's corresponding equivocation on whether he should stay or go, and this disaster and equivocation in turn appear—in a form of circular illogic—as a product of Green's initial intrusive presence. What transpires after the torturous dinner scene—Pollunder's daughter Klara's sexualized aggression, Karl's humiliation in the face of Klara's fiancé Mack's superior masculinity, the labyrinthine and endlessly under construction passages of the house itself, the supplication to Green and Pollunder for return, and the bizarre musical reconciliation with Klara and Mack—is in fact merely displacement or postponement of, or indeed "play" within, what is the scene's simultaneous premise and conclusion.

For again, the necessity of the letter's delivery and final message of the letter itself is presaged constantly and explicitly from the very first scenes of the chapter. Upon entering the house, Green's first act, like the act of some overzealous archangel, is the shutting of the glass doors against Karl's pleasure at breathing in the house's edenic—Green and Pollinated—garden. In this can be recognized a continuation of the expulsion from paradise motif of which the famous sword-wielding Statue of Liberty at the novel's beginning (*V* 7) is the clearest symbol.[90] In both cases, Kafka's technique is to make the normal temporal chain of cause and effect an atemporal self-sufficient circle, placing the expulsion not just at the end but also at the beginning. Karl is already cast out from paradise at the very moment he enters it.[91] Meanwhile, the yet-to-be revealed contents of the letter that sends Karl once again into exile are alluded to already during the conversation at dinner in Green's story of his aged manservant: "'My God,' cried Klara, 'what loyalty!' ['Mein Gott,' rief Klara, 'ist das eine Treue!'] 'Yes, there is still loyalty in this world,' said Mr. Green and placed a morsel in his mouth, where his tongue, as Karl chanced to notice, gripped the food in one sweep. He felt nearly sick and stood up" (*V* 82). Lack of loyalty, of course, is precisely the accusation later lobbed against Karl by his uncle (signed, in a final twist of the knife, "Your loyal uncle Jakob [Dein treuer Onkel Jakob]" [*V* 123]), an accusation of which, moreover, Green clearly displays his foreknowledge in his greeting to Karl at a moment past midnight, "You are indeed not a man of your word [Sie sind tatsächlich kein Mann von Wort]" (*V* 121).

"[I am] thoroughly a man of principles [ein Mann von Principien]" (*V* 122): thus begins the letter that closes (and, effectively, opens) the chapter. In other words, Uncle Jakob—and the world over which he holds sway—operates on the transcendental plane of pure reason, whereas Karl largely persists in operating on the immanent plane of practical reason. But perhaps the clearest sign that something else is in force in this scene than the logic of cause and effect upon which both empirical reality and standard situation comedy depend is the fact that at the end of the chapter, time, the very essence of the contingent and causal (see, e.g., *CPR* 299–300; 621), is here subordinated to the timelessness of principle itself. "Now it's a quarter past twelve," says Green, putting Karl off on his stated wish to return to his uncle's posthaste,

> I can finish discussing my business with Mr. Pollunder, for which your presence would only be a disturbance, and you can pass a little time [ein hübsches Weilchen] with Miss Klara. Be here at twelve on the dot, when you will receive the necessary information. (*V* 113)

Two pages later, standing before Klara's door, Karl asks the servant who has accompanied him for the time: "'Just now it was half past eleven.' 'Half past eleven,' repeated Karl wonderingly, as if terrified at these numbers" (*V* 115). Two pages still later (after a long conversation with Klara on the lateness of the hour and the shabbiness of his piano-playing), Karl asks the same servant the time yet again: "'Almost quarter to twelve,' said the servant," to which Karl replies, "'How slowly the time passes'" (*V* 117); and on the following page asks again, "'How late is it?' [. . .]. 'Quarter to twelve.' 'Then I still have a little time [Dann habe ich noch ein Weilchen Zeit]'" (*V* 118). When the clock finally chimes midnight and Karl rushes to receive his letter from Green, however, what would ordinarily be a suspense-building technique of counting down the minutes turns out to be nothing more than a ruse that highlights an actual stasis of the always-already. ("Then it's high time," says Karl on page 118; "High time" on page 121.) For the envelope that—literally—seals Karl's fate specifies that Karl is to be given the letter only at midnight, a letter of whose message Green, idly playing with the object at the very moment he exercises his delaying tactics, is "bound by higher orders to reveal nothing to [Karl] before midnight" (*V* 112). That is: Karl's fate is *not* contingent upon either his actions or the actions of others; rather—in every sense of the phrase—*it is written.* Time, which in a situation comedy still retains the power to unwrite, here serves merely an expressive or even a deceptive purpose, creating a parody of madcap comedy by occurring, as if unwittingly, within a technically timeless situation of transcendental law. *Unlike* the standard situation comedy that it appears to resemble, then, the comedy here can no longer be located on the immanent plane of cause and effect, of actions (usually at cross-purposes) leading to more actions. And yet neither is it a comedy of philosophical errors, in which Karl emerges as laughingstock because he has failed the test of Kantian ontology. (And as far as a comedy that would exist purely on the transcendent plane, this is impossible by definition.) The comedy is located rather in the irresolvable tension *between* the planes of immanence and transcendence,[92] those planes that in the Kantian schema manage to coexist in their provisional separateness, but in the Kafkan universe are brought—if in betrayal of the spirit of Kantian philosophy, then faithful to its letter—conclusively together.

Indeed, directly upon his learning of his banishment toward the end of the chapter, Karl appears at least temporarily to acknowledge the fact of this impossible coexistence, thus momentarily annulling the comedy of the scene (if also simultaneously creating a different sort of comic effect, a more usual one of violated expectations). Karl's sudden absolute and unperturbed acceptance of the situation— "'Are you ready,' asked Green. 'Yes,' said Karl, 'have you brought my suitcase and umbrella?' 'Here it is,' said Green" (*V* 123)—demonstrates that Karl, too, has the capacity to be, so to speak, in on the transcendental game. His playing along allows him not only to take in the contents of the letter without dismay or even surprise, but also to dilate on the virtues of his suitcase and crack jokes about his own absentmindedness. This harmonizing moment of being able to play both sides of the antinomy without them coming into contact—an ability which, it should be noted, if maintained would bring with it the consolation prize of a new life in San Francisco, "in the East [*sic*]" (*V* 124)[93]—is decidedly short-lived, however, as Karl quickly slips back into a search for reasons, causes, and responsible parties:

> There is still one thing you have to explain to me. On the envelope of the letter that you were to give me, it's written merely that I should receive it at midnight, wherever I'm to be found. So why did you keep me here, referring to this letter, when I wanted to leave at quarter past eleven? You went beyond your orders there [. . .]. If you had been too tired, perhaps you wouldn't have even been able to follow after me, or, though even Mr. Pollunder denied this, by midnight I would have already arrived back at my uncle's, or it would have ultimately been your duty to take me back to my uncle's in your automobile, something which suddenly no longer came up in conversation, considering that I was so insistent on returning. Doesn't the heading on the envelope imply that midnight was my last deadline? And it's you who bears the guilt for making me miss it. (*V* 125–26)

Here too Karl is mistaken, for the question of who is to bear the blame is actually a non-question. Karl is caught from the very beginning in an impossible situation, that is, the situation of transcendent necessity, in which perhaps only the search for empirical causes and effects, for a consistent ground of personal action, can be considered a blameworthy act.[94] "Not another word!" yells Green after Karl's attempt to get to the bottom of things, "in a tone of voice as if he was interrupting Karl, who in fact had been silent for some time" (*V* 126–27). But in fact Karl *has* monopolized the preceding conversation with his mistaken search for real empirical motives; the episode therefore comes to an end, and "Karl stood astonished in the open [Karl stand erstaunt im Freien]" (*V* 127), for a moment free of both pure *and* practical reason and therefore temporarily also free of plot. For if there is to be a question of error or indeed a question at all, it can at most be one, again, of "an error in the original fettering": that is, of the very concept of a heavenly law that apparently has no direct connection to the earthly one and is only connected indirectly through the mediation of the acting subject, whose innocent neck nevertheless hangs on both systems simultaneously.

In this way, the structure of the "almost necessary" reveals itself essentially as the structure of the double bind: no longer the antinomy of pure reason, but its aporia.[95] Kant's "both may be true [sie (können) beiderseits wahr sein]" (*CPR* 316; 644) appears in Kafka as no less than a version of Freud's "kettle logic": a "mutual canceling-out [Einanderaufheben] of multiple thoughts, each of which is in itself perfectly valid" (*JRU* 205, translation modified; 234). But whereas in Freud's joke, the rational and disinterested observer can see that only one of the options (if indeed any at all) can actually be the case, in Kafka reigns a kettle logic for which there is no outside, no "rational" observer or joke-teller, and thus no recourse to the punch line of a judgment that would in some way satisfy the requirements of rational truth, and one could say that, rather than seeking refuge in the oneiric or the absurd, Kafka is simply taking the joke of Kantian ontology at face value.[96] Just as Karl experiences "freedom" in the very moment of suspension before he bums it out to his occidental captivity in Ramses, in this real-life kettle logic, one can only exist as a paradoxical "free and secure citizen" of two mutually exclusive realms, whose freedom and fettering alike refer back to an original comic error that is not even precisely identifiable, much less resolvable or correctible. Here is where the aporia of Kantian ontology intersects with the Jewish implications of the Christian doctrine of original sin: that is, how one is to understand a concept created to justify the immanence of the Messiah, if the Messiah is not in fact to be understood as immanent. As the always-already-fallenness of Karl Roßmann's situations show, for Kafka, the only possible answer is that it is *the double bind itself* that is original, and yet not a "sin" in any Pauline sense but rather the joking ruin of dialectics that frees and fetters all action, the aporia and the a priori of historical being all at once. In this sense too, the Theater of Oklahama chapter can indeed be considered a proper resolution, as it presents a kind of end to history—"Everything he had done before was forgotten, no one would reproach him for it" (*V* 388)—and thus, even if only within the eternal static mechanisms of a fantastic bureaucracy, a proper denouement of the double bind of action.

With this, however, Kafka should not be seen merely as writing religious ideology critique or shifting the story to the solemn sphere of the purely transcendent. Instead, with these series of nested aporias (or perhaps just the ultimate combining of the venerable traditions of the lawyer joke and the Jewish joke) Kafka raises the stakes of the comic. For as Kant never tires of reminding his readers, there can be no actual situation of transcendental law: the attempt to create such a thing is a perfect example of what Kant calls "subreption" or category error between two spheres that must remain separate in order to hang together.[97] Such a crossing of the lawfulness of the transcendent with the randomness of the quotidian is however precisely what the set pieces of Kafka's novels, the "Landhaus" chapter foremost among them, dramatize with a kind of relentless bemusement. Thus they perform natural law as situation comedy and situation comedy as natural law, in both cases cutting off the actions of the main characters before they are even begun and making a mockery of the very notion of the "protagonist" around which the history of the novel constructs itself.[98]

But even this does not exhaust the issue. For just as Kafka's aphorisms diverge from conventional paradox in their lack of a stable truth to turn wittily on its head, there is not even an actual transcendent logic against which worldly events could collide, but only a seeming one or the idea of one. ("And if this concerns the essence of the law," writes Derrida, "it is that the latter has no essence" ["Before the Law" 206].) And just as the fatedness of tragedy relies on a certain kind of order in distinction from the *Trauerspiel* (for which a *lack* of order is the prerequisite), so too does Kafka's work distinguish itself both from tragedy and the deterministic comedy that is its counterpart. Kafka may of course be said to parodically *imitate* such tragedy, easily leading to the mistaken conclusion that it *is* this, and parodically imitate such comedy, leading to the idea that Kafka's clowning around is that of the ordinary, that is, the purely situational kind. Benjamin notes that "the martyr-drama [the precursor to the *Trauerspiel*] was born from the death of Socrates *as a parody of tragedy.*"[99] But not only is the parody of tragedy the death of classical tragedy and the beginning of the modern *Trauerspiel;* the *Trauerspiel* (perhaps precisely because of its origins in parody) also prepares a place for an ensuing or indeed a coexisting *Lustspiel.* And where Benjamin speaks of the "secularization" of the medieval passion plays in the baroque *Trauerspiel*—in which, not insignificantly, "the official [die beamtete Person]" now fills the intriguer function formerly performed by the devil (*Origin* 126; *Ursprung* 107)—in Kafkan comedy we can speak, again according to the durable Marxian model of farcical repetition, of a *second* secularization.

In Kafka appears the comic secularization of the Kantian attempt to recuperate transcendental ideals for an age of Enlightenment in the wake of early modern secularization and the subsequent spread of empiricist and proto-positivistic philosophies. Kafka's comedy is thus not even only—although it also still is—the correctible comedy of subreption, the erroneous attempt to demand of the transcendent that it appear in the empirical world, expressed by Friedrich Theodor Vischer in the punchy formula, "the comic is the sublime made *explicit* [das Komische sei ein *deutlich* gemachtes Erhabenes]" (*UEK* 160). It is also the irony of this comedy, that is, a comedy of the loss of grounds for even the meta-comic comedy of category error. Vischer's ensuing, not quite anti-idealist argument—at one point he calls his study a "metaphysics of the comic" (*UEK* 166)—provides not only an insight into the comedic history of Kant reception but also an instructive hint for the reading of Kafka's own comic aspects:

> One can go further and *admit* that only an apparent sublime can be forfeited to laughter, but to that one would have to add that *there is nothing really sublime* and that even a truer sublime, in comparison with mere pomposity, is in fact not absolutely sublime, and that therefore the spirit of the comic only adds to it that which already belongs to it by rights, when it fails to spare it as well. (*UEK* 165)

In other words: the operation of forcing together the transcendent and the immanent, itself a form of comic business, leads to the permanent diminishment of the transcendent. Or rather, it leads to a collision of the transcendent and the immanent that is no longer a category error at all, but simply fact.[100]

Kafka's comedy is thus a comedy of the regulative ideal without regulative ideal, both a lacking comedy and a comedy of lack. In the establishing of a comedy of the transcendent within the immanent, the sphere of transcendence is demolished, thus also demolishing the possibility for that comedy itself.[101] And yet out of the ruins of this comedy emerges once again a space of comic possibility—more, a comic almost-necessity. Deleuze and Guattari note that Kafka's insertion of "humor" into the Kantian moral law gives one more rotation to the Copernican turn: out of Kant's self-justifying and self-perpetuating law is made an "entirely different sort of machine which needs this image of the law only to align its gears and make them function together with 'a perfect synchronicity'" (43). However, the case is not even so much that Kafka puts humor "into" the Kantian conception of law, as that this law already forms the basis of Kafka's humor, or indeed, is structurally indistinguishable from the mechanism of the comic itself.[102] Thus the double bind of the Kantian system, rather than leading to immobilization, melancholia, or crisis, in fact furnishes the opportunity for the proliferation of its own comedy. It is in *this* sense that Kafka's humor achieves the level of a "liberation for play," a "pleasure in nonsense" (see Neumann, "Paradox,"

744): as the perpetual repetition of the paradoxes of the law in the absence of the law's telos. It is not incidental that Karl, although he first resists Klara's jujitsu erotic advances and protests that "I am, if I'm to be honest, glad that it's too late for playing [music], for I still can't do anything" (*V* 116), in the end yields at least partially to her temptation to "play." From the standpoint of empirical causality this might be interpreted as a terrible succumbing every bit on the magnitude of Eve's acceptance of the apple, which leads, just as in the biblical story, to Karl's irrevocable exile from his Lower Manhattan Eden. But since the chapter utterly resists and indeed parodies just such moral-psychological interpretation, the delay and postponement that Karl is made to undertake at first through coercion, then through will, is of no decisive importance; or rather, its importance lies not so much in the fact that this is some sort of fatal flaw or original sin, but that in the absence of a moral law guaranteeing the essential meaningfulness of the universe and the importance of individual action, delay and postponement is in fact all there is.[103] (As the exemplary American Mack says, Karl may have "made a few mistakes, but I still enjoyed it very much, not even taking into account the fact that I don't look down my nose at anyone's playing [daß ich das Spiel keines Menschen verachte]" [*V* 120].) Once again the *bildende* claims of the bourgeois novel are undone in a parodic exaggeration of the fact that a narrative only exists by virtue of its unresolved complications, its eternal continuation or proliferation of comic business. In the stalling of the Kantian grounds for rational *Handeln,* every action is *Lustspiel.*[104]

Such questions are, moreover, not merely a matter of idle metaphysical speculation for Kafka. In his professional processing of claims for the Workmen's Accident Insurance Institute, the question is always that of who bears responsibility. Even more, and more paradoxically still, the question is who bears responsibility for *accident,* that for which, at least by definition, no one can bear responsibility: who has caused—and ultimately, who pays for—the *Zufall* of the *Unfall.*[105] At the same time, once again, Kafka's job also involves the fairly recent practice of the systematic fostering of methods for risk assessment and accident prevention. Thus on the one hand, Kafka's work entails a humanitarian effort to control workplace injury and loss of life by way of the most cool-headed observations and most modern technological means, and to hold some actor accountable when the necessary precautions fail to have been taken. On the other hand, however, such work involves a calculation of risk factors according to statistical norms, and the dispersal of the individual subject along a cross-section of the population. Here causality and potentiality; there probability and statistical necessity: Kant's "euthanasia of pure reason [Euthanasie der reinen Vernunft]" (*CPR* 231; 513), his name for an unreflective and aggressively empirical skepticism, is thus ironically reinscribed in the algorithms of actuarial tables and risk assessment. The empirically unprovable yet logically and ontologically indispensable force that Kant locates in the laws of practical reason and, from there, in a supreme being, is now to be found in nothing so much as the calculation of statistical averages (a praxis, moreover, into whose esoteric laws Kafka as *juris doctor* had literally an initiate's insight).[106]

Among the several conclusions to be drawn from this is the fact that the business of risk assessment collapses Kantian ontology yet again, perhaps this time definitively, as a codified, ultra-secular, biopolitically motivated empiricism reaches the levels, not only of pure mathematics, but also of pure reason. Kafka's professional duty—which in this sense is effectively a satanic one—is the almost unthinkable or (in the Kantian sense) undutiful duty of taking the laws of probability to task, to alter them or, in the case that they cannot be altered, to seek an often elusive source of accountability. Yet, as a consequence of his occupation, Kafka also thus manages to occupy one of the few patches of *Spielraum* between random accident and statistical probability, a space (however practically limited) of reordering or at least of imagining things otherwise.[107] The recognition of this position adds a further valence to Kafka's designation of the "almost necessary" as "slightly lamentable [leicht kläglich]": it is, also, literally the space of the *Klage,* the legal or professional grievance—with which, it should be recalled, in Karl's vain advocacy for the Stoker *Der Verschollene* effectively begins. The grievance—which, for Dr. Kafka, was more often than not a written document—also shapes the letter to Elsa Taussig, in the form of a parody of the genre of the lover's plaint, specifically the circularly paradoxical complaint that by furnishing "all the conditions for the necessary and thereby also for the superfluous [alle Voraussetzungen des Notwendigen und damit des Überflüssigen]" for the writing of the letter, she has prevented the occurrence of that rare and amusing thing, the almost necessary, of which the letter she is reading is in fact a living specimen. And lastly, it can be said that a whole cycle of complaint, in this case in highly lapidary form, makes up the essence of the third and fourth chapters of the Bible—and thus the essence of the very origin of Judeo-Christian history—as the serpent first brings charges against God, then God accuses Adam and Eve, Adam blames Eve, Eve blames the serpent, God denounces Cain, and Cain, finally, registers his grievance with God. These attempts at attributing guilt and rectifying wrongs are just as futile as Karl's arguing on behalf of the Stoker—who is identified by the captain as "a well-known malcontent [ein bekannter Querulant]" (*V* 24)—or seeking rational causes for his intra-American exile; as in all cases, a logic of contingency comes into comic conflict with the unknowable will of the divinity—be it a divinity of theology, of power, of statistics, or of Kafka's own hesitations that keep his writing hand in check. As Kafka writes with obvious exasperation in a 1915 report: "The complaints come in from all sides [Die Klagen laufen von allen Seiten ein]" (*Amtliche Schriften* 255). Rarely, however—but this "rarely" is also an "only on this condition"—such a conflict manages to provide the impetus for action, for history,[108] for situation, for writing, for beginning, in a comedy of the comedy of the comic's own becoming.

"Well of Course I've Been Playing a Comedy"[109]

That the above considerations on the comic are not just descriptions of "superfluous" amusements, but inherent—or rather, "almost necessary"—components of Kafka's work can be further demonstrated by pointing out the existence of a crucial yet all too easily overlooked character in *Der Verschollene,* one who, like the serpent of the Old Testament, effectively sets the entirety of the action in motion. The novel gets going on the first page when Karl, about to disembark, realizes he has forgotten his umbrella and turns, in typical Kafkan countermotion, against the tide of passengers to retrieve it:

> A young man with whom he had become casually acquainted during the journey said to him as he passed by, "So, you don't feel like getting off yet?" "I'm almost done," said Karl, laughing, and, out of high spirits and because he was a strong lad, hoisted his suitcase up onto his shoulder. But when he looked over at his acquaintance, who, swinging his walking stick a little as he went, was already starting to make his way with the others, he realized that he had forgotten his umbrella down below in the ship. He asked his acquaintance, who didn't seem too pleased with the request, to be so good as to stay by his suitcase for a moment, quickly surveyed the situation so as to be able to later find his way back, and hurried off. (*V* 7–8)

A few pages later, in the Stoker's room, he suddenly recalls the reason for his return to the ship's bowels and his stick-swinging, suitcase-guarding acquaintance above:

> Karl crawled in as well as he could and laughed loudly at his first useless attempt to swing himself over. Hardly was he inside than he cried, "My goodness, I've completely forgotten about my suitcase." "Where is it then?" "Up on the deck, an acquaintance of mine is watching it. What was his name again?" And he drew a calling card from out of a secret pocket that his mother had sewed into the lining of his coat for the trip. "Butterbaum, Franz Butterbaum." (*V* 10)

It is a surprising fact that where so much attention has been paid to the myriad Ks dotting Kafka's literary landscape, little notice has been taken of this "Franz" who leaves his signature behind on a slip of paper and with his walking stick gives Kafka's first long prose work its initial push. Stanley Corngold has pointed out the existence of a different "Franz," one of the two police officers in the opening scene of *The Trial* (see Corngold, *Lambent Traces,* 53; Kafka, *Der Proceß,* 9), and a "Franz" also shows up in the unpublished story fragment "Die städtische Welt" ("The Urban World") as the cocky brother of the worried Oskar and sharer of Karl Roßmann's own presumptive profession of "engineer" (see *T* 151–58). Thus not once but multiple times does "Franz" appear in Kafka's works as the catalyst of the action. In the context of the Kantian God of the regulative ideal, it may also be noted that there is something indeed decidedly satanic or serpentine in the improbable family name of this first instigator figure, which seems to recall a kind of particularly lubricious tree of the knowledge of good and evil to send Karl down the slippery slope of potential perdition.[110] And in fact, the interventions of Herr Butterbaum and his namesakes may be read as a parodically literalized, profane incarnation of the "*original* action [ursprüngliche Handlung]" (*CPR* 305, translation modified; 629) whose existence Kant himself rejects (or more precisely, maintains is "not to be found in the causal concatenation of phenomena" [*CPR* 305, translation modified; 629]).

In and of themselves, of course, the interventions of Franz Butterbaum are essentially random, significant only insofar as they set the workings of the plot in motion. Recalling with regret his nights on the ship spent keeping vigil over the now-missing suitcase, Karl mutters to himself, in indirect free speech, "That Butterbaum, if he should ever run into him again" (*V* 17). Karl will, of course, *not* meet Franz a second time; even when his suitcase is returned to him at the end of the "Landhaus" chapter, its recovery is attributed to "a certain Schubal" (*V* 124), and if Franz Butterbaum is to be the First Cause or Original Adversary, he is clearly of the absentee variety.[111] Yet by portraying the nonexistent original cause in literal (if literary) flesh and blood, Kafka once again draws attention to the aporia of pure reason—the fettering of action between the transcendent and the immanent—as the basis of *Handlung* itself. Karl's laughing answer to Franz Butterbaum's question of whether he plans to start his American adventure, "I'm almost done [Ich bin doch fertig]," is thus yet another joke on the chain of causes and events: Karl is already finished, finished before he even starts within a universe that cannot decide if actions happen as a consequence of an obscurely authorized universal law or as a series of accidents set off by unreliable traveling companions.

Significant, then, is the fact that, in both this passage and the scene in the Stoker's cabin—that is, the two major moments in which the figure of Franz Butterbaum appears—Karl is described, precisely, as *laughing*. As Peter Rehberg has shown, not only comedic elements but also the *presentation* of moments of laughter and laughing characters is of decisive importance for Kafka's work. Yet rather than reading this laughter as an "inaccessible outside, by which the text is influenced and whose illusionless negativity it makes readable" (Rehberg, *Lachen Lesen,* 154), such moments of laughter's thematization can be seen as a signal that the action of Kafka's novels falls initially or rather *originally* under the sign of the comic. Not just *Der Verschollene* but all three of Kafka's novel fragments provide an explicit reference to comedy or the comic at their start. The Stoker's travails, although earnestly understood by Karl, appear to the ship's crew as "a joke [. . .] whose laughableness didn't even stop in front of the Captain" (*V* 52). Joseph K. names his future trial a "bad joke [groben Spaß]" and a comedy with which he has to play along at the very moment of his arrest (*Der Proceß* 11–12), and K.'s exasperated identification in *The Castle* of the comedy of his situation appears as early as the third page of the novel. Deleuze and Guattari have written of Kafka that "everything leads to laughter, starting with *The Trial*" (*Kafka* 42), but from this list, it is just as clear that everything also begins with laughter, starting (at least) with *Der Verschollene.* In the examples from *The Trial* and *The Castle* in particular, Kafka is obviously playing with the high degree of semantic drift of the word "Komödie" as not only that which is generally amusing, but also spectacle and theatricality per se.[112] This association between "comedy" as that which is funny and "comedy" as theatrical staging is precisely the point, however, for the "comedy" highlighted at the beginning of all the novels expresses precisely the combination of paradox, performance, and action that Kafka's work exemplifies.

"Franz" appears at least one more time in connection with laughter in Kafka's works, in an early, unfinished sketch from the time of the writing of *Der Verschollene* (situated directly between "Die städtische Welt" and part of an early version of *Der Verschollene*'s Stoker chapter). The sketch, a tale of four young friends, is written in a realistic and anecdotal style unusual for Kafka. Just as unusual is the autobiographical nature of the piece, not only in the names "Franz" and "Max," but also in the names of the other two friends, "Robert" and "Samuel": clear analogues of the "Richard" and "Samuel" who stand in for Kafka and Brod in their unfinished co-written eponymous roman à clef (see *DL* 419–40). Here Kafka brings the two identical twosomes together in a jovial *Freundeskreis,* in a passage that confirms, but also complicates, the biographical reports of Kafka's humor by his contemporaries:

> They laughed so much on these evenings that once on the way home Max said that this constant laughing was actually quite unfortunate, because through it you forgot about all the serious things, of which everyone certainly had plenty to bear. When you were laughing you figured that for the serious matters there was still plenty of time. But this wasn't correct, because the serious matters were naturally much more demanding and it was of course perfectly clear that in the company of friends you were able to take on greater demands than you were on your own. One should laugh at the office, because one didn't accomplish much more than that there anyway. This opinion was directed at Robert, who worked long hours in the artists' club that he was helping to revive and at the same time entertained his friends with the most comical observations. As soon as he would get started, the friends would get up from their seats and place themselves around him or sit on the table, and Max and Franz especially would laugh with such abandon [so selbstvergessen] that Samuel would move all the glasses over to a side table. (*T* 164)

In this debate about the nature of laughter, "Max" stands as the representative of the ordinary kind of paradoxical wit, which inverts normal logical assumptions to create humor out of this (temporary) inversion. Laughter is frivolous, but friendship is serious; thus one should laugh only at work, where, as Max humorously (and thus somewhat self-contradictorily) claims, nothing serious actually happens. For his part, "Robert" does not contradict this through a simple reversal of Max's paradox back to the received truth it attempts to overturn, that is, that work is serious and thus one should not laugh at the office but rather only in one's leisure time with one's friends. He instead *diverts* Max's paradox, maintaining that both work *and* friendship are comical: or rather, that work and friendship are comical and serious simultaneously, and that serious friendship, a friendship in which one can be amused to the point of forgetting oneself, requires the recounting of work's comical aspect. Whereas for Max, laughter is a mere diversion and pleasant pastime when one has nothing better to do, for Robert, laughter is not only coextensive with work (specifically, with *artists'* work), but is also the basis of the social, an agent of the disintegration of the subject, and, not least, the condition of the possibility of narrative. For Kafka, in other words, narrative begins where one laughs, where in the midst of and out of serious work the "most comical" things are noted, a position that he declares by writing laughter and comedy literally into the first pages of all his novels, and signing his own name into the bargain.

The "Verschollene" of Kafka's America-novel is in this sense not just the young migrant Karl Roßmann, but also the comic, which, like the suitcase-stealing Franz Butterbaum, initiates the action and then disappears, if only to be writ large later in the nature theater of Kafka's subsequent body of work. Kafka begins his writing career from the overdetermined premise that in the comic lies the origin, not just of his own literary production, but indeed of the very order of things and the history of humankind itself. If the comic is play with non-sense in the strict meaning of the term, then the history of humankind is nothing more or less than the playing-out of its own original non-sense in an eternally varying parade of forms. "How could fools grow tired? [Wie könnten Narren müde werden?]" (*DL* 14) ends the opening piece in Kafka's first printed book, *Betrachtung* (*Contemplation*). As *The Castle*'s exhausted straight-man K. can attest, the attempt to reach the seriousness that would put an end to events wears one out. In contrast, a body of writing meant to take the indefatigability of the comic into account will be nothing less than the continuing ironic comedy of the comic, the comic telling of the story of how things, comically, happen.

Chapter Four

✦

Bearing Wit to History: Joseph Roth

> Precisely a philosophy of concrete life must not withdraw from the exception and the extreme case, but must be interested in it to the highest degree. The exception can be more important to it than the rule, not because of a romantic irony for the paradox, but because the seriousness of an insight goes deeper than the clear generalizations inferred from what ordinarily repeats itself.
>
> —Carl Schmitt, *Political Theology*

> This close succession of everyday objects of widows and momentous current events upon which verges all the significance of the historical makes, indeed, a well-nigh comical impression. On the one hand a coffee-spoon-affair, a footboy's deliciously clandestine course of action, and on the other a newspaper announcement sending ripples throughout the whole civilized world.
>
> —Robert Walser, *The Robber*

Casuistry Belli

In 1914, in the literary journal *Zeit-Echo: Ein Kriegstagebuch der Künstler* (*Time-Echo: An Artists' Diary of the War*), Max Brod publishes a short essay entitled "Gefühl von einer Verwandlung des Staates" ("Feeling of a Transformation of the State").[1] The piece, an impressionistic commentary on the recently begun war (named allusively but unmistakably as "these events [diese Ereignisse]"), is structured around the metaphysical conceit of the two—prewar and wartime—"faces" of the Habsburg Empire. Given that two-facedness is usually seen as a sign of a split within identity, and thus functions as a metaphor for duplicity, hypocrisy, or an irony not exactly benign, both the title of the essay and its organizing trope would at first seem to suggest a certain critical or ambivalent position in regard to the Austro-Hungarian state. Certainly, Brod's opening gambit flirts with the rhetoric of critique: "It seems to me as if the state had two faces, or rather, as if since the start of these events it has acquired a new face, whereas previously, with its other, gloomy and, to say it straight out, untrue face it had always annoyed more than frightened, but certainly never gladdened us." And yet what Brod generates from this conceit is something quite other than the satire or philippic it initially seems to be, much less a tragicomedy of the kind his friend Franz Kafka found in the same concept of "Verwandlung" two years previous,[2] and what will emerge from the state's two-faced metamorphosis is indeed not a narrative of resistance or ambiguity, but a dialectical fable of a unity all the stronger for its apparent contradiction.

Following upon the presentation of its central conceit, the essay continues in almost wistful mode, looking back on Brod's youthful (and, implicitly, disavowed) thoughts on the state:

> Before, whenever I thought about what the state meant to me, —how was it that each time the only symbol that occurred to me was that of a streetlamp's nighttime illumination of some drowsily patrolling night watchmen, whose purpose, I imagined, could just as well be fulfilled by a small pocket flashlight? Why did the state's face, when it happened to show itself to me, seem only a familiar and unpleasant hodgepodge, whose individual components manifested themselves in more or less the same fashion as the scowls of bad-tempered and half-awake but still sternly probing professors at one of those innumerable official exams, as the look of one of those government officials, who out of pure good will and unselfconsciousness even sits himself on the edge of the table like an old school buddy while he pronounces his terrible words of refusal? Yes, the state had always treated us with arrogance and imperiousness, and in return we treated it like something one prefers not to think about.

Thus ends the first paragraph, the paragraph of youth and the old world. At this point in Brod's piece, however, there occurs much more than just a line break. Bursting forth in the lacuna between the first and second paragraphs are the previously alluded-to "events" of the war, which bring not just a change of face, but also, for Brod, a change of heart:

> Then came the time in which one neither can nor wants to think about anything *but* this cold and unfriendly state. But wait, a miracle! The state was no longer unfriendly; it began to speak to me, to solicit me, to exhort me in every newspaper, on every street corner; it began to show me its beautiful new face, it did away with the commands that one had previously followed without feeling and issued new ones,

> which said: You, the individual, and I, the state, we are one and the same, —do not just obey me begrudgingly, but know that everything I do I do for you and your honor and your soul alone. . . That was the great transformation. The state began to love its citizens; or rather, it had always loved them, and, correctly understood, its whole existence had never been anything other than a deep love, but it was only now that the state also showed and said this, and the foolish citizens, who had previously failed to understand, now loved the state back with a boundless and sincere love. The state humbled itself before us and we not only tolerated this but humbled ourselves before it in return. We saw a great father standing over us, full of concern and far more prudent and forward-looking than we. In this way the new face of the state also became an image of the most sublime youthfulness, combining within itself wisdom and love in a way that we had never experienced with any human being. Indeed, it was precisely something superhuman that had come over us; and here I am not even speaking about the feeling of those truly lucky ones, for whom this war is a national German war, but only of those who can feel in this war only the force, the sorrow, the triumph of the state organism like us in multilingual Austria. I have been to neither Lemberg nor Czernowitz and I will probably visit a hundred Italian cities before it would ever occur to me to travel to Galicia. But as soon as someone wanted to take Lemberg and Czernowitz away from me, I felt in my body that they belonged to me by rights and that I can on no account do without them. I suddenly understood all the tribulation and cares of the state from the inside out; indeed, there was little lacking for me to also understand why before the state always had to regard me so sternly.

Thus the two faces of the state are ultimately revealed to be, not deception or difference, but the necessary self-representation of a "great father" in the charge of his children, judiciously adjusted to serve the historical contexts of, respectively, peacetime and war. First is the stern, professorial, testing father of the prewar years, Oedipal in the sense that he can be, if not overthrown, than at least ignored in the youthfully arrogant thought that the illumination that it provides can be achieved just as well "by a small pocket flashlight"; then comes the benevolent but imperiled father who rallies his beloved children in time of danger. Brod's small text thus reads as a kind of condensed Holy Bible of political theology: in the New Testament's galvanizing Passion of God the Son is the identity of the judging God of the Old Testament fulfilled. Or else, in Hegelian terms, the duty of obedience that the state requires from its citizens, while experienced only as a burdensome repression in one's childhood, in one's maturity—Brod's professor/student analogy is surely not incidental—is finally recognized as the Universal and Substantial that it in fact is. It is in this way that Brod can feel an affinity to the denizens of

Czernowitz, Lemberg, and Galicia—even though, as he admits, he still prefers Italy as a vacation spot.[3]

Regardless of exactly what hermeneutic model is used to interpret the piece, however, it is clear that by the end the two faces of the state, the scolding/professorial one and the beseeching/fatherly one, have been reconciled in an intimate, internalized image of state authority. (Significant for the success of Brod's metaphor is that the Austro-Hungarian Empire is the "Dual Monarchy" of Trans- and Cisleithania, whose emblem, moreover, is the double-headed eagle; thus the idea of two-facedness is built *already* into the Habsburg Empire's own self-representation.) Or rather, these two faces are *almost* reconciled, as Brod concludes enigmatically that "there was little lacking for me to also understand why before the state always had to regard me so sternly." What is it that is still wanting, then? It may be no less than the crucible of war itself that is finally able to justify the state's peacetime cultivation of disciplinary unease, turning what had once seemed a merely arbitrary subjugation into the accomplished interpellation of the subject. In this way, Brod's piece is not just a concentrated allegory of political theology, but also a political Bildungsroman in miniature and an illustration *avant la lettre* of Althusser's distinction between "the repressive state apparatus" and "the state ideological apparatus" (clearly corresponding to Brod's first and second "faces" of the state, respectively).[4] The oddness of Brod's piece in this context is that it first appears to expose the state's ideological interpellation as a masquerade, and then subsequently embraces this ideological interpellation as the innermost truth of Brod's being. One may consequently speculate that the small thing that is lacking for Brod to understand the state's repressive face together with its imploring one is *also* the recognition that he was in fact *always* answering the state's appeal, regardless of the face it wore, and that both faces, far from being in contradiction with one another, are distinct but necessary moments in the state's performance of its own authority.

Despite (or because of) these unresolved complications, Brod's piece offers a valuable insight into the nationalism that took hold in many intellectual and artistic circles at the dawn of the First World War.[5] It also provides a useful point of contrast to the postwar writings of his younger contemporary and fellow (former) subject of the emperor, Joseph Roth. Together with thousands of his peers, Roth heeded the call of Brod and others, in 1916 volunteering for military service in the Austrian army. During this time Roth was also employed as a military war reporter, beginning his official career as a writer.[6] Although the tenure was brief—in 1917 the organ shut down, in part due to government censorship[7]—Roth clearly gained good practice in comparing his personal experiences with the prevailing talk of imperial solidarity. For Roth, the two faces of the state—if indeed it is only *two* faces—do not merge to form the unified disciplinarian-caretaker of Brod's imagination; instead, they fall away from one another, in the process revealing that they were actually always only masks, and the state a state only by virtue of its play with them. And where Brod sees the state as essential in its irony—in other words, as *dialectical*—Roth will draw the opposite conclusion, understanding it as *ironic in essence*.

This chapter will trace this ironic essence in Roth's writing, with particular attention to the feuilletons he wrote in the hundreds for a diverse range of newspapers and journals from the years 1915 to 1939. The feuilleton, a relatively new and in many ways vexed genre, provides the protean form in which Roth both practices his particular art of the comic and places expected forms of comedy under question in light of the dramatic political and media-technical transformations of his time. For despite the earnest moral import of much of Roth's writing, he is also serious about the ironies of the world, and even more, about the necessity of preserving the legacy of irony in the face of increasing calls for renewed earnestness and the bogus "'jokes' of indigenous pathos-monger[s]" (*JRW3* 417).[8] It is only when one fails to recognize where the real joke lies, Roth suggests, that the consequences are somewhat less than funny.

Wise Cracks

Roth's first documented prose piece, "Herbstwindes Kriegsgeschichten ("War-Tales of the Autumn Wind") (*JRW1* 3–5), published in December 1915, bears witness already to the change in mood since the early days of the war. Whereas in 1914 Brod emphasizes his spiritual and political kinship with people and lands he has never even seen, one year later, Roth recounts the war in a series of mordant anecdotes emphasizing the themes of miscommunication and distance despite physical proximity. The little boy strutting about playing soldier pays no heed to his returned father's actual tales of war; a dog, "who understands nothing of fatherlands and heroic deaths" (3), searches in vain for his dead master; a mother writes a letter to her only son, unaware that he has only just died on the field of battle. The leitmotif of the blowing wind (the "narrator" of the piece) serves, despite the manifest sentimentality of the conceit, not to unify but rather to emphasize the tragic irony of discontinuity within simultaneity.

Helen Chambers has described the difference between Roth's feuilletons and the journalistic news article as one "comparable to that between the novel and historiography," commenting, "[Roth's] process of composition involves reducing and filtering events in order to arrive at a human perspective, which is the level at which the reader can grasp the dynamics of a situation and in so doing gain a better understanding of the bigger picture."[9] Roth's humanism is explicit (and something to which he expressly lays claim in much of his writing), but it is nevertheless highly unclear, both in this text and many others, exactly what sort of "bigger picture" we as readers are supposed to receive here. Indeed, the opposite is the case: despite the piece's panoramic views, no reconciling bigger picture or general "dynamics of a situation" is on offer, unless, indeed, it is that of the loss of a cohesive dynamic itself. Stéphane Pesnel has interpreted Roth's writing along precisely these lines, drawing the opposite conclusion to Chambers that Roth's fictive world is "always a world of the absence of totality, of the disappearance of the immanence of sense, in which characters never succeed in identifying principles of meaning and constantly run up against an opacity of the real."[10] The last sentence of Roth's early piece—"The poor woman jumped up in fright and stared silently into the night . . ." (*JRW1* 5)—dramatizes such "opacity of the real" in striking fashion: if Brod concludes his call to arms with sudden illumination, Roth's war report ends in the literal shock of darkness.

Even if patriotism as meaning-making will appear later in Roth's works in the form of nostalgia and legitimism—those aspects of Roth's work and life to which the most critical attention has so far been paid[11]—such an attitude is still largely foreign to his work prior to 1929, and indeed, Roth's fabled nostalgia for Felix Austria may itself be more complex than is usually acknowledged.[12] And though, admittedly, the maudlin tone of "Herbstwindes Kriegsgeschichten" does not at first promise much in the way of hilarity, Roth is nevertheless far from being merely the master of post-Habsburg pathos or despairing critic of modern society that much scholarship still portrays him as.[13] One small but telling indication of this is the fact that, while Roth's first feuilleton is a tragicomic portrayal of the cruel ironies of war, his second—published just five weeks later in the same journal, the *Österreichs Illustrierte Zeitung*—is entitled "Über die Satire: Eine Plauderei" ("On Satire: A Confabulation") (*JRW1* 6–8). "It would be mistaken," writes Roth, "to think that satire wants to laugh at things. No, it laughs because it has to" (6). Despite the stated theme of the piece, what Roth here calls "satire" has little in common with the caustic mockery made so famous by fellow Austrians such as Karl Kraus. Georg Lukács, in his 1932 essay "Zur Frage der Satire" ("On the Question of Satire"), describes the basis of the satirical method in Hegelian terms as "the *direct* contrast of essence and appearance [der *unmittelbare* Gegensatz von Wesen und Erscheinung],"[14] a contrast, moreover, that is eventually to find its fulfillment in the "growing hatred, the increasing outrage and scorn of the proletariat" (Lukács, "Satire," 107). In this interpretation, satire is nothing more than the antithetical moment that comes between the earnestness of error and that of its resolution. For Roth, on the other hand, this double-sided earnestness is precisely the "perfection [Vollkommene]" of which satire is the "revenge" (*JRW1* 8). In part, Roth's conception of satire bears similarities to the Jean Paulian and Nietzschean humor of gods and higher beings, in which earthly travails are reduced to inconsequence from the perspective of eternity.[15] In even greater measure, however, Roth's "satire" is a satire on (the Lukácsian version of) satire itself: not that which laughs—be it cruelly or magnanimously—from a position on high, but an immanent and co-implicated laughter which makes such judgments from on high strictly impossible. It is in this sense telling that Roth provides as examples of his kind of satire the decidedly counterintuitive ones of *Hamlet* and *Faust*. Hamlet in particular is for Roth the exemplary figure of satire, or rather of irony,[16] in that his inability to take anything fully seriously, his Kierkegaardian reflection of reflection (see *CI* 242), is what causes him, in the end, to meet his downfall.[17] Hamlet's situation can lead only to irresolute and ironic role-play, but this irresolute and ironic role-play is the opposite of the heroic single-mindedness necessary to put an end to his situation. Thus "his tragedy is his satire" (*JRW1* 7): Roth's Hamlet—and, by extension, "humanity" itself—is caught in a version of Jean Paul's "circle of wit [witziger Zirkel]," "this true *causa sui*" (*VA* §46, 47; 179) in which the joke is no longer an exception, but a pure logical tautology that encompasses the whole of reality.

Despite this emphasis on the universality of the comic, however, the works of Joseph Roth, perhaps more even than those of Kafka or Walser, seem to resist interpretation as comedic texts. Yet at least in his feuilletons—aimed, after all, at a mass audience and designed for quick, enjoyable consumption—Roth's highlighting of comic techniques and humorous situations, as well as his frequent recourse to comedic themes and tropes, is at least as prominent as it is in the works of either of the two other authors. Foolery, games, and play are celebrated in many of Roth's feuilletons;[18] caricature, droll observations, and witty ornaments of speech are made frequent use of; and the figure of the clown once again makes an appearance.[19] Such features of Roth's writing are, by and large, freely acknowledged in the critical literature; yet they are also most often classed immediately under the categories of satire or "the grotesque"—both of which hide a serious message (as the "real" content) beneath their amusing surfaces, while simultaneously providing for the evocation of laughter as the consoling supplement to the satirized bad world.[20]

The logical inconsistencies of this position and its unsuitability for a general definition of the comic have been discussed already in chapter 1. For the present, therefore, it will suffice to examine the specific character and implications of Roth's comic techniques themselves. One of the most frequent of these techniques, already deployed in "Herbstwindes Kriegsgeschichten," is the unexpected or inappropriate juxtaposition, taken by a long tradition to be the very definition of joking and wit. Examples abound: in the 1920 piece, "Irrungen, Wirrungen: Überraschende Entdeckungen im Telefonbuch" ("Delusions, Confusions: Surprising Discoveries in the Telephone Book") (*JRW1* 358–59), Roth turns Fontane's novel of crossed relationships and social classes into a world of crossed wires and phone book entries, such that it appears that "the goal of the telephone book is to provide false connections" (*JRW1* 358).[21] In the *Minima Moralia*-esquely titled "Ruhr-Totenfeier mit Shimmyklang ("Ruhr Funeral Procession with Shimmy-Sound") (*JRW1* 993–94), Roth writes of the distant strains of jazz music from a neighboring dance hall audible during a showing of a newsreel on the burial of those killed in the 1920 Ruhr workers' uprising: "All those who have eyes to see and ears to hear will recognize in this convergence of shimmy and death the meaning of these times" (*JRW1* 994). The oft-discussed piece "Spaziergang" ("Going for a Walk") (*JRW1* 564–67) is a veritable *ars poetica* of this technique, not only comprising a list of seriocomic juxtapositions[22]—but also thematizing these vis-à-vis both a pathos-laden monumental worldview—"the broad, all-encompassing arm-sweep of the world-stage hero" (565)—and the no longer accessible experience of unmediated nature.

Such a technique of incongruous juxtaposition is not only a classical component of wit, however; it is also essentially identical to what Benjamin, with respect to Baudelaire, describes as that *shock* so definitive for the experience of urban modernity. It is indeed likely that Roth, as fellow self-styled flâneur, partakes of that same "sensation of modernity" gained only at the price of "the disintegration of the aura in immediate shock experience [die Zertrümmerung der Aura im Chockerlebnis]."[23] Indeed, Roth says as much in his concluding lament for a non-commercialized, non-domesticated nature ("The day nature became a health resort, it was all over" [*JRW1* 567]). And yet the city-going speaker of Roth's feuilleton brings a very different sensibility to his walk than that of the Baudelairean dandy. For if aura and the enchantment of the world are lost, then the incongruity of urban experience can no longer be experienced traumatically as the loss of aura. Insofar as the catastrophe has already occurred, the urban observer is now, like the contented sanatorium inmates of Roth's "Das Haus der 100 Vernünften ("The House of the Hundred Sane Men") (*JRW1* 929–31) or like the characters of Robert Walser's novels in Benjamin's assessment, "*geheilt.*"[24] Roth's *Spaziergänger* understands the shock of the everyday in fact as a form of *respite* from those forms of experience not yet triumphant in Baudelaire's time, namely, news journalism and commercial advertising. Both of these, in their different ways, are invested in the smoothing-out of quotidian contradictions into a generalized and consistent master narrative. In contrast to such narratives, then, the shock of contradictory sensations no longer connotes the danger of traumatic interruption, but provides a refuge from the dishonest idealizations of the mass media, and it is in protest against the latter that Roth states, "Only the small details of life"—just that which cannot be so easily idealized away—"are important" (*JRW1* 565).

That these tiny incongruous details imply in turn a positive valuation of what in Benjamin's essay remain the traumatic fragments of experience is obvious. This is not to say that all the images that Roth describes are *themselves* always cheerful, of course; but the particular *mode* of perception, at least, is now privileged. And if wit is, in Kant's definition, the bringing-together of antitheses or seeming antitheses, then such a technique of bringing incongruities together is emphatically a species of wit, even when the image itself is at times too piteous to actually raise a smile. Yet unlike the comparative and accretive joking that, for Kant, sophomorically "snatches at sudden inspiration [hascht nach Einfällen]" (*ANTH* §55, 116; 130) and thus is "not enough for awakening and enlivening the ideas of reason that are required for insight into important affairs" (*ANTH* §55, 118; 133),[25] Roth's ambulant observation presents itself as a specifically objective or journalistic—even, a *photo*journalistic[26]—wit, which derives its force not from a facile play with dreamt-up antitheses, but from the raw contradictions thrown up by real, everyday life. In this Roth is closer to Jean Paul, for whom wit has the quality of a "miraculous birth of our creative self [Wundergeburt unsers Schöpfer-Ich]," an idea "both freely created through our will and determination and necessary, for otherwise the creator would have seen the creation before he made it, that is, before he saw it" (*VA* §43, 121; 171). However, Roth takes this description one step further than Jean Paul, playing, as he did already in "Über die Satire," with the notion that this is a wit *wholly* of necessity, indeed to the point of effacing the "creative self" entirely, as he writes for example in the introduction to his "Harzreise" ("Travels in the Harz Mountains") (*JRW3* 270–346):[27] "It's not me who exaggerates and overemphasizes. The things themselves take themselves too far [treiben sich selbst auf die Spitze], a destructive satirist created them. The way I see it, I'm just transcribing [Es ist mir, als schreibe ich sie nur ab]" (273). Roth thus frees himself from Kant's aforementioned charge that witty inspiration is incompatible with serious thought. Whereas for Kant, wit is a distortion—done for the purposes of puerile amusement and cheap shock effect—of an essentially rational world, for Roth, *judgment* and *reason* are the abstract deformations of a reality that consistently refuses to line up.

Of course, Roth's claim to merely report the comical combinations he finds lying around must also be recognized as disingenuous, given his insistence elsewhere on the creative and especially the *created* aspect of not just the feuilleton but *all* language and representation. And even if it is assumed that modern, urban life is essentially characterized by the ever more rapid succession of ever more disparate images, the selection and assortment of these images, and their specific staging as wit, must not (as the comparison with Benjamin's Baudelaire-interpretation already shows) be taken for granted. Roth's assertion that not he but the world is making the jokes is thus not to be understood as historical fact, but instead as epistemological claim. What is new in Roth is less the argument for wit's value (for which there is no lack of honorable precedents) than his insistence on the identity of wit and, if not exactly reason, then at least a certain *reasonableness* and clarity of perception. As already mentioned in the first chapter of this book, Kant significantly follows his discussion on wit in the *Anthropology* with an excursus on the virtues of the experimental method (see *ANTH* §56, 118–19; 133–34). Roth's speculative journalism, necessarily tied to the contingent, is clearly not the same thing as the aptitude for systematic investigation that Kant praises (indeed, Kant makes a distinction between research and the dumb luck of stumbling upon things). But, precisely by virtue of this contingency, it is also just as removed from the subjective arbitrariness that determines mere whimsicality, and it is this uncomfortably near distance from shrewd discovery on the one hand and arbitrary find on the other that makes the feuilleton such a troubling new genre or form of representation.

At this point in the *Anthropology*, Kant has occasion to speak of genius (*Genie*) as a sort of happy medium between the free play of the creative imagination and the "appropriateness of the product to the underlying idea; that is, *truth* in the presentation of the object," which "must be learned by means of school rigor [muß nun mit Schulstrenge gelernt werden]" (*ANTH* §57, 120; 135). If the latter, however necessary, is also merely an "effect of imitation [Wirkung der Nachahmung]" (*ANTH* §57, 120; 135), incapable of producing anything new, the former "might deliver original folly [würde vielleicht originale Tollheit abgeben]" (*ANTH* §57, 120; 135), but never anything of "exemplary" and thereby of lasting value.[28] At issue, predictably, is the abiding rivalry between French and German culture, marked for all eternity by the double meaning of *esprit* as both "Geist" and "Witz" (see *ANTH* §57, 120–21; 135–36). Consequently, what is at stake in Roth—that well-known Francophile—is not just the reimplementation in a new key of the familiar idea of wit as the juxtaposition of like unlikes, but also an increasing tension between the rhetoric of wit and the rhetoric of reality, in Kant basically antithetical, in Roth complimentary or rather interdependent terms. That is: on the one hand Roth claims that reality is essentially—and accidentally—witty; on the other hand, he argues that reality is already and inherently a matter of creation, whose "truth in presentation" cannot be learned in any school, because it is the presentation that creates the truth in the first place. Here a documentary comedy, in the form of a wittiness that is nevertheless "real"; there a comedy of documentary, in the form of the performativity of truth and reality themselves. And yet in Kant, too, is already the notion that genius consists above all in the power to create new realities, to go beyond the possibilities allowed for by common sense: this is one way, at least, of reading genius's "exemplary" force.[29] If this is the case, then *Witz* and *Geist* may not be so far from each other as Kant would have them, and Roth's merging of wit and documentation represents a conscious shift towards an *episteme* in which the dividing lines between norm and invention, reality and imagination begin definitively to blur.

Kant, of course, did not have anything like Roth's feuilletons in mind when he wrote his paragraphs on the "talent for inventing" (*ANTH* §57, 120; 134). He refers to the reading of newspapers just once in the *Anthropology*, namely as an occasional "distraction" for weary heads (*ANTH* §47, 101; 112), indeed for weary heads "after strenuous rumination over a philosophical point" (*ANTH* [German only] §47, 112, note to line 21). The newspapers are so much the opposite of genius that the reading of them constitutes no less than the mind's vacation from itself. It is all the more curious, then, that it is just this kind of happy medium, hybrid genre, or belletristic monstrosity—depending on one's sympathies—between fact and fiction, objectivity and subjectivity, norm and distortion that has structured much of the debate on both the feuilleton in general[30] and Roth in particular.[31] Carl Schorske describes the feuilleton as the transformation of the "objective analysis of the world into subjective cultivation of personal feelings" and portrays it, with no little moral censure, as a product of fin-de-siècle Viennese culture's liberal-bourgeois turn inward: "The feuilletonist exemplified the cultural type to whom he addressed his columns: his characteristics were narcissism and introversion, passive receptivity toward outer reality, and, above all, sensitivity to psychic states."[32] In his disdain for the medium, Schorske is following the lead of Karl Kraus, who in the 1910 broadside "Heine und die Folgen" ("Heine and the Consequences") derides both the Prussian "hell" of instrumentalized art and the French "hell" of art as ornament. Far worse than either of these on their own, however, is the combination of the two together, in the hybrid—but at bottom "Parisian"—genre of "Impressionsjournalistik."[33] Kraus takes the feuilleton to task—together with its supposed progenitor Heine—for its mixing of substance and style, "German purpose [deutschen Zweck]" and "French wit [französischen Geist]" (Kraus 189); the feuilleton is "the implementation of journalism with the elements of wit," a generic amalgam which leads only to "an even more catastrophic confusion" than both alone (Kraus 191–92). (Schorske, less acid than Kraus but if possible even more critical, for his part considers the feuilleton part of the same aestheticized culture in whose apoliticalness National Socialism was able to take root.)

Roth is certainly not unaware of the new *Lebensformen* (see Kraus 220) created by the daily feed of the mass media, but his own criticism tends in a quite different direction from that of Kraus. His scorn is reserved, not for the "vermin of humor [das Ungeziefer des Humors]" (Kraus 218) and the "degradation of practical life through ornament [Verschweinung des praktischen Lebens durch das Ornament]" (Kraus 191), but for the arrogance of a presumed *objectivity* and a journalism ostensibly *without* subjective distortions of personality. As he writes in the 1929 piece "Die Tagespresse als Erlebnis: Eine Frage an deutsche Dichter ("The Daily Press as Experience: A Question for German Writers") (*JRW3* 101–2): "If the newspaper were as immediate [unmittelbar], as sober, as rich, as easily controllable as reality, then the former, like the latter, could indeed communicate experience. But the newspaper offers only an untrustworthy, screened [gesiebte] reality—and an inadequately formed one—that is to say: a bogus one. For there is no other objectivity but artistic objectivity [Denn es gibt keine andere Objektivität als eine künstlerische]. Only it is capable of representing the facts truthfully. Every other kind of representation is a private, that is to say, an incomplete [unvollkommene] one" (*JRW3* 101). Even if Roth here claims that reality is "immediate" and "easily controllable," this must be read primarily as a provocation in light of the received wisdom that the newspaper adequately reflects and filters a multifarious world. In contrast to the alleged veracity of reportage, Roth's spirited defense of his own medium turns the opposition between objectivity and subjectivity, truth and fiction, genius and *esprit*—and above all, the enforcement of these terms *as* opposites—on its head.

The necessity of putting into question the assumptions behind such terms is essentially the same point Roth makes just a few months later in the same journal, in the celebrated polemic "Schluss mit der 'Neuen Sachlichkeit'!" ("Enough with 'New Objectivity'!") (*JRW3* 153–64). "The real," complains Roth, "started to be taken as true, the documentary as genuine, the authentic as valid" (153). The ideology of autonomous art, always problematic,[34] now achieves its vulgar apotheosis in the new requirement to unambiguously distinguish between "life" and "art," the sociological and the fantastic, reportage and escapism (see 156), indeed to the point where "'objectivity' starts to replace and to repress 'purposiveness' [Die 'Sachlichkeit' beginnt, die 'Zweckmäßigkeit' zu ersetzen und zu verdrängen]" (163)—which is as much to say that the classicist separation of art from life has merely been reversed into a pseudo-modernist separation of life from art.[35] In contrast to this craze for the real, Roth here champions "verisimilitude [Wahrscheinlichkeit]" (157). If the word has a certain implicitly Aristotelian and humanist tenor, what is in fact being defended is ultimately the literariness of the literary as such and the gaps, ironies, and "nuances" (164) that this entails, exemplarily expressed in the "Mischprodukt" of the feuilleton.[36]

It is however much earlier, in the self-referentially titled "Feuilleton" (*JRW1* 616–19), that Roth takes his most specific aim at the anti-feuilleton faction.[37] Although in 1921 a rather belated response to Kraus's attack, it is nevertheless an explicit one, not only mentioning Kraus by name, but also deploying several of Kraus's own metaphors and arguments against him. Roth's main and relatively uncontroversial point in this piece, dispatched between parentheses, is that Kraus confuses the sins of individual writers with a deficiency of the whole genre. Yet Roth is also aware that something more is at stake in the genre of the feuilleton than the question of a few bad apples. Assuming a tone of ironic self-deprecation, Roth characterizes the feuilleton as so many "soap bubbles," over which "only women and those who have remained children might [. . .] rejoice. Men, in contrast, maintain that they only concern themselves with eternal things" (616). "The feuilleton," writes Roth, "is said to have come about out of the desire for entertainment, or even less: amusement. And a muckety-muck is never amused. Pooh! [Und ein Würderich amüsiert sich nicht! Pfui!]" (616). Beyond this cheeky rejection of the consensus on seriousness, however, is the understanding that wit and irony also furnish their own kinds of truths, indeed truths more valid than those of the literal-minded "drum majors in the marching-bands of culture [Tambourmajore der Kulturmarschkapellen]" (616). Responding to the claim that Heine's travel reports are inaccurate, Roth writes, "The degenerate *Homo sapiens* [who has criticized a previous feuilleton of Roth's for being "dishonest" (617)] would have studied statistics on Paris for ten years and then published a boring, therefore immoral, book. Heine might have lied around a few small facts [hat vielleicht kleine Tatsachen umgelogen], but in this way he saw the facts exactly as they ought to be. For his eye consisted of more than just an instrument of vision and optic tracts" (617). Roth's use of the word "umlügen" hedges strategically on Heine's fabrications: facts are neither fabricated nor attacked head-on, but instead *circumambulated* in service of a higher, more true form of truth.[38]

This critique—that an imaginative and witty creativity with facts is more ethically justified, and indeed, more *correct* than an unadorned and ultimately self-deceptive objectivity—is *the* leitmotif of Roth's journalistic work, and structures his relationship not just to wittiness and the comic, but also to the specific place of the comic in the representation of "reality." Roth positions himself between the sentimentalism of would-be litterateurs who, in Roth's metaphor, as dogs to the moon, "bark at [God], because he is out of reach" (*JRW1* 618), and the positivists for whom "the use of a new pronoun is [. . .] a sin" (*JRW1* 617), between the hackneyed clichés of a bygone romanticism and the modern confidence game of fact. In the middle of these two literary subterfuges lies that literary half-breed of *esprit* and *Geist,* the ambiguous play of the comic, that creates its own terms: "See: that was already a 'joke.' A 'paradox.' A 'feuilleton' " (*JRW1* 618).

Accidents of Bread in Cheese

Roth is explicit about the seriousness with which he regards such joking matters. In the 1921 feuilleton "Lauter Juxen" ("Jokes Galore") (*JRW1* 442–43), he waxes enthusiastic about the recently renewed boom in the invention of novelty articles, which, he remarks, "during the war was suspended [. . .] almost completely [. . .]. *Inter arma silent musae*" (442). Now, however, "with each passing year the development of carnival culture strides indefatigably forward [Rastlos schreitet mit jedem Jahr die Entwicklung der Karnevalkultur vorwärts]" (442). The evocation of "carnival culture" is not infrequent in Roth's work, and makes Roth a clear forerunner of Bakhtin in the latter's thinking on "carnival laughter" in early modern Europe. But Roth's understanding of "carnival culture" in this feuilleton is more complex, or at least more equivocal and ironic, than that of Bakhtin. In contrast to the medieval pastoral-cyclical temporality of Bakhtin's carnival,[39] Roth's modern, technological carnival culture "develops" and "strides forward": terms borrowed from a vocabulary more often used to describe a historical teleology in which war is precisely the high point, *not* the hiatus. Hegel, for example, describes war in the *Philosophy of Right* as "that condition in which the vanity of temporal things and temporal goods [. . .] takes on a serious significance [. . .] the moment in which the ideality of the particular attains its right and becomes actuality" (*PR* §324, 361; 492). The "ethical health of nations [sittliche Gesundheit der Völker]" (*PR* §324, 360; 492–493) that for Hegel emerges only through the seriousness of war, comes to be for Roth, in contrast, through the discovery of objects that are not only in the philosophical but also in the everyday sense wholly frivolous. Against the militaristic hygiene practiced by those whom Roth elsewhere names "the children of Hegel, father of spiritual gymnastics [die Kinder des geistigen Turnvaters Hegel],"[40] the cultivation of willful naughtiness, as represented by the magic egg and the trick collapsing nail, is the true benchmark of civilization.

It is significant, then, that Roth goes on to note that it is specifically *war invalids* who are now responsible for advances in the development of joke products. This new wave of progress in the novelty product industry began "in the last years of the war," that is, after a large number of soldiers had been injured and thus rendered unfit for military service. "Today," remarks Roth, "approximately two thousand war invalids are employed in the manufacture and fabrication of novelty items [Juxartikeln]" (*JRW1* 442). While in another author such a statement might occur as a bitter condemnation of a society that has no better use for its veterans than to employ them in the production of gag-items, Roth's piece evinces only an unqualified approval for these objects, that are (in a way similar to the joke in Freud), "like folk songs" passed down with "ever greater perfection, ever finer effect as an essential cultural treasure" (*JRW1* 442; see also *JRU* 15; 13). Thus it is clear that for Roth, "carnival culture" does *not* offer a temporary hygienic release from normality and the ecstatic counterpart to a hegemonic disciplinary solemnity in the manner of Bakhtin; it *itself* is the order, not just of everydayness, but of ennobled labor and spiritual development, indeed, the "original" genius of a whole culture (see *JRW1* 442).

In this way, the laughter of "the grown-up" who appears in the final paragraph at the three boys who accidentally break their toy, much like the laughter of the fabled Thracian maid who laughs at the impracticality of speculative philosophy, redraws the line between fooling and normativity that the toy itself erases. Roth's subsequent belittling description of the adult's appearance is an implicit polemic against his order of things, further emphasized by Roth's shift to an imitation of children's language: "The grown-up has bushy eyebrows. He has whole pine tree forests over his eyes. I hate him" (*JRW1* 443). While Roth's insistence on the grotesquerie of the adult's appearance certainly raises the question of just who should be laughing at whom, it also shows the contaminating power of the normative order, insofar as Roth's sulky ridicule of the laughing adult displays an internalization of the same laughter of contempt that the adult exemplarily incarnates. The piece thus ends on a melancholy note, displaying the double victory of meanness over childish joy: the first, in the man's mockery itself; the second, in the socialization of the child, who, wounded, learns to turn from the gratuitous laughter of play to the defensive laughter of power.

Despite this conclusion, which makes Roth's piece no less than a tragedy of the comic in the narrative of the comic's fateful loss of innocence, the purpose of the feuilleton is still to defend and promote this earlier form of laughter, not as a state of exception within cyclical temporality or as the negative element of dialectical historiography, but as the simultaneous amalgam and reversal of both forms of time, a progress *into* comic pleasure after the fallow period of war. It is in this context that Roth's meditations in the fifth paragraph of the feuilleton should be read, beyond their merely expository quality. In an abrupt transition from the paragraph that precedes it, the section begins:

> The inventor of the first exploding "frog" was a Triestine Slav. His name was Ivan Krak and he was a watchmaker by trade. He lived in the second half of the nineteenth century. (*JRW1* 442)

Roth's attention to this fabled toymaker's nationality—he is a Slav of unspecified type from Trieste, the former Habsburg shipping and trade center, annexed to Italy in 1920 (one year before the feuilleton's publication)—is consistent with his support for the multiethnicity of the former Habsburg empire against the linguistic and cultural homogeneity of the nation-state. Even more significant, however, is the fact that the toymaker Krak is by trade a "watchmaker": a living embodiment of *the* privileged Enlightenment metaphor of calculated rationality, divine order, and a lawfully regulated universe.[41] Here, however, the crowning achievement of this human analogue of a rationalist God—and by extension, the guarantor for the rational structure of the universe as a whole—is no more and no less than a mechanical exploding frog, an object not only useless by any rational standard, but also something unpredictable and sudden, the very opposite of the watch's uniform motion. Unlike the regular and sequential temporality of the clock, emblem of a well-maintained cosmos, the toy frog bursts with the same explosive and ephemeral force as that of laughter.

The real significance of this paragraph for a consideration of Roth's comic irony, however, lies in its second part, in which Roth philosophizes on the seemingly incidental and random detail of said watchmaker's family name:

> It's thoughtful of the man that he was named "Krak." Really: "Krak!" This is why the exploding frog was for a long time called a "Krak-Krak." A piece of evidence for the existence of a regulative power of designation in human affairs. Here an event does not call forth an onomatopoeic designation; instead, the onomatopoeia of a name brings about an event. (*JRW1* 442)

The above lines are notable in Roth's work—indeed, nearly unique—in their unsparing praise of the *adequacy of language*. Almost nowhere else does Roth care to speak of a "piece of evidence for the existence of a regulative power of designation in human affairs [Ein Beweis für die Existenz einer regulierenden Bestimmungsmacht im menschlichen Geschehen]."[42] To the contrary: in most cases, not only is there for Roth no proof of a regulating determinative force in human affairs to be found in language, but dissonance, discrepancy, non-sense, and even the wholesale breakdown of meaning are fully the rule of linguistic utterance.[43] It has been claimed that behind Roth's frequently voiced skepticism with regard to language lies "an almost mystical belief," in which the "profanation of the meaning of words" is the sign of the most grievous cultural and historical degeneration—a claim that would appear to find confirmation in Roth's critiques of Nazi propaganda or the distortions of the mass media, respectively, in such pieces as "Der Apokalyptische Redner" ("The Apocalyptic Orator") (*JRW3* 798–801) and "Am Ende ist das Wort" ("In the End is the Word") (*JRW3* 837–40), as well as in satirical riffs on advertising-speak such as "Der Merkantile Superlative" ("The Mercantile Superlative") (*JRW2* 200).[44] Yet Roth's awareness of language's lability extends to more than just the vulnerability of words to their manipulation for nefarious purposes. It also refers to the possibility—in the manner of Mr. Krak's onomatopoetic frog—of the creation of reality *out of* language.[45]

For if Kraus blames Heine for having "loosened the bodice of the German language to such an extent [. . .] that nowadays any little clerk can feel her up" (Kraus 195), Roth wants rather to show that the German language was never really all that chaste to begin with.[46] Indeed, many of Roth's more distinctive rhetorical constructions are those that play on the indeterminacy of language itself.[47] One of these constructions, used to specifically comic effect in Roth's feuilletons, could be described as a kind of meta-zeugma—the rhetorical trope designating the application of the same word to two different and dissimilar contexts—that will here be termed the "nicht/doch" construction. The basic form of this construction is easily discernible in the following passage, from the 1919 piece "Volkscafé" ("People's Café") (*JRW1* 200–203):

> In this café, you can get for cheap, for very cheap, a white coffee. It's not quite as white as it was in peacetime. It's actually not white at all, but rather brown. But it's called "white coffee," and so it *is* white coffee. It's just the same with things as with people. They are what they're called. (200–201)

The form is as follows: first, Roth declares the existence of "white coffee"; this phrase is just as soon negated as it is proposed, however, and the coffee is declared to be actually brown. Then, without actually rescinding this statement (i.e., denying that the coffee is brown), Roth reconfirms the first assertion, at the same time diverting the discussion to a different level. That is: without marking the shift in discourse, Roth moves from the *noumenal* to the *phenomenal* to the *nominal*. What at first appears as an anecdote about a local coffeehouse becomes an exposition of the quality of postwar coffee, which in turn becomes a debate about semiotics, all the while leaving the language designating the object of discussion unchanged.[48]

A similar use of the *nicht/doch* construction occurs in "Preishog'lziag'n" (*JRW1* 225–27), which begins: "*Preishog'lziag'n* is actually called *Preishake-lziehn* [competition finger-pulling, i.e., as bar game]. But actually it's really called *Preishog'lziag'n*. Mysterious relationships exist between the Viennese dialect and the noble sport of *Hakelziehen*" (*JRW1* 225). The 1920 piece "Chiromanten" (*JRW1* 284–85) takes this figure perhaps to its farthest extreme, asserting difference within total linguistic identity:

> There are chiromancers and there are chiromancers. So you see: the story isn't as simple as it looks. Even apart from the fact that the word comes from the Greek, that is, from "cheir," and—but that's a side issue. (284)
>
> For what was it that I said before? "There are chiromancers and there are chiromancers." The man is—also a chiromancer. (285)

In this example, Greek etymology functions in the same way as the *actually* brown coffee and the *actual* word "Preishakelziehn." All three are attempts to appeal to some kind of evidentiary claim that would ground the word as concept and the concept as word. In all three cases, however, precisely that which would seem to be able to justify distinction appears, as "side issue [Nebensache]," as the mobile hinge between the conceptual and the linguistic itself, and if Roth possesses a "mystical belief" in language, as has been claimed, it must be in the sense not of monotheistic origin but of pagan magic: just as the fortune-telling machine literally "reads" the unsignifying lines of the hand and translates them into words indicating an entire history and future, just as in the con man's enigmatic "curious! [merkwürdig!]" a "whole world is contained" (*JRW1* 285), naming makes it so.[49]

Additionally, at the dawn of innovative design movements such as Constructivism and Bauhaus, Roth is also one of the first to explicitly thematize the communicative power of the non-linguistic aspects of mass media.[50] "I see typography grown into a worldview [Ich sehe die Typographie zur Weltanschauung entwickelt]" (*JRW1* 565), writes Roth in 1921 in the aforementioned "Spaziergang," and in the 1929 "Nonpareille aus Amerika" ("Nonpareille from America") (*JRW3* 39–42) he remarks, in the context of the hierarchy of newspaper content, that "nonpareille is the typeface of everything unimportant" (39). Here not even an already ambiguous language but the wholly non-denotative suggestiveness of graphic design furnishes meaning, serving, for example (in the illustration that Roth provides) to consign a story about punishment by whipping in American prisons to insignificance and oblivion. Similarly, from the other end of the power spectrum, in "Das Denkmal" ("The Monument") (255–59), the glory of the nation is conveyed through a pompous typeface that is "Antiqua, Rune and Gothic all in one" (255). Perhaps most tellingly of all, in "Unsere Setzerei" ("Our Typesetting Shop") (*JRW2* 521–24) Roth writes of the printing press workers who, through their daily manipulation of lead type, "know [. . .] the irony of the work [. . .]. Only once paper is laid down does the original backwardness acquire the appearance of rational meaning" (522–23).

This "irony of the work," however, is not just the distance or disconnect that Roth thematizes in the above lines between truth and its representation as wittily allegorized in the inversive process of the printing press; it is also the arbitrariness of that representation, the infinite potentiality of linguistic combination and thus of the creative power of language itself. Roth's complaint in regard to the newspapers is thus not about the arbitrariness of language, but about this arbitrariness's presumed *cancellation*. Accordingly, "Unsere Setzerei" also contains a comic fantasia on the possibility of imagining the actions of letters otherwise:

> All sorts of different typefaces live inside the drawers [of the print shop], ready to give weak thoughts a beautiful shape, a garment, a form, an expression [Ausdruck]. The drawers have all been provided with names like the compartments for spices in a kitchen, for pepper, cinnamon, and paprika. Where are they from, the names Nonpareille, Colonel, Petit, Bourgeois, Garamond, Cicero, Mittel, Tertia, Text, Doppel Mittel; Italic, Century, Roman Narrow, Kaleidoscope? They are names for the imagination. [Es sind Namen für die Phantasie.] They could just as well be the names of toys or hobgoblins. What do they do at night, Kaleidoscope, Dido, and Century, when no one is there, when down below in the printing room the machines are already recklessly and inexorably impressing the law on hundreds of thousands of sheets of paper? They hop out of their drawers, these alphabets, and that most eternal of all hierarchies is demolished, from A to Z. (*JRW2* 523)

Letters and language can play, or they can be set down in seeming inevitability in the pseudo-facticity of journalism and the portentous phrases of the powers that be. For the newspaperman knows: words do indeed have lawgiving force; the real question, however, is that of *which* laws will be ratified.

Language's power to *make* meaning rather than merely *reflect* stable concepts is treated in the 1920 feuilleton "Das Urteil der Geschichte" ("The Judgment of History"), mock-seriously subtitled, "Who is to blame for the war?—The encyclopedia brings the answer to light" (*JRW1* 332–33). Even if the 1920 edition of the *Meyers Handlexikon,* whose publication forms the occasion for the feuilleton, has of course been written by the *losing* side of the First World War, Roth's piece nevertheless recalls Benjamin's famous pronouncement in "On the Concept of History" that "whoever has emerged victorious participates to this day in the triumphal procession in which current rulers step over those who are lying prostrate [. . .]. There is no document of culture which is not at the same time a document of barbarism."[51] Here the "document of culture" in question is the literal historiographical document of the encyclopedia itself; that which is (re-)established in Meyer's "first peacetime encyclopedia" (333)—"admittedly, only a handbook" (333)—is the conservative worldviews of Wilhelmine Germany and late Habsburg Austria that, predating the war, also survive it (almost) intact. Despite this ideological continuity, however, Roth's piece also marks a period of transition and undecidability (or a premonition of its own *Zwischenkriegszeitlichkeit:* the penultimate paragraph is a wry complaint that this supposedly comprehensive encyclopedia still does not include the word "swastika"). For while Roth is clearly sending up the Meyer encyclopedia's ideological (bourgeois, nationalist, and implicitly revanchist) underpinnings, he is also implicitly acknowledging that there *are* no words yet for that which has just taken place in Europe and which, like Brod and indeed like the Meyer encyclopedia itself, he euphemistically calls merely "Events [Ereignisse]."[52]

Without an established narrative, there is not yet an established interpretation. Roth's sarcastic recapitulation of the encyclopedia's solemn explanations resemble nothing so much as the sped-up literature summaries of Walser's *Bleistiftgebiet*: a story deprived of affect, context, and causality, that is, of all that ordinarily makes a story coherent and thus meaningful. The difference from Walser, perhaps, is that Roth takes as his object a text that already puts narrative coherence profoundly into question. The terse, dispassionate (but nevertheless latently propagandistic) language of the encyclopedia makes a mockery of the human cost and catastrophic impact of the recent war. It is certainly not hard to see what Roth might find objectionable in passages like the following:

> Caught btwn. Fr. and Rus., Ger. declared war on both countries on 1 Aug. to retain the advantage of rapid mobilization and invaded Belgium on 4 Aug., which Engl. immediately took as grounds for war [Eingeklemmt zw. Frankr. u. Rußl. erklärte Deutschl., um den Vorteil der raschen Mobilmachung zu wahren, 1. 8. an beiden den Krieg u. marschierte 4. 8. In Belgien ein, was Engl. sofort zum Kriegsgrund nahm].[53]

While the encyclopedia's self-exonerating, self-justifying interpretation of the war (an interpretation that was indeed later to have disastrous consequences) is clearly a target of Roth's ire, the comedy of the piece has less to do with the encyclopedia's interpretations of historical facts than with the very claim to interpretive authority that the encyclopedia, by virtue of its *being* an encyclopedia, makes. What is at stake here is no less than the discipline of historiography itself, specifically the conflict between the historian and the philosopher of history as described by Hayden White in his analysis of historiographical tropes. The historian, White claims, may be ironic towards the *documents* of history insofar as they are objects of hermeneutical analysis; yet "once he thinks he has extracted the truth from the documents, he may then abandon his Ironic posture and write his histories [. . .] in the firm conviction that he is telling *the truth about* 'what really happened' in the past, with more or less Ironic condescension toward his audience, but not with respect to what he himself 'knows.' "[54] The philosopher of history, on the other hand, "seeks to determine the extent to which a given historian's work (and indeed, the whole historiographical enterprise) may still be undergirded by unacknowledged presuppositions or assumptions—that is to say, to identify the *naive* element in historical thinking, the extent to which a given historical work has failed to maintain a critical attitude *with respect to itself*" (White, *Metahistory,* 376).

For White, the philosopher of history then attempts to find a system or narrative framework (or in his terminology, an "emplotment") that would eliminate also *this* irony, without, however, falling into the same trap of naïveté. Roth, however, in this feuilleton at least, is not trying to find a new form of history to supersede the presumably faulty one of the Meyer encyclopedia. His interest is rather in letting the irony of historiography itself, its real lack of objective narrative models, stand in all its nakedness.[55] Roth's technique is correspondingly to highlight the quasi-causal relation—in fact, a causality of reversed temporality—between the establishment of new terminology and the happening of the event. In this particularly egregious hermeneutical circle, belatedness paradoxically precedes priority, as Roth remarks cheekily, "The encyclopedia also calls the World War the World War and so now there can be no more doubt. It truly was a World War. Now I can confidently start writing my memoirs: Reminiscences of the World War" (*JRW1* 333); and on the encyclopedia's explanation that "sincere attempts at intercession on the part of the Germans and the English came to naught faced with the inevitability of the system of alliances and Russia's conscious determination to go to war [Ernstgemeinte deutsche und englische Vermittlungsversuche scheiterten an der Zwangsläufigkeit des Bündnismechanismus und dem bewußten russischen Kriegswillen]" (*JRW1* 333; see also *Handlexikon* 760), Roth exclaims, "So it was *inevitability* [Also die Zwangsläufigkeit war's]" (333). Roth's faux-naive acceptance of the encyclopedia's far from innocent word points out how a simple choice of idiom allows a particular interpretation of recent history to achieve the status of a self-evident truth, whose retelling then not only forms the basis of the understanding of the past, but also lays the ground for the politics of the present and future.

In the next sentence, however, Roth considers the implications of the word "Zwangsläufigkeit" in a different light: "That is still a malicious denunciation of inevitability against the League of Nations" (*JRW1* 333). In a parenthesis, Roth comments on his own (mis-)interpretation: "But we won't hold it against him, that Meyer. Otherwise he's *actually* objective [Wir nehmen's ihm aber nicht übel, dem Meyer. Er ist sonst *wirklich* objektiv]" (*JRW1* 333). The first joke here, of course, consists in Roth's reading of subversive messages (as much regarding the old European system of alliances that led to war as the newly created League of Nations meant to forever prevent it) into a text that presents itself as a definitive repertoire of objective information—the encyclopedia's subtitle reads: "A Reference Work of General Knowledge"—and whose political stance, moreover, is doubtless as far from subversive as it is possible to be. The joke also lies in Roth's temporarily playing the role of the offended patriot, a role manifestly in contrast to the bemused cynicism of his preceding paragraphs. Roth makes the conservative worldview of the encyclopedia speak against itself, then makes comedy out of pretending to forgive the ideological sins that he himself has read into the text.

So much seems clear. However, the second sentence of this remark complicates matters, in a way that comically puts into question the grounds of the simple or satirical comic of the previous two paragraphs. For Roth does not write "Er ist sonst objektiv," a sober (if here also ironic) critical judgment. Instead, what he writes is: "Er ist sonst *wirklich* objektiv." The addition of this pleonastic "wirklich" (for what is objectivity if it is not real objectivity? but this is precisely the question), not to mention the over-compensating typographical emphasis, is not just an interpretive aid for the irony-impaired reader. Rather, it marks a limit or an aporia in Roth's text—indeed, in his whole body of work—and while Roth's piece begins as a not so gentle satire on the encyclopedia's claim to provide the conclusive interpretation of history, within this local satire lie the greater problems of language and narration themselves. Roth does not wish to claim, for example, that the information "Liebknecht was shot; Luxemburg murdered [Liebknecht ist erschossen, die Luxemburg ermordet worden]" (*JRW1* 333; see also *Handlexikon* 433 and 446) is factually false; yet there is something clearly not right with the lapidary, context-poor presentation of these facts that the encyclopedia offers. Thus what is at issue, once again, is *not* the choice between "truth" and "untruth," but the fissures within "truth" itself and language's role in its production—particularly in the context of the dissolution of the old world order and hence also the collapse of a system able to authorize language's truth claims. Roth's comment that "the authority of the Meyer Encyclopedia has already [. . .] taken possession of the most recent events [hat sich schon (. . .) der allerletzten Ereignisse bemächtigt]" (*JRW1* 332–33) only emphasizes the vacuum that the disappearance of *political* authority has left behind, in which a strange amalgamation of popular opinion and ghostly expertise, implied in the word "Konversationslexikon" itself, strains to deliver judgment on current affairs.[56]

And yet this very judgment, as Roth also wittily reveals, is already a dual condemnation, not only of the encyclopedia's historiographical authority, but also of the authority of the in fact defeated and humiliated nation in whose continued affirmation (despite all evidence to the contrary) the encyclopedia's own authority might alone be said to inhere. In this context, it is significant that Roth singles out as a target of his sarcasm the passage in the encyclopedia attributing the war to "Zwangsläufigkeit." This word has clearly been chosen by the encyclopedia's authors to signal the innocence of the Central Powers vis-à-vis the Entente nations' bellicosity—although perhaps even more, to signal the innocence of *all* interested parties in the face of a mechanized Realpolitik that functions here as a veritable secularized analogue of the ancient conception of fate.[57] In thus placing the guilt of the war with inhuman and "inevitable" forces, however, the encyclopedia does not just open itself to ridicule; it also unintentionally affirms the very opposite of what it itself is attempting to maintain. For to attempt to explain history in any way other than as a product of a sovereign will is already to cede authority, not just *to* someone or something else, but entirely. As Louis Marin notes in his study of historiographical discourse in the reign of Louis XIV,

> The *occasus* of history, the *casus belli,* is not and cannot be simply the disequilibrium of antagonistic forces in Europe [n.b., precisely the Meyer encyclopedia's claim], which could be the object of a de facto description. The objective report of the forces present, their conflict and the outburst of this conflict, is one with the justice and right—of the king. To explain the causes of the war is to unfold the "political will" [*vouloir politique*], that is, the will of history's agent, the king.[58]

The historical narrative that would support monarchial power must not inquire into objective causes at all, "inevitable" or no. This is all the more pressing when what is at stake is the explanation of war—again, according to a certain view, the very proving grounds of the state as political and conceptual entity and thus the proof, indeed the substance, of sovereign power.[59] Roth's joke on the encyclopedia's version of history is to point out that actually to speak of "Zwangsläufigkeit" in regard to the political order is a reproof tantamount to treason, for a governing body that can be coerced—be it by the external enemy or merely the relentless machinery of international alliance—is not fit to govern, has already ceased to govern. As the above passage from Marin makes clear, the mere application of normal laws of causality to matters of state is already a blasphemy against political theology: "L'état, c'est moi" means that, as concerns the state, the will of the sovereign alone—unencumbered by profane causal determinations—is immediately both dogma and fact.

Naturally, there is a world of difference between the centralized absolutism of Louis XIV and the bourgeois monarchies of the Belle Époque (not to speak of the international collectivism of a League of Nations). Nevertheless, the conclusion remains the same: for authority, the question "why" is, already, implicitly its negation. Roth's tautological insistence that "der Meyer" is "sonst *wirklich* objektiv" thus *not only* indicates a serious loss of criteria for judging objectivity (that is, for judging objectivity objectively), it also drives home the point that the very notion of "objectivity" implies the loss of criteria for judging by its very nature, and the attempt to establish objectivity is only a sign for the onset of doubt, just as a certain kind of doubt is itself dependent on a notion of metaphysical objectivity.[60] (By way of contrast, consider that in the milieu with which Marin is concerned, the phrase "*wirklich* objektiv" would be unthinkable.)

In the long essay "What Is Authority?" Hannah Arendt similarly hints that the loss of distinction with regard to the definition of certain political terms—not least among which is "authority" itself—is already the most conspicuous sign of a crisis *in* authority. The fact of "a common world where the words we have in common possess an unquestionable meaningfulness" is as conditional upon the existence of authority as it is determinate of it, and the loss of one implies or entails the loss of the other.[61] In this context, it is hardly a coincidence that that paradigmatic treatise on political absolutism, Hobbes's *Leviathan,* begins not, as one might expect, directly with an approach to the theory of the state, but rather with the long introductory chapter "Of Man," essentially a compendium of terminological definitions. In a passage—with obvious polemic undertones—specifically engaging with the question of "Non-sense," Hobbes writes: "And therefore if a man should talk to me of a *round Quadrangle;* or *accidents of Bread in Cheese;* or *Immateriall Substances;* or of *A free Subject; A free-Will;* or any *Free,* but free from being hindred by opposition, I should not say he were in an Errour; but that his words were without meaning; that is to say, Absurd."[62] Even where Hobbes's definitions are at least apparently more ideologically neutral, the implication is clear: before a compromised order can be pieced back together again, before the decapitated sovereign can be restored as the irremovable head of the new collective political body, the definitions of words must be agreed upon. Yet Hobbes's nominalism—"There being nothing simply and absolutely so; nor any common Rule of Good and Evill, to be taken from the nature of the objects themselves; but from the Person of the man (where there is no Common-wealth;) or, (in a Common-wealth) from the Person that representeth it; or from an Arbitrator or Judge, whom men disagreeing shall by consent set up, and make his sentence the Rule thereof" (120–21)—forces him almost immediately to run up against the same impasse that Arendt points out: there must be a sovereign authority (of one kind or another) to decide upon the meaning of words, but it is the stable definition of words—and by implication, a common anthropology and worldview—that alone gives legitimacy to the sovereign.

Roth's own insistent nominalism is thus a product of the recognition that not only is there no longer a king or an emperor whose word is law, but also that any efforts to reinstate such authority must either openly acknowledge their performativity or perish by it.[63] Just as Hobbes's need for getting things straight once and for all cannot but betray the profound anxiety behind his stabilizing project, the weak and indeed self-contradictory authority of a Meyer encyclopedia (as Roth's smart-alecky reading against the grain demonstrates) only barely suffices to hide its latent hermeneutic anarchy. The only place in which Roth does allow for a self-identical, onomatopoetically appropriate language is, precisely, in the *abandonment* of sovereignty that takes place in *play.* The name of the inventor of the exploding frog appears as a seeming inevitability that nevertheless contrasts radically to the "Zwangsläufigkeit" of international alliances that were to set off an explosive "Ereignis" far less innocuous than the sporadic blasts of Mr. Krak's creation. But if a play culture exceptionally causes sense to emerge from nonsense, outside of the realm of play—for example, in the Hobbesian Commonwealth or the world of the bushy-eyebrowed adult, where laugher arises not from the ludic handling of irony but from an "apprehension of some deformed thing in another" (Hobbes 125)—the search for essential lexicographical, narratological, or political meaningfulness only confirms the absence of that which it would require, making it absolutely vulnerable to its own satirical laughter of power just where it has eliminated the happy laughter of the powerless.

Statisms of Exception

Roth follows the association of the breakdown of political authority and the questioning of the status of language literally to the letter in the 1925 piece "Kaiserliche Orthographie" ("Imperial Orthography") (*JRW2* 339–41). In this piece, Roth dryly observes that among the many interesting things to be learned from the recent publication of Kaiser Wilhelm II's manuscripts is the fact that "he couldn't spell [Er schrieb fehlerhaft]" (339). In possession neither of the genius's sovereign carelessness toward rules of language, nor of the excusable poor spelling of the uneducated, the kaiser, far more humiliatingly, "wrote with the orthography of the semi-educated petit bourgeoisie [schrieb die Orthographie des halbgebildeten Kleinbürgertums]" (340). After registering, in a classically humorous syllepsis, the irony that "the Kaiser commanded sixty million subjects, but not proper spelling [der Kaiser zwar sechzig Millionen, aber nicht die Rechtschreibung beherrschte]" (340), Roth offers his public a close reading of one imperial misspelling of particular significance:

> The Kaiser wrote the word "Konflikt" in the following way:
>
> "*Conflickt*"
>
> An uncommonly charming way of writing this pleasant word, at whose sound one thinks anyway of Wilhelm II. O, he was a splendid conflict-virus, a conflict-bacterium, a whole conflict-epidemic, a conflict-plague. No one has more of a prerogative to write the word "Konflikt" incorrectly than the Kaiser. You will note how he adorns the word, festoons it, makes it exotic by means of the antique "C" at the beginning, and how he places another "c" before the "k" in the middle, thus so to speak charging the whole thing with extra weight. He will not be satisfied by a simple, garden-variety "Konflikt." He must have his "Conflickt." With Wilhelm II, every conflict becomes heavy and labored. Every "Conflickt" gives birth to "Conflickts." (*JRW2* 340)

Here Roth might at first seem to be paying heed to the implications of Pellisson's letter in Marin's analysis: whichever way the kaiser writes is the correct way, or is at the very least a unique, inimitable, nonstandard but therefore even more rich and proper way, a sovereign stamp on a word to which, as Roth wryly notes, the kaiser of all people should have a right. But Roth has already established that Wilhelm II—now, after the war, in exile in Holland, deprived of that very thing that would have given his misspellings legitimacy—never even possessed the genial courage to err in grand style, but made only mistakes that were "overblown, inauthentic, hollow, pathetic [gespreizt, unecht, hohl, pathetisch]" (*JRW2* 340). Here authority is no longer merely defeated or defunct; worse—it is *trivial*. And it is also not too difficult to hear, in the "sound" of the kaiser's "petit bourgeois" spelling errors, an echo of the petit bourgeois—yet all too imperial—trivial-tragic error of entering into the war.

To make fun of the bad spelling of a kaiser, even a deposed one, is clearly to place oneself within the great tradition of the wise fool who at once speaks truth to power and ignores the world-historical forest in favor of the trees of personal idiosyncrasy. However, far more than just a mockery of the formerly powerful, Roth's impudence relates to his concern with the question of authority and its loss that is one of the most consistent themes of his oeuvre. Roth's most famous work, the 1932 novel *Radetzkymarsch* (*The Radetzky March*), is remembered for what has become the emblematic scene of the end of the Habsburg Empire, as the sudden announcement of the assassination of the Archduke Franz Ferdinand brings a precipitous end, not just to the Trottas' gala dinner in celebration of the dragoon regiment to which the family belongs, but to the entire European order that this symbolizes. Yet the young lieutenant Carl Joseph von Trotta's Oedipal announcement that "the monarchy is dead" (*JRW5* 429) is not nearly as sudden or as climactic in the context of the novel as it is occasionally made to seem. In the chapter that directly precedes this scene, no less a personage than the revered Emperor Franz Joseph himself appears, but he is now a senile old man with a runny nose, so clearly in no way superior to the supplicant subject in front of him that "it seemed to the emperor as if he was standing before his own mirror image" (*JRW5* 407).[64] Indeed, the disenchantment of political theology begins already in the first pages of the novel, where the heroic act of the soon to be ennobled Joseph Trotta—the act which will form both the leitmotif of the novel and the founding myth of the von Trotta line—consists only in saving the emperor from his own *Schaulust*-induced stupidity (see *JRW5* 140).

If the ironies of authority contained in *Radetzkymarsch* are nevertheless related with a certain bitter pathos (even more so in the novel's 1938 sequel, *Kapuzinergruft* [*The Emperor's Tomb*]), in 1920 Roth is still more concerned with unsentimentally revealing such nostalgia as "Potemkinschen Ludendörfer"[65] and children's-book kitsch. The feuilleton "Lesebuch gegen Weltgeschichte" ("School Primer versus World History") (*JRW1* 429–31), for example, a critique of German history textbooks (similar to the attack on the Meyer encyclopedia four months earlier), reads almost as advance self-criticism for any imperial nostalgia of which Roth might later be found guilty. The piece begins, with unmistakable sarcasm:

> The old mendacity of idyllic notions about the paternalistic relationship between sovereign and subject, superiors and subalterns, shoulder to shoulder and loyal to the crown, the whole schoolbook arsenal of *Orgescherichs*[66] and all the Potemkin *Ludendörfer* has been preserved: in the primers and textbooks of the democratic middle schools of Prussia. (429)

The mawkish heroic narrative that Roth subsequently cites as example of the textbooks' propaganda, in which a dying soldier revives just long enough to salute his kaiser—"Yes, your majesty! I shall remember you for all eternity! Also there up above! [Ja Majestät! Ich werde Ihrer ewig gedenken! Auch dort oben!]" (431)—upon the latter's writing a last remembrance in the former's diary, is precisely the *parody* of the "painfully longed-for order" that Claudio Magris has attributed to Roth of the "hypothetical" but no less desired "presence of a unified and unifying value in its various manifestations" (Magris, *Unauffindbare Sinn,* 7). Roth's matter-of-fact comment on the textbook's anecdote belies such an interpretation well in advance: "Go ahead and try to tell this syrupy story to a fifth-year whose father fell in battle or who's seen classmates of his die. His sister, who'd been a nurse in the hospital, could quote you quite different utterances from the mouths of dying soldiers" (431).

The ideology of *pro patria mori,* magnified to ridiculous sublimity in the school history textbook and returned cruelly to the profane (in both senses of the word) by Roth's acerbic commentary, is not just the call to which millions of soldiers marched to their death in the trenches of World War I; it is also one of the cornerstones of state religion itself. In Ernst Kantorowicz's celebrated analysis of sovereignty in the Middle Ages, the doubleness of the king's body emerges as a result of the impasse between the king as Christ figure who sacrifices himself in battle for the good of the state, and the king as representative head of state, who demands that others sacrifice themselves for him. This self-sacrifice of the foot soldiers for the *patria* is only justified if the *patria* is an analogue of the Kingdom of Heaven, and authority is conferred upon the sovereign insofar as "the value of immortality or continuity upon which the new politic-centered rulership would thrive [is] vested in the *universitas* 'which never dies,' in the perpetuity of an immortal people, polity, or patria, from which the individual king might easily be separated, but not the Dynasty, the Crown, and the Royal Dignity."[67] When this *universitas* dies indeed—as the Habsburg Empire did in spectacular fashion after the First World War—the king's immortal body dies with it, and the sacred martyrdom held within the idea of *pro patria mori* finally becomes (in Wilfred Owen's famous phrase) "the old Lie."[68]

If Roth criticizes political theology as "outdated ideals [unzeitgemäße Ideale]" (*JRW1* 429) in "Lesebuch gegen Weltgeschichte," and in *Radetzkymarsch* exposes its bitter ironies, in the 1921 feuilleton "Autoritäten" ("Authorities") (474–76), he turns these ironies into the deceptively simple stuff of comedy. The bulk of the text is dedicated to a seemingly simple paradoxical reversal of the notion of authority; whereas "the scales of opportunity lift and let fall government officials like waves beneath the planks of a ship" (476), those vested with *true* authority are the school janitors, weather forecasters, street magicians, doormen, tram conductors, maître d'hôtels, waiters and cashiers, the lackeys and dregs of society. Or as Roth states outright: "He who is born to authority will not become a politician or a professor, but rather something arbitrary, subordinate" (475). Despite the conventional comedy of this inversion, however, the conceit of this piece already works to set a more profoundly ironic comedic machine in motion. For to attribute authority to those who are subordinate is clearly already to render the concept of "authority" unstable, and even when one is prepared to grant the paradoxical aptness of Roth's attribution of authority to cranks, hucksters, and members of the service professions, it is hard to know what "authority," so prominently blazoned in the feuilleton's title, *is,* exactly. The "weather-prophet," at first "laughable as a novelty item [lächerlich wie ein Scherzartikel]" (475), achieves the rank of authority and is consulted on all matters relating to the weather because, so Roth speculates, once his prediction of rain, when rain seemed most unlikely, happened to come true. Roth does *not* write that the man's subsequent predictions have ever actually been borne out. Nor does he speak about how the man came to make the original correct prediction in the first place. The man's authority just rests on a certain event in the archaic past, which itself is only something that

Roth imagines, literally puts in front of himself, "sich vorstellt" (475). The foundational moment of authority, if indeed it ever really took place at all, now resides in the realm of myth and of legend, and the weather-prophet has become simply "an authority by virtue of his umbrella and the will of God" (475).

Thus what at first appears to be little more than classical comic diminishment on Roth's part turns out to be *also* an accurate political assessment. The self-constitution of authority has not disappeared; it has simply moved into the property owners, bureaucrats, and state functionaries who now indeed hold the reins of power:

> Authority is granted by God himself. Its external attributes are rarely scepters and orbs, but rather for the most part objects of daily use, simple workaday things such as for example a moustache or gold braid. (*JRW1* 474)

> Whatever a civil engineer in street clothes says doesn't have to be right. But a man with a desk, a moustache, and a cravat knows all. For someone with muttonchops, an error is quite out of the question. (*JRW1* 476)

Even when the performative force of royal regalia is here transferred into the accouterments of bourgeois respectability, the message is the same: the divine right of kings exists in a relationship with its symbolic presentation that is as reciprocal as it is paradoxical. The symbols of authority must be believed in to be in force, but the power to compel belief in these symbols is what alone constitutes authority. Thus in other feuilletons Roth addresses the uncanniness of symbols of authority *deprived* of their credibility. In "Kaisers Geburtstag" ("The Kaiser's Birthday") (*JRW2* 335–37), for example, Roth exults over the emptied-out form of the titular holiday, in light of whose obsolescence of which the kaiser's image now appears as one which had "consisted in the main of two blond beard prongs and which in its facial features had buried the marks of the German petit bourgeoisie under a higher, Salieri-like power" (335). In *Homo Sacer,* Giorgio Agamben asks the rhetorical question: "What, after all, is a State that survives history, a State sovereignty that maintains itself beyond the accomplishment of its *telos,* if not a law that is in force without signifying?"[69] Roth's depiction of the exiled kaiser and the trappings of his reign presents what is possibly an even more extreme case of Agamben's political death-in-life: not just a non-signifying law, but the remnant even of this, the non-signifying signification of the law no longer able to be in force, a *pure signification* without efficacy or the possibility of efficacy. The posthumous remains of the State that has in point of fact *not* survived history are the spectacular ruins of a sovereignty itself always-already spectacular.

Similarly, in the 1922 piece "Persönlichkeitsrecht" ("The Right to Personality") (*JRW1* 849–51), Roth describes—in the context of a report on a civil suit between the deposed Kaiser Wilhelm and the publisher of a drama about Bismarck—what could be called the fateful transition from *sovereignty* to mere *fame.* The latter, with respect to the former, is characterized by a state of affairs in which the Great Man is no longer identical with his public persona, but split between his "public" and "private" life, which is then essentially available for the relativizing pens of biographers and playwrights. "He has become 'matter' [Er ist 'Stoff' geworden]," Roth comments of Bismarck, "appearance, material. Whether he was the tool of history or its master, object or subject, negative or positive, harmful or beneficial—he belongs to the public" (851). Such a public but inessential posterity (with its corresponding private but essential humanness) clearly implies an entirely different sort of historiography than that proposed by the biographer of Louis XIV. In the biography of the famous man, the symbolic cohesion that a royal historiography demands becomes a mere constellation of dead symbols, as deprived of use value as a sentimentally preserved piece of shrapnel or the pyramids of Egypt.[70]

It is as a reverse of the monarchial comedowns of "Persönlichkeitsrecht," "Kaisers Geburtstag," and "Kaiserbilder," then, that in "Autoritäten" Roth presents the bureaucratization, or rather the proletarianization, or rather the *lumpenproletarianization* of divine authority. This reversal of divine authority into the humble and poor, however, does not thereby entail authority's relegitimation. Roth is after all not advocating for a government of eccentrics and waiters (which would anyway already be a scandal for any conventionally revolutionary politics). Nor does he present—even assuming such a thing were possible—the final delegitimation of the concept of divine authority. Again, a double comic operation is being performed here: first, in the paradoxical claim—in essence a witty play on the semantic difference (in German as in English) between "authority" and "authorities"—that "real" authority inheres not in great monarchs but in the petty officialdom of the everyday, but second, in the consequent undermining of the notion of "authority" itself. The feuilleton thereby exists in a space of conceptual confusion, indeed a double bind of its own compositional principle, and Roth's witty paradox of authority in which the first is last and the last is first undoes *itself,* insofar as authority is by definition the one thing in which Jesus's famous chiasmus cannot hold valid.[71]

And yet, at the same time—in a third and final comic operation—the authority of the amateur weather forecaster and the like can in fact *not* be claimed to be false, neither for reasons of its triviality nor because of any supposed emptiness of the concept of authority. If either of these two claims were the whole story, Roth's piece would be a relatively straightforward satire: in the case of the former, an elitist satire on the humble folk who puff themselves up with their scrap of importance; in the case of the latter, a leftist satire on the effective bankruptcy of political or disciplinary power. Both of these satires, ideologically at odds though they may be, are certainly in operation here. Yet there is something more. For *despite* the parodic insignificance of the figures Roth describes, and *despite* the fact that authority is revealed as being dependent on its representation, one fact remains, the last turn of the comic screw: this authority is *real*. It is real in the sense that Arendt defines authority: as something that relies neither on coercion and violence, nor even on persuasion and reason,[72] but on a hierarchical system leading to "an obedience in which men retain their freedom" (106). In this sense, the trappings of authority are not fake or superficial, not a deception to be mocked; but nor are they the exterior signs of any real inherent force, rectitude, or competence. What they are is *authority itself*, authority as self-referential performative, devoid of specificity and empirical justification alike.

Here the aforementioned *nicht/doch* structure of Roth's play with language and episteme is writ politically large. Authority is in fact not-authority—or not-authority is actually authority—and *also* (n.b., *not* "but still") *authority is authority*. Indeed, it is the very fact that authority is authority that enables the two previous and seemingly contradictory statements to both be true, for if authority is authority—that is, if authority is as such tautological—then anything may potentially be true of it. As with the meaning-determining "authority of the Meyer encyclopedia" (*JRW1* 332), no fundamental characteristic, but the mere act of positing authority makes authority come to be. Traditional authorities, however, make the mistake of claiming for themselves a singularity, an absoluteness, and a foundation that the "constantly abiding within the world-historical changing of positions" (*JRW1* 474) type of authority gladly forgoes. And whereas the claim to singularity within tautology is a logical contradiction, tenable only to the extent that the tautological structure of authority remains unrecognized, the unqualified embrace of the performative tautology of authority—"by virtue of his umbrella and the will of God" (*JRW1* 475)—creates an authority safeguarded from the need to provide any justification for itself beyond the fact of its own being.[73]

Clearly, the recognition of this performative tautology also creates a crisis in authority. Or rather: it *is* the crisis in authority.[74] If authority were real without being empty, it could continue undisturbed and unquestioned; if authority were empty without being real, its lack would be of no consequence. That it is both at once, however, creates a genuine dilemma. Precisely this dilemma is what "Autoritäten" reveals; yet Roth, significantly, does not attempt to resolve the problem, but instead suspends the question in favor of "Scherzartikel" potentates and "Tricks" of command, a comic play with power that both echoes and answers to the ostensibly serious equivocality of the meaning of authority. This triply tautological comedy of authority is not only inseparable from Roth's attention to language and representation, it is also essential for an understanding of why this attention is neither language critique à la Hofmannsthal nor Krausian satire of linguistic convention. The latter would correspond to a belief in genuine authority combined with the conviction that the wrong people were in power,[75] the former roughly to the denial that authority was ever or could ever be in force, in analogy to a language that can never adequately correspond to reality. Neither of these beliefs are to be found in Roth, however. The weather-prophet appears "as if he didn't exist in actuality, but instead effectively within quotation marks" (*JRW1* 475); the words of the man with muttonchops "stride forth in march time to an inaudible military music, filing in perfect formation directly towards a destination become a 'directorate'" (*JRW1* 476). Roth's metaphorical evocation of scare quotes in the former passage and his actual use of scare quotes in the latter indicate clearly what the rest of the feuilleton already implies: authority—or rather "authority"—is always a citation of itself.[76] But, precisely *as* self-citation, it is also in force. Such a structure moves Roth's comic technique definitively away from a dialectical form of comedy, that is, that "comedy" which sets up paradoxes only in order to demonstrate their overcoming.[77] Instead, in Roth not only are thesis and antithesis suspended in their mutual validity, they also exist simultaneously as their own combination, in a permanent joke in which oscillate apparent contradiction and apparent resolution.[78]

In other words, while Roth's humorous pieces do sometimes set up the antithetical structures of satire or traditional paradox, more often than not—in a way not dissimilar to Kafka's "sliding paradoxes"—they go a step further than traditional satire or paradox allow. This step—the crucial step of comic irony—is the one that crosses over into a space in which no actual authority holds sway, the space of deauthorized representation in which "nothing *is*, everything is called [Nichts *ist*, alles heißt]" (*JRW1* 566). The two anti-ironic fallacies, then, would be the false completeness of a journalistic language that imagines itself to have expunged the last traces of rhetoric, and the sentimental leftovers of a discredited *Spießbürgertum* in which the self-satisfied *idée reçue* and the cheap humor of simple paradox are equally at home.[79] What all of these options have in common, despite their manifest differences, is a hermeneutic security which is able to fold even sallies of wit and local paradoxes into a coherent interpretive system. In the context of the paradoxes of authority that Roth diagnoses, however, both *Sachlichkeit* and humanist sentimentality are merely complementary forms of kitsch,[80] tacitly assuming an order that can no longer—if indeed it ever could—be said to exist. Given these circumstances, Roth opts instead for what Carl Schmitt disparagingly calls romanticism's figure of the "child who plays with all possibilities," for whom, in contrast to "the rationalistic, mechanical state" and the "man already limited by his profession and accomplishments,"[81] authority is nothing but a toy.[82] Once authority is understood to refer only to itself, however, to inhere in nothing but the persuasiveness of its self-representation, the comedy of the "suspension of every decision" that constitutes "the origin of romantic irony" (Schmitt, *Political Romanticism,* 56) rings far truer than the serious, grown-up need to arrive at a conclusion.

The Irony of Objectivity

Marin argues that the historian's self-effacement as subject in his narration of history leads, paradoxically, ultimately to the historian's absolute *resurgence,* "not however as *narrator, act producing the narrative, narration,* but as history itself and its absolute agent, performed in the discourse of the reader that much more strongly, more powerfully, more absolutely because the uttering subject, the narrator, has been more radically and more completely excluded and denegated in the narrative" (79). This self-effacement of the royal historian is the opposite of the chatty, personable, personalized style of the feuilletonist—but not for the expected reason that the one disappears within his work while the other jumps affably out of it. As Susan Bernstein has observed in her study of the figure of the virtuoso, the material conditions of journalism (that is, as collaborative and, especially, as *commercial* venture), together with the feuilleton's brevity and occasional nature, lead to an inherent "discursive irresponsibility"[83] and promotion of stylistic play over "expressive" language: the very thing disdained by Hegel as "subjective humor,"[84] and derided by Karl Kraus as the "French disease" that Heine brings back from Paris.[85] Writes Bernstein:

> The relationship between the *I* of Heine's individual entries and the editorial *I* cannot be read in terms of a unified subject or brought into line with the stable chronology of a life. This divided *I* has much in common with the virtuoso, an unstable and performing figure that can give only the temporary unification of aggregation, a unity not proceeding from an ideal structure but with a technical origin in spatial position on the stage and on the page. The virtuoso belongs to the guild of the rhapsode, a problematic figure standing at the beginning—and not the origin—of literature, the scribe whose tongue or pen makes possible the emergence of the author and the ideal origin of speech. His public appearance, interrupting and punctuating an errant and disappearing existence, is not a distortion or repetition but is his very emergence. (33)

The feuilletonist presents the worst of both worlds: in his work can be found neither an authentic imaginative expression pulled from the emotive depths of his personality, nor the sober, objective, and trustworthy documentation of journalistic reportage. His work is made up of subjective impressions without a real subject, objective observation without the guarantee of objectivity:

"Journalistic virtuosity is precisely the failure of reference, for it does not faithfully report about its world. But nor does it oppose reference by presenting itself as an idealized 'other' language of transcendent expression" (Bernstein 13–14). Such a lack of either reference or expressivity means not only that virtuosity, in default of these two options, thereby "produces and exposes the mundane and material conditions of production—need, greed, egotism, and calculation—common to both the journalistic page and the virtuoso's face" (Bernstein 14); it also means that feuilleton journalism muddies the distinction between real and ideal, content and expression, or rather, complicates the dialectic between these terms to the point where they lose meaning entirely.

Thus in the feuilleton, as practiced by virtuosi such as Heine and Roth, Hegel's dream of "objective humor" once again runs up against its own contradictions. The first of these is that it is only through contact with an ostensibly objective reality that the subject acquires subjectivity, but at the same time, this objective reality is only apprehensible by the already constituted, symbolically representing, and emotionally reactive subject. The second contradiction is that in "objective humor" the artist takes himself, his subjective being, as object, and yet this "object" must remain itself uncontaminated by subjectivity. The dangerous irony lurking within the notion of "objective humor" is the very charge leveled again and again against the feuilleton: that is, that this self-examination (compounded by the pressures of the mass media) leads ultimately to a literary *mise en abyme,* in which a promiscuous use of language does not just stand in for but *is* the vacuous content of the empty subject.[86] To this accusation Roth counters—with respect both to standard journalism and the Neue Sachlichkeit movement that might provisionally be described as objective humor's humor*less* self-purging—"The eyewitness account [. . .] is information *about* the event. The report reproduces the event itself. Indeed, it *is* the event" (*JRW3* 155). The demand for narrative objectivity forecloses the event-like quality of texts and occludes the conditions of objectivity's production, making it, in fact, the least "objective" literature of all.

Roth addresses the issue of literary rhetoric from the opposite but complementary angle in the 1922 "Nachruf auf den Lieben Leser" ("Obituary for the Dear Reader") (*JRW1* 854–57). "The dear reader is dead," Roth announces at the outset of the piece. "Now there are only just readers [Es leben nur noch Leser schlechthin]" (854). With these lines, Roth turns the obsolete rhetorical convention of apostrophizing the reader as "Dear Reader" into a figure endowed with substance and individuality, a "real" individual who can die an individual's death. But if, as Roth writes, "'style' is determined by the relation of the creator to his environment" and thus "a change of style means a change of this relation" (856), then the death of the "dear reader" in favor of the "reader without attributes" (855) is also the death of the ontotheological ("schaffenden") author and the individualized affective relationship to the surrounding world (including his readership) that such a figure permits. The former intimate connection between author and reader is reduced to a relationship of alienated consumption in which the newly *non*-addressed reader becomes a "receptor without echo [Empfänger ohne Widerhall]" (856). Roth attributes this change to the commercialization of literature (meanwhile keeping silent on the fact that the piece, published under Roth's initials in the *Berliner Börsen-Courier,* takes part in just this process), which is in turn linked to the technologization and depersonalization of modern life. This change is equated with a "break with 'romantic irony'" (856), defined as an attitude toward literature that "valued the producer over the work [den Erzeuger höher werten ließ als das Werk]" (856): the end of romantic irony means the end of creative genius and the beginning of a literature that is instrumentalized, dehumanized, fungible as any other commercial product.

And yet Roth's critique of the changing values of literature is not as straightforward or as sentimental as it may initially appear. The depersonalized grammar of the opening passage—"An announcement which ought to alarm no one [Eine Kunde, bei der niemand zu erschrecken braucht]" (*JRW1* 856)—as well as the neutral formula "Es leben," hint already at the uncanny truth of Roth's figure of speech, in which the highly formalized and impersonal grammatical constructions function as performative speech acts in a negating *and* in an affirming sense. The use of the impersonal voice "calls" "mere readers" into being, but these "mere readers" or "readers per se," defined precisely by their un-addressability, can only be apostrophized *in the lack of* direct apostrophe.[87] The alternative—which Roth's piece continually promises only to withhold—would be to *actually* address his own readers (whom he has however already consigned to attributelessness) as "dear readers" in defiance of current fashion. But Roth himself dismisses this possibility as an act of "mere irony, the result of a repressed and shame-impeded heartiness [nur Ironie, Folge verdrängter und durch Scham gehemmter Herzlichkeit]" (855), what Jonathan Culler has elsewhere called the "genuine embarrassment" of the apostrophe.[88] Roth bypasses this embarrassment, then, by addressing the reader through precisely a *lack* of address, that is, by addressing the reader's non-addressability and death as a subject. Henceforth the reader will be, not individualized *person,* but statistical *consumer:* since the very idea of apostrophe means that there must be a person to apostrophize, the disappearance of the apostrophe marks the disappearance of the person, but this "person," as Roth also freely admits, was only ever "the object of a constant apostrophizing" (854). Roth's eulogy for the "dear reader" is thus a eulogy for the apostrophe as such (the exact opposite of the "reader as such") and thus a eulogy for community, solidarity, the political, all that whose possibility is precisely what apostrophe apostrophizes.[89] Despite the ostensible nostalgia of Roth's argument, however, this eulogy means that the dear reader was always only the "dear reader," a trope which was itself a cipher, a *personification* (for community, etc.).[90] This fictional or figurative nature of the apostrophe means that the "dear reader" *already* assumes the non-presence or, indeed, the death of the "dear reader"; the personification of the abstract actuality of listening/speaking community *is* the "dear reader"'s very actuality and presence.

If the "dear reader" is thus simultaneously object of apostrophe and the very possibility of this apostrophe, the "mere reader" is at once the sign for the impossibility of apostrophe and the paradoxically apostrophized object of apostrophe-less speech. The word "apostrophe," from the Greek morphemes *apo,* "from," and *strophein,* "to turn" (of the same origin as the word "trope"), literally indicates a turning away. If this is originally meant as a turning from the dramatic action to address the audience, Roth's piece may be interpreted as a turn away from the "dear reader" to address his lack, and thus—as has been demonstrated above—the paradoxical act of apostrophizing no one in the impossibility of apostrophizing what has been revealed to be nothing more than apostrophe as such. It is the belated intimation of this "apostrophe as such," of the very figurative nature of the "dear reader," that, more than anything, contributes to bring about its death, as Roth himself admits in the acknowledgment that the "apostrophizing nevertheless outlived its object by several years" (*JRW1* 855). As the tautological "object of a constant apostrophizing" (*JRW1* 845), the object of the "dear reader" is in fact nothing but the fiction of itself. Culler's "embarrassment" of the apostrophe is just this embarrassment of being forced to acknowledge the text's rhetorical character over or indeed to the exclusion of its mimetic "reality." It is the "sign of a fiction which knows its own fictive nature."[91] In this sense, the death of the "dear reader" is not the death of something like a real symbiotic relationship between writer and consumer, as Roth might initially seem to imply, but rather the final going underground of the fictionality of the fictional. The death of the "dear reader" is for Roth the self-deception of a literature that thinks it can do without literary effects.

The apparently defunct literary device of the apostrophe—which, invoked by Roth, continues to haunt the piece from beyond—also recalls that other paradigmatic trope of literariness, that is, the rhetorical figure of *parabasis.* Indeed, the apostrophe's function is effectively identical with that of parabasis, insofar as both are a form of "the author's intrusion that disrupts the fictional illusion."[92] This connection lends a new and more substantial validity to Roth's claim that the death of the "dear reader" is concomitant with the break with romantic irony. For the author-subject of romantic irony is not identical with "himself," but rather with artworks' process of formation, in the words of Lacoue-Labarthe and Nancy: "insofar as the Subject is envisaged as operator, or as operation itself [. . .] it must come to itself as *artifet* [. . .], as the very artificiality of the process of the work's production."[93] Roth's implication that romantic irony is defined as the literary mode that "valued the producer over the work" (*JRW1* 856) should thus not be taken as a plea for the consideration of the author as personalized, humanist human subject. For, "contrary to what the customary banalizing imagery might lead one to believe, romanticism effectuates the Subject's decisive break with all 'naturality'" (Lacoue-Labarthe and Nancy 104), and despite Roth's lament for the fact that hardly anyone anymore seems to be interested in the author as person, what is performed in the figures of parabasis and apostrophe alike is *not* the breaking through of the real within a text, but an interruption of the text that "serves to prevent the all too readily mystified reader from confusing fact and fiction and from forgetting the essential negativity of the fiction" (de Man, "Temporality," 219).[94] The self-presentation of the author as author—and the dear reader as "dear reader"—disturbs the illusion of self-contained, authoritative narrative and thus also a text's claims to unmediated truth.[95] Roth's own continually renewed arguments against Neue Sachlichkeit must be read in this light. For Roth, Neue Sachlichkeit is the epitome of literary mystification in the de Manian sense of the term. Explicitly encouraging the reader to identify fiction and fact, Neue Sachlichkeit seeks to deflect charges of literariness (or in de Man's words, "the negativity of the fiction") and authorial subjectivism alike. Its documentary self-assurance requires no apostrophizing evocation of a receptive reader, because its texts are merely the neutral presentation of already available facts.

The contrast to this personality-less empiricism is, precisely, the figure of the genius—or else that translation of the genius into the age of mass media, the figure of the virtuoso, who in place of genial depth substitutes masterful execution and artistic play.[96] This is very close to what Roth is getting at with his reference to a "romantic irony" that "inhered eternally in the poet" (*JRW1* 857). If on the surface Roth appears to wholeheartedly embrace the pathos of the cult of genius and of origin, declaring in crescendo tones that "the word, fleshlier, more human than iron, steel, and type wheel, always betrayed the humanity of its origin" (857), it should also be recalled that the process of such humanistic revealing of the origin of the word is the same as the disruptive, interruptive apostrophe itself. Thus the figure which seems to confirm both the objectivity of the real and the real subjects at either end of the literary operation instead not only confirms the representational nature of both self and world, but also suggests the non-identity and the potential for buffoonish disruption that lies within or indeed constitutes representation, making self and world, as it were, ironic by definition.

In this way, just as Nietzsche's lines on the death of God are only the announcement of something that already long since happened,[97] Roth's death notice for the "dear reader" is but an announcement that the relationship of the creative, originating, writing subject to the personalized, receptive, reading subject-object (the "dear reader," writes Roth with erotic verve, "filled up with well-nigh bodily warmth the cool, isolated world of the poet" [*JRW1*

854]) was always opposed, not only to the self-satisfied illusions of a supposedly unmediated reportage but also to the closed circle of the relationship between author and reader itself. It is thus no coincidence that the last sentence of Roth's piece—"The 'dear reader' must, in a manner of speaking, certify his own existence as addressee [Der 'liebe Leser' muß gewissermaßen seine eigene Richtexistenz bescheinigen]" (857)—has buried within it the very word that in the German tradition signifies that play of appearances which prevents unmediated access to the real: *Schein.* The existence of the "dear reader" as "dear reader" is only so by virtue of his *Selbst-Bescheinigung:* not just his "self-certification" or "self-authentication"—or perhaps his "self-authorization"—but also, literally, his "self-appearancing" or indeed "self-semblancing." Like the suspect non-I I of the virtuoso performer, the "dear reader," together with the author who interrupts the fiction of his narrative to address him, exists in a liminal zone of subjectivity, a space of textual play devoid of either the blunt earnestness of Neue Sachlichkeit or the empathic realism of "objective humor." It is rather the defenders of *Sachlichkeit* in its various forms and the *murderers* of the "dear reader" who represent the latest assertion of individual subjectivity and personality, this time not in showy displays of technical skill but precisely in the claim to neutrality and transparence that hides an actual tendentiousness and disavowed rhetoricity. So long as it lived, the figure of the "dear reader" helped to keep this irony of objectivity on the surface, demystified and tongue-in-cheek. With the death of the "dear reader," however, this comedy of the irony of representation goes underground.

Laugh-Cabinets, or an Elegy for Irony

Nevertheless, for Roth, this rhetoric of objectivity is—once again—showing its cracks: "The scenery has been torn down. That is the—provisional—outcome of the year 1918 [Die Kulissen sind zerstört. Das ist das—vorläufige—Ergebnis des Jahres 1918]" (*JRW2* 337). Roth's metaphor in this passage echoes that of Carl Schmitt in his nearly contemporaneous description of the modern condition: "Today the 'backstage' that conceals the real movement of reality is constructed everywhere. This betrays the insecurity of the time and its profound sense of being deceived" (Schmitt, *Political Romanticism,* 14). Roth's own complaint, however, is *not* about the construction of spectacular theater flats which hide a "real movement of reality," but instead precisely about these flats' *destruction.* Unlike Schmitt, Roth's conception of authority—both political and literary/linguistic—is emphatically a theatrical, or rather a post-theatrical one, in which the performance alone grants validity, even as this validity is prevented by its performativity from ever claiming definitiveness. It is in *this* sense that Roth can speak, in the short story "Die Büste des Kaisers" ("The Bust of the Emperor") (*JRW5* 655–76), of a Habsburg Empire done in by its jokesters more than its revolutionaries":[98] performativity is *of* irony, but irony destroys the naturalism of the performance it helps to bring about.

One of Roth's major emblems for the destruction of such naturalism, to which he returns repeatedly in his feuilletons over the span of several years, is the *panopticon.*[99] This is not the panopticon of Bentham's model prison or Foucault's disciplinary paradigm, but the far more profane institution of the wax cabinet as popular spectacle (specifically, the famous Castan's Panopticon, which stood on Berlin's Schloßplatz from 1869 to 1922). *Theatrum mundi* and memento mori all at once, the panopticon gathers together the wax simulacra of historical personages side by side with tableaux of criminal or pornographic acts. The dead but permanent materiality of the panopticon's figures makes the institution already one in which one can see "how segments of world history, formed in wax, are released from the pitiless law of the fleetingness of all that happens" (*JRW1* 640). This elegiac, or rather death-in-life, nature of the panopticon is moreover magnified by the fact that, by the time of Roth's writing, the panopticon is also a form of entertainment *in decline,* whose slightly shabby pleasures have been superseded by more spectacular forms of spectacle such as the cinema and the live nude revue. This doubly defunct quality of the panopticon, however, does not mean that in his feuilletons Roth mourns the authenticity of a lost form. For the panopticon itself, as Roth makes clear, was always ever a spectacle and a copy, whose "sole merit [. . .] was the unintentional comedy with which it balanced out the pathos of the world and transformed it into a kind of laugh-cabinet" (*JRW1* 939). As in Vischer's conception of theism's rigid Godhead (see *UEK* 166–67), a world representing itself in all seriousness, especially when replicated in the cheesy immobility of the waxworks, in the end makes itself that much more vulnerable to ridicule.

Despite this inherent risibility of the panopticon, Roth's evocation of its outmoded *theatrum mundi* also calls to mind Benjamin's image of a world in ruins as reflected in the baroque *Trauerspiel*, together with his description of allegory as the exemplary figure of this ruination, particularly in contrast to the symbol's promise of "organic totality."[100] Such a potential has not escaped the attention of Claudio Magris, who, citing Benjamin, maintains that Roth's early novels constitute "an allegory whose unambiguousness makes possible a reaction to the modern confusion of signs, and which instead presents clear, unambiguous signs that—far removed from the polyvalence of the symbol—assert their secure meaning."[101] This brief citation suffices to demonstrate that Magris's notion of allegory is precisely the kind *criticized* by Benjamin and complicated definitively by de Man, in which concrete images stand in, rebus-like, for equally fixed concepts.[102] Besides the fact that what Magris calls the "unambiguous signs" and "secure meaning" of Roth's writings—not to mention his "unadorned style" (Magris, *Mythos*, 259)—is a matter of no little doubt, after the work of Benjamin and de Man it is plain that the presence of allegory must be understood not as the mark of a self-enclosed and stable literature, but, much to the contrary, as the mark of a literature whose own inner irony has finally become manifest.

Likewise, the panopticon as it appears in Roth's feuilletons is no simple emblem for the end of history, its ruins an image in miniature of the ruins of empire, but is rather a doubling of this emblem or indeed an "allegory of irony" in the de Manian sense (see "Temporality," 228), the ruined *theater* of the *theater* of the imperial performance. Indeed, Castan's Panopticon, once the presentation of the whole world in its seeming totality, is not only ruined but also transformed on the auction block into the modern virtuality (and, arguably, totality) par excellence: that is, into *capital*. The auctioning-off of the panopticon into its liquid assets gives the final lie to its claim to be a microcosm of the world at large, even as it continues to function as a sign for the loss of metaphysical coherence in an increasingly commercialized world. Roth's tale of the panopticon's end is thus also two-faced, albeit in a manner quite different from Brod's (in 1914 still imperial) state. On the one hand, of course, is the panopticon as image of the world as fragment and ruin; but on the other hand, there is the fragmentation of the metaphor for the world that is the panopticon itself, a fragmentation of the metaphorical legibility of the world that was, moreover, always already there as the world's own condition of possibility.

In this way, the end of the panopticon's *theatrum mundi* and its pretensions to a transcendent total representation *also* offers the possibility for a humor that "realizes [. . .] in the brokenness of the medium of reflection, in the deficiency of subjective refraction, the very contingency of the creation of forms,"[103] and from there the possibility of an ironic comedy of the very contingency of form in all its applications. Against every pathos of authenticity and stability of meaning, Roth's celebrated "nostalgia" is (at least in his feuilletons) in fact a future-looking nostalgia for illusion, for play, for the sustained ironies that, like all other forms of "miscegenation [Mischehen]" (*JRW1* 8), the world in which he lived appeared less and less willing to tolerate. Like Hamlet, Roth's tragedy is his irony; not, however, in the fact that he had ever come under its influence, but in the fact that the forces of history and the deformations of posterity alike gradually conspired to deny him access to it. And if Roth's novels, as so many have observed, draw attention to the figure of the wanderer and the exile, the person without state, homeland, or legal order,[104] perhaps the first order from which Roth is cast out is that of the "right of residence of the imagination [Heimatsrecht der Phantasie]" (*JRW2* 516), of jokes, of play, of the comic. As Roth, strolling around the toy fair, rhetorically asks: "The thrones on which the gods used to sit have been smashed to pieces. But *must* gods sit on thrones?" (*JRW2* 516). Yes, Roth answers himself: but only the ridiculous gods, those that would attempt to rescue us from the ironies from which we are not actually to be saved.

Conclusion

✦

Last Laughs

> As soon as irony is related to a conclusion, it manifests itself as comic.
>
> —Søren Kierkegaard, *The Concept of Irony*

A short fable by Heinrich von Kleist runs as follows:

> Two honest gun dogs, who, having been made clever fellows in the school of hunger, went for everything on the ground they could catch sight of, came across a bird. The bird, embarrassed to be caught out of his element, hopped all around, now here, now there, and his antagonists were already celebrating their triumph; but just at that moment, too violently pressed, the bird bestirred his wings and vaulted into the air. The other two, those heroes of the hunt, stood there like oysters and tucked their tails between their legs, gaping up at him.
>
> ———
>
> Wit, when you raise yourself into the air: how the sages all stand and stare after you![1]

What so often appears potentially graspable in certain theories of wit, humor, jokes, and the comic is perhaps only a result of having removed the comic temporarily from its "proper element": that is—as Hugo von Hofmannsthal once observed and as I have attempted in this book to prove—the element of irony.[2] The promise of the comic's terrestrial capture is thus only a short-lived victory, for the taking-flight of the comic happens in just that loss of solid ground for which irony is, precisely, the figure. At the same time, just as the actual density of the atmosphere is usually only perceivable insofar as it lifts up buoyant bodies, the omnipresent "element" of irony, otherwise seemingly ethereal, becomes only truly discernible in those moments when the comic suddenly takes flight within it. For, as Friedrich Schlegel points out, irony has almost as many modes and manifestations as the air itself.

What begins in the schools of rhetoric of ancient Greece as a means of strategically manipulating denotative meaning becomes, in the wake of Kant's epistemological revolution, the privileged term for the utopian potential of the subject to continually create the world through the sheer vitality of his or her power of imagination. The post-Enlightenment optimism expressed in this term was as localized as it was fleeting, however, and it was not long before such continuous creation came to be seen, falsely or not, no longer as "the actual infinity, by means of the fragmentary apparatus, of the very process of truth,"[3] but instead as a *merely* fragmentary apparatus or indeed as fragments per se, haphazard shards of phenomena deprived of both the conceptual cohesion and the material reality that might establish moral value or cognitive intelligibility. In such a view—exemplified by but hardly confined to the post-romantic backlash—irony can be nothing but nonsense. Indeed, for this view, irony literally *is* nonsense, the total flouting of the order of things or the destruction of the comprehensibility of everything existing, and if there is a laughter that can be ascribed to it all, it is only that of contempt.

Such cultural lines in the sand have survived well into the present day. As both academic subject and cultural attitude, irony is perpetually being declared to be over, superseded at long last by a reawakened interest in emotional sincerity, logical clarity, or empirical reference. And yet, despite how it may often seem, irony is a matter neither merely of university politics nor of generational fashions, but instead refers to something far more basic, with effects and aftereffects that are, indeed, "incredibly long-lasting" (*OI* 267; 208). As irony's most formidable adversary, Hegel, knew, irony is thoroughly a question of *knowing and its foundations*—and, even more, the lack thereof. Irony as *problem* thus emerges when perception and understanding are thrown back onto the subject and his or her spatiotemporal conditions (which subsequent challenges to the position of the subject do not remove but only compound), when there are no longer any "things in themselves" to count on, nor origins to which to take recourse or eschatons to be foreseen. Schlegel's "progressive universal poetry" and Hegel's "world spirit" are but fraternally twinned solutions—the one under the sign of an infinitely unleashed geniality, the other of the slow-grinding mills of God—to the problem Kant's philosophy (though not just Kant's philosophy) unwittingly unleashed on the world of how to think phenomena in the absence of metaphysical certainty without ending up in either solipsism or nihilism, egoism or despair. And yet both of these proposed solutions—as Schlegel emphatically came to realize, and as Hegel vigorously tried to deny—are in the end only *deferrals* of the problem of irony in favor of a not-yet-present fullness of signification, or even irony *itself* as the present lack of such fullness—and *not* irony's conclusion.

For *as soon as irony is related to a conclusion, it manifests itself as comic* (*CI* 145). Irony's conclusion is comic, of course, in part because conclusion is seemingly the one thing that the anti-conceptualism (or, in Kierkegaardian terms, the "negativity") of irony cannot allow. And yet at the same time it is only in its being *related* to a conclusion, in *its manifestation as comic,* that irony reveals its true nature.[4] In the comic, irony achieves its "eternal validity" (see *CI* 329): not, indeed, as the "humor" which keeps its reserve from the phenomenal world in more or less direct reference to a higher transcendence, nor as a mere limited "mastery over irony [. . .] within the strictly localized sphere of aesthetic production,"[5] but rather, as a *fundamentally* aesthetic, that is to say, a *manifest* irony which toys in every sense of the word with the forms of phenomena and the relations between them. The "conclusion" to which this irony is related is not its ending or its decision—least of all its settling down in the lumpy armchair of humorous forbearance—but rather its fixing in a performative moment, its being made to show itself as determinate representation that is *of* and *about* irony at one and the same time.

This is the staging of irony, the *comic irony* that has been at issue throughout these pages. As the ironic staging of itself, comic irony is an irony that avoids irony's three major anti-ironic temptations: the utopian/romantic (or indeed, "messianic"), which gathers irony despite everything into the purity of a hoped-for holism; the melancholic/modernist, which looks out (be it in condemnation or bitter assent) onto the broken remnants of a bygone meaningfulness; and the sentimental/humanist, which validates irony insofar as it speaks to the inherent finitude of the individual vis-à-vis the absolute and the correspondingly bittersweet destiny of humankind. To be sure, these are oversimplifications of the various position-takings in regard to irony of the past two and a half centuries, and among all of these stances there is not only overlap, complication, and dialectical tension, but also historical relevance and import. To every age its irony. And yet, despite the inexhaustibility of the shapes that irony may take, it can perhaps also be said that comic irony alone maintains the privilege of being the only form of irony that is still actually *ironic.* If wit or the comic is that moment when the heterogeneity of thought takes flight in a particular and succinct formation, then irony is the sustaining element of this heterogeneity, the real impossibility of a positive absolute meaning. Some, of course, have regarded this impossibility as, variously, a cause for sorrow, a confirmation of madness, or a rallying cry to pick up the pieces. However, for those who subscribe to the ethos of comic irony, this impossibility also appears as an opportunity—more, as the *necessity*—to play. *Comic irony is play in the ruins of absolute meaning.* The "ends" of irony are the performances of this play: those moments in which, eluding mourning and reconciliation alike, irony, finally in its own element, makes its comic appearance.

NOTES

Introduction

1. Hofmannsthal, "Drei kleine Betrachtungen," 40–55.

2. Hofmannsthal's hoax has taken in more than a few unsuspecting readers, who failed to suspect the irony of his own philology. See, e.g., Altenhofer, *"Die Ironie der Dinge,"* esp. 31 and 37–38, as well as 186 in the editor's afterword. For an exposure of Hofmannsthal's hoax, as well as a discussion of the things Novalis *did* say about comedy, see Endres, "Novalis und das Lustspiel."

3. See *VA* §54, 143; 201: "[Wit] takes interest in no being, only in relationships [Der Witz (. . .) nimmt an keinem Wesen Anteil, sondern nur an dessen Verhältnissen]."

4. Schopenhauer, *World as Will and Representation,* vol. 1, §13, 58–60; also Schopenhauer, *World as Will and Representation,* vol. 2, 91–92.

5. Schlegel's list is worth quoting at length: "The first and most distinguished [kind of irony] is coarse irony. It is to be found in the real nature of things and is one of the most widespread of substances; it is properly at home in the history of mankind. Next there is fine or delicate irony; then extra-fine [. . .]. This kind of irony is also to be found in poets, as well as straightforward irony, a type that flourishes most purely and originally in old gardens where wonderfully lovely grottoes lure the sensitive friend of nature into their cool wombs only to besplash him plentifully from all sides with water and thereby wipe him clean of delicacy. Further, dramatic irony; that is, when an author has written three acts, then unexpectedly turns into another man and now has to write the last two acts. Double irony, when two lines of irony run parallel side-by-side without disturbing each other: one for the gallery, the other for the boxes, though a few little sparks may also manage to get behind the scenes. Finally, there is the irony of irony [. . .]. For example, if one speaks of irony without using it, as I have just done; if one speaks of irony ironically without in the process being aware of having fallen into a far more noticeable irony; if one can't disentangle oneself from irony anymore, as seems to be happening in this essay on incomprehensibility" (*OI* 266–67; 369).

6. This phrase refers, not insignificantly, to the character of Hamlet, who similarly appears in Hegel's *Phenomenology* as a marker of the transition between tragic and comic consciousness that precedes philosophy (see *PS* §737, 446–47; 537–38). See also Haverkamp, "Im Auge des Orkans. Shakespeare und die Philosophen," esp. 72 on the "discovery of the modern, romantic 'character' " as a product of the German romantics' Shakespeare reception.

7. Compare 2 Cor. 3:17: "Denn der HERR ist der Geist; wo aber der Geist des HERRN ist, da ist Freiheit" (Luther Bible); "Now the Lord is that Spirit: and where the Spirit of the Lord is, there is liberty" (King James Bible).

8. See e.g., Jean Paul's statement that "the comic is thus the enjoyment, or imagination and poetry, of the whole understanding released and at liberty, which develops playfully, dancing to and fro among the three syllogistic or flowery chains [Das Komische ist also der Genuß oder die Phantasie und Poesie des ganz für das Freie entbundnen Verstandes, welcher sich an drei Schluß- oder Blumenketten spielend entwickelt und daran hin- und widertanzt]" (*VA* §30, 86; 122).

9. For a lucid summary of the critique of romantic irony from within the ironic tradition (particularly in Nietzsche, Derrida, and de Man), see Colebrook, *Irony,* esp. 95–110.

10. De Man, naturally with reference to Kierkegaard, denies that irony is a concept *sensu stricto,* in that it can not only not be subsumed under a distinct unit of meaning, but is the very troubling of all such units of meaning. See de Man, "Irony," esp. 163.

11. See Schopenhauer, *World as Will and Representation,* vol. 1, 59–60.

12. Bergson's theory of the comic is discussed in greater detail in chapters 1 and 3.

13. On pun and ambiguity, see Schopenhauer, *World as Will and Representation,* vol. 1, §13, 61. On intention, censorship, morality, and the social function of jokes, see *World as Will and Representation,* vol. 2, 99–101.

14. Jeffrey Mehlman argues that the comic as Freud conceives it "is quite simply *identical* to the structure of the narcissistically constituted ego," whereas the triangulation necessary to the joke represents a melancholic admission of loss and thus a certain emotional maturity. See Mehlman, "How to Read Freud on Jokes," 458.

15. A point on which Freud is emphatic in his conclusion to the *Interpretation of Dreams*: "the unconscious must be assumed to be the general basis of psychical life. The unconscious is the larger sphere, which includes within it the smaller sphere of the unconscious. Everything conscious has an unconscious preliminary stage; whereas what is unconscious may remain at that stage and nevertheless claim to be regarded as having the full value of a psychical process. The unconscious is the true psychical reality." Freud, *Interpretation of Dreams,* 612–13.

16. Alenka Zupančič suggests that the reason why the joke should be funny at all is because the *punch line* distracts from the joke's real significance as a "joke about the very functioning of our symbolic universe as constituted through signifiers." That is, whereas Freud posits the joke-work as a semantic diversion from its moral *content,* Zupančič posits the joke's moral content as a diversion from its semiotic *work.* Zupančič, *The Odd One In,* 142.

17. Incidentally, as Falke himself notes in his memoirs, this museum was the first museum for applied art and design on the European continent. See Falke, *Lebenserinnerungen,* 187–188.

18. Freud repeats two of Falke's retold Irish jokes (both, curiously enough, having to do with the Duke of Wellington): one in the footnote on *JRU* 61; 64, and another on *JRU* 71; 75–76.

19. See, e.g., Oring, *The Jokes of Sigmund Freud.* Oring's book, however, amounts mainly to an argument for the latent anti-Semitism, and thus fallaciousness, of Freud's theories, an argument all the more strange in that Oring uses a vulgarized version of a supposedly discredited psychoanalysis to support it.

20. Sarah Kofman interprets Freud's focus on Jewish jokes as, on the one hand, a "prime de séduction," a setup, by which Freud's gentile readership is seduced

into uncomfortable truths through the (false) assurance that the joke is not on *them,* and on the other hand, a symptom of the refused/desired debt to the father in the fetishized stereotype of the neurotic Jew. See Kofman, *Pourquoi rit-on?* esp. 27–48.

21. Wittgenstein, *Wittgenstein's Lectures,* 39–40.

22. Compare Lüdemann, *Mythos und Selbstdarstellung,* esp. 171–72.

23. In the programmatic essay "The Resistance to Theory," de Man both indirectly answers Wittgenstein's charge and grants it a qualified truth when he writes: "if the condition of existence of an entity is itself particularly critical, then the theory of this entity is bound to fall back into the pragmatic. The difficult and inconclusive history of literary theory indicates that this is indeed the case for literature in an even more manifest manner than for other verbalized occurrences *such as jokes, for example, or even dreams.*" De Man, "The Resistance to Theory," 5, emphasis added.

24. Let it be said that Freud's compositional method in this book—particularly the techniques of delay, displacement, and analogy—also highly resemble his own description of the joke-work, whose punch line is then nothing less than psychoanalysis itself.

25. Felman, *The Scandal of the Speaking Body,* 86; on the joke as linguistic/cognitive phenomenon, see also Preisendanz, *Über den Witz,* esp. 17–31.

26. Samuel Weber argues that the presence of the joke "is not that of a representation, but of the *process of representing 'itself.'* " Weber, "Laughing in the Meanwhile," 705–6.

27. Compare Fenves, "*Chatter,*" 114: "To question whether wordplay [. . .] and thus the word that falls prey to such play, constitutes the essence of language, to question whether the interrogative mood determines the mode of language through which one can relate to oneself as a self-same being, is jest. To jest in all seriousness is to question whether language itself, and not that questionable language whose seriousness can never be assured, has indeed come into being." On the joke as a "meaningful discourse about the *crisis* of signification," see also Virno, *Multitude,* 106, also 165–67.

28. Freud himself notes the close affinity between jokes and slips of the tongue. See Freud, *On the Psychopathology of Everyday Life,* 77–80.

29. In his translation of *Jokes and Their Relation to the Unconscious,* James Strachey has—consciously or unconsciously—picked up on the compulsive punning of Freud's language, felicitously rendering the bath joke's "Verbum mit unabgeschwächter Bedeutung" (*JRU* [German] 50) as "the verb with its sense unwatered down" (*JRU* [English] 49).

30. Weber, *The Legend of Freud,* 123.

31. See Blumenberg, *Das Lachen der Thrakerin.* This book is an expanded version of Blumenberg's opening essay for the Poetik und Hermeneutik group's volume on the comic, "Der Sturz des Protophilosophischen."

32. See *JRU* 14; 11 and Kofman 61. The decisive point here is the fact that a theory of the joke, like that of psychoanalysis in general, must proceed by example rather than logical speculation. As Freud states in the first sentence of the main body of his text: "Let us follow up a lead presented to us by chance and consider the first example of a joke that we came across [Wir folgen einem Winke des Zufalls und greifen das erste Witzbeispiel auf]" (*JRU* 16; 14).

33. The French language, of course, renders this mirroring/caricature particularly conspicuous, as the word *esprit* translates both *Witz* and *Geist.*

34. See Nancy, "Laughter, Presence"; also Davis, *Breaking Up [at] Totality,* esp. 28.

35. On repetition in the comic/the joke, see *JRU* 226; 258; also Weber, *Legend,* 130–36; Zupančič, *The Odd One In,* 149–82.

36. Weber finds the radical implications of Freud's joke theory best elaborated in the joke-type to which Freud himself only devoted a footnote, the explicitly anti-synthetic "shaggy dog joke" ("Unsinnswitz" or "Aufsitzer"): "If the joke then refuses to provide the meaning it dangles before the listener, then its operation cannot be described as pure and simple nonsense. For such jokes 'play' games with the desire of the listener to find 'an intelligible context,' the desire that, as we have seen, is at the origin of 'secondary elaboration.' This desire involves nothing less than the narcissistic striving of the ego to unify, bind, and synthesize, and thereby to construct that meaningful, self-contained subject, a self-consciousness." Weber, *Legend,* 153. For Freud on the shaggy dog joke, see *JRU* 169–70; 154–55, note 1.

37. Ted Cohen describes what he calls "critical" or (to my mind problematically) "Jewish" humor as a joke whose critique is at once outward-aimed and self-implicating. While such jokes obviously exist, Cohen's emphasis on the joke's ridiculing function—be it two-pronged—still keeps it situated on the level of judgment and normative meaning. See Cohen, *Jokes,* 67–68.

38. Another way of understanding the "subversiveness" of the joke, of course, is in relation to the criteria of objectivity and normativity themselves to which Felman (speaking with Lacan and Nietzsche), for example, points (see Felman 84–111). Even in this case, however, the notion of "subversion" may be misleading, lending itself to precisely the kind of overcoming that it would seek to avoid.

39. Its ur-form, however, is perhaps the carnival as conceived by Bakhtin, whose structure as the exact inversion of forms of solemnity and periodic exception to the rule makes it both a less emancipatory and less universally applicable model than is often assumed.

40. See, e.g., La Farge, "Comedy's Intention," esp. 135–36.

41. Thus Deleuze, *Logic of Sense,* 72: "We do not seek in Freud an explorer of human depth and originary sense, but rather the prodigious discoverer of the machinery of the unconscious by means of which sense is produced always as a function of nonsense." See also the discussion of Lacan's "The Agency of the Letter in the Unconscious, or Reason Since Freud" in chapter 1.

42. Compare Kierkegaard: "as soon as irony is related to a conclusion, it manifests itself as comic, even though in another sense it frees the individual from the comic" (*CI* 145). See also the conclusion to the present work.

43. Massimo Cacciari, in his analysis of fin-de-siècle Vienna (from which Freud, incidentally, is conspicuously absent), describes the premises of Wittgenstein's *Tractatus Logico-Philosophicus* thus: "It is impossible to name a simple object; it is impossible to describe the totality of the world. Language can only denote situations or construct tautologies—that is, logical propositions. All that can be sensibly expressed resides within these limits." Cacciari, *Posthumous People,* 14. In this context, the "fundamentality" of which Cacciari accuses the Wittgenstein

of the *Tractatus* can be seen as an attempt to sidestep the whole problem of irony that the language of jokes has as its condition of utterance.

44. Novalis, *Schriften,* 425.

45. Emphatically *not* meant is also what Northrop Frye, in *Anatomy of Criticism,* calls "ironic comedy." Frye's anthropological definition of comedy as the genre of "playing at human sacrifice" centered on the institution of the *pharmakos* is basically indebted to the common punitive/cathartic notion of comedy, which will be critiqued below. See Frye, *Anatomy of Criticism,* esp. 36–46.

46. See Sigmund Freud, "Humor." In a different way, the term has also been strongly marked by Deleuze, who opposes it to irony (including romantic irony) as a horizontal comic of particularity versus a vertical comic of ideality. See Deleuze, *Logic of Sense,* 134–41. Still, Deleuze's hope that "nonsense and sense [will do] away with their relation of dynamic opposition in order to enter into the co-presence of a static genesis" and his definition of humor as "the coextensiveness of sense with nonsense" (*Logic of Sense* 140–41) is not entirely dissimilar to what is here meant by "comic irony," even if the story he tells is a somewhat different one.

Chapter One

1. Kierkegaard particularly emphasizes the moment of the *emergence* of the phenomenon of irony, namely "the historical turning point where subjectivity made its appearance for the first time" (*CI* 264) in the figure of Socrates. See also Newmark, *Irony on Occasion,* 11–12 and 65 on irony and history (or rather historicity) in Kierkegaard and generally.

2. Lukács, *Theory of the Novel,* 90. As is well known, Lukács's paradigmatic example of novelistic irony is Cervantes' very funny *Don Quixote,* but other of his examples, such as Goethe's *Wilhelm Meisters Lehrjahre* and Tolstoy's *Anna Karenina,* could hardly be accused of raising a chuckle.

3. De Man, "The Rhetoric of Temporality," 216.

4. Hobbes, *Leviathan,* 125.

5. See, e.g., Bakhtin 5–12 on the "utopian character of festive laughter" (12) and 73–96 on medieval laughter's "indissoluble and essential relation to freedom" (89); and *JRU* 117–28; 131–43, on the joke in relation to the overcoming of inhibition.

6. Baudelaire's emphasis on laughter as a byproduct of the human condition (usually divested of its air of scandal) has been taken up by more than one theorist of the comic in the century or so following. See, e.g., Plessner, *Lachen und Weinen*; Ritter, "Über das Lachen"; Critchley, *On Humour,* esp. 25–38 on the relation of human beings to their non-human animal counterparts; and Heller, *Immortal Comedy,* esp. 199–214. Alenka Zupančič, meanwhile, helpfully modifies the usual anthropological thesis to argue that the comic is not simply a product of human beings' situatedness between the animals and the gods, the body we have and the soul we are, but rather that even "our finitude is always a *failed finitude*—one could say a finitude with a leak in it." Zupančič, *The Odd One In,* 52.

7. Benjamin, *Origin of German Tragic Drama,* 186. Benjamin specifically names this symbolic totality—in an observation that will become relevant with

the discussion of "objective humor," below—as that which classical humanism "venerated [. . .] in the human figure" (*Origin* 186).

8. See Geulen, *The End of Art,* esp. 21–22.

9. See, e.g., *A* 8–11; *AI* 21–26. See also Hamacher, "(The End of Art with the Mask)," esp. 114–18; and Agamben, *The Man Without Content,* esp. 53–56.

10. On romantic criticism as the "conjoint sublation of philosophy and of poetry," see Lacoue-Labarthe and Nancy, *The Literary Absolute,* particularly chapter 4, 101–19, here 119.

11. Schlegel, *Gespräch über die Poesie,* 324.

12. See Benjamin, *Origin of German Tragic Drama,* esp. 159–63 and 174–77; and de Man, "Rhetoric of Temporality," esp. 188–92 and 207–8.

13. Compare de Man, "Sign and Symbol in Hegel's *Aesthetics,*" 104, on allegory in Hegel as a split between the generality of grammar (or the grammatical subject) and the specificity of predication: "For discourse to be meaningful, this separation has to take place, yet it is incompatible with the necessary generality of all meaning," thus "allegory functions, categorically and logically, like the defective cornerstone of the whole system."

14. Manfred Frank defines Schlegel's concept of allegory concisely, if not incontestably, as "the tendency towards the absolute in the form of finitude itself." Frank, "Allegorie, Witz, Fragment, Ironie," 129. See also Christoph Menke, *Die Souveränität der Kunst,* 39–43.

15. Such as those—among the myriad attempts to think a possible future for art after Hegel—suggested by Dieter Henrich in "Art and Philosophy of Art Today: Reflections with Reference to Hegel."

16. See Kierkegaard's similarly inclined (if more nuanced) comments on irony and "mood" in *The Concept of Irony,* esp. the chapter entitled "Irony after Fichte" (*CI* 272–323). Of particular interest is that where Hegel sees jokes and fancy as the null point of art, Kierkegaard, in his discussion of Tieck, adjudges that romantic poetry ultimately devolves into "the musical element" as exemplified by nursery rhymes: "Such poems must now, of course, be considered the ultimate, because here mood—and mood, after all, is all-important—has absolute sway and is utterly free, since all content is negated" (*CI* 307).

17. See Preisendanz's etymology of "humor" in the *Reallexikon der deutschen Literaturwissenschaft.* Preisendanz contends that at least the German usage of the term "humor" as a category related to comedy and laughter begins strictly with Jean Paul, and that all attempts to apply the term in this sense to previous eras are anachronistic.

18. Also worth noting in this context is Hegel's basic distrust of laughter: "Laughing as such is an outburst which yet ought not to remain unrestrained if the Ideal is not to be lost [Lachen überhaupt ist der Ausbruch des Herausplatzens, das jedoch nicht haltungslos bleiben darf, wenn nicht das Ideal verlorengehen soll]" (*A* 159; *AI* 210). Certain kinds of smiling, as well as the tranquil laughter of the gods, are, however, permitted.

19. See also *A* 295–96; *AI* 381–82. As in the passage quoted above, Jean Paul is here the exemplary target.

20. Karl Heinz Bohrer further notes the nationalistic impetus of the discourse on wit, specifically in terms of German idealism's backlash against the culture

of the French *âge des Lumières*. See Karl Heinz Bohrer, "Sprachen der Ironie—Sprachen des Ernstes," esp. 34.

21. See Preisendanz, *Über den Witz*, 7–8.

22. See Nancy, "*Menstruum Universale*," 253: "The first *Witz*, then, is knowledge that cannot be acquired, that is unprovable (as opposed to *mathemata*), knowledge that perceives [*savoir-voir*], that grasps the *idea* at a glance and distinguishes with lucidity."

23. Such an observation allows the Kantian commonplace that laughter is "an affect resulting from the sudden transformation of a heightened expectation into nothing [der plötzlichen Verwandlung einer gespannten Erwartung in nichts]" (*CPJ* §54, 209; 229) to be read as a more than merely empirical claim.

24. Adding, "in the coupling of reason and caprice emerges humor [wo sich Vernunft und Willkühr paaren, Humor]." Novalis, *Schriften*, 425.

25. Nancy, "*Menstruum Universale*," 255. Perhaps the most prominent example of wit or funniness as a product of the crisis of judgment is Foucault's famous opening to *The Order of Things*, in which an outburst of laughter in response to Borges's "Chinese Encyclopedia" "shattered [. . .] all the familiar landmarks of my thought [. . .] breaking up all the ordered surfaces and all the planes with which we are accustomed to tame the wild profusion of existing things." Foucault, *The Order of Things*, xvi. In the context of Foucault's subsequent discussion of the shift from analogical to analytical thinking in the age of the Enlightenment, this century's especial interest in the phenomenon of wit becomes strikingly clear: wit is the residue of analogy in the age of analysis.

26. Hegel does not rule out entirely the role of originality in art, but maintains that, in opposition to "mere manner [bloßer Manier]" (*A* 291; *AI* 380), "the genuine originality of the artist, as of the work of art, lies solely in his being animated by the rationality of the inherently true content of the subject matter" (*A* 298; *AI* 385). The difference between Kant and Hegel in this respect, meanwhile, may be one of quantity and not quality: where Kant sees mere aberration, Hegel sees real threat.

27. See, e.g., *A* 1174–81; *AIII* 495–504, "Verhältnis des dramatischen Kunstwerks zum Publikum ("Relation of the Dramatic Work of Art to the Public"). It may also be noted that Hegel is here explicitly if unintentionally contradicting himself, specifically in his earlier designation of Jean Paul as a "favorite [beliebter] humorist" (*A* 601; *AII* 230).

28. See Aristotle, *On Interpretation*, esp. 117.

29. Benjamin, *Origin of German Tragic Drama*, 178. Making the connection between romantic irony/humor and baroque allegory still more explicit, Benjamin further calls Jean Paul "the greatest allegorist in German literature" (*Origin* 188).

30. Jacques Lacan, "The Agency of the Letter in the Unconscious," 175; "L'instance de la lettre dans l'inconscient," 508.

31. See Flieger, *The Purloined Punch Line*, esp. 24–39 and 53.

32. See Weber, *Rückkehr zu Freud*, 89–96; also Haverkamp, *Metapher*, 73–74.

33. Compare Zupančič 214–16, although she rather locates play's suspension "between life and signifier" (215).

34. This dynamic is repeated in Adorno's assessment of art after the "catastrophe of meaning [Katastrophe des Sinns]," although Adorno no longer frames it in

terms of a possible reversion to nonsense but as a dialectic of "absolute responsibility" and "absolute irresponsibility," in which the latter is mere creative play in disregard of historical and epistemological disaster. Adorno, *Aesthetic Theory,* 22 and 39; *Ästhetische Theorie,* 40 and 64. See also Weitzman, "No *Fun*: Aporias of Pleasure in Adorno's Aesthetic Theory."

35. Schiller, *On the Aesthetic Education of Man,* 105; *Über die ästhetische Erziehung des Menschen,* 236.

36. Jean Paul also calls irony "epic humor," although, in contrast to Hegel, he distinguishes irony's "epic," "objective" quality from what he calls the "lyric" or "subjective" aspect of the comic. See *VA* §37, 107–11; 148–54.

37. Schlegel, *Philosophische Fragmente,* 85.

38. Cicero, *De Oratore,* §203, 163. Compare Quintilian, *The Orator's Education,* 8.6, 457–59.

39. Quintilian observes that the importance, in (verbal) irony, of knowing the frame of reference "is true of most Tropes [. . .] because the thing said may be literally true in another context." Quintilian, *The Orator's Education,* 8.6, 457.

40. See Booth, *A Rhetoric of Irony,* esp. 11–14.

41. This demand for a "rigorously logical certainty" would be what those attacking and those defending irony on pragmatic grounds alike reject, arguing that hermeneutics is always a relative matter anyway, and the demand for interpretive certainty—or the radical questioning of hermeneutics in the default of same—is thus a reductio ad absurdum. See, e.g., Booth, *A Rhetoric of Irony,* 216–21, and, in a more sympathetic vein, Rorty, *Contingency, Irony, and Solidarity,* esp. 3–22. This objection has merit; nevertheless, the rejection of irony's deeper implications poses more problems than it solves—not least of which is the problem of the source of the normative claims that a controlled irony would require. For an overview of the terms of this debate, see Colebrook, *Irony,* esp. 16–21 and 41–46.

42. Werner Hamacher has elaborated the political threat that irony holds for Hegel: "If the irony of the natural shape lies in its dissolution into the purposes of self-consciousness and in the loss of itself as figure, then the irony of communal existence, of the polis, lies in the contrast between its claims to universality and the particular interests it falls victim to [. . .]. Thus once again, as immanent contrast, irony shatters the figure—in this case, that of the demos organized in the polis—and liberates its elements, political individuals: they become actors in a political comedy who self-consciously use the masks of the abstract legal person for their own ends." Hamacher, "'End of Art,'" 119.

43. Compare Kierkegaard's distinction between irony and mere "dissimulation": unlike the latter, irony "also denotes the subjective pleasure as the subject frees himself by means of irony from the restraint in which the continuity of life's conditions holds him [. . .]. Irony [. . .] has no purpose; its purpose is immanent in itself and is a metaphysical purpose. The purpose is nothing other than the irony itself" (*CI* 255–56). See also Ronell, *Stupidity,* 148 on the philosophical affinities between Schlegel and Georges Bataille and the necessary "pornographic accent" of their twin challenges to understandability.

44. See Goethe, *Faust,* 20, lines 376–85: "Drum hab' ich mich der Magie ergeben, / Ob mir durch Geistes Kraft und Mund / Nicht manch Geheimnis würde kund; / Daß ich nicht mehr mit saurm Schweiß / Zu sagen brauche, was ich nicht

weiß; / Daß ich erkenne, was die Welt / Im Innersten zusammenhält, / Schau' alle Wirkenskraft und Samen / Und tu' nicht mehr in Worten kramen [Therefore I have devoted myself to magic / To see if through spirit's strength and mouth / Secrets might not be made known / So that I no longer, with sour sweat / Need to speak of what I myself do not know; / So that I understand that which the world / Holds together most intimately, / Observe all the power and seed of all activity / And no longer rummage about in words]."

45. See Schlegel, *Friedrich Schlegel's* Lucinde *and the Fragments,* 129: "Now the soul understands the lament of the nightingale and the smile of the newly born babe, understands the deep significance of the mysterious hieroglyphs on flowers and stars, understands the holy meaning of life as well as the beautiful language of nature." On the baroque era's consideration of hieroglyphs as manifestations of divine speech, see Benjamin, *Origin of German Tragic Drama,* 167–74.

46. Kittler, *Discourse Networks 1800/1900,* 4.

47. See de Man, "Temporality," 225–26 on irony as the "mode of the present," which "knows neither memory nor prefigurative duration" (226).

48. Schumacher, *Die Ironie der Unverständlichkeit,* 195, also 187–89. The above passage in specific refers to Adam Smith's concept of labor value vis-à-vis commodities as alluded to by Schlegel.

49. See also Ronell on the ethics of ironic incomprehension: "Thinking one has understood fully not only is the kiss of death—who but an idiot has really understood?—but also the end of all irony, which [. . .] brings an abrupt halt to any illusion of having understood." Ronell, *Stupidity,* 156. See also Comstock, "'Transcendental Buffoonery': Irony as Process in Schlegel's 'Über die Unverständlichkeit.'"

50. Lacoue-Labarthe and Nancy have emphasized what might be called the paradox of romanticism: that revealed truth is nevertheless to be conceived "in *art*—and in *form.*" Lacoue-Labarthe and Nancy, *The Literary Absolute,* 76–77. In this way, a self-generating *poesis* becomes the substance of the absolute; infinity of form comes to stand in for the "form" of infinity. See also Benjamin, *Concept of Criticism,* 138; Hamacher, "'End of Art,'" esp. 105–6 and 121–24.

51. Allemann is one of the few to have recognized this, though he reads Schlegel's irony of irony merely as a wry announcement of his supposed retirement from irony, and not as the emergence of a new form of irony itself.

52. Hegel already foresees this dilemma in his analysis of the two potential consequences of irony's "negativity": on the one hand, "the vanity of everything factual, moral, and of intrinsic worth, the nullity of everything objective and absolutely valid" and on the other, a "yearning and a *morbid* beautiful soul [krankhafte Schönseelischkeit und Sehnsüchtigkeit]" (*A* 66–67; *AI* 96) in mourning for what was never actually to be attained.

53. Literature then has a privileged place for de Man, as the thing that was, so to speak, "undone" from the start. See de Man, "Criticism and Crisis," esp. 17–18.

54. See Ronell, *Stupidity,* 145–46. Ronell further suggests that de Man balks here at the practical and psychological implications of his own argument, preferring to leave it on the comparatively safer level of literary debate. Of course, given the jocular tone and comparatively late date of de Man's own essay, one

should not exclude the possibility that it *itself* is an ironic citation of Schlegel's ironic farewell to irony.

55. See Schumacher, *Die Ironie der Unverständlichkeit,* 222–28; on Schlegel's Socratic turn in particular, see 224–25. See also Mergenthaler, *Zwischen Eros und Mitteilung,* esp. 40–41 and 52–53.

56. Compare Kierkegaard: "Enthusiasm is not always bound up with endurance; on the contrary, enthusiasm is a consuming zeal in the service of possibility. Therefore, an ironist is always an enthusiast, except that his enthusiasm never accomplishes anything, for he never goes beyond the category of possibility" (*CI* 192). In these terms, "On Incomprehensibility" can be described as Schlegel's self-condemnation for not having gone beyond mere possibility in the *Athenäum* group, while still continuing to refuse to go beyond mere possibility.

57. Adorno, "Ist die Kunst Heiter?" 605. The difference between these two art forms may be summed up in Schlegel's hermeneutic "catastrophe" of universal readership versus Adorno's "historical catastrophe" which art may—or may not—survive. See also chapter 1, footnote 34. Preisendanz similarly posits a "deconstructive humor that implies a self-judgment on the vis comica" as characteristic of German postwar fiction. Preisendanz, *Reallexikon,* 102. See also Preisendanz's essay, "Zum Vorrang des Komischen bei der Darstellung von Geschichtserfahrung in deutschen Romanen unserer Zeit."

58. On late Schlegel, see Allemann, 77–82; Schumacher, 253–54.

59. Preisendanz himself cites Joachim Ritter's and Helmuth Plessner's theories of laughter approvingly, although once again in the context of an attempt to differentiate humor from either romantic irony or the comic. See *HDE* 13–14.

60. Preisendanz—rhetorically—asks precisely this question: "What separates the descent into one's own breast, which discovers *Humanus* as a new saint, from the abstract, unreconciled subjectivity of irony and subjective humor?" (*HDE* 125).

61. Booth, *A Rhetoric of Irony,* 6.

62. Allemann, *Ironie und Dichtung,* 16.

63. Lukács, *Theory of the Novel,* 78.

64. See Terence, *The Self-Tormentor,* 104. Quoted in *A* 46; *AI* 70.

65. See Ritter, "Über das Lachen," esp. 90–91 on "humor" in relation to the "late Middle Ages discovery of the individual as belonging to being."

66. See Agamben, *The Man Without Content,* 57–58: "art is the annihilating entity that traverses all its contents without ever being able to attain a positive work, because it cannot identify with any content. And since art has become the pure potentiality of negation, nihilism reigns in its essence [. . .]. The essence of nihilism coincides with the essence of art at the extreme point of its destiny insofar as, in both, being destines itself to man in the form of nothingness."

67. Benjamin attempts to reconcile this dilemma by dividing irony into, on the one hand, what he calls the "irony of the material," which "rests on a subjective, playful reflection of the author" in the manner of subjective humor, and on the other hand, what he calls "formal irony," which "opens up a heaven of eternal form, the idea of forms," and which Benjamin—not so far from both Hegel and Schlegel—locates in criticism and aesthetic reflection. Benjamin, *Concept of Criticism,* 164–65.

68. Hegel's restriction helps to explain Preisendanz's repeated insistence on humor as an exclusively aesthetic phenomenon (see *HDE* 16), especially in contrast to the comic, which is defined not as a mode of representation but as a situation, event, character, or condition *to be* (re-)presented. One might say that for Preisendanz, humor is an aesthetic problem, whereas comedy is, as it were, merely an ontological one. This distinction—essentially similar to Hegel's own between objective and subjective humor—moreover results in the incongruous situation that, whereas serious content may be portrayed with "epic humor" in the novel, comic content must always be presented "seriously."

69. Geulen argues that not only does Hegel not succeed (even assuming he wished to succeed) in giving the final blow to art, but, with art's museumization, in fact inaugurates the "(re)birth of modernity" in the anachronistic and historicizing—and thus, the ironicizing—relation to art's past. Geulen, *End of Art*, 39.

70. Adorno, as is well known, is particularly eloquent on this point. For example: "In the history of art, the dialectic of the ugly has drawn the category of the beautiful into itself as well; kitsch is, in this regard, the beautiful as the ugly, taboo in the name of that very beauty that it once was and which it now contradicts in the absence of its own opposite." Adorno, *Aesthetic Theory*, 47–48.

71. The synthesis, to speak in Hegelian terms, of these two "end" forms of art—that is, kitsch and nihilism—would be, precisely, *camp:* in Susan Sontag's description, "the sensibility of failed seriousness, of the theatricalization of experience." Sontag, "Notes on Camp," 290. In this context, camp would not exactly be an improvement on irony, as Sontag indeed suggests at one point, but rather the "purely aesthetic" ironization of and ironized aesthetic love for a humanist sentimentality and a classical standard of beauty grown insipid.

72. Though Hegel avails himself of Terence's truism without much thought for its context, it is significant in this sense that he takes recourse, for the aphorism that essentially bookends his lectures, to the opening lines of a *comedy*: thereby directly—if also unintentionally—combining the notion of a humanist aesthetics with that of the human being as (mere) play.

73. Here lies one of several points of similarity between Hegel's *comedy* and Kierkegaard's *irony*, as potentially beneficial methods of purification within a dialectical historical process (though Kierkegaard's idea of irony naturally manifests far less certainty than Hegel's comedy concept as to what is to be jettisoned and what retained). This purifying function of comedy/irony is why Socrates is such a crucial figure for Kierkegaard, as the "*accoucheur*" (*CI* 211) of world history and "the nothing from which the beginning must nevertheless begin" (*CI* 198). See also *CI* 128–53 on Aristophanes' comical Socrates portrayal.

74. Mark W. Roche has particularly stressed the significance of comedy within the Hegelian dialectic, even if his basically conventional and characterological argument (i.e., comedy as the satire of individual foibles, as in the farces of Molière) ignores both the problem of unhappy consciousness and the role it plays in the *Aesthetics* as the auto-destruction of art itself. See Roche, "Hegel's Theory of Comedy in the Context of Hegelian and Modern Reflections on Comedy." A longer version of the same thesis, including an extended typology of comedy illustrated with examples from literature, is presented in Roche's *Tragedy and Comedy: A Systematic Study and Critique of Hegel.*

75. Aristotle, *Poetics* 3.4, 9.

76. Roche cites Karl Rosenkranz's concept of the ugly to argue that the comic exists as "the aesthetic counterpart to evil." Roche, "Hegel's Theory of Comedy," 426. The association between the comic and evil (or the demonic) is not wholly unwarranted, but is also far more complex than Roche's analysis allows for. Meanwhile, Rosenkranz himself actually designates the ugly as "the *midpoint* between the concept of the beautiful and the concept of the comic," and not, as Roche would have it, as an analogue of the comic whereby both would be simply *opposed* to the beautiful and the good. See Rosenkranz, *Ästhetik des Häßlichen,* 5, emphasis added.

77. These contradictions are not quite rectified by the various well-meaning attempts to privilege self-deprecating humor—what Simon Critchley, with reference to Freud's humor concept, calls the laughter of "super-ego II"—over the aggressive humor of ridicule. Although on an ethical level this is surely to be preferred, structurally speaking, even laughing at one's own errors remains laughing at error. See Critchley, 102–6.

78. Hegel's reading of Aristophanes, however, brings the idea of comedy as moral corrective to the forefront again. See *A* 1220–22; *AIII* 552–55.

79. Such a form of comedy is not entirely unlike Jean Paul's description of the "annihilating or infinite idea of humor" (*VA* §33, 91–94; 129–30) or—in a further contribution to terminological confusion—"ironic distance," which, in Beda Allemann's words, "displays itself as the translucence and detachment of a poetic world in which all things stand in mild autumnal light and clear air." Allemann, *Ironie und Dichtung,* 17.

80. See Corngold, "Some Theoretical and Historical Complications in Hegel's Aesthetics of Comedy," esp. 33, 37–38.

81. See Ritter, "Das Lachen," 76 on laughter as the "secret belonging of the negative to being [geheime Zugehörigkeit des Nichtigen zum Dasein]."

82. On Jean Paul's own revision of the sublime in distinction from both Kantian and romantic conceptions, see Fleming, *The Pleasures of Abandonment,* esp. 47–49.

83. It should be stated that Vischer's analysis also effects a certain distortion of Hegel's argument here, placing the *sublime* where Hegel has the *actual* and the *necessary.*

84. On the "irony in the center of Hegel's own philosophy," see also Behler, *Irony and the Discourse of Modernity,* 85–91, here 89.

85. See Haverkamp, "Humor," 180: "If humor reenacts the judgment of the world as a judgment on itself as a mimesis gone astray [. . .], the only thing that can help again is irony, from which the *vis comica* can then indeed arise, to establish this going astray as the only appropriate relation." The allusion is to Preisendanz's concept of "deconstructive humor," noted in chapter 1, n57.

86. Szondi, "Friedrich Schlegel und die romantische Ironie," 8.

87. Manfred Frank makes a similar argument in his essay on Schlegel, concluding, in Hegelian tones, "Thus irony laughingly corrects the false valuation of an atomized world, in that it—for the time being, only in the realm of the imaginary—ridicules as null everything that spreads itself out as substantial reality." Frank, "Allegorie, Witz, Fragment, Ironie," 142. Frank sets romantic irony between allegory—itself allegorized as a striving for the absolute—and a *Witz* identified with the fragment. Frank's error—which ultimately leads him, like

Szondi, to the conclusion that irony is in fact not-irony—is to overlook the real and complicated affinities between allegory and *Witz* and the fragment and the whole. Thus irony becomes, according to an old story, merely the "synthesis of wit and allegory" (Frank 140) as the dialectical reconciliation of fragmentation and unity, absolute and particular.

88. See, e.g., Plessner 125: "The laughing person is open to the world. The consciousness of his elevation and abstraction [Abgehobenheit und Herausgehobenheit], that often presents itself as the consciousness of superiority, implies at once remove from a given situation and openness, flexibility." In similar fashion, Heller argues that "keeping a distance is the first constituent of rationality in laughter. There is no sentimental laughter," and Kottman maintains that the crucial difference between tragedy and comedy is that comedy refuses the empathic affect which tragedy demands. See Heller, *Immortal Comedy*, 25; and Kottman, "Slipping on Banana Peels," esp. 8. The ban on sentimentality and pathos in comedy is perhaps true enough; however, it is to be asked if the only opposite of these is superiority and rational distance.

89. See Hamacher, "'End of Art,'" 106. Or in de Man's own words: "Making the language that denies the self into a center rescues the self linguistically at the same time that it asserts its insignificance, its emptiness as a mere figure of speech. It can only persist as self if it is displaced into the text that denies it. The self which was at first the center of the language as its empirical referent now becomes the language of the center as fiction, as metaphor of the self." De Man, "Rhetoric of Tropes," 111–12.

90. See de Man, "Temporality," 213–14 and 218–19; see also Hamacher, "Unlesbarkeit," esp. 11–14.

Chapter Two

1. For example, Ehrich-Haefeli, "'Gaukler sein wäre schön'"; and Wägenbaur, "Robert Walsers Geste des Schreibens und die Komik des 'interface,'" 484–85. See also Fuchs, *Dramaturgie des Narrentums*, esp. 62–63, and Greven, "'Mit seiner deutschen Sprache jonglieren gelernt.'"

2. Walser, "Wenn ich neben meinem Mädchen einhergehn würde wie der!" (*AB1* 70–73, here 72).

3. Schiller, *On the Aesthetic Education of Man*, 101; *Über die ästhetische Erziehung des Menschen*, 233–35.

4. On Walser's complicated relation to his Swissness, see Greven, "'Mit seiner deutschen Sprache jonglieren gelernt,'" esp. 26–27; and Böhler, "Dichten aus der Peripherie des Schreibens."

5. Paradigmatic in this regard is Rodewald, *Robert Walsers Prosa. Versuch einer Strukturanalyse*; see also Jürgens, *Robert Walser. Die Krise der Darstellbarkeit* (in particular, on what he calls Walser's "crisis of subjectivity," 137–49); and Avery, *Inquiry and Testament*.

6. Fuchs, *Dramaturgie des Narrentums*, 172. Fuchs bases her analysis primarily on Bakhtin's idea of the carnivalesque, with nods to Plessner's theory of "eccentric subjectivity" in *Lachen und Weinen* and Preisendanz's description of comic role play. See Plessner, *Lachen und Weinen*; and Preisendanz, "Humor als Rolle."

7. Massimo Cacciari, in his analysis of Viennese modernism, offers a third (and equally misleading) interpretation of Walser as quasi-Buddhistic Jugendstil

aesthete, e.g.: "Walser's idler knows the art of Zen painting and flower arranging very well. From his first work, *The Themes of Fritz Kocher,* the method of an authentic 'small' master is described with minute attention, along with 'reverential respect for everything that exists' [. . .]. Consider the praise of calligraphy in 'The Class Theme Paper,' the recommendations on how to sit quietly in your seat and on what paper to use. Consider the recurrent motif of courtesy, of fascination with the norm that prevents 'originality,' and the imperceptible changes in the ceremony." Cacciari, *Posthumous People,* 167–68. Similarly, see Kellenberger, *Der Jugendstil und Robert Walser,* esp. 61–62. For a trenchant argument *against* the idea of Walser as a "Jugendstil version of the Romantic good-for-nothing," see Martin Walser, "Der Unerbittlichkeitsstil: Zum 100. Geburtstag von Robert Walser," here 129.

8. Walser, "Wie die sich so selber fallen ließ" (*AB1* 33–35, here 33).

9. Benjamin, *The Concept of Criticism,* 122.

10. This joke on the novelistic conventions of the "found" manuscript is continued from the title page of the book's first edition, which presents the collection as "Fritz Kocher's [*sic*] Aufsätze, mitgeteilt von Robert Walser ("Fritz Kocher's Essays, Presented by Robert Walser").

11. A possible source text is Johann Karl August Musäus's *Volksmärchen der Deutschen,* in which the title character of the tale "Ulrich mit dem Bühel" is led into a "wohl angelegten Lustgarten" during a respite from his adventures. Musäus, *Volksmärchen der Deutschen,* 202.

12. As recorded for example in the 1873 *Deutsches Sprichwörter-Lexikon: Ein Hausschatz für das deutsche Volk* (ed. Wander), 594.

13. Rodewald speaks of the "subjunctive dimension" (123–24) of the Kocherian schoolroom.

14. On a similar pedagogical temporality in the novel *Jakob von Gunten,* see Kreienbrock, *Kleiner. Feiner. Leichter,* 166–68.

15. Shelley, *A Defense of Poetry,* 46.

16. See de Man, "Rhetoric of Persuasion (Nietzsche)," 131: "Considered as persuasion, rhetoric is performative but when considered as a system of tropes, it deconstructs its own performance."

17. Ernst Robert Curtius gives a succinct description of the kind of schooling to which Walser himself was no doubt submitted: "To us, [rhetoric] has become unfamiliar. As an independent subject it has long since vanished from the curriculum. Some scanty scraps of rhetorical knowledge were still offered to the nineteenth-century German grammar-school pupil when he was taught to turn out German themes. He was expected to draw up a preliminary 'outline,' divided into introduction, main body, and conclusion. The introduction had to contain a generalization. One must on no account pass directly on to the theme, but must find a suitable 'transition.' These transitions were a torment [. . .]. The grammar-school student encountered rhetoric again when he studied Latin poetry (and Schiller's too)—here metaphors, metonyms, hyperboles, and the like were to be found in abundance." Curtius, *European Literature and the Latin Middle Ages,* 62.

18. Zmegac, "Robert Walsers Poetik in der literarischen Konstellation der Jahrhundertwende," 24.

19. Benjamin, "Robert Walser," 259.

20. This phrase is mis- or overtranslated in Cacciari as "a song of too many voices singing too high" (168), turning Fritz's merely florid metaphor into a statement of explicit disapprobation.

21. Adorno writes that parataxes "evade the logical hierarchy of a subordinating syntax." Adorno, "Parataxis: On Hölderlin's Late Poetry," 131.

22. The dangers of reading Walser as a programmatically political author are demonstrated by Valerie Heffernan's study, *Provocation from the Periphery: Robert Walser Re-examined.*

23. On the complications involved in periodicizing Walser, see Evans, "Der Dichter als Räuber: Robert Walser zwischen Modernismus und Avantgardismus."

24. Hegel's program for art on the following page is worth quoting in full in this context: "What we may regard as necessary here is rather a sensitive abandonment of the heart in the object [ein empfindungsvolles Sichergehen des Gemüts in dem Gegenstande], which is indeed unfolded but remains a *subjective* spirited movement of imagination and the heart—a fugitive notion, but one which is not purely accidental and capricious but an inner movement of the spirit devoted entirely to its object and retaining it as its content and interest" (*A* 609; *AII* 240).

25. In a comment from July 24, 1944, Carl Seelig recalls how Walser "warms to the theme of the 'comical masterliness [drolligen Meisterlichkeit]' of a Charles Dickens or a Gottfried Keller, with whom you never really knew if you should cry or laugh. This [he says] is surely a sign of genius." Seelig, *Wanderungen mit Robert Walser,* 82. See also Walser's own biographical-critical-anecdotal sketch "Gottfried Keller," in *Aus dem Bleistiftgebiet,* vol. 4, 228–32.

26. Keller, *Der Grüne Heinrich,* 397. On the preceding pages, Keller (or rather his avatar), gives a concise summary of Hegel's warning against subjective humor, in the context of his own artistic education: "in regard to much that I once called poetic, I now learned that the ungraspable and impossible, the fantastic and the rhapsodic is not poetic [. . .], in a word, that one must not confuse art's so-called purposelessness with groundlessness" (395–96).

27. Benjamin; "Surrealism: The Last Snapshot of the European Intelligentsia," 209.

28. Taussig, *Mimesis and Alterity,* 23.

29. This immediacy of realism is also reflected in terms of language, as Benjamin observes in relation to Breton: "the belief in a real separate existence of concepts [. . .] has always very quickly crossed over from the logical realm of ideas to the magical realm of words." Benjamin, "Surrealism," 212.

30. That is, as the narrative presentation of the confrontation between ideal structures or concepts and multidimensional human reality, the "privilege of the human being to be able to see two sides of things" (*HDE* 213).

31. Consider the following lines from "Und dann und so kam Bertha von Suttner mit ihrem 'Waffen nieder!'" (*AB1* 261–62): "All the girls were burning again for romance [Die Mädchen glühten wieder für Romantik]. Who could hold it against them? Rogues and beautiful women came into fashion in the literary sector. The salons figured they had been bored long enough. The word was completely free, and we writers made a comfortable use of our unrestricted license. Has society changed since then? How could I venture to judge?" (*AB1* 261).

32. On the text/image relationship in Walser's work, see Siegel, *Aufträge aus dem Bleistiftgebiet,* in particular 120–25. Siegel furthermore draws attention to

the concrete or graphical aspect of Walser's microgram, so to speak the reverse of the ekphrastic relation: not images expanding into words, but words turning into images.

33. Certain of the compositions, such as "Der Feuersbrunst" ("The Fire") (*FKA* 12–14), "Jahrmarkt" ("Fair") (*FKA* 40–42), and, counterintuitively, "Aus der Phantasie" ("From the Imagination") (*FKA* 26–28), do, however, follow a more standard pictorial logic.

34. Compare Hegel's uncannily similar lines on Dutch painting: "This is as it were an objective music, a peal in colour [Es ist dies gleichsam eine objektive Musik, ein Tönen in Farben]" (*A* 599–600; *AII* 228).

35. Walser, "Ein Maler," 67.

36. See Burwick, *Mimesis and Its Romantic Reflections.* Burwick usefully points out that despite its seeming opposition to literary realism, "the Romantic endeavor to redefine the function of art as the expression of the individual artist simply relocate[s] the same proprietary ideology [of materialist mimesis]" (11).

37. Auerbach, for example, explicitly includes within the purview of mimesis (here in the context of the modernist novel) the "process of formulation and interpretation whose subject matter is our own self." Auerbach, *Mimesis,* 549.

38. The last of these is Jürgens' final thesis in *Krise der Darstellbarkeit*: see 150–74. On Walser's "literary autism," see Jürgens, 147–48.

39. Burwick follows his discussion of the "doubly damned" structure of romantic mimesis with a mention of Grabbe's 1822 *Lustspiel, Scherz, Satire, Ironie, und tiefere Bedeutung,* quoting from the—decidedly proto-Walserian—scene in which the character Rattengift writes a poem about not being able to write a poem: "RATTENGIFT: [. . .] So I sit here, drink coffee, chew pens, write down, cross out, and still find no thoughts, no thoughts!—Hm, how can I capture it, then?—Soft, soft! what idea is that that arises before me?—Splendid! divine! I'll write a sonnet precisely about the thought that I can't find any thoughts, and truly, this thought about having no thoughts is the most genial thought that could have come to me! [RATTENGIFT: (. . .) Da sitze ich, trinke Kaffee, kaue Federn, schreibe hin, streiche aus und kann keinen Gedanken finden, keinen Gedanken!—Ha, wie ergreife ich's nun?—Halt, halt! was geht mir da für eine Idee auf?—Herrlich! göttlich! eben über den Gedanken, daß ich keinen Gedanken finden kann, will ich ein Sonett machen, und wahrhaftig, dieser Gedanke über die Gedankenlosigkeit ist der genialste Gedanke, der mir nur einfallen konnte!]" Grabbe, *Scherz, Satire, Ironie, und tiefere Bedeutung,* act 2, scene 2, 255–56. Walser, naturally, removes the specifically satirical aspect of Grabbe's lines; thus he no longer "ridicules the solipsistic entrapment of self-reflexivity" (Burwick 12) as Grabbe does, but in a way affirms it and carries it to its logical ends.

40. See Benjamin, *Origin of German Tragic Drama,* 191: "Because of its obsession with earnestness the German *Trauerspiel* never mastered the art of using allegory inconspicuously. Only comedy accorded the allegorical the rights of citizenship in the secular drama; but when comedy moves in seriously, then the consequences are unexpectedly fatal."

41. Agamben, while not particularly interested in the comic aspects of Walser's work, has described this tension with admirable accuracy: "Ontotheological pathos—both in the form of unsayability and in the (equivalent) form of absolute sayability—always remained foreign to [Walser's] writing, which maintained

a delicate balance between 'modest imprecision' and a mannerist stereotype." Agamben, *The Coming Community,* 58.

42. It is precisely the *neglect* of this secondary or tertiary nature of much of Walser's writing that allows for the prevalence of pathetic, not to say tragic, interpretations of Walser's work. Exemplary in this regard are the oft-discussed short prose pieces "Der heiße Brei" (roughly translatable as "The Bush," as in "beating around") in Walser, *Es war einmal,* 89–92, and "Für die Katz" (approximately, "For the Birds"), in Walser, *Für die Katz,* 430–32, both of which have been privileged as allegories for Walser's alleged mimesis issues. On "Der heiße Brei," see for example Rodewald, 55; Jürgens, 119–24; Bungartz, *Zurückweichend vorwärtsschreiten,* 161–65; and Heffernan, 173–80. On "Für die Katz," see Rodewald, 237–38; Jürgens, 167–74; and Bungartz, 193–99.

43. The quotations in this passage are from Friedrich Schlegel's review article "Zu Jean Pauls Vorschule der Ästhetik," 668 and 657. It should be noted that Schlegel himself, on page 668 of this essay, poses not "humor," but rather *irony* as the antidote to materialism and "sentimentalism."

44. See Haverkamp, "Humor. Die Latenz der Form."

45. See Fleming, *The Pleasures of Abandonment,* esp. 30–36. As Fleming also notes, however, Jean Paul's "humor" already exemplarily displays a certain "permanent tension" (154), precisely as a result of the limitations on fantasy and—with reference to Vischer—the "fissure at the heart of the world" (155).

46. In the same fragment, Schlegel further connects this "highest law" to the inherent expressivity of the novel: "there is [. . .] no form so fit for expressing the entire spirit of an author: so that many artists who started out to write only a novel ended up by providing us with a portrait of themselves" (*F* 175; 182).

47. Starobinski, *Portrait de l'artiste en saltimbanque,* 9.

48. Thus also (in Peter Bürger's words) the "avant-garde protest, whose goal is to return art to life praxis,"whose unintentional result is a further reiteration of the realization of the "connection between autonomy and inconsequence." Bürger, *Theorie der Avantgarde,* 29.

49. Benjamin is perhaps the first to emphasize this connection, at the same time noting—what has often been neglected—the significant *difference* between Walser and mere clownery: "If Polonius, the model for all windbags, is a juggler, then Walser is a Bacchus who wreathes himself in linguistic garlands that then trip him up." Benjamin, "Robert Walser," 258.

50. Walser also often speaks of artistic freedom in a quite practical and quotidian—that is to say, a professional—sense, for example in the following comment to Seelig: "Wherever artists don't stand in a tense relation to human society, they quickly grow slack. They mustn't let themselves be mollycoddled, because then they feel obliged to cling to existing conditions [sich den gegebenen Verhältnissen anzuschmiegen].—No, not even in times of the greatest poverty would I have allowed myself to be bought. My personal freedom was always dearer to me." Seelig, *Wanderungen mit Robert Walser,* 124.

51. Schopenhauer, *World as Will and Representation,* vol. 1, §36, 191.

52. This decadent moment of subjective humor is precisely the one in which Agamben's *The Man Without Content* is situated, in the context of which the artist "has no other identity than a perpetual emerging out of the nothingness of

expression and no other ground than this incomprehensible station on this side of himself." Agamben, *The Man Without Content,* 55.

53. As Starobinski himself ultimately does, ruefully commenting that "when social order deteriorates, the presence of the clown on stage or on the canvas becomes weaker; but it is then that the clown goes out into the street: he is now all of us. There are no more limits, thus there are no more transgressions." Starobinski, *Portrait de l'artiste en saltimbanque,* 144.

54. Walser's (mis-)appropriation of Kocher's name eventually prompted an irate letter to Insel Verlag from the latter's daughter, Margit Wyss-Kocher, who, apparently *without* irony, writes: "I kindly request an explanation in this matter. I'd so like to enjoy this charming little book with the familiar expressions in my father's compositions, but which part is actually true? The 'Introduction' or the essays?" Quoted in Müller, *Mit Fritz Kocher in der Schule der Moderne,* 17; see also Müller 10 and footnote, 12.

55. See Fuchs, *Dramaturgie des Narrentums,* 133. Surprisingly, Fuchs does *not* mention *Fritz Kochers Aufsätze* in this context. It should also be emphasized that for Plessner, the phrase "eccentric subjectivity" technically does not refer to a particular kind of self-conscious and self-ironizing subject, but is rather his definition of the human condition as such, of which laughing is then the exemplary or limit condition.

56. See Hamacher, "'End of Art,'" 129.

57. Hegel's thoughts on language in the *Phenomenology* are the clear background to de Man's thinking here: "Language is self-consciousness existing *for others* [das *für andere* seiende Selbstbewußtsein], self-consciousness which *as such* is immediately *present,* and as *this* self-consciousness is universal. It is the self that separates itself from itself, which as pure 'I' = 'I' becomes objective to itself, which in this objectivity equally preserves itself as *this* self, just as it coalesces directly with other selves and is *their* self-consciousness. It perceives itself just as it is perceived by others, and the perceiving is just *existence which has become a self* [das Vernehmen ist eben das *zum Selbst gewordene Dasein*]" (*PS* §652, 395; 478–79). What permits the difference between these two ideas of language is that Hegel thinks only of language as a unity, whereas de Man's rhetorical approach takes for granted the fact that language has an internal dynamic proper to *it,* and therefore it cannot be understood as a simple medium for consciousness, in itself undivided.

58. The discovery of these works by Greven and Jürgens in 1972 and their painstaking deciphering by Werner Morlang and Bernhard Echte from 1985 to 1999 have already become the stuff of scholarly legend.

59. Walser, *Briefe,* 301. Interesting to compare in this context is an unfinished note of Saussure, in which he complains of a "pathological fear of the pen," written precisely around the same time as he begins his research into cryptic writing and the anagram. See Starobinski, *Les mots sous les mots,* 13.

60. This danger is already present in the *Aufsätze,* where Fritz—significantly, in the composition entitled "Freithema" ("Free Topic")—writes, "I don't love this kind of freedom. I like to be restricted to pre-given material [Ich liebe diese Art von Freiheit nicht. Ich bin gern an einen vorgeschriebenen Stoff gebunden]" (*FKA* 24).

61. See, e.g., Walser's letter to Hermann Hesse, dated November 15, 1917: "People are all talking about how Robert Walser is living the life of a first-class

fool's-paradise-lazybones and village philistine, instead of 'fighting.' [Es ist laut geworden, daß Robert Walser ein vornehmes Schlaraffen-Faulpelz- und Spießbürgerleben führe, anstatt zu 'kämpfen.'] The politicians are displeased with me. But what do people want, really? And what sort of great and good things are supposed to be achieved with articles in newspapers and magazines? If the time is out of joint, the efforts of twenty thousand mad Hamlets are worth little to nothing. Every day I read a little French, because it's such a beautiful language. Does that make me a scoundrel? Also, just for fun, every day I have to stroll around a little in the winter landscape. Do I prove thereby that I am indifferent to great suffering? I think you of all people should understand why I like to be quiet and take things slow. Kind regards from the marble palace in which I reside." Walser, *Briefe,* 117.

62. Bernstein, *Virtuosity of the Nineteenth Century,* 91. See also Utz, "Die Kalligraphie des 'Idioten,'" esp. 115–17.

63. Such a dynamic obviously has significance for Walser's similarly largely self-imposed confinement in mental institutions for the majority of his adult life. See Utz, "Avant-Propos," in *Robert Walser, l'écriture miniature,* and in the same volume, Morlang, "Magie du camouflage micrographique."

64. Walser, "Der Commis," 54.

65. Walser, *Jakob von Gunten,* 8.

66. See Greven, *Figur am Rande,* 37 on Walser's specific challenge to the culture of the Bildungsroman, particularly in light of Walser's Swissness and imposed early exit from the educational system.

67. Campe, "Robert Walsers Institutionenroman *Jakob von Gunten,*" 238 and 243.

68. Compare Malevich, *The Non-Objective World: The Manifesto of Suprematism,* 68: "No more 'likenesses of reality,' no idealistic images—nothing but a desert! But this desert is filled with the spirit of non-objective sensation which pervades everything."

69. Aristotle, *Poetics* 3.4, 9.

70. This is of course already implied by Aristotle's subsequent assertion that "the laughable is an error or disgrace that does not involve pain or destruction" (*Poetics* 3.4, 9)—pain and destruction being precisely consequences that the comic, at least traditionally, may not allow. I have argued that the comic does in fact have consequences, indeed profound ones; nevertheless, these are naturally of a different kind than those meant by Aristotle.

71. Walser, "Mon Repos-Schlösser schlummern mir im erneuerungsscheuen Kopf" (*AB1* 39–42, here 39). The "not [nicht]" in brackets has been suggested by the editors.

72. Agamben, *Infancy and History,* 60.

73. The only long text of the *Bleistiftgebiet* manuscripts, the novel *The Robber,* plays with narrative aimlessness in particularly explicit fashion, establishing with the very first words—"Edith liebt ihn. Hievon nachher mehr [Edith loves him. More on this later]"—a pattern of withholding against traditional narrative development and mechanisms of suspense. Walser, *Der "Räuber"-Roman,* 173. See also Frederick, *Narratives Unsettled,* 25–97; on *The Robber* in particular, 78–80. On hesitation and suspension in literature generally as immanent "analytical method," see Vogl, *Über das Zaudern,* 61.

74. Morlang notes that "Walser's marginality is always defined by his refusal to enter the world of adults." Morlang, "Magie du camouflage micrographique," 17.

75. Walser, "Das laß ich mir aber nicht auch nehmen!" (*AB1* 271–72, here 272).

76. Benjamin, "Robert Walser," 259. Similarly, see Cacciari, *Posthumous People,* 148–56.

77. Agamben, *Coming Community,* 6.

78. Agamben, *Coming Community,* esp. 35–37 and 58–59.

79. Walser, "Spät bis alle Nacht herumziehende Jünglinge" (*AB1* 43–45, here 43).

80. See Nietzsche, *Also Sprach Zarathustra,* 139–41.

81. Walser, "Ein Etwas richtet sich boltzengerade in mir auf" (*AB1* 281–89, here 283).

82. Walser, "Usually I first put on a prose piece jacket," 59–62; for original, see Walser, "Sonst zieh' ich immer erst einen Prosastückkittel, also eine Art Schriftstellerjacke an" (*AB1* 65–68).

83. Walser's "prose piece jacket" also potentially evokes the image of the laborer or (recalling Walser's description of the microscript system's "office-like" quality) the clerk, whose rote labors, once again, are the precise opposite of genial creation.

84. In the English translation, the requirement of a pronoun ("them") necessarily removes the ambiguity contained in the German.

85. Freud, *Beyond the Pleasure Principle,* 17; *Jenseits des Lustprinzips,* 15.

86. See Weber on Freud's play concept as one underwritten by the "interests of the narcissistic ego bent on reducing alterity to a variation of identity." Weber, *Legend of Freud,* 136.

87. Freud, "Creative Writers and Day-Dreaming," 146: "A child's play is determined by wishes: in point of fact by a single wish—one that helps in his upbringing—the wish to be big and grow up. He is always playing at being 'grown up,' and in his games he imitates what he knows about the lives of his elders." See also Freud, *Beyond the Pleasure Principle,* 16–17.

88. Unlike Freud, Huizinga argues for play as something that "resist[s] any attempt to reduce it to other terms." Huizinga, *Homo Ludens,* 6. Indeed, in the chapter "Play-Forms in Art," Huizinga implicitly reverses Freud's schema, making *mimesis* a form of *play* rather than play a form of mimesis (see especially Huizinga 162). Huizinga's reversal, however, is nevertheless also in service of a teleological story—indeed, one even more emphatically teleological and pedagogical than that of Freud—in which a primary play serves as the origin of "the antithetical and agonistic basis of civilization" (Huizinga 75) all the way up to juridical contests and even war.

89. Similarly, the appellation of the woman as "this ideal of a lady [diesem Ideal von Dame]" marks the romantic (in the weak sense) subplot squarely as a literary convention, indeed a thorough citation from the vast and storied repertoire of the theme of courtly love: once again making that which seems most authentic in fact the most quoted, the most clichéd.

90. Freud describes fetishism as the giving of sexual value to ordinarily nonsexual objects "in which the sexual aim, whether normal or perverse, is entirely abandoned [mit Verzicht auf ein normales oder perverses Sexualziel]." Freud, "Three Essays on Sexuality," 153; "Drei Abhandlungen zur Sexualtheorie," 52.

See also Greven, *Figur am Rande,* 98, for an (in this case pathologizing) application of the fetish concept to Walser's work. On the other hand, in support of the idea that "to write means to *perpetually* go or wander around a *main matter*"—specifically, in relation to the paradigmatic piece "Der heiße Brei" (also discussed in footnote 42, this chapter)—see also Kreienbrock, *Kleiner. Feiner. Leichter,* 16.

91. See Freud, "Creative Writers and Day-Dreaming," 144. Freud seems to be alluding to Schlegel's *Athenäum* fragment 419, which begins, "The world is much too serious, but seriousness is nevertheless a rather rare phenomenon. Seriousness is the opposite of play" (*F* 231; 245).

92. "Ob Sie glauben oder nicht: Eines Tages mutete mir Bruno Cassirer zu, ich solle Novellen wie Gottfried Keller schreiben. Ich brach in schallendes Gelächter aus." Seelig, *Wanderungen mit Robert Walser,* 29.

Chapter Three

1. Kafka, *Das Schloß,* 416–26.

2. On puns in *Das Schloß,* see Haverkamp, "Kafkas Pannen: Poetik des Landstreichens im dichtgemachten Text."

3. Brod, *Über Franz Kafka,* 42. For a catalog of biographical anecdotes of Kafka's sense of humor, see Petr, *Kafkas Spiele,* esp. 14–21.

4. Weltsch, *Religion und Humor im Leben und Werk Franz Kafkas,* 79. Similarly, see Wallace, "Laughing with Kafka."

5. There is of course also no lack of readings against even this novel's lightness. Peter-André Alt, for example, typically considers the "irony" of Kafka's novel only as a "subversive narrative process" in the service of deadly earnest social critique. See Alt, *Der ewige Sohn,* 366.

6. Sokel, *Franz Kafka—Tragik und Ironie,* 9.

7. See Dentan, *Humour et création littéraire dans l'œuvre de Kafka,* esp. 19.

8. In this I must take issue with Maurice Blanchot, who asserts in a footnote that "the diaries speak to us of a Kafka at that preliminary stage where there were not yet any opinions and where there was hardly a Kafka." Blanchot, *De Kafka à Kafka,* 95. Blanchot instead clearly prefers the version of Kafka as melancholic sage, as presented, for example, in Janouch's *Gespräche mit Kafka.* Blanchot's statement, however, begs the question of what "Kafka" is or ought to be. Even Brod admits that "the whole situation of those conversations of which Janouch gives his account and naturally sees only one side, from another perspective, regarded from the opposite side, appears not without a few demonic drops of irony [erscheint nun nicht ohne einige Teufelströpfchen von Ironie]," further noting that these conversations date from the time of Kafka's unhappy love affair with Milena Jesenská. Brod, *Über Franz Kafka,* 189.

9. For example, Collignon, "Kafka's Humor," 53–54: "Kafka's humor [. . .] does not correspond in the least to the variety exemplified by Rabelais, Fielding and good-natured people who delight in after-dinner jokes [. . .]. It is the humor of a man both oppressed and depressed who smiles not in order to forget but to assert his independence, and makes plain his determination not to be overwhelmed by hardships."

10. Kafka alludes to his reworking of Dickens in a diary entry some years after the composition of *Der Verschollene* in an assessment both revealing and (at least

as regards his own work and abilities) somewhat inaccurate: "Dickens's Copperfield ('The Stoker' pure Dickens imitation, the planned novel even more so. Suitcase anecdotes, all that cheer and charm [der Beglückende und Bezaubernde], the menial labor, the sweetheart in the country manor, the dirty houses, et al., but above all the method. Now I see that my intention was to write a Dickens novel, only enhanced by the brighter lights that I must have gotten from the current times, and the dull ones that I fitted on from out of myself. Dickens's abundance and unhesitating powerful current, but in consequence also passages of dreadful feebleness, where he just keeps tiredly stirring together that which has already been achieved. The whole senseless thing makes a barbaric impression, a barbarism that I avoided thanks to my own weakness and the lessons of my status as epigone)." Also of note is the end of the same parenthetical remark: "Walser's connection with him in the imprecise use of abstract metaphor" (*T* 840–41).

11. Thus I take a different approach than Mark Spilka, who, in his comparative study *Dickens and Kafka: A Mutual Interpretation,* argues for what he calls a "transcendent comedy" common to both authors, defined as "an infantile perspective which reflects the terrors and absurdities of internal and external traps, and yet still allows for the play of conscious feeling." Spilka, *Dickens and Kafka,* 243.

12. On the "horizontal" and "vertical" models of Kafka's architectonics, see Neumann, "Chinesische Mauer und Schacht von Babel. Franz Kafkas Architekturen." Other "railings [Geländer]"—functioning almost universally as portents of border transgression or phase-change—feature prominently in Kafka's writing, for example in the opening paragraphs of *Der Verschollene,* where they form the line between the modern verticality of New York and the horizontality of ship, ocean, and Old Europe. "Geländer" also and perhaps most famously appear in "The Judgment" (whose composition is contemporaneous to the America-novel), where the penultimate lines read: "he held fast to the railing, like a hungry man to food [. . .]. Still holding on with hands growing weaker and weaker, through the bars of the railing he caught sight of an omnibus that would easily drown out the noise of his fall, called out softly: 'Dear Parents, I really did always love you,' and let go" (*DL* 61).

13. Compare Stach, *Kafka: Die Jahre der Entscheidungen,* 195–96.

14. On "proliferation of series" in Kafka, see Deleuze and Guattari, *Kafka,* 53–62; see also Ronell, "Doing Kafka in *The Castle,*" esp. 188–89.

15. Karl's obsession with the photograph of his parents (see *V* 134–35 and 166–69) could thus be read as a homesickness for an earlier form of literature, unavailable in the novel in which he finds himself.

16. Wolf Kittler maintains that "the scenes with Klara are the satyr play to the tragedy of Karl's seduction into fatherhood in his parents' house." Yet not only does Karl's seduction by the maid Johanna Brummer not actually take place in the time of the novel, one would also be hard-pressed to consider the seduction itself anything but a parodic reversal of the usual seduction scenario, and thus a satyr play in its own right. See Kittler, "Dead Beat Father," 170.

17. See Zischler, *Kafka geht ins Kino*; and Alt, *Kafka und der Film.*

18. See Beck, *Kafka and the Yiddish Theater*; and Massimo, *Franz Kafka, Jizchak Löwy und das jiddische Theater.* Beck's book in particular is an attempt to show, through analogical comparisons between the Yiddish theater's dramatic

repertoire and Kafka's own works, that from 1911 to 1914 Kafka's writing style radically changed as a result of the Yiddish theater's direct influence.

19. Benjamin is the one to have introduced the theme of the *gestural* (as opposed to the narrative) in Kafka scholarship, noting that the Theater of Oklahama chapter "harks back to Chinese theater, which is a theater of gesture. One of the most significant functions of this theater is to dissolve events into their gestural components." Benjamin, "Franz Kafka: On the Tenth Anniversary of his Death," 801. See also Benjamin's comment in the *Trauerspiel* book that "the *Trauerspiel* is conceivable as pantomime; the tragedy is not." Benjamin, *Origins of German Tragic Drama,* 118.

20. The claims of Beck and Massimo, respectively.

21. Corngold, *Lambent Traces,* 70. On such "stage business" in Kafka, see also Neumann, "Ritual und Theater"; and Benay, "De la secondarité romanesque chez Franz Kafka."

22. Corngold points out the double meaning of *Prozess* as both "trial" and "process," also noting that "In the Penal Colony" was written during a difficult patch in the composition of *The Trial,* that is, when the writing process of *Der Proceß* literally breaks down. See Corngold, *Lambent Traces,* 42 and 71.

23. See for example Sokel, 313; Dentan, 84–85; Spilka, 138–49 and 172–73; and Stach, 279–81.

24. See for example Vogl, *Ort der Gewalt,* 31; Alt, *Ewige Sohn,* 369–74; Jahn, 92–93 and 101; and Nicolai, 238–43.

25. See Weber, *Theatricality as Medium,* 76–96. Weber, however, reads the "Theater of Oklahama" chapter less as the becoming-theatrical of Kafka's novel and more as a certain becoming-Kafkaesque of theater, indeed, ultimately even a dark premonition of German fascism (see esp. 95–96).

26. Similarly, Karl's old friend from the Hotel Occidental, Giacomo, is "hired not as an actor, but as an elevator boy" (*V* 414), the very position he had occupied in his non-theatrical life.

27. See Wellnitz, "La théâtralité dans *Le Disparu* de Franz Kafka: du Grand Théâtre d'Oklahoma au *theatrum mundi*?" Wellnitz's application of the baroque trope of the world theater to Kafka is apt, though his main thesis—that the "Oklahama" chapter thereby presents a denunciatory image of "art deformed by modern society" (Wellnitz 85)—clearly differs from the argument developed here.

28. See Benjamin, "Franz Kafka: On the Tenth Anniversary of his Death," 801: "One can go even further and say that a good number of Kafka's shorter studies and stories are seen in their full light only when they are, so to speak, put on as acts in the 'Nature Theater of Oklahoma.' "

29. Kafka, *Der Verschollene. Apparatband (Critical Appendix),* 272.

30. Compare Arthur Holitscher's description of the American theater—or as he puts it, "The American theater, God have mercy! [Das amerikanische Theater, daß Gott erbarm!]"—in his travelogue *Amerika Heute und Morgen*: "The American theater should be trimmed to fit the mental elasticity and receptivity of the salesman who after his 8- to 10-hour workday graciously consents to put off his bedtime for an hour and thus becomes the patron and protector of the dramatic arts. The contemporary American theater probably operates according to the motto: just nothing too exciting, nothing that would upset anyone;

business and politics during the day, politics and business in the evening behind the missing fourth wall. In point of fact, in all these months I have seen in the theater only the selfsame play, over and over, in six or seven variants." Holitscher, *Amerika Heute und Morgen,* 412. Exceptionally, Holitscher praises the Yiddish theater in America for its "astonishing accumulation of acting talent and of raw material, that is moreover not spoiled by the typical Broadway replaying of the same nonsense for the five hundredth time" (414). The unusual extravagance of Holitscher's praise here—in a passage which likely did not fail to attract Kafka's attention—must also be read in the context of the complicated polemic running through his book about Jews in America and, by extension, in Europe.

31. See for example Rehberg, *Lachen Lesen. Zur Komik der Moderne bei Kafka.* Despite its title, Rehberg's book is less concerned with the comic than with laughter as anti-hermeneutic allegory. Telling, for example, is the reflexive dismissal of the scene in "In the Penal Colony" in which the condemned prisoner clowns around for the amusement of the attendant soldier. Rehberg comments, "even if the scene [. . .] is 'comic,' this comicalness remains foreign and isolated in relation to the story, because it follows no narrative economy [. . .]. The scene is almost annoying. It falls out of the frame" (129).

32. Derrida, "The Theater of Cruelty," 235.

33. Artaud, *The Theater and Its Double,* 86.

34. Paradigmatic in this regard is the short story "Josephine, the Singer, or the Mouse Folk," in which the title figure's great art is great precisely in its *lack* of aesthetic consummation.

35. Robinson's eulogies can also be interpreted as particularly tongue-in-cheek instances of Kafkan wordplay. Brunelda's "Herrlichkeit" obviously evokes her domination of the trio as well as a certain ambiguous sexuality. The connection between Brunelda's "Größe" as a singer and her own physical size is clear, even if Kafka had not further emphasized it by writing that Robinson subsequently "rolled a great chunk of candy around on his tongue [eine große Bonbonmasse auf der Zunge wälzte]" (*V* 304). Meanwhile, the entire Brunelda episode can be taken as the comic literalization of the word "Frauenzimmer": "Brunelda" is truly the name for *woman* and *room* simultaneously. On literalized metaphors and catachreses in Kafka, see also Corngold, *Franz Kafka: The Necessity of Form,* 94–98; Corngold, *Lambent Traces,* 74; Pasley, "Kafka's Semi-Private Games," esp. 117; and Dentan, 178–80.

36. On blocks and blockages as compositional principle in Kafka, see Deleuze and Guattari, *Kafka,* 72–80.

37. Compare this with the equally lengthy (and similarly placed) description of the rococo "Schreibschrein" in Stifter's *Der Nachsommer,* 82–83. In Stifter's paradigmatic Bildungsroman, the desk's charm and novelty consists not in its technical ingeniousness but in the fineness of its ornamentation, that is, in its *aesthetic* rather than its *functional* value.

38. Might not the (already anyway overdetermined) names of Kafka's most famous protagonists be the best possible joke played on statist sovereignty? That is, in their names is reinscribed each and every moment that the worthy employee of the Workmen's Accident Insurance Institute for the Kingdom of Bohemia in Prague marked something as k. k. (*kaiserlich und königlich* [imperial and royal]: the designation for all official entities of the Habsburg Empire), secretly signing

for his fictional creations within the very name of empire and the name of empire within his fictional creations.

39. The political free-for-all in the street is meanwhile later echoed by the domestic free-for-all in the apartment (see *V* 335–38).

40. See also Neumann on the function of windows in Kafka as spaces marking the "continual oscillation and alternation between acting and observing, between performative and constative acts." Neumann, "Kafkas Architekturen," 461.

41. In *Homo Ludens,* Huizinga singles out repetition as a "very positive feature" of play, insofar as it "creates order, *is* order. Into an imperfect world and into the confusion of life it brings a temporary, a limited perfection." Huizinga, *Homo Ludens,* 10. Of course, such repetition may also be conceived in quite another sense, namely as static *disorder* and the *undoing* of teleological development.

42. "Humor Risk" (also known as "Humorisk" and "Humoresque") is the title of the Marx Brothers' first film, now presumed lost. See Mitchell, *The Marx Brothers Encyclopedia,* 149–50.

43. Janouch, *Gespräche mit Kafka,* 177.

44. See Kafka, *Briefe 1900–1912,* 202–205.

45. Chaplin's first films appeared in 1914, obviously postdating the writing of *Der Verschollene.*

46. Schiller, "On Grace and Dignity," 125; "Über Anmut und Würde," 142.

47. See for example *CPJ* §17, 116–20; 86–93. For Kant at least, the ability to construe beauty, and ultimately the real site of the beautiful, lies in the cognitive powers of the human spectator, that is, in the ideas of perfection, proportion, telos, and so on, encompassed within the faculty of judgment.

48. Kleist, "Über das Marionettentheater," 343–44.

49. Bergson, *Laughter,* 84.

50. See Aristotle, *Parts of Animals,* 673a, 281: "human beings [are] the only creatures that laugh." This far-reaching statement of Aristotle's in fact occurs as an incidental remark within a general discussion of the biological function of the diaphragm.

51. Indeed, in contrast to Kleist, Bergson finds the anthropomorphism of marionettes to be comic per se: "let us follow the imperceptible progress by which [the playing child] makes his puppets grow, inspires them with life, and brings them to that state of final indecision in which, without ceasing to be puppets, they have yet become human beings. We thus obtain figures of comedy." Bergson, *Laughter,* 105, translation modified. See also Fraenger, *Formen des Komischen,* 49–52.

52. Kafka, *Briefe 1900–1912,* 108. Brod, quoting this same letter in his biography of Kafka, remarks that the passage has the "humoristic form of a foreseen Chaplin film." Brod, *Über Franz Kafka,* 80.

53. Kracauer, "Silent Film Comedy," 31.

54. Vogl, "Kafkas Komik," 81.

55. See Bergson: "rigidity is the comic, and laughter is its punishment." Bergson, *Laughter,* 74, translation modified.

56. Here "soul" should be taken in the sense, going back to Aristotle, of "the cause and first principle of the living body," both origin and telos of the living organism. See Aristotle, *De Anima,* 18.

57. Kracauer, *Theory of Film,* 62.

58. Poser, *Museum der Gefahren,* 103.

59. K. A. Lindner, *Denkschrift,* quoted in Poser, *Museum der Gefahren,* 157.

60. As Beck notes, "By locating Ramses in the Promised Land, Kafka creates a paradoxical image of bondage in freedom." Beck, *Kafka and the Yiddish Theater,* 130. It is clear that the Book of Exodus is one of the several prominent source texts of *Der Verschollene.* However, contrary to Beck's opinion, it is not the case that the biblical tale is being used in Kafka's novel to give a contemporary story "universal" (or "Jewish") relevance; the force of allusion goes rather in the other direction, with *Der Verschollene* as a burlesqued, profane retelling of the sacred ur-narrative of servitude, exile, and redemption.

61. "Blue-black masses of stone sped by the train in sharp hunks, one leaned out of the window and tried in vain to find their peak, dark narrow lacerated valleys opened up, one pointed out the direction where they lost themselves to view, broad mountain streams came rushing in a great wave out of the undulating bedrock and spread out into a thousand tiny ripples of foam, they plunged under the bridges over which the train was going and were so near that their cool mist made one's face shiver" (*V* 418–19).

62. Wagner, "Kafkas Poetik des Unfalls," 439. This article also appears translated and in modified form in Corngold and Wagner, *Ghosts in the Machine,* 177–202.

63. See Aristotle, *Poetics* 5.5, 16.

64. In regard to Kafka's comment on Walser see also Kreienbrock, *Kleiner. Feiner. Leichter,* 24–45.

65. Wagner deliberately misreads this phrase to refer, not to Walser, but to Kafka's evaluation of his own job at the Prague Workmen's Accident Insurance Institute, also making the images of the jumping and the falling horses an allegory for Kafka's current place of employment versus his former one: an interpretation that is certainly suggestive, but also in no way actually supported by the letter itself. See Wagner, "Poetik des Unfalls," 440; Corngold and Wagner, *Ghosts in the Machine,* 193.

66. In the annotated English edition of Kafka's office writings, this passage is read somewhat unconvincingly as an allegory of new relations of property ownership and commodity fetishism: "The reader acquainted with the historical background of automobile insurance could see in this facet of Kafka's fantasy of America a grandiose parody of the legal realities of Old Europe. The cars' eagerness to get to their owners may very well allude to the strange legal ties between vehicles and their 'owners' when the latter have become the economic and legal subjects of their 'firms.'" Corngold, Greenberg, and Wagner, eds., *Franz Kafka: The Office Writings,* 88.

67. Also relevant is the gruesome photograph reproduced by Holitscher in his book of what is presumably a lynch mob, posing next to the still-hanging corpses of their two victims. Holitscher's sarcastic caption reads: "Idyll from Oklahama [*sic*]." Holitscher, *Amerika Heute und Morgen,* 367. Such a connection, of course, could be and has been read as proof that Kafka thinks of Karl's end as a fatal trap indeed. However—beyond the fact that Kafka usually takes an extremely free hand with his source material—it may also be noted that on the next page, Holitscher expresses the wish that African Americans might rise up against the injustice exercised upon them, especially since "the colored man in the lift [can]

often rival in intelligence the white man in the office." Holitscher, *Amerika Heute und Morgen,* 370.

68. Holitscher's remark may be understood with all its biopolitical and anthropological implications intact. According to most sources, the word "cretin" derives from a Swiss patois of *chrétien,* "Christian," used originally to refer to people afflicted with a particular form of dwarfism and mental retardation once typical in the Alps region. As the *OED* entry for this word further specifies, "Christian" in this context is intended to signify "'human creature' as distinguished from the brutes; the sense being here that these beings are really human, though so deformed physically and mentally."

69. See, e.g., Wagner, "Die Versicherung des Übermenschen," esp. 293–94; Hermsdorf, "Arbeit und Amt als Erfahrung und Gestaltung," 45–46; and Corngold, Greenberg, and Wagner, *The Office Writings.*

70. See Wagner, "'. . .in der Fremde, aus der Sie kommen. . .' Die Geburt des Schreibens aus der Statistik des Selbstmords," 223; also Corngold and Wagner, *Ghosts in the Machine,* 35–55; Vogl, "Kafkas Komik," 85.

71. See, for example, Kafka's not exactly sympathetic portrayal of Bohemian-born illustrator Alfred Kubin and his enthusiasm for a certain cure-all laxative (*T* 40–41 and 45).

72. Kracauer, "The Mass Ornament," 84.

73. On the historical affinity between Kafka and Chaplin's Little Tramp, see Weissberg, *Hannah Arendt, Charlie Chaplin und die verborgene jüdische Tradition.* Similar to the phenomenon in which, as Weissberg describes, many in Chaplin's day (not least of whom Hannah Arendt) simply assumed Chaplin to be of Jewish origin, Holitscher explicitly considers the American hobo as a Jew in contrast to the go-getting, upwards-striving, vigorous American Gentile: "The poor Jewish worker, already enervated, beaten before the battle starts, grown anemic from the pogroms back home, arrives in the land of freedom and victorious energy, can't, it goes without saying, keep up the pace. He has the choice between suicide, death by exhaustion, madness, and crime. He opts for the open road [Landstreicherei]." Holitscher, *Amerika Heute und Morgen,* 311.

74. On Kafka's quasi-scientific dramatization of anthropological border-categories, see Neumann, "Kafka als Ethnologe."

75. Thus Hanns Zischler is incorrect when he cites this passage as evidence of Kafka's "pleasure in early films" and describes Kafka's words as an "urgent film recommendation." Zischler, *Kafka geht ins Kino,* 16. To the contrary, it is clear that the recommendation being given here is anything but urgent (and indeed, not even really a recommendation at all). And while Kafka's pleasure here is obvious, it is less the pleasure of an enthusiastic moviegoer than that of a bemused observer of popular culture, an all-around ladies' man, and—above all—an inveterate player with words and logic.

76. See Neumann, "Umkehrung und Ablenkung: Franz Kafkas 'Gleitendes Paradox,'" esp. 744.

77. Zischler's book provides facsimiles of the original Pathé frères' publicity cards with plot summaries for both films mentioned by Kafka. Adding to an understanding of Kafka's playfulness in the letter to Elsa Taussig is the fact that while *Der durstige Gendarm* is clearly a crude burlesque, *Der galante Gardist*

appears to be the purest of high melodrama—complete with love affair, murder, an innocent falsely accused, and a last-minute salvation from the gallows—and the laughter it would evoke likely to be only of the unintentional kind. See Zischler, *Kafka geht ins Kino,* 18–19.

78. Compare Kierkegaard, *Either/Or,* 234: "The occasion is always the accidental, and the prodigious paradox is that the accidental is absolutely just as necessary as the necessary. In the ideal sense, the occasion is not the accidental as, for example, when I think the accidental in the logical sense, but the occasion is the accidental in the sense of fetishism, and yet in this accidentality it is the necessary."

79. On *Der Verschollene* in relation to the Bildungsroman, see Neumann, "Ritual und Theater," esp. 66; and Scheffel, "Paradoxa und kein Ende. Franz Kafkas Romanprojekt 'Der Verschollene,'" esp. 22.

80. Scheffel quotes Blanckenburg's stipulation that in the successful novel, characters and actions "must [. . .] be so bound to one another that they are at once both cause and effect [. . .] so that the end, the result of the work is the necessary effect of all that has come before [eine nothwendige Wirkung alles des Vorhergehenden]." Blanckenburg, *Versuch über den Roman,* 381, quoted in Scheffel, 23–24.

81. See Bubner, "Die Aristotelische Lehre vom Zufall," esp. 7.

82. Schopenhauer criticizes Kant's account of causation on precisely these grounds. See Schopenhauer, *World as Will and Representation,* vol. 2, 285–88. See also Schopenhauer, *World as Will and Representation,* vol. 1, 463–71 and 501–7.

83. Kafka, *Nachgelassene Schriften und Fragmente II,* 127–28.

84. See, e.g., Weltsch, 86–93. See also the section, "The Comic Treatment of Contingency," in Hegel's *Aesthetics* (*A* 590–92; *AII* 216–18); Rosenkranz, *Ästhetik des Häßlichen,* 205–6; and Preisendanz, "Komik als Komplement der Erfassung von Kontingenzen."

85. See Siegfried J. Schmitt on comedic plot as "the thematized simultaneity of different worlds in a single communication situation." Schmitt, "Komik im Beschreibungsmodell kommunikativer Handlungsspiele," 187.

86. Among the several aphorisms addressing this topic, perhaps the most explicit is the piece on the "triplicity of free will [Dreierlei des freien Willens]," which concludes similarly, "but it is also the case that the triplicity is a unicity [ein Einerlei] and it is so fundamentally a unicity [im Grunde so sehr Einerlei] that there is no place left for will, neither free nor unfree." Kafka, *Nachgelassene Schriften und Fragmente II,* 138.

87. See Kafka, *Der Proceß,* 208.

88. See Zilcosky, *Kafka's Travels,* esp. 52–54.

89. The possibility that Green's phrase is an obscene joke on Kafka's part—thus making Karl the excrement expelled from the bowels of good society—should not be ruled out. The same phrase also occurs in *Der Proceß* as Joseph K.'s description of his trial. See Kafka, *Der Proceß,* 168. On excreta and *allotria* or random play in Kafka (specifically, on the latter as a form of waste *activity* to match the former as waste *product*) see Corngold, *Lambent Traces,* 72–73.

90. Beck is of the opinion that the weaponized Statue of Liberty is a "playful" move on Kafka's part, a whimsical touch to bring together the contradictory motifs

of the American myth of freedom and the biblical Fall of Man. See Beck, *Kafka and the Yiddish Theater,* 125. As suggested by the argument of the present chapter, however, it may be pointed out that freedom and the Fall are not contradictory at all, but rather, and indeed according to the words of the Bible itself—"And the LORD GOD said, Behold, the man is become as one of us, to know good and evil" (Gen. 3:22, King James Bible)—the expulsion from Eden is at once freedom's *origin* and *necessary condition.* Kafka's conflation of these two images would then be not simply an irreverent incongruity, but an ironic appropriation of the American freedom myth to explore ideas of human freedom and knowledge per se.

91. Another of the 1918 aphorisms treating the concept of original sin, whose relevance to *Der Verschollene* seems clear, runs as follows: "The expulsion from Paradise is in its main part eternal: thus the expulsion from Paradise is indeed final and life in the world inevitable, yet the eternity of the process means it remains possible that we not only could have stayed in Paradise permanently, but indeed are permanently there, regardless of whether we here know it or not." Kafka, *Nachgelassene Schriften und Fragmente II,* 127.

92. It is perhaps not incidental that the uncle's business is described as a "Zwischenhandel" (*V* 66).

93. Kafka's curious geographical error can be clarified by a look at Genesis 4:16: "And Cain went out from the presence of the LORD, and dwelt in the land of Nod, on the east of Eden" (King James Bible). This reference sheds further light on Karl's chosen appellation "Negro" in the Theater of Oklahama chapter, as well as the fact that, despite Karl's own status as "fugitive and vagabond" (Gen. 4:14), no truly grievous harm befalls him—although it should also be noted, against any merely analogic reading, that the marked Karl in fact does *not* go "east" to San Francisco.

94. Also significant is the fact that, in the paragraph directly after the uncle's reluctant approval—which will of course turn out to be no approval at all—in which Karl and Pollunder try in vain to parse the uncle's motivations, the word "trotzdem" appears three times in the space of seven lines (see *V* 73).

95. See Derrida, "Before the Law," esp. 26; see also Vogl, *Ort der Gewalt,* 175–76 on Kafka's approach to the double bind in Kantian *ethics,* which, as Vogl notes, "also provides an occasion for comical and ironic twists" (177).

96. See Lacan's couched allusion to Kafka in "The Agency of the Letter in the Unconscious": "Madness, you are no longer the object of the ambiguous praise with which the sage decorated the impregnable burrow [*terrier*: the word used in French to translate Kafka's *Bau*]; and if after all he finds himself tolerably at home there, it is only because the supreme agent forever at work digging its tunnels is none other than reason, the very logos that he serves." Lacan, "The Agency of the Letter in the Unconscious," 192; compare Lacan, "L'instance de la lettre dans l'inconscient," 526.

97. See especially *CPR* 317–18; 647: transcendental ideas "detach themselves completely from experience and construct for themselves objects, the material of which has not been presented by experience, and the objective reality of which is not based upon the completion of the empirical series, but upon pure a priori conceptions. The intelligible object of these transcendent ideas may be conceded, as a transcendental object. But we cannot cogitate it as a thing determinable by certain distinct predicates relating to its internal nature, for it has no connection

with empirical conceptions; nor are we justified in affirming the existence of any such object. It is, consequently, a mere product of the mind alone."

98. This structure bears similarities to what Vogl, following a distinction made by Deleuze, describes in Kafka as the crossing of humor (as a downwards movement towards the particular) with irony (as an upwards movement taking aim at the general). See Vogl, "Kafkas Komik," 84.

99. Benjamin, *Origin of German Tragic Drama,* 113, emphasis added. On Socratic vs. tragic irony, see *Origin of German Tragic Drama,* 117–18.

100. See also *UEK* 176: "The sublime is not denied, not annihilated: that would be frivolous [. . .]. The sublime and the infinitely small play within one another, and this play is the comic." Vischer's refinement of his own thesis acts as a warning against conceiving of Kafka's comedy merely as anti-ontotheological satire.

101. In an interpretation of the opening scenes of *The Trial,* Neumann argues for a "split in Kafka's work between sublimity and the comic." Neumann, "'War es eine Komödie, so wollte er mitspielen,'" 106. With Vischer, however, I would like to claim that the comic exists not in contrast to the sublime, but as a breach within the sublime itself.

102. See Kafka's brief and enigmatic note: "Laughableness re: Kant [Lächerlichkeit betr. Kant]." Kafka, *Nachgelassene Schriften und Fragmente I,* 423.

103. It may be recalled that the two forms of legal proceedings available to Joseph K.—besides the execution that puts the novel to a summary end—are "ostensible acquittal" and "postponement." As the painter Titorelli aptly (and punningly) comments, "Those are the only things that can come into question [Um die allein kann es sich handeln]." Kafka, *Der Proceß,* 208.

104. On "unlimited postponement" as a result of "the mutual immanence of a decoded law and a deterritorialized desire," see Deleuze and Guattari, *Kafka,* 51–52.

105. On the many valences and appearances of the German word "Fall," see de Man, "Aesthetic Formalization: Kleist's *Über das Marionettentheater,*" esp. 289–90. For the historical context of Kafka's desk job, see Wagner, "Kafka's Office Writings: Historical Background and Institutional Setting," 19–46.

106. Hermann Lübbe calls religion a "culture of the management of absolute contingency." Lübbe, "Kontingenzerfahrung und Kontingenzbewältigung," 43. See also Wagner, "Statistik des Selbstmords," esp. 203.

107. See, e.g., Kafka's mordantly witty remark in a report on safety measures in rock quarries: "Fig. V. Here the reversed ridge formation is so prevalent that one would almost be tempted to say the quarry would comply better with protective regulations than it does now if it were turned upside-down." Kafka, *Amtliche Schriften,* 260.

108. Consider the fact that at the moment Karl comes under Uncle Jakob's protection, "no one laughed, everyone listened patiently and seriously." As the narrative explains, "After all, one doesn't just laugh at a senator's nephew at the first opportunity that presents itself" (*V* 39). Post-lapsarian history (which is history per se) could then be said to begin again for Karl in the following chapter, when "at one of his expressions all the gentlemen fell over themselves laughing and Karl was afraid that he had made some sort of crude blunder, but no, as Mr. Pollunder explained to him, he had in fact said something very apt" (*V* 69).

109. "Ja freilich habe ich Komödie gespielt" (*DL* 58): this outburst, coming from the father in "The Judgment," continues, "Comedy! A good word! What other consolation does an old widowed father have left to him?" (*DL* 58).

110. Also of note is the fact that the name of the town to which Delamarche and Robinson first propose traveling is "Butterford" (*V* 137).

111. The name Schubal, containing within in it the word "Schub"—"push, impulse"—naturally also includes the ship's machinist within this dynamic. The notion of a vanished antagonistic impetus is a repeated motif in Kafka's writing: in a diary entry of January 19, 1911, Kafka describes an early, unfulfilled plan to write a novel, "in which two brothers struggle against one another, of whom one traveled to America, while the other sat in a European prison." Besides the theme of migration to America, and the Cain and Abel motif of the "good" and "bad" brother, which finds itself indeed in anagrammatic form in *Der Verschollene,* the diary entry (a description of a family luncheon in which Kafka writes a scene for the first novel) hints at other possible germs of the novel, including "an uncle who liked to laugh," and who mocks the young Kafka's literary ambitions (see *T* 146–47).

112. Also of interest in terms of Kafka's wordplay with "Komödie" are the compounds "Hundekomödie" and "Affenkomödie," both meaning something like "buffoonery, burlesque" and which, taken literally, can be seen to expand into the epistemological fables "Investigations of a Dog" and "A Report to an Academy," respectively.

Chapter Four

1. Brod, "Gefühl von einer Verwandlung des Staates," 30–31.

2. *The Metamorphosis (Die Verwandlung)* was written in 1912 and published in 1915 by Kurt Wolff Verlag. In his 1912 letters to Felice Bauer, Kafka frequently mentions work on a new story, without however divulging the title; the novella is first mentioned by name in Kafka's papers on April 4, 1913, in a letter to the publisher Kurt Wolff. See Kafka, *Briefe 1913–März 1914,* 156.

3. Also significant for the polemical import of Brod's piece is the fact that the three areas of Austria-Hungary that he names are ones known for their large Jewish populations. This not only allows Brod to synecdochically express his affinity to the Habsburg Empire as a whole, but also, more importantly, functions as an appeal to his fellow cosmopolitan Jews for solidarity with their non-urban coreligionists, and serves as a reminder to ethnically German Austrians ("those truly lucky ones, for whom this war is a national German war") that the shtetls of the East, too, must be counted as imperial lands and thus equally worth fighting for.

4. Althusser, "Ideology and Ideological State Apparatuses," esp. 170–77.

5. Not just Brod but also Robert Walser, Hesse, Hofmannsthal, Rilke, Thomas Mann, Elsa Lasker-Schüler, Oskar Kokoschka, Paul Klee, Martin Buber, Georg Trakl, Franz Werfel, Alfred Kubin, and Paul Scheerbart, among many others, made contributions to the pages of *Zeit-Echo.* As such a list might suggest, the contributions vary widely in content, style, and ideological orientation. Brod's essay is in fact far from the most egregiously propagandistic of the contributions to the journal: see, for example, Felix Stössinger's "Deutschland und Europa," which concludes that a fulfilled greater German nation-state would be inherently and inevitably a "nation of virtue." Stössinger, "Deutschland und Europa," 278. Despite such early

nationalist drum-banging, the magazine became increasingly critical of the war during the course of its brief existence, and eventually, in its third and last year in Swiss exile under the editorship of Ludwig Rubiner, explicitly revolutionary in tone. See Grötzinger, *Der Erste Weltkrieg im Widerhall des "Zeit-Echo."*

6. See Bronson, "Die journalistischen Anfänge Joseph Roths," esp. 37–38.

7. See Westermann, "Nachwort," esp. 1109–10.

8. In "Witzbold im Goethe-Jahr" (*JRW3* 415–18). This late piece is a response to the claim of a fellow columnist that Roth—in the previous "Ursachen der Schlaflosigkeit im Goethe-Jahr" (*JRW3* 413–15)—failed to see that the nationalist comments of the former's report on the 1932 Schmeling-Sharkey boxing match were meant "ironically." Roth responds: "Naturally it was never my ambition to understand the 'joke' of an indigenous pathos-monger [den 'Witz' eines autochthonen Pathetikers] [. . .]. When he makes one of his 'jokes,' I feel like crying" (*JRW3* 417).

9. Chambers, "Signs of the Times: Joseph Roth's Weimar Journalism," 102. See also Aristotle's crucial passage on tragedy and historiography in the *Poetics* 5.5, 16.

10. Pesnel, *Totalité et fragmentarité dans l'œuvre romanesque de Joseph Roth*, 6 and 11.

11. This imbalance is largely a result of the work of Claudio Magris. See Magris, *Der habsburgische Mythos in der österreichischen Literatur,* esp. 255–65; Magris, "Joseph Roth: Der Aufbruch auf der Suche nach dem Bekannten"; and Magris, *Der Unauffindbare Sinn. Zur österreichischen Literatur des 20. Jahrhunderts.* On the "Habsburg Myth" and the cultural milieu of pre- and postwar Austria more generally, see Schorske, *Fin-de-Siècle Vienna*; Le Rider, "Pour une histoire interculturelle de la production littéraire de langue allemande en Europe centrale," esp. 25; and Le Rider, *Modernity and Crises of Identity,* esp. 15–29.

12. Roth draws down a surprising amount of ire for his lack of a systematic politics, and, especially, his later turn to monarchism and Catholicism. Such ire generally takes the form of an attempt to discredit Roth's work wholesale, attributing his political and religious conversions to a latent bourgeois romanticism, when not indeed to outright personality disorder. See, e.g., Sieg, *Zwischen Anarchismus und Fiktion*; Sasse, "Der Prophet als Außenseiter"; Schweikert, "'Der rote Joseph' "; Goltschnigg, "Zeit-, Ideologie- und Sprachkritik in Joseph Roths Essayistik"; Aquiatas, "Satires et pamphlets dans les écrits journalistiques de Joseph Roth"; and Kiefer, *Braver Junge—gefüllt mit Gift. Joseph Roth und die Ambivalenz.*

13. Magris once again remains the critic most influential in promoting this viewpoint. See also, e.g., Trommler, *Österreich im Roman*; and Matthew, *Ambivalence and Irony in the Works of Joseph Roth.*

14. Lukács, "Zur Frage der Satire," 90.

15. See *VA* §33, 91–94; 129–32; and Nietzsche, *Also Sprach Zarathustra,* esp. 752–54, also quoted in the preface added by Nietzsche to *Die Geburt der Tragödie,* "Versuch einer Selbstkritik," esp. 17.

16. "His self-irony—a garment of satire—demolishes the thought-palaces of his spirit and allows him to build new ones" (*JRW1* 7).

17. This is essentially the same interpretation offered by Friedrich Schlegel in a letter to his brother August. As he writes: "Were [Hamlet] less great, he would

be a hero [Wäre er weniger groß, so würde er ein Heroe sein].” Quoted in Szondi, “Friedrich Schlegel und die romantische Ironie,” 7.

18. See, among others, “Der 70jährige Kadelburg” (*JRW1* 619–21); “Der Lausbub: Zur Psychologie Eulenspiegels” (*JRW1* 1046–48); and “Spielzeug” (*JRW2* 514–16). Roth’s praise, however, is by no means unequivocal. The ambiguity of his take on “carnival culture,” for example, is particularly in evidence in “Karneval” (*JRW1* 771–73) and “Stunde in Rummel” (*JRW1* 995–98), where Roth—in a manner that anticipates Adorno’s ambivalent critique of the “culture industry”—denounces the amusement park as the degradation of the spirit of real play.

19. Admittedly often—in the late romantic vein described by Starobinski (see chapter 2 of this book)—as tragic hero. See, e.g., “Der Tod im Zirkus” (*JRW1* 453–55); “Vormittagsprobe im Zirkus” (*JRW1* 1043–45); “Grock” (*JRW2* 299–301); “Der Mann, der die Ohrfeigen bekommt” (*JRW3* 118–21); and “Der Unbekannte Clown von Barcelona” (*JRW3* 888–89).

20. See, e.g., Sültemeyer, *Das Frühwerk Joseph Roths,* 74–76; Matthew, *Ambivalence and Irony,* 24–25; Plank, *Joseph Roth als Feuilletonist,* 51–73; and Powell, “Joseph Roth, Ironic Primitivist.”

21. On the telephone book as “the other book of books, a name which registers all the names of history, if only to attend the refusal of the proper name,” see Ronell, *The Telephone Book,* 5. If this is so, then Roth’s feuilleton also bears witness to the scrambling of the historical record, as will be discussed in greater detail below.

22. For example: “A war invalid who has found a nail file. Someone, a lady, lost the file just at the place where the invalid is sitting. So the beggar begins to file his nails. With this coincidence that has played a nail file into his hands and by means of the insignificant action of nail-filing, he has symbolically leapt over a thousand social levels” (*JRW1* 565). I note in passing the threefold pun between the beggar’s literal (and now manicured) hand, the coincidence that “played” the nail file “into his hand [in die Hand gespielt hat]” and the “action [Handlung]” entailing his social advancement.

23. Benjamin, “On Some Motifs in Baudelaire,” 343; Benjamin, “Über einige Motive bei Baudelaire,” 653.

24. See *JRW1* 929; and Benjamin, “Robert Walser” (German), 327. While the time lag between Roth’s feuilleton and Benjamin’s review—1923 to 1929—is considerable, it is nevertheless not outside the realm of possibility that Benjamin is indirectly alluding to Roth’s feuilleton—particularly considering the fact that Walser entered the Waldau mental clinic on January 25, 1929, approximately eight months before the publication (in *Das Tagebuch,* September 28, 1929) of Benjamin’s essay.

25. This phrase occurs in the context of Kant’s critique of Samuel Johnson, in which Kant disparagingly contrasts Johnson’s wittiness in trivial matters to his “coarseness [Grobheit]” in weightier subjects, which in turn proves a “great inability to unite wit with profundity in the same thought [großes Unvermögen eines in demselben Gedanken mit Gründlichkeit vereinigten Witzes]” (*ANTH* 118; 132).

26. Especially in Barthes’ sense of the “*trouvaille,*” “a ‘natural’ scene which the good reporter has had the genius, i.e., the luck, to catch.” Barthes, *Camera Lucida,* 33. Compare Roth’s statement in the 1924 feuilleton “Wiederbelebung

durch 20 000 Zinnsoldaten" (*JRW2* 247–49): "It's not the first time that a trivial event takes on the historical significance of a symptom; still, it doesn't happen every day that a particular trend reveals the whole misery of its spiritual condition in a single triviality so appropriately, so *self-appropriately,* that even the caricaturist has nothing left to do but take a photograph" (*JRW2* 247).

27. Roth's "Harzreise" is naturally a tribute to Heine's work of the same name.

28. Paul Fleming examines this paradox from the other side, showing how the example-giving character of genius gives rise to the idea of autonomous art, at the same time that the "sensus communis" necessary to art's reception precludes exceptionality. See Fleming, *Exemplarity and Mediocrity,* esp. 28–36.

29. See *VA* §43, 121–22, translation modified; 171: "Wit alone invents, and indeed directly; thus Friedrich Schlegel is right to call it fragmentary genius [. . .]. It used to refer to genius altogether; accordingly in several languages its synonyms are *Geist, esprit,* spirit, *ingeniosus.*"

30. See for example Otto Groth, who in his magisterial study of the periodical as medium, writes: "When, in a feuilleton, content and form merge in an aesthetically pleasing unity, the result is a fine piece of craftsmanship; depending on its truth content and epistemic value, it might even be able to approach the level of a scholarly paper. But the ultimate achievements of art or scholarship will always be denied to it; in exchange, the feuilleton may enjoy its reputation [. . .] of being the loveliest blossom on the tree of journalism." Groth, *Die unerkannte Kulturmacht,* 136.

31. Schweikert, for example, accuses Roth of a "contradiction in the undecided coexistence of sentimentally romanticized subjectivism and political objectification," paralleled "formally in the alternation between feuilleton and reportage." Schweikert, "'Der rote Joseph,'" 48.

32. Schorske, *Fin-de-Siècle Vienna,* 9.

33. Kraus, "Heine und die Folgen," 188–89.

34. See, e.g., Roth's parody of the idea of autonomous art in his novel *Die Flucht ohne Ende* (*Flight Without End*), where the brother of the main character Franz Tunda, a well-off provincial bandleader, pronounces, "Art is something sacred, removed from the everyday [. . .]. Can you picture someone giving a political speech and then directing *Parsifal*?" (*JRW4* 455).

35. Jürgen Heizmann points out that Neue Sachlichkeit's notion of "objectivity" can also be understood more charitably as a *heuristic* category, indicating the movement's rejection of what it considered to be the febrile pathos of a culturally dominant Expressionism. See Heizmann, *Joseph Roth und die Ästhetik der Neuen Sachlichkeit,* 27–28.

36. See Wildenhahn, *Feuilleton zwischen den Kriegen,* 20–21 and 46.

37. On this justly oft-discussed piece, see Plank, *Joseph Roth als Feuilletonist,* 17–22; Sültemeyer, *Das Frühwerk Joseph Roths,* 62–63; Wirtz, *Joseph Roths Fiktionen des Faktischen,* 33–35; Hackert, *Kulturpessimismus und Erzählform,* 144; and Schroeder, *Experimente des Erzählens,* 79–80.

38. I am indebted to Sophie Witt for this observation.

39. See Bakhtin, *Rabelais,* 24–25; also 11 on carnival culture's "pathos of change and renewal."

40. In "Die Hinrichtung Österreichs" (*JRW3* 922–25, here 924).

41. For example, in the following passage from the seventeenth-century scientist and inventor Robert Boyle's "An Essay Containing a Requisite Digression, Concerning Those That Would Exclude the Deity from Intermeddling with Matter," 159–60: "Methinks we may without absurdity conceive that God [. . .] did divide (at least if he did not create it incoherent) that matter which he had provided into an innumerable multitude of very variously figured corpuscles [. . .] and put them into such motions, that, by the assistance of his ordinary preserving concourse, the phenomena which he intended should appear in the universe must as orderly follow [. . .]. As, in the formerly mentioned clock of Strasbourg, the several pieces making up that curious engine are so framed and adapted, and are put into such a motion, that [. . .] each performs its part in order to the various ends for which it was contrived, as regularly and uniformly as if it knew and were concerned to do its duty."

42. Two exceptions also have to do with comic coincidences in proper names. In "Flug nach Dortmund" (*JRW1* 651–54), Roth observes, "The pilot that flew the plane was called Kurt Ungewitter [Kurt Thunderstorm]. A pilot could hardly have a better name" (*JRW1* 652). A less innocuous coincidence appears in "Ludendorff und das Schlachtvieh" ("Ludendorff and the Animals to the Slaughter") (*JRW2* 79–81), where a cattle transport firm bears the same name as that of the famous World War I general. Roth comments: "The German present is rich in witty occurrences [. . .]. If people in Germany had more of a feeling for the terrific mordancy of happenstance, we wouldn't have to fight so hard for revolution" (*JRW2* 79).

43. See Beug, "Sprachkrise und Sprachgläubigkeit im Werk Joseph Roths."

44. Heizmann, *Joseph Roth und die Ästhetik der Neuen Sachlichkeit,* 117; see also Pesnel, *Totalité et fragmentarité dans l'œuvre romanesque de Joseph Roth,* 314. Heizmann's own language would seem to indicate that he has Roth's eventual conversion to Roman Catholicism in mind.

45. While onomatopoeia is traditionally considered a form of fairly uncomplicated mimesis, indeed, "a particularly concentrated and effective product of a deep-seated need to coordinate words with things" (Breden, "Onomatopoeia as a Figure and a Linguistic Principle," 566), a more considered reading of the trope understands it as a mutual constitution *between* sound and sense, and thus an example of the "*work of bringing meaning into being.*" Attridge, "Language as Imitation: Jakobson, Joyce, and the Art of Onomatopoeia," 1134.

46. Compare Hughes, *Facing Modernity,* 29. Against the notion of Roth as linguistic irredentist, Hughes argues that Roth is "broadly" a "nominalist" in the tradition of Simmel and Hofmannsthal: "By embracing the relativity of language and meaning, their indetermination (what Derrida terms 'undecidable'), the narrator of [Roth's travelogue] *Die weißen Städte* begins a process of questioning which will lead him ultimately to the hope of a world in which ambivalence and ambiguity, in the form of racial mixing to the point that 'race' ceases to be a recognized category, become the norm."

47. On Roth's use of "linguistically concentrated figures of speech based on contrast and contradiction," see Chambers, "Signs of the Times," 111.

48. Later in the same piece, Roth repeats the figure in the other direction: "the undetermined ones [among the café's patrons] don't have names, so I can imagine how they are called: Mr. Day-Laborer, Mr. Jinxed, Mr. Unemployed, Mr.

Tubercular. So long as I don't know them, people are just called what they are [Solange ich sie nicht kenne, heißen die Menschen so, wie sie sind]" (*JRW1* 201).

49. As the narrator of *Die Flucht ohne Ende* comments: "Writers experience everything through the medium of language; they have no experience without putting it into words [Schriftsteller erleben alles durch das Mittel der Sprache, sie haben kein Erlebnis ohne Formulierung]" (*JRW4* 407). It is a particular irony, of course, that this comment appears in the same novel subtitled "A Report [Ein Bericht]," of which Roth, in the brief foreword, asserts, "I've invented nothing, composed nothing. It's no longer about 'fiction' [Ich habe nichts erfunden, nichts komponiert. Es handelt sich nicht mehr darum zu 'dichten']" (*JRW4* 391).

50. See also Chambers, "Signs of the Times," 114–15.

51. Benjamin, "On the Concept of History," 391–92.

52. The first sentence of the foreword to the 1916 *Kriegsnachtrag* of the *Meyers Großes Konversations-Lexikon* (n.b. *not* the work that Roth is citing) reads, "The world-shaking events of the present day affect all those now living [Die welterschütternden Ereignisse der Gegenwart bewegen alle Lebenden]." *Meyers Großes Konversations-Lexikon. Kriegsnachtrag,* v.

53. *Meyers Handlexikon. Siebente gänzlich veränderte und neubearbeitete Auflage,* 760.

54. White, *Metahistory,* 375–76. See also Wirtz, *Fiktionen des Faktischen,* 114–19 on the "question of the narratability of the world" in Roth in terms of White's analysis.

55. As Paul Fussell observes: "the Great War was perhaps the last to be conceived as taking place within a seamless, purposeful 'history' involving a coherent stream of time running from past to present to future"; consequently, in the war's aftermath, "there seems to be one dominating form of modern understanding; that it is essentially ironic." Fussell, *The Great War and Modern Memory,* 21 and 35.

56. The first version of the Meyer *Konversations-Lexikon* appeared in 1839. My claim is not that the encyclopedia has any more or less authority in 1920 than it did at the time of its first publishing, only that authority *itself* is now more deeply in question.

57. The 1986 edition of the Meyer *Lexikon,* while offering a rather more nuanced version of the causes of the war than the 1920 edition, nevertheless preserves this word in anagrammatized form within the phrase, "So geriet Deutschland in Zugzwang [Thus Germany's hand was forced]." *Meyers großes Universallexikon,* 341.

58. Marin, *Portrait of the King,* 58–59.

59. The exemplary exponent of this view is of course Carl Schmitt, e.g.: "in the orientation towards the possible extreme case of an actual battle against a real enemy, the political entity is essential, and it is the decisive entity for the friend-or-enemy grouping; and in this (and not in any kind of absolutist sense) it is sovereign. Otherwise the political entity is nonexistent." Schmitt, *The Concept of the Political,* 39.

60. This is the famous paradox of Cartesian skepticism. See, e.g., Blumenberg, *Die Legitimität der Neuzeit,* 20 and 74–76; also Williams, "Descartes and the Metaphysics of Doubt," esp. 135.

61. Arendt, "What Is Authority?" 95. See also Ronell, *Loser Sons,* esp. 24–34 and 69.

62. Hobbes, *Leviathan,* 113.

63. It is no doubt in *this* sense that for Roth Habsburg (and Catholic) pageantry succeeds where a Bismarckian and Protestant austerity falls short. See, e.g., "Seine k. und k. apostolische Majestät" (*JRW2* 910–15), in which Roth praises the Habsburg Empire for the gift of a "strongly felt sense for ceremony and representation" (*JRW2* 911).

64. Magris describes Roth's emperor—who not only confuses the elder Trotta with Trotta's long-dead father, but also mixes up past and present entirely—as "Cassandra-like and death-betokening, clumsy and childishly sly." Magris, *Habsburgische Mythos,* 264. From Roth's actual description of the scene, however, it is plain that the old emperor is being portrayed, not as "childishly sly [kindlich schlau]," but, in fact, fully in his second childhood.

65. An untranslatable pun, combining "Potemkinschen Dörfer [Potemkin villages]" with the name of German general Erich Ludendorff, one of the chief military commanders of World War I.

66. The Orgesch (short for "Organisation Escherich," after its founder, Bavarian politician and forester Georg Escherich) was a far-right paramilitary group active from 1920 to 1921. See Vincent, *A Historical Dictionary of Germany's Weimar Republic,* 115–16.

67. Kantorowicz, *The King's Two Bodies,* 272.

68. "If you could hear, at every jolt, the blood / Come gargling from the froth-corrupted lungs, / Obscene as cancer, bitter as the cud / Of vile, incurable sores on innocent tongues, / My friend, you would not tell with such high zest / To children ardent for some desperate glory, / The old Lie; Dulce et Decorum est / Pro patria mori." Owen, "Dulce et Decorum Est," 117.

69. Agamben, *Homo Sacer,* 60.

70. Both of these are used as analogies for royal ceremonial in "Kaiserbilder." In other feuilletons, Roth also lashes out at forms of *republican* political presentation: see, e.g., "Die Stimme seines Herrn" (*JRW1* 602–5); "Wahlkampf in Berlin" (*JRW2* 169–70); and "Ein Unpolitischer Geht in den Reichstag" (*JRW2* 191–94).

71. See Mark 9:35 and 10:31, Matthew 19:30 and 20:16, and Luke 13:30. Naturally, the decisive difference is that Jesus's proverb contains an eschatological element that Roth's piece and, arguably, the concept of authority itself both lack.

72. See Arendt, "What Is Authority?" 93: "authority precludes the use of external means of coercion; where force is used, authority itself has failed. Authority, on the other hand, is incompatible with persuasion, which presupposes equality and works through a process of argumentation. Where arguments are used, authority is left in abeyance."

73. Thus Brod's attempt to reconcile the "two faces of the state" is to a certain degree justified, since there is no "original" or "real" authority in contrast to which one could accuse his two-faced state of hypocrisy or satirically play one face against the other. Unlike Roth, however, Brod reverts to claiming the actual identity of these two aspects and thus to affirming a state authority that is in the end real, intrinsic, and essential.

74. This is in fact the central problematic of Arendt's essay, as she traces the attempt throughout history—from Plato, Aristotle, Roman law, and institutional Christianity to Machiavelli and the ideology of modern revolutions—to ground what is in the end just this tautology. She concludes with an implicit plea for what might be termed a politics *without* authority: "For to live in a political realm with neither authority nor the concomitant awareness that the source of authority transcends power and those who are in power, means to be confronted anew, without the religious trust in a sacred beginning and without the protection of traditional and therefore self-evident standards of behavior, by the elementary problems of human living-together." Arendt, "What Is Authority?" 141.

75. More than one critic has attributed just such a belief to Roth. This is understandable, given Roth's eventual vocal support for the renewal of the Habsburg monarchy; yet even if one could hardly blame Roth for finding Franz Joseph to be a better option than Hitler, the fact that this support developed mainly *after* the Anschluss suggests that Roth is a believer not in authority so much as in "authority": that is, since authority is always anyway provisional and performative, in the face of the Austrian republic's failure and the impending Nazi rise to power, a revival of the notion of the divine right of kings would seem to be the least of several evils.

76. See also Cavell, foreword to *The Scandal of the Speaking Body,* xviii: "Yet when [. . .] Austin guards against the sound of flippancy by declaring that 'Surely the words must be spoken "seriously" and so as to be taken "seriously,"' it turns out that his scare quotes around 'seriously,' far from helping to provide safeguards against flippancy, are symptoms that he has, and knows he has, turned away from the founding question he has raised concerning what it is to say something."

77. This is Hackert's interpretation (via Beda Allemann) of Roth's "irony." For a critique of precisely this dialectical neutralization of irony, see de Man, "Irony," esp. 169–70.

78. Compare Jean Paul on the "witziger Zirkel": "In this form of nonfigurative or reflective wit an idea first opposes itself then makes a peace of similarity, but not of equality, with its non-self" (*VA* §46, 127; 179).

79. See the 1922 piece "Paradoxie" (*JRW1* 857–60), in which Roth denounces Ewald Gerhard Seeliger's *Handbuch des Schwindels* for its cheap and lame—not to mention anti-intellectual and anti-Semitic—humor.

80. Or in Roth's words: "'Kitsch' is the literary expression of socially accepted forms and manifestations of life. 'Convention' is applied kitsch" (*JRW1* 586).

81. Schmitt, *Political Romanticism,* 69. See also Schumacher, *Die Ironie der Unverständlichkeit,* 23.

82. Virno, with reference to Schmitt, if not exactly in his spirit, speaks of the *joke* as "the state of exception of discourse": not in the sense of an affirmation of Schmittian decisionism, but rather in terms of joke's capacity to highlight the grounds of its own contingency and thus—theoretically—to lead to new forms of ethico-political action. See Virno, *Multitude,* 123.

83. Bernstein, *Virtuosity of the Nineteenth Century,* 17. "Irresponsibility" is naturally to be understood here as a formal textual attribute, and not as an authorial defect.

84. In which, again, the artist "starts from his own subjectivity and continually comes back to it, so that the actual object of representation is treated only as an external occasion for giving free play to witticisms, jokes, fancies, and the

extravagances of his most subjective mood. But since this is so, the matter and this subjective quality fall apart from one another, and the material is treated in an absolutely arbitrary fashion, indeed so that the particularity of the artist himself flashes forth as the chief thing" (*A* 295, translation modified; *AI* 381).

85. Kraus, "Heine und die Folgen," 189. See Hackert, *Kulturpessimismus und Erzählform,* 27–42 on the rivalry between Kraus and Roth, especially 33 on Kraus's desire "to take the world at its word" through the elimination of figurative speech and the re-literalization of metaphor.

86. The semi-anonymity of the feuilletonist is marked in concrete fashion by the practice of reducing bylines to initials or pseudonyms, as is the case in many of Roth's articles. See also Wildenhahn, *Feuilleton zwischen den Kriegen,* 34–37 on the relation between this inherent authorlessness of the feuilleton and editorial efforts to standardize newspaper reading practices.

87. Compare Roth's later description of the development of the "Leser schlechthin": "The dear reader was already long gone, but he was still appealed to. He stood there in the lines of text like a telephone subscriber in an old phone book. You called, and no one answered. He had become a stock phrase, a figure of speech, a fixed expression, an apostrophization-husk with nothing inside. [. . .] Once writers realized, late enough, how useless their attempts to make a connection were, they ceased calling vanished names and became reserved, cool, and businesslike" (*JRW1* 855).

88. Culler, *Pursuit of Signs,* 137.

89. This aspect is highlighted by Derrida at the beginning of *Politics of Friendship,* in his evocation of Montaigne's similarly paradoxical vocative.

90. The complement to the trope of the "dear reader" is that of prosopopoeia, the figure of giving of voice to the absent or dead: if prosopopoeia is the fiction of the presence of the absent or nonexistent speaking subject, then apostrophe is the fiction of the presence of the absent subject who has ears to hear. See Bettine Menke, *Prosopopoiia,* esp. 138.

91. Culler, *Pursuit of Signs,* 146. On prosopopoeia's similar dynamic, see Bettine Menke, *Prosopopoiia,* 167–68.

92. De Man, "The Rhetoric of Temporality," 218–19.

93. Lacoue-Labarthe and Nancy, *The Literary Absolute,* 104.

94. Significantly, Hegel frowns upon this practice in the dramatic arts, where the presence of the author still remains an open question (as opposed to lyric, where the author is present by definition, and epic, where he is entirely invisible). The sole exception to this prohibition on dramatic parabasis is in the case of *comedy,* where "from the very beginning the ruling principle is the contingency and caprice of subjective life" (*A* 1180; *AIII* 504).

95. See Hughes, *Facing Modernity,* 171 on the "emphasis upon the diegetic, rather than the mimetic" in Roth's early novels, which "has the side-effect of undermining the 'authority' of the narrator within the fictional sphere of his own narrative. The bridges to the 'real' world, to the past as it 'actually' happened, are burnt at the outset, leaving the text to function solely according to its own internal dynamics, not 'Geschichte' but 'eine Geschichte.' "

96. See Bernstein, *Virtuosity of the Nineteenth Century,* 28: "Through playful articulation, a particular self or point of view is smuggled into the generality of

public discourse—a private self is published. But these utterances cannot be conflated with the immediate experience of an *I.*"

97. See Nietzsche, *Die fröhliche Wissenschaft,* esp. §108, 145; §125, 158–60; and §343, 255–56.

98. "Perhaps he suspected even then, long before the fall of the monarchy, that facetious jokes could be deadlier than the assassination attempts of criminals or the solemn speeches of ambitious and insurrectionary do-gooders [. . .]. For the old Austro-Hungarian monarchy did not die of the hollow pathos of revolutionaries, but of the ironic skepticism of those who should have been its faithful upholders" (*JRW5* 659).

99. For example, in "Amüsement" (*JRW1* 640–641); "Abschied von Castans Panoptikum" (*JRW1* 737–39); "Philosophie des Panoptikums" (*JRW1* 939–41), "Der Friedhof des Panoptikums" (*JRW2* 201–2); and "Panoptikum am Sonntag" (*JRW2* 931–34).

100. See Benjamin, *Origin of German Tragic Drama,* 176. On the *theatrum mundi* motif in general, see Quiring, ed., *Theatrum Mundi,* esp. introduction, 7–30.

101. Magris, "Joseph Roth," 290. See also Heath, "The Legacy of the Baroque in the Novels of Joseph Roth," which, however, deals less with questions of form than with thematic motifs (specifically: death, women, the search for order) supposedly common to both Roth and the literature of the German baroque period.

102. See Benjamin, *Origin of German Tragic Drama,* esp. 159–63; and de Man, "Temporality," esp. 205–8 and 222–26.

103. Haverkamp, "Humor," 177.

104. Magris calls Roth's early novels the equivalent of the *Odyssey* for postwar Europe's Jews. Magris, "Joseph Roth," 277. More speculatively, Cacciari describes the loss of *Heimat* in Roth as "a surrender of any possible return to conditions of experience." Cacciari, *Posthumous People,* 93.

Conclusion

1. Kleist, "Die Hunde und der Vogel," 324–25.

2. See Hofmannsthal, "Drei Kleine Betrachtungen," 40, and the introduction to this book.

3. Lacoue-Labarthe and Nancy, *The Literary Absolute,* 45.

4. Kierkegaard's sentence refers, paradigmatically, to Aristophanes' portrayal of Socrates in *The Clouds.*

5. Pattison, "Beyond the Grasp of Irony," 363.

WORKS CITED

Adorno, Theodor W. *Aesthetic Theory*, translated by Robert Hullot-Kentor. Minneapolis: University of Minnesota Press, 1997.

———. *Ästhetische Theorie*. Frankfurt am Main: Suhrkamp, 1970.

———. "Ist die Kunst Heiter?" In *Noten zur Literatur, Gesammelte Schriften*, vol. 2, edited by Rolf Tiedemann, 599–606. Frankfurt am Main: Suhrkamp, 1974.

———. "Parataxis: On Hölderlin's Late Poetry." In *Notes to Literature*, vol. 2, translated by Shierry Weber Nicholsen, 109–49. New York: Columbia University Press, 1992.

———. "Parataxis: Zur späten Lyrik Hölderlins." In *Noten zur Literatur, Gesammelte Schriften*, vol. 11, edited by Rolf Tiedemann, 447–91. Frankfurt am Main: Suhrkamp, 1974.

Agamben, Giorgio. *The Coming Community*. Translated by Michael Hardt. Minneapolis: University of Minnesota Press, 1993.

———. *Homo Sacer: Sovereign Power and Bare Life*. Translated by Daniel Heller-Roazen. Stanford, Calif.: Stanford University Press, 1998.

———. *Infancy and History: On the Destruction of Experience*. Translated by Liz Heron. London: Verso, 2007.

———. *The Man Without Content*. Translated by Georgia Albert. Stanford, Calif.: Stanford University Press, 1999.

Allemann, Beda. *Ironie und Dichtung*. Tubingen: Günther Neske Pfullingen, 1956.

Alt, Peter-André. *Franz Kafka: Der ewige Sohn: Eine Biographie*. Munich: Beck, 2005.

———. *Kafka und der Film. Über kinematographisches Erzählen*. Munich: Beck, 2009.

Altenhofer, Norbert. "*Die Ironie der Dinge." Zum späten Hofmannsthal*. Edited by Leonhard M. Fiedler. Frankfurt am Main: Peter Lang, 1995.

Althusser, Louis. "Ideology and Ideological State Apparatuses (Notes Towards an Investigation)." In *Lenin and Philosophy and Other Essays*, translated by Ben Brewster, 127–86. New York: Monthly Review, 1971.

Aquiatas, Christine. "Satires et pamphlets dans les écrits journalistiques de Joseph Roth (1915–1920): Der 'rote' Roth?" In *Écritures et langages satiriques en Autriche (1914–1938)/Satire in Österreich (1914–1938)*, edited by Jeanne Benay and Gilbert Ravy, 277–93. Bern: Lang, 1999.

Arendt, Hannah. "What Is Authority?" In *Between Past and Future: Six Exercises in Political Thought*, 91–141. New York: Penguin Classics, 2006.

Aristotle. *De Anima*. Translated by D. W. Hamlyn. Oxford: Clarendon, 2002.

———. *On Interpretation.* In *The Categories, On Interpretation, Prior Analytics,* translated by Harold P. Cook and Hugh Tredennick, 111–79. Cambridge, Mass.: Harvard University Press, 1962.

———. *Parts of Animals.* Translated by A. L. Peck. Cambridge, Mass.: Harvard University Press, 1961.

———. *Poetics.* Translated by Malcolm Heath. London: Penguin, 1996.

Artaud, Antonin. *Le théâtre et son double.* Paris: Gallimard, 1964.

———. *The Theater and Its Double.* Translated by Mary Caroline Richards. New York: Grove, 1958.

Attridge, Derek. "Language as Imitation: Jakobson, Joyce, and the Art of Onomatopoeia." *MLN* 99, no. 5 (December 1984): 1116–40.

Auerbach, Erich. *Mimesis: The Representation of Reality in Western Literature.* Translated by Willard R. Trask. Princeton, N.J.: Princeton University Press, 2003.

Avery, George C. *Inquiry and Testament: A Study of the Novels and Short Prose of Robert Walser.* Philadelphia: University of Pennsylvania Press, 1968.

Bakhtin, Mikhail. *Rabelais and His World.* Translated by Hélène Iswolsky. Bloomington: Indiana University Press, 1984.

Barthes, Roland. *Camera Lucida: Reflections on Photography.* Translated by Richard Howard. New York: Noonday, 1981.

Baudelaire, Charles. "De l'essence du rire, et généralement du comique dans les arts plastiques." In *Œuvres complètes,* vol. 2, edited by Claude Pichois, 525–43. Paris: Gallimard, 1976.

Beck, Evelyn Torton. *Kafka and the Yiddish Theater: Its Impact on His Work.* Madison: University of Wisconsin Press, 1971.

Behler, Ernst. *Irony and the Discourse of Modernity.* Seattle: University of Washington Press, 1990.

Benay, Jeanne. "De la secondarité romanesque chez Franz Kafka." In *Franz Kafka, Der Verschollene: Le Disparu/L'Amérique—Écritures d'un nouveau monde?* edited by Philippe Wellnitz, 27–49. Strasbourg: Presses Universitaires de Strasbourg, 1997.

Benjamin, Walter. *Briefe I.* Edited by Gershom Scholem and Theodor W. Adorno. Frankfurt am Main: Suhrkamp, 1978.

———. *The Concept of Criticism in German Romanticism.* In *Selected Writings, vol. 1: 1913–1926,* edited by Marcus Bullock and Michael W. Jennings, 116–200. Cambridge, Mass.: Harvard University Press, 1996.

———. *Der Begriff der Kunstkritik in der deutschen Romantik.* In *Gesammelte Schriften,* vol. 1, book 1, edited by Rolf Tiedemann and Hermann Schweppenhäuser, 7–122. Frankfurt am Main: Suhrkamp, 1974.

———. "Der Surrealismus: Die letzte Momentaufnahme der europäischen Intelligenz." In *Gesammelte Schriften,* vol. 2, book 1, edited by Rolf Tiedemann and Hermann Schweppenhäuser, 295–310. Frankfurt am Main: Suhrkamp, 1977.

———. "Franz Kafka: On the Tenth Anniversary of his Death." In *Selected Writings, vol. 2: 1927–1934,* edited by Michael W. Jennings, Gary Smith, and Howard Eiland, 795–818. Cambridge, Mass.: Harvard University Press, 2005.

———. "Franz Kafka. Zur zehnten Wiederkehr seines Todestages." In *Gesammelte Schriften,* vol. 2, book 2, edited by Rolf Tiedemann and Hermann Schweppenhäuser, 409–38. Frankfurt am Main: Suhrkamp, 1977.

———. “On Some Motifs in Baudelaire.” In *Selected Writings, vol. 4: 1938–1940*, edited by Howard Eiland and Michael W. Jennings, 313–55. Cambridge, Mass.: Harvard University Press, 2003.

———. “On the Concept of History.” In *Selected Writings, vol. 4: 1938–1940*, edited by Howard Eiland and Michael W. Jennings, 389–400. Cambridge, Mass.: Harvard University Press, 2003.

———. *The Origin of German Tragic Drama*. Translated by John Osbourne. London: Verso, 1998.

———. “Robert Walser.” In *Gesammelte Schriften*, vol. 2, book 1, edited by Rolf Tiedemann and Hermann Schweppenhäuser, 324–28. Frankfurt am Main: Suhrkamp, 2000.

———. “Robert Walser.” In *Selected Writings, vol. 2: 1927–1934*, edited by Michael W. Jennings, Gary Smith, and Howard Eiland, 257–61. Cambridge, Mass.: Harvard University Press, 2005.

———. “Surrealism: The Last Snapshot of the European Intelligentsia.” In *Selected Writings, vol. 2: 1927–1934*, edited by Michael Jennings, Gary Smith, and Howard Eiland, 207–21. Cambridge, Mass.: Harvard University Press, 2005.

———. “Über den Begriff der Geschichte.” In *Gesammelte Schriften*, vol. 1, book 2, edited by Rolf Tiedemann and Hermann Schweppenhäuser, 691–704. Frankfurt am Main: Suhrkamp, 1974.

———. “Über einige Motive bei Baudelaire.” In *Gesammelte Schriften*, vol. 1, book 2, edited by Rolf Tiedemann and Hermann Schweppenhäuser, 605–53. Frankfurt am Main: Suhrkamp, 1974.

———. *Ursprung des deutschen Trauerspiels*. Frankfurt am Main: Suhrkamp, 1978.

Bergson, Henri. “Laughter.” In *Comedy*, edited by Wylie Sypher, 61–190. Baltimore: Johns Hopkins University Press, 1956.

———. *Le Rire*. Paris: Presses Universitaires de France, 1961.

Bernstein, Susan. *Virtuosity of the Nineteenth Century: Performing Music and Language in Heine, Liszt, and Baudelaire*. Stanford, Calif.: Stanford University Press, 1998.

Beug, Joachim. “Sprachkrise und Sprachgläubigkeit im Werk Joseph Roths.” In *Joseph Roth und die Tradition*, edited by David Bronsen, 345–63. Darmstadt: Agora, 1975.

Blanchot, Maurice. *De Kafka à Kafka*. Paris: Gallimard, 1981.

Blanckenburg, Christian Friedrich von. *Versuch über den Roman*. Stuttgart: Metzler, 1965.

Blumenberg, Hans. *Das Lachen der Thrakerin. Eine Urgeschichte der Theorie*. Frankfurt am Main: Suhrkamp, 1987.

———. “Der Sturz des Protophilosophischen. Zur Komik der Reinen Theorie—Anhand einer Rezeptionsgeschichte der Thales-Anekdote.” In *Poetik und Hermeneutik VII: Das Komische*, edited by Wolfgang Preisendanz and Rainer Warning, 11–64. Munich: Fink, 1976.

———. *Die Legitimität der Neuzeit*. Frankfurt am Main: Suhrkamp, 1996.

Böhler, Michael. “Dichten aus der Peripherie des Schreibens. Theoretische Prolegomena zur Frage nach Robert Walsers kulturpolitischem Ort im deutschsprachigem Raum.” In *Wärmende Fremde: Robert Walser und seine Übersetzer im Gespräch*, edited by Peter Utz, 31–45. Bern: Lang, 1994.

Bohrer, Karl Heinz. "Sprachen der Ironie—Sprachen des Ernstes: das Problem." In *Sprachen der Ironie—Sprachen des Ernstes,* 11–35. Frankfurt am Main: Suhrkamp, 2000.

Booth, Wayne C. *A Rhetoric of Irony.* Chicago: University of Chicago Press, 1974.

Boyle, Robert. "An Essay Containing a Requisite Digression, Concerning Those That Would Exclude the Deity from Intermeddling with Matter." In *Selected Philosophical Papers of Robert Boyle,* edited by M. A. Stewart, 155–75. Manchester: Manchester University Press, 1979.

Breden, Hugh. "Onomatopoeia as a Figure and a Linguistic Principle." *New Literary History* 27, no. 3 (Summer 1996): 555–69.

Brod, Max. "Gefühl von einer Verwandlung des Staates." *Zeit-Echo: Ein Kriegstagebuch der Künstler* 1, no. 3 (1914): 30–31.

———. *Über Franz Kafka.* Frankfurt am Main: Fischer, 1974.

Bronson, David. "Die journalistischen Anfänge Joseph Roths. Wien 1918–1920." *Literatur und Kritik* 41 (1970): 37–54.

Bubner, Rüdiger. "Die Aristotelische Lehre vom Zufall. Bemerkungen in der Perspektive einer Annäherung der Philosophie an die Rhetorik." In *Poetik und Hermeneutik XVII: Kontingenz,* edited by Gerhart von Graevenitz and Odo Marquard, 3–21. Munich: Fink, 1998.

Bungartz, Christoph. *Zurückweichend vorwärtsschreiten. Die Ironie in Robert Walsers Berner Prosa.* Frankfurt am Main: Lang, 1988.

Bürger, Peter. *Theorie der Avantgarde.* Frankfurt am Main: Suhrkamp, 1974.

Burwick, Frederick. *Mimesis and Its Romantic Reflections.* University Park: Pennsylvania State University Press, 2001.

Cacciari, Massimo. *Posthumous People: Vienna at the Turning Point.* Translated by Rodger Friedman. Stanford, Calif.: Stanford University Press, 1996.

Campe, Rüdiger. "Robert Walsers Institutionenroman *Jakob von Gunten.*" In *Die Macht und das Imaginäre. Eine kulturelle Verwandtschaft in der Literatur zwischen früher Neuzeit und Moderne,* edited by Rudolf Behrens and Jörn Steigerwald, 235–50. Würzburg: Königshausen & Neumann, 2005.

Cavell, Stanley. Foreword to *The Scandal of the Speaking Body,* by Shoshana Felman, xi–xxi. Stanford, Calif.: Stanford University Press, 2002.

Chambers, Helen. "Signs of the Times: Joseph Roth's Weimar Journalism." In *German Novelists of the Weimar Republic: Intersections of Literature and Politics,* edited by Karl Leydecker, 101–24. Rochester, N.Y.: Camden House, 2006.

Cicero, *De Oratore,* book III. Translated by H. Rackham. Cambridge, Mass.: Harvard University Press, 1968.

Cohen, Ted. *Jokes: Philosophical Thoughts on Joking Matters.* Chicago: University of Chicago Press, 1999.

Colebrook, Claire. *Irony.* London: Routledge, 2004.

Collignon, Jean. "Kafka's Humor." *Yale French Studies* 16 (1955): 53–62.

Comstock, Cathy. "'Transcendental Buffoonery': Irony as Process in Schlegel's 'Über die Unverständlichkeit.'" *Studies in Romanticism* 26, no. 3 (Fall 1987): 445–64.

Corngold, Stanley. *Franz Kafka: The Necessity of Form.* Ithaca, N.Y.: Cornell University Press, 1988.

———. *Lambent Traces: Franz Kafka.* Princeton, N.J.: Princeton University Press, 2004.

———. "Some Theoretical and Historical Complications in Hegel's Aesthetics of Comedy." In *After Poststructuralism: Writing the Intellectual History of Theory,* edited by Tilottama Rajan and Michael O'Driscoll, 25–42. Toronto: University of Toronto Press, 2002.

Corngold, Stanley, Jack Greenberg, and Benno Wagner, eds. *Franz Kafka: The Office Writings.* Princeton, N.J.: Princeton University Press, 2009.

Corngold, Stanley, and Benno Wagner, eds. *Franz Kafka: The Ghosts in the Machine.* Evanston, Ill.: Northwestern University Press, 2011.

Critchley, Simon. *On Humour.* London: Routledge, 2002.

Culler, Jonathan. *The Pursuit of Signs: Semiotics, Literature, Deconstruction.* Ithaca, N.Y.: Cornell University Press, 1981.

Curtius, Ernst Robert. *European Literature and the Latin Middle Ages.* Translated by Willard Ropes Trask. Princeton, N.J.: Princeton University Press, 1983.

Davis, D. Diane. *Breaking Up [at] Totality: A Rhetoric of Laughter.* Carbondale: Southern Illinois University Press, 2000.

Deleuze, Gilles. *The Logic of Sense.* Translated by Mark Lester and Charles Stivale. New York: Columbia University Press, 1990.

Deleuze, Gilles, and Félix Guattari. *Kafka: Toward a Minor Literature.* Translated by Dana Polan. Minneapolis: University of Minneapolis Press, 1986.

de Man, Paul. "Aesthetic Formalization: Kleist's *Über das Marionettentheater.*" In *The Rhetoric of Romanticism,* 263–90. New York: Columbia University Press, 1984.

———. "The Concept of Irony." In *Aesthetic Ideology,* edited by Andrzej Warminski, 163–84. Minneapolis: University of Minnesota Press, 1996.

———. "Criticism and Crisis." In *Blindness and Insight,* 3–19. Minneapolis: University of Minnesota Press, 1983.

———. "The Resistance to Theory." In *The Resistance to Theory,* 3–20. Minneapolis: University of Minnesota Press, 1986.

———. "Rhetoric of Persuasion (Nietzsche)." In *Allegories of Reading: Figural Language in Rousseau, Nietzsche, Rilke, and Proust,* 119–31. New Haven, Conn.: Yale University Press, 1979.

———. "The Rhetoric of Temporality." In *Blindness and Insight,* 187–228. Minneapolis: University of Minnesota Press, 1983.

———. "Rhetoric of Tropes (Nietzsche)." In *Allegories of Reading: Figural Language in Rousseau, Nietzsche, Rilke, and Proust,* 103–18. New Haven, Conn.: Yale University Press, 1979.

———. "Sign and Symbol in Hegel's *Aesthetics.*" In *Aesthetic Ideology,* edited by Andrzej Warminski, 91–104. Minneapolis: University of Minnesota Press, 1996.

Dentan, Michel. *Humour et création littéraire dans l'œuvre de Kafka.* Geneva: Librairie Droz; Paris: Librairie Minard, 1961.

Derrida, Jacques. "Before the Law." In *Acts of Literature,* edited by Derek Attridge, 181–220. New York: Routledge, 1992.

———. *The Politics of Friendship.* Translated by George Collins. London: Verso, 2005.

———. "The Theater of Cruelty and the Closure of Representation." In *Writing and Difference,* translated by Alan Bass, 232–50. Chicago: University of Chicago Press, 1978.

Ehrich-Haefeli, Verena. "'Gaukler sein wäre schön.' Fritz Kochers Aufsätze—ein Modell subversiver Anpassung bei Robert Walser." In "*Verbergendes Enthüllen." Zu Theorie und Kunst dichterischen Verkleidens. Festschrift für Martin Stern,* edited by Wolfram Malte Fues and Wolfram Mauser, 329–44. Würzburg: Königshausen & Neumann, 1995.

Endres, Johannes. "Novalis und das Lustspiel. Ein vergessener Beitrag zur Geschichte der Gattung." *Goethezeitportal.* 19 January 2004.

Evans, Tamara S. "Der Dichter als Räuber: Robert Walser zwischen Modernismus und Avantgardismus." In *Traditionalismus und Modernismus: Kontroversen um den Avantgardismus,* edited by Walter Haug and Wilfried Barner, 235–39. Tubingen: Niemeyer, 1986.

Falke, Jacob von. *Lebenserinnerungen.* Leipzig: Meyer, 1897.

Felman, Shoshana. *The Scandal of the Speaking Body: Don Juan with J. L. Austin, or Seduction in Two Languages.* Translated by Catherine Porter. Stanford, Calif.: Stanford University Press, 2002.

Fenves, Peter. "*Chatter*": *Language and History in Kierkegaard.* Stanford, Calif.: Stanford University Press, 1993.

Fleming, Paul. *Exemplarity and Mediocrity: The Art of the Average from Bourgeois Tragedy to Realism.* Stanford, Calif.: Stanford University Press, 2008.

———. *The Pleasures of Abandonment: Jean Paul and the Life of Humor.* Würzburg: Königshausen & Neumann, 2006.

Flieger, Jerry Aline. *The Purloined Punch Line: Freud's Comic Theory and the Postmodern Text.* Baltimore: Johns Hopkins University Press, 1991.

Foucault, Michel. *The Order of Things: An Archeology of the Human Sciences.* London: Routledge, 2002.

Fraenger, Wilhelm. *Formen des Komischen. Vorträge 1920–1921.* Dresden: Fundus, 1995.

Frank, Manfred. "Allegorie, Witz, Fragment, Ironie. Friedrich Schlegel und die Idee des zerrissenen Selbst." In *Allegorie und Melancholie,* 124–46. Frankfurt am Main: Suhrkamp, 1992.

Frederick, Samuel. *Narratives Unsettled: Digression in Robert Walser, Thomas Bernhard, and Adalbert Stifter.* Evanston, Ill.: Northwestern University Press, 2012.

Freud, Sigmund. *Beyond the Pleasure Principle.* In *The Standard Edition of the Complete Psychological Works of Sigmund Freud,* vol. 18, translated by James Strachey, 3–64. London: Hogarth, 1955.

———. "Creative Writers and Day-Dreaming." In *The Standard Edition of the Complete Works of Sigmund Freud,* vol. 9, translated by James Strachey, 143–50. London: Hogarth, 1959.

———. "Der Dichter und das Phantasieren." In *Gesammelte Werke,* vol. 7: *Werke aus den Jahren 1906–1909,* 213–23. Frankfurt am Main: Fischer, 1993.

———. "Der Humor." In *Gesammelte Werke,* vol. 14, *Werke aus den Jahren 1925–1931,* edited by Anna Freud, 383–89. London: Imago, 1948.

———. *Der Witz und seine Beziehung zum Unbewussten.* In *Gesammelte Werke,* vol. 6, edited by Anna Freud. London: Imago, 1940.

———. *Die Traumdeutung.* In *Gesammelte Werke,* vols. 2 and 3, edited by Anna Freud, 1–642. London: Imago, 1948.

———. "Drei Abhandlungen zur Sexualtheorie." In *Gesammelte Werke,* vol. 5, *Werke aus den Jahren 1904–1905,* edited by Anna Freud, 27–145. London: Imago, 1942.

———. "Humor." In *The Standard Edition of the Complete Psychological Works of Sigmund Freud,* vol. 21, translated by James Strachey, 161–66. London: Hogarth, 1961.

———. *The Interpretation of Dreams (Second Part).* In *The Standard Edition of the Complete Psychological Works of Sigmund Freud,* vol. 5, translated by James Strachey. London: Hogarth, 1953.

———. *Jenseits des Lustprinzips.* In *Gesammelte Werke,* vol. 13, edited by Anna Freud, 3–68. London: Imago, 1955.

———. *Jokes and Their Relation to the Unconscious.* In *The Standard Edition of the Complete Psychological Works of Sigmund Freud,* vol. 8, translated by James Strachey. London: Hogarth, 1960.

———. *On the Psychopathology of Everyday Life.* In *The Standard Edition of the Complete Psychological Works of Sigmund Freud,* vol. 6, translated by James Strachey. London: The Hogarth Press, 1960.

———. "Three Essays on Sexuality." In *The Standard Edition of the Complete Psychological Works of Sigmund Freud,* vol. 7, translated by James Strachey, 123–245. London: Hogarth, 1953.

———. *Zur Psychopathologie des Alltagslebens.* In *Gesammelte Werke,* vol. 4, edited by Anna Freud. London: Imago, 1941.

Frye, Northrop. *Anatomy of Criticism: Four Essays.* In *Collected Works of Northrop Frye,* vol. 22, edited by Robert Denham. Toronto: University of Toronto Press, 2007.

Fuchs, Annette. *Dramaturgie des Narrentums: Das Komische in der Prosa Robert Walsers.* Munich: Fink, 1993.

Fussell, Paul. *The Great War and Modern Memory.* New York: Oxford University Press, 2000.

Geulen, Eva. *The End of Art: Readings in a Rumor After Hegel.* Translated by James McFarland. Stanford, Calif.: Stanford University Press, 2006.

Goethe, Johann Wolfgang von. *Faust.* In *Werke,* vol. 3: *Dramatische Dichtung I,* edited by Erich Trunz. Munich: Beck, 1986.

Goltschnigg, Dietmar. "Zeit-, Ideologie- und Sprachkritik in Joseph Roths Essayistik." *Literatur und Kritik,* no. 243/244 (April/May 1990): 124–36.

Grabbe, Christian Dietrich. *Scherz, Satire, Ironie, und tiefere Bedeutung.* In *Werke in zwei Bänden,* vol. 1, 227–95. Berlin: Aufbau, 1987.

Greven, Jochen. "'Mit seiner deutschen Sprache jonglieren gelernt': Robert Walser als Imitator, Parodist, Stilexzentriker." In *Wärmende Fremde: Robert Walser und seine Übersetzer im Gespräch,* edited by Peter Utz, 19–30. Bern: Lang, 1994.

Groth, Otto. *Die unerkannte Kulturmacht: Grundlegung der Zeitungswissen (Periodik), vol. 2, Das Sein des Werkes.* Berlin: de Gruyter, 1961.

Grötzinger, Vera. *Der Erste Weltkrieg im Widerhall des "Zeit-Echo" (1914–1917). Zum Wandel im Selbstverständnis einer künstlerisch-politischen Literaturzeitschrift.* Bern: Lang, 1993.

Hackert, Fritz. *Kulturpessimismus und Erzählform. Studien zu Joseph Roths Leben und Werk*. Bern: Lang, 1967.

Hamacher, Werner. "(The End of Art with the Mask)." In *Hegel After Derrida,* edited by Stuart Barnett, 105–30. London: Routledge, 1998.

———. "Unlesbarkeit." Foreword to *Allegorien des Lesens,* by Paul de Man, translated by Werner Hamacher and Peter Krumme, 7–26. Frankfurt am Main: Suhrkamp, 1988.

Haverkamp, Anselm. *Figura Cryptica. Theorie der literarischen Latenz.* Frankfurt am Main: Suhrkamp, 2002.

———. "Humor. Die Latenz der Form." *Deutsche Vierteljahrsschrift für Literaturwissenschaft und Geistesgeschichte,* no. 2 (2002): 171–180.

———. "Im Auge des Orkans. Shakespeare und die Philosophen." In *Diesseits der Oder: Frankfurter Vorlesungen,* 67–82. Berlin: Kadmos, 2008.

———. "Kafkas Pannen. Poetik des Landstreichens im dichtgemachten Text." In *Schloß-Geschichten: Zu Kafkas drittem Romanplan—eine Diskussion,* edited by Peter Henninger, Rainer Nägele, and Bart Philipsen, 110–18. Eggingen: Edition Isele, 2007.

———. *Metapher. Die Ästhetik in der Rhetorik.* Munich: Fink, 2007.

Heath, John. "The Legacy of the Baroque in the Novels of Joseph Roth." *Forum of Modern Language Studies* 40, no. 3 (2004): 329–38.

Heffernan, Valerie. *Provocation from the Periphery: Robert Walser Re-examined.* Würzburg: Königshausen & Neumann, 2007.

Hegel, G. W. F. *Elements of the Philosophy of Right.* Translated by Allen W. Wood. Cambridge, Eng.: Cambridge University Press, 1991.

———. *Grundlinien der Philosophie des Rechts.* Edited by Eva Moldenhauer and Karl Markus Michel. Frankfurt am Main: Suhrkamp, 1970.

———. *Hegel's Aesthetics: Lectures on Fine Art,* vol. 1. Translated by T. M. Knox. Oxford: Oxford University Press, 1975.

———. *Hegel's Aesthetics: Lectures on Fine Art,* vol. 2. Translated by T. M. Knox. Oxford: Oxford University Press, 1975.

———. *Phänomenologie des Geistes.* Edited by Eva Moldenhauer and Karl Markus Michel. Frankfurt am Main: Suhrkamp, 1970.

———. *The Phenomenology of Spirit.* Translated by A. V. Miller. Oxford: Oxford University Press, 1977.

———. *Vorlesungen über die Ästhetik I.* Edited by Eva Moldenhauer and Karl Markus Michel. Frankfurt am Main: Suhrkamp, 1970.

———. *Vorlesungen über die Ästhetik II.* Edited by Eva Moldenhauer and Karl Markus Michel. Frankfurt am Main: Suhrkamp, 1970.

———. *Vorlesungen über die Ästhetik III.* Edited by Eva Moldenhauer and Karl Markus Michel. Frankfurt am Main: Suhrkamp, 1970.

Heizmann, Jürgen. *Joseph Roth und die Ästhetik der Neuen Sachlichkeit.* Heidelberg: Mattes, 1990.

Heller, Agnes. *Immortal Comedy: The Comic Phenomenon in Art, Literature, and Life.* Lanham, Md.: Lexington Books, 2005.

Henrich, Dieter. "Art and Philosophy of Art Today: Reflections with Reference to Hegel." In *New Perspectives in German Literary Criticism,* edited by Richard E. Amacher and Victor Lange, 107–33. Princeton, N.J.: Princeton University Press, 1979.

Hermsdorf, Klaus. "Arbeit und Amt als Erfahrung und Gestaltung." In *Amtliche Schriften,* by Franz Kafka, edited by Klaus Hermsdorf, 9–87. Berlin: Akademie-Verlag, 1984.
Hobbes, Thomas. *Leviathan.* New York: Penguin, 1982.
Hofmannsthal, Hugo von. "Drei kleine Betrachtungen." In *Gesammelte Werke in Einzelausgaben, Prosa IV,* 40–55. Frankfurt am Main: Fischer, 1955.
Holitscher, Arthur. *Amerika Heute und Morgen. Reiseerlebnisse.* Berlin: Fischer, 1912.
Hughes, Jon. *Facing Modernity: Fragmentation, Culture, and Identity in Joseph Roth's Writing in the 1920s.* London: Maney, 2006.
Huizinga, Johan. *Homo Ludens: A Study of the Play-Element in Culture.* Boston: Beacon, 1950.
Jahn, Wolfgang. *Kafkas Roman "Der Verschollene" ("Amerika").* Stuttgart: Metzler, 1965.
Janouch, Gustav. *Gespräche mit Kafka. Aufzeichnungen und Erinnerungen.* Frankfurt am Main: Fischer, 1981.
Jürgens, Martin. *Robert Walser: Die Krise der Darstellbarkeit: Untersuchungen zur Prosa.* Kronberg: Scriptor, 1973.
Kafka, Franz. *Amtliche Schriften,* edited by Klaus Hermsdorf. Berlin: Akademie-Verlag, 1984.
———. *Briefe 1900–1912.* Edited by Hans-Gerd Koch. Frankfurt am Main: Fischer, 1999.
———. *Briefe 1913–März 1914.* Edited by Hans-Gerd Koch. Frankfurt am Main: Fischer, 1999.
———. *Das Schloß.* In *Kritische Ausgabe,* edited by Malcolm Pasley. Frankfurt am Main: Fischer, 2002.
———. *Der Proceß.* In *Kritische Ausgabe,* edited by Malcolm Pasley. Frankfurt am Main, Fischer, 2002.
———. *Der Verschollene.* In *Kritische Ausgabe,* edited by Jost Schillemeit. Frankfurt am Main: Fischer, 2002.
———. *Der Verschollene. Apparatband.* In *Kritische Ausgabe,* edited by Jost Schillemeit. Frankfurt am Main: Fischer, 2002.
———. *Drucke zu Lebzeiten.* In *Kritische Ausgabe,* edited by Wolf Kittler, Hans-Gerd Koch, and Gerhard Neumann. Frankfurt am Main: Fischer, 2002.
———. *Nachgelassene Schriften und Fragmente I.* In *Kritische Ausgabe,* edited by Jost Schillemeit. Frankfurt am Main: Fischer, 1993.
———. *Nachgelassene Schriften und Fragmente II.* In *Kritische Ausgabe,* edited by Jost Schillemeit. Frankfurt am Main: Fischer, 2002.
———. *Tagebücher.* In *Kritische Ausgabe,* edited by Hans-Gerd Koch, Michael Müller and Malcolm Pasley. Frankfurt am Main: Fischer, 2002.
Kant, Immanuel. *Anthropologie in pragmatischer Hinsicht.* Hamburg: Meiner, 2000.
———. *Anthropology from a Pragmatic Point of View.* Translated by Robert B. Louden. Cambridge, Eng.: Cambridge University Press, 2006.
———. *Critique of Pure Reason.* Translated by J. M. D. Meiklejohn. Amherst, N.Y.: Prometheus, 1990.
———. *Critique of the Power of Judgment.* Translated by Paul Guyer and Eric Matthews. Cambridge, Eng.: Cambridge University Press.

———. *Kritik der reinen Vernunft*. Hamburg: Meiner, 1998.

———. *Kritik der Urteilskraft*. Hamburg: Meiner, 2006.

Kantorowicz, Ernst H. *The King's Two Bodies: A Study in Mediaeval Political Theology*. Princeton, N.J.: Princeton University Press, 1957.

Kellenberger, Irma. *Der Jugendstil und Robert Walser: Studien zur Wechselbeziehung von Kunstgewerbe und Literatur*. Bern: Francke, 1981.

Keller, Gottfried. *Der Grüne Heinrich, Zweite Fassung*. Edited by Gustav Steiner. Zurich: Diogenes, 1993.

Kiefer, Sebastian. *Braver Junge—gefüllt mit Gift. Joseph Roth und die Ambivalenz*. Stuttgart: Metzler, 2001.

Kierkegaard, Søren. *The Concept of Irony, with Continual Reference to Socrates*. Translated by Howard V. Hong and Edna H. Hong. Princeton, N.J.: Princeton University Press, 1989.

———. *Either/Or, Part I*. Translated by Howard V. Hong and Edna H. Hong. Princeton, N.J.: Princeton University Press, 1987.

Kittler, Friedrich. *Discourse Networks 1800/1900*. Translated by Michael Metteer. Stanford, Calif.: Stanford University Press, 1992.

Kittler, Wolf. "Dead Beat Father. Zu Kafkas Roman *Der Verschollene*." In *Für Alle und Keinen. Lektüre, Schrift und Leben bei Nietzsche und Kafka*, edited by Friedrich Balke, Joseph Vogl, and Benno Wagner, 161–75. Zurich: Diaphanes, 2008.

Kleist, Heinrich von. "Die Hunde und der Vogel." In *Sämtliche Werke und Briefe*, vol. 2, edited by Helmut Sembdner, 324–25. Frankfurt am Main: Deutsche Taschenbuch Verlag, 2008.

——— "Über das Marionettentheater." In *Sämtliche Werke und Briefe*, vol. 2, edited by Helmut Sembdner, 337–45. Frankfurt am Main: Deutsche Taschenbuch Verlag, 2008.

Kofman, Sarah. *Pourquoi rit-on? Freud et le mot d'esprit*. Paris: Galilée, 1986.

Kottman, Paul A. "Slipping on Banana Peels, Tumbling into Wells: Philosophy and Comedy." *diacritics* 38, no. 4 (Winter 2008): 3–14.

Kracauer, Siegfried. "Das Ornament der Masse." In *Das Ornament der Masse*, 50–63. Frankfurt am Main: Suhrkamp, 1977.

———. "The Mass Ornament." In *The Mass Ornament: Weimar Essays*, translated by Thomas Y. Levin, 75–86. Cambridge, Mass.: Harvard University Press, 1995.

———. "Silent Film Comedy." *Sight and Sound* 21, no. 1 (August/September 1951): 31–32.

———. *The Theory of Film: The Redemption of Physical Reality*. New York: Oxford University Press, 1960.

Kraus, Karl. "Heine und die Folgen." In *Untergang der Welt durch schwarze Magie*, 188–222. Munich: Kösel-Verlag, 1960.

Kreienbrock, Jörg. *Kleiner. Feiner. Leichter. Nuancierungen zum Werk Robert Walsers*. Zurich: Diaphanes, 2010.

Lacan, Jacques. "The Agency of the Letter in the Unconscious, or Reason Since Freud." In *Écrits: A Selection*, translated by Alan Sheridan, 161–97. London: Routledge, 1977.

———. "L'instance de la lettre dans l'inconscient ou la raison depuis Freud." In *Écrits*, 493–528. Paris: Seuil, 1966.

Lacoue-Labarthe, Philippe, and Jean-Luc Nancy. *The Literary Absolute.* Translated by Philip Barnard and Cheryl Lester. Albany: State University of New York Press, 1988.

La Farge, Benjamin. "Comedy's Intention." *Philosophy and Literature* 28, no. 1 (April 2004): 118–36.

Le Rider, Jacques. *Modernity and Crises of Identity: Culture and Society in Fin-de-Siècle Vienna.* Translated by Rosemary Morris. New York: Continuum, 1993.

———. "Pour une histoire interculturelle de la production littéraire de langue allemande en Europe centrale." In *Les Littératures de langue allemande en Europe centrale: Des Lumières à nos jours,* edited by Jacques le Rider and Fridrun Rinner, 21–48. Paris: Presses Universitaires de France, 1998.

Lübbe, Hermann. "Kontingenzerfahrung und Kontingenzbewältigung." In *Poetik und Hermeneutik XVII: Kontingenz,* edited by Gerhart von Graevenitz and Odo Marquard, 35–47. Munich: Fink, 1998.

Lüdemann, Susanne. *Mythos und Selbstdarstellung. Zur Poetik der Psychoanalyse.* Freiburg: Rombach, 1994.

Lukács, Georg. *The Theory of the Novel.* Translated by Anna Bostock. Cambridge, Mass.: MIT Press, 1999.

———. "Zur Frage der Satire." In *Werke,* vol. 4: *Essays über Realismus,* 83–107. Neuwied: Luchterhand, 1971.

Magris, Claudio. *Der habsburgische Mythos in der österreichischen Literatur.* Translated by Madeleine von Pásztory. Salzburg: Müller, 1966.

———. *Der unauffindbare Sinn. Zur österreichischen Literatur des 20. Jahrhunderts.* Klagenfurt: Carinthia, 1978.

———. "Joseph Roth: Der Aufbruch auf der Suche nach dem Bekannten." Translated by Jutta Prasse. *Literatur und Kritik* 75 (1973): 277–91.

Malevich, Kasimir. *The Non-Objective World: The Manifesto of Suprematism.* Translated by Howard Dearstyne. Mineola, N.Y.: Dover, 2003.

Marin, Louis. *Portrait of the King.* Translated by Martha M. Houle. Minneapolis: University of Minnesota Press, 1988.

Massimo, Guido. *Franz Kafka, Jizchak Löwy und das jiddische Theater.* Translated by Norbert Bickert. Frankfurt am Main: Stroemfeld/Nexus, 2007.

Matthew, Celine. *Ambivalence and Irony in the Works of Joseph Roth.* Frankfurt am Main: Lang, 1984.

Mehlman, Jeffrey. "How to Read Freud on Jokes: The Critic as *Schadchen.*" *New Literary History* 6, no. 2 (Winter 1975): 439–46.

Menke, Bettine. *Prosopopoiia. Stimme und Text bei Brentano, Hoffmann, Kleist und Kafka.* Munich: Fink, 2000.

Menke, Christoph. *Die Souveränität der Kunst. Ästhetische Erfahrung nach Adorno und Derrida.* Frankfurt am Main: Suhrkamp, 1991.

Mergenthaler, May. *Zwischen Eros und Mitteilung. Die Frühromantik im Symposion der "Athenaeums-Fragmente."* Paderborn: Schöningh, 2012.

Meyers Großes Konversations-Lexikon. Ein Nachschlagewerk des allgemeinen Wissens. Kriegsnachtrag, Erster Teil. Leipzig: Bibliographisches Institut, 1916. Reprint 1920.

Meyers großes Universallexikon, vol. 15. Mannheim: Bibliographisches Institut, 1986.

Meyers Handlexikon. Siebente gänzlich veränderte und neubearbeitete Auflage. Leipzig: Bibliographisches Institut, 1920.

Mitchell, Glenn. *The Marx Brothers Encyclopedia.* London: Reynolds & Hearn, 2003.

Morlang, Werner. "Magie du camouflage micrographique." In *Robert Walser, l'écriture miniature,* 13–26. Carouge: Éditions Zoe, 2004.

Müller, Andreas Georg. *Mit Fritz Kocher in der Schule der Moderne: Studien zu Robert Walsers Frühwerk.* Tubingen: Francke, 2007.

Musäus, Johann Karl August. *Volksmärchen der Deutschen,* vol. 4. Gotha: Ettinger, 1788.

Nancy, Jean-Luc. "Laughter, Presence." In *The Birth to Presence,* 368–93. Stanford, Calif.: Stanford University Press, 1993.

———. "*Menstruum Universale.*" In *The Birth to Presence,* 248–65. Stanford, Calif.: Stanford University Press, 1993.

Neumann, Gerhard. "Chinesische Mauer und Schacht von Babel. Franz Kafkas Architekturen." *Deutsche Vierteljahrschrift für Literaturwissenschaft und Geistesgeschichte,* no. 3 (September 2009): 452–71.

———. "Kafka als Ethnologe." In *Odradeks Lachen. Fremdheit bei Kafka,* edited by Hansjörg Bay and Christof Hamann, 325–45. Freiburg: Rombach, 2006.

———. "Ritual und Theater. Franz Kafkas Bildungsroman *Der Verschollene.*" In *Franz Kafka, Der Verschollene: Le Disparu/L'Amérique—Écritures d'un nouveau monde?* edited by Philippe Wellnitz, 51–78. Strasbourg: Presses Universitaires de Strasbourg, 1997.

———. "Umkehrung und Ablenkung: Franz Kafkas 'Gleitendes Paradox.'" *Deutsche Vierteljahrschrift für Literaturwissenschaft und Geistesgeschichte* 42, Sonderheft (November 1968): 702–44.

———. "'War es eine Komödie, so wollte er mitspielen.' Zu Kafkas Inszenierung des Anfangs im Prozeß-Roman." In *Vom Erhabenem und vom Komischen. Über eine prekäre Konstellation,* edited by Hans Richard Brittnacher and Thomas Koebner, 97–106. Würzburg: Königshausen & Neumann, 2010.

Newmark, Kevin. *Irony on Occasion: From Schlegel to Kierkegaard to Derrida and de Man.* New York: Fordham University Press, 2012.

Nicolai, Ralf R. *Kafkas Amerika-Roman "Der Verschollene." Motive und Gestalten.* Würzburg: Königshausen & Neumann, 1986.

Nietzsche, Friedrich. *Also Sprach Zarathustra.* In *Kritische Studienausgabe,* vol. 4, edited by Giorgio Colli and Mazzino Montinari. Munich: Deutsche Taschenbuch Verlag, 1988.

———. *Die fröhliche Wissenschaft.* In *Kritische Gesamtausgabe,* vol. 5, book 2, edited by Giorgio Colli and Mazzino Montinari, 41–335. Berlin: de Gruyter, 1973.

———. "Versuch einer Selbstkritik." In *Werke,* 9–17. Munich: Hanser, 1981.

Novalis. *Schriften,* vol. 2, edited by Richard Samuel. Stuttgart: Kohlhammer, 1981.

Oring, Elliott. *The Jokes of Sigmund Freud: A Study in Humor and Jewish Identity.* Philadelphia: University of Pennsylvania Press, 1984.

Owen, Wilfred. "Dulce et decorum est." In *The Poems of Wilfred Owen,* edited by Jon Stallworthy, 117–18. London: Hogarth, 1985.

Pasley, Malcolm. "Kafka's Semi-Private Games." *Oxford German Studies,* no. 6 (1971): 112–31.

Pattison, George. "Beyond the Grasp of Irony." In *International Kierkegaard Commentary: The Concept of Irony*, edited by Robert L. Perkins, 347–64. Macon, Ga.: Mercer University Press, 2001.

Pesnel, Stéphane. *Totalité et fragmentarité dans l'œuvre romanesque de Joseph Roth*. Bern: Lang, 2000.

Petr, Pavel. *Kafkas Spiele. Selbststilisierung und literarische Komik*. Heidelberg: Winter, 1992.

Plank, Ilse. *Joseph Roth als Feuilletonist. Eine Untersuchung von Themen, Stil und Aufbau seiner Feuilletons*. Dissertation, Friedrich-Alexander-Universität, Erlangen-Nürnberg, 1967.

Plessner, Helmuth. *Lachen und Weinen. Eine Untersuchung nach den Grenzen menschlichen Verhaltens*. Munich: Lehnen, 1950.

Poser, Stefan. *Museum der Gefahren. Die gesellschaftliche Bedeutung der Sicherheitstechnik. Das Beispiel der Hygiene-Ausstellungen und Museen für Arbeiterschutz in Wien, Berlin und Dresden um die Jahrhundertwende*. Munster: Waxmann, 1998.

Powell, Ward H. "Joseph Roth, Ironic Primitivist." *Monatshefte für Deutschen Unterricht, Deutsche Sprache und Literatur* 53 (1961): 115–22.

Preisendanz, Wolfgang. "Humor." In *Reallexikon der deutschen Literaturwissenschaft*, edited by Harald Fricke, 100–103. Berlin: de Gruyter, 2000.

———. *Humor als dichterische Einbildungskraft: Studien zur Erzählkunst des poetischen Realismus*. Munich: Eidos, 1963.

———. "Humor als Rolle." In *Poetik und Hermeneutik VIII: Identität*, edited by Odo Marquard and Karlheinz Stierle, 423–34. Munich: Fink, 1979.

———. "Komik als Komplement der Erfassung von Kontingenzen." In *Poetik und Hermeneutik XVII: Kontingenz*, edited by Gerhart von Graevenitz and Odo Marquard, 383–401. Munich: Fink, 1998.

———. *Über den Witz*. Konstanz: Druckerei und Verlagsanstalt Konstanz, 1970.

———. "Zum Vorrang des Komischen bei der Darstellung von Geschichtserfahrung in deutschen Romanen unserer Zeit." In *Poetik und Hermeneutik VII: Das Komische*, edited by Wolfgang Preisendanz and Rainer Warning, 153–64. Munich: Fink, 1976.

Quintilian, *The Orator's Education*. Edited and translated by Donald A. Russell. Cambridge, Mass.: Harvard University Press, 2001.

Quiring, Björn, ed. *Theatrum Mundi. Die Metapher des Welttheaters von Shakespeare zu Beckett*. Berlin: August, 2012.

Rehberg, Peter. *Lachen Lesen. Zur Komik der Moderne bei Kafka*. Bielefeld: Transcript, 2007.

Richter, Jean Paul. *Horn of Oberon: Jean Paul Richter's "School for Aesthetics."* Translated by Margaret R. Hale. Detroit: Wayne State University Press, 1973.

———. *Vorschule der Ästhetik*. Edited by Wolfhart Henckmann. Hamburg: Meiner, 1990.

Ritter, Joachim. "Über das Lachen." In *Subjektivität: Sechs Aufsätze*, 62–92. Frankfurt am Main: Suhrkamp, 1974.

Roche, Mark W. "Hegel's Theory of Comedy in the Context of Hegelian and Modern Reflections on Comedy." *Revue Internationale de Philosophie* 56, no. 221 (March 2002): 411–30.

———. *Tragedy and Comedy: A Systematic Study and Critique of Hegel*. Albany: State University of New York Press, 1998.

Rodewald, Dierk. *Robert Walsers Prosa. Versuch einer Strukturanalyse*. Bad Homburg: Gehlen, 1970.

Ronell, Avital. "Doing Kafka in *The Castle*." In *Finitude's Score*, 183–206. Lincoln: University of Nebraska Press, 1994.

———. *Loser Sons: Politics and Authority*. Urbana: University of Illinois Press, 2012.

———. *Stupidity*. Urbana: University of Illinois Press, 2002.

———. *The Telephone Book: Technology, Schizophrenia, Electric Speech*. Lincoln: University of Nebraska Press, 1989.

Rorty, Richard. *Contingency, Irony, and Solidarity*. New York: Cambridge University Press, 1989.

Rosenkranz, Karl. *Ästhetik des Häßlichen*. Edited by Dieter Kliche. Stuttgart: Reclam, 1990.

Roth, Joseph. *Werke 1. Das journalistische Werk 1915–1923*. Edited by Klaus Westermann. Cologne: Kiepenheuer & Witsch, 1989.

———. *Werke 2. Das journalistische Werk 1924–1928*. Edited by Klaus Westermann. Cologne: Kiepenheuer & Witsch, 1990.

———. *Werke 3. Das journalistische Werk 1929–1939*. Edited by Klaus Westermann. Cologne: Kiepenheuer & Witsch, 1991.

———. *Werke 4. Romane und Erzählungen 1916–1929*. Edited by Fritz Hackert. Cologne: Kiepenheuer & Witsch, 1989.

———. *Werke 5. Romane und Erzählungen 1930–1936*. Edited by Fritz Hackert. Cologne: Kiepenheuer & Witsch, 1990.

Sasse, Sonja. "Der Prophet als Außenseiter. Rezeption von Zeitgeschehen bei Joseph Roth." *Text und Kritik: Zeitschrift für Literatur. Sonderband: Joseph Roth*, edited by Heinz Ludwig Arnold (1974): 76–89.

Scheffel, Michael. "Paradoxa und kein Ende. Franz Kafkas Romanprojekt 'Der Verschollene.'" In *Franz Kafka, Der Verschollene: Le Disparu/L'Amérique—Écritures d'un nouveau monde?* edited by Philippe Wellnitz, 7–25. Strasbourg: Presses Universitaires de Strasbourg, 1997.

Schiller, Friedrich. "On Grace and Dignity." In *Schiller's "On Grace and Dignity" in Its Cultural Context: Essays and a New Translation*, edited by Jane V. Curran and Christopher Fricker, 123–70. Rochester, N.Y.: Camden House, 2005.

———. *On the Aesthetic Education of Man, In a Series of Letters*. Translated by Elizabeth M. Wilkinson and L.A. Willoughby. Oxford: Clarendon, 1967.

———. "Über Anmut und Würde." In *Werke*, vol. 4, 141–92. Frankfurt am Main: Insel, 1966.

———. *Über die ästhetische Erziehung des Menschen in einer Reihe von Briefen*. In *Werke*, vol. 4, 193–286. Frankfurt am Main: Insel, 1966.

Schlegel, Friedrich. *Fragmente*. In *Kritische Friedrich-Schlegel-Ausgabe*, vol. 2, *Charakteristiken und Kritiken I (1796–1801)*, edited by Hans Eichner, 147–272. Munich: Schöningh, 1967.

———. *Friedrich Schlegel's* Lucinde *and the Fragments*. Translated by Peter Firchow. Minneapolis: University of Minnesota Press, 1971.

———. *Gespräch über die Poesie*. In *Kritische Friedrich-Schlegel-Ausgabe*, vol. 2, *Charakteristiken und Kritiken I (1796–1801)*, edited by Hans Eichner, 284–351. Munich: Schöningh, 1967.

———. *Lucinde*. In *Kritische Friedrich-Schlegel-Ausgabe*, vol. 5, *Dichtungen*, edited by Hans Eichner, 1–92. Munich: Schöningh, 1962.

———. *Philosophische Fragmente*. In *Kritische Friedrich-Schlegel-Ausgabe*, vol. 18, *Philosophische Lehrjahre (1796–1806)*, edited by Ernst Behler, 1–422. Munich: Schöningh, 1962.

———. "Über die Unverständlichkeit." In *Kritische Friedrich-Schlegel-Ausgabe*, vol. 2, *Charakteristiken und Kritiken I (1796–1801)*, edited by Hans Eichner, 363–72. Munich: Schöningh, 1967.

———. "Zu Jean Pauls Vorschule der Ästhetik." Edited by Ernst Behler. *Der Neue Rundschau* 68 (1957): 654–72.

Schmitt, Carl. *Der Begriff des Politischen*. Berlin: Duncker & Humblot, 2002.

———. *The Concept of the Political: Expanded Edition*. Translated by George Schwab. Chicago: University of Chicago Press, 2008.

———. *Political Romanticism*. Translated by Guy Oakes. Cambridge, Mass.: MIT Press, 1986.

———. *Politische Romantik*. Munich: Duncker & Humblot, 1925.

Schmitt, Siegfried J. "Komik im Beschreibungsmodell Kommunikativer Handlungsspiele." In *Poetik und Hermeneutik VII: Das Komische*, edited by Wolfgang Preisendanz and Rainer Warning, 164–89. Munich: Fink, 1976.

Schopenhauer, Arthur. *Die Welt als Wille und Vorstellung*, vol. 1. Edited by Ludwig Berndl. Munich: Müller, 1912.

———. *Die Welt als Wille und Vorstellung*, vol. 2. Edited by Ludwig Berndl. Munich: Müller, 1912.

———. *The World as Will and Representation*, vol. 1. Translated by E. F. J. Payne. New York: Dover, 1969.

———. *The World as Will and Representation*, vol. 2. Translated by E. F. J. Payne. New York: Dover, 1969.

Schorske, Carl E. *Fin-de-Siècle Vienna: Politics and Culture*. New York: Vintage, 1981.

Schroeder, Irene. *Experimente des Erzählens: Joseph Roths frühe Prosa 1916–1925*. Bern: Lang, 1998.

Schumacher, Eckhard. *Die Ironie der Unverständlichkeit*. Frankfurt am Main: Suhrkamp, 2000.

Schweikert, Uwe. "'Der rote Joseph.' Politik und Feuilleton beim frühen Joseph Roth (1919–1926)." *Text und Kritik*, edited by Heinz Ludwig Arnold (Sonderband 1982): 40–55.

Seelig, Carl. *Wanderungen mit Robert Walser*. Frankfurt am Main: Suhrkamp, 1990.

Shaftesbury, Anthony Ashley Cooper, 7th Earl of. *Sensus Communis: An Essay on the Freedom of Wit and Humour*. In *An Old-Spelling, Critical Edition of Shaftesbury's* Letter Concerning Enthusiasm *and* Sensus Communis: An Essay on the Freedom of Wit and Humour, edited by Richard B. Wolf, 129–208. New York: Garland, 1988.

Shelley, Percy Bysshe. *A Defense of Poetry*. Edited by Albert S. Cook. Boston: Ginn, 1903.

Sieg, Werner. *Zwischen Anarchismus und Fiktion. Eine Untersuchung zum Werk von Joseph Roth*. Bonn: Bouvier Verlag Herbert Grundmann, 1974.

Siegel, Elke. *Aufträge aus dem Bleistiftgebiet. Zur Dichtung Robert Walsers*. Würzburg: Königshausen & Neumann, 2001.

Sokel, Walter H. *Franz Kafka—Tragik und Ironie. Zur Struktur seiner Kunst.* Munich: Albert Langen Georg Müller, 1963.

Sontag, Susan. "Notes on Camp." In *Against Interpretation and Other Essays,* 275–92. New York: Farrar, Straus and Giroux, 1966.

Spilka, Mark. *Dickens and Kafka: A Mutual Interpretation.* London: Dobson, 1963.

Stach, Reiner. *Kafka. Die Jahre der Entscheidungen.* Frankfurt am Main: Fischer, 2003.

Starobinski, Jean. *Les mots sous les mots: Les anagrammes de Ferdinand de Saussure.* Paris: Gallimard, 1971.

———. *Portrait de l'artiste en saltimbanque.* Geneva: Éditions d'Art Albert Skira, 1970.

Stifter, Adalbert. *Der Nachsommer.* Frankfurt am Main: Fischer, 2008.

Stössinger, Felix. "Deutschland und Europa." *Zeit-Echo* 1, no. 18 (1914/1915): 276–78.

Sültemeyer, Ingeborg. *Das Frühwerk Joseph Roths 1915–1926. Studien und Texte.* Vienna: Herder, 1976.

Szondi, Peter. "Friedrich Schlegel und die romantische Ironie: Mit einer Beilage über Tiecks Komödien." In *Satz und Gegensatz,* 5–24. Frankfurt am Main: Suhrkamp, 1976.

Taussig, Michael. *Mimesis and Alterity.* New York: Routledge, 1993.

Terence. *The Self-Tormentor.* In *The Comedies,* translated by Betty Radice, 93–155. New York: Penguin, 1976.

Trommler, Frank. *Österreich im Roman. Eine Untersuchung zur dargestellten Wirklichkeit bei Joseph Roth, Robert Musil und Heimito von Doderer.* Munich: Dissertations-Druckerei Charlotte Schön, 1965.

Utz, Peter. "Avant-Propos." In *Robert Walser, l'écriture miniature,* translated by Marion Graf, 5–11. Carouge: Éditions Zoe, 2004.

———. "Die Kalligraphie des 'Idioten.'" *Text + Kritik,* no. 12/12a (October 2004): 106–19.

Vincent, C. Paul. *A Historical Dictionary of Germany's Weimar Republic, 1918–1933.* Westport, Conn.: Greenwood, 1997.

Virno, Paolo. *Multitude: Between Innovation and Negation.* Translated by Isabella Bertoletti, James Cascaito, and Andrea Casson. Los Angeles: Semiotext(e), 2008.

Vischer, Friedrich Theodor. *Über das Erhabene und Komische.* Frankfurt am Main: Suhrkamp, 1967.

Vogl, Joseph. "Kafkas Komik." In *Kontinent Kafka. Mosse-Lectures an der Humboldt-Universität zu Berlin,* edited by Klaus R. Scherpe and Elisabeth Wagner, 71–87. Berlin: Vorwerk 8, 2006.

———. *Ort der Gewalt. Kafkas literarische Ethik.* Munich: Fink, 1990.

———. *Über das Zaudern.* Zurich: Diaphanes, 2008.

Wägenbaur, Thomas. "Robert Walsers Geste des Schreibens und die Komik des 'interface.'" *MLN,* no. 115 (2000): 482–501.

Wagner, Benno. "Die Versicherung des Übermenschen." In *Für Alle und Keinen: Lektüre, Schrift und Leben bei Nietzsche und Kafka,* edited by Friedrich Balke, Joseph Vogl, and Benno Wagner, 259–94. Zurich: Diaphanes, 2008.

———. "'. . . in der Fremde, aus der Sie kommen. . .' Die Geburt des Schreibens aus der Statistik des Selbstmords." In *Odradeks Lachen. Fremdheit bei Kafka,* edited by Hansjörg Bay and Christof Hamann, 193–228. Freiburg: Rombach, 2006.

———. "Kafka's Office Writings: Historical Background and Institutional Setting." In *Franz Kafka: The Office Writings,* edited by Stanley Corngold, Jack Greenberg, and Benno Wagner, 19–46. Princeton, N.J.: Princeton University Press, 2009.

———. "Kafkas Poetik des Unfalls." In *Die Unordnung der Dinge. Eine Wissens- und Mediengeschichte des Unfalls,* edited by Christian Kassung, 421–54. Bielefeld: Transcript, 2009.

Wallace, David Foster. "Laughing with Kafka." *Harper's Magazine* (July 1998): 23–27.

Walser, Martin. "Der Unerbittlichkeitsstil: Zum 100. Geburtstag von Robert Walser." In *Liebeserklärungen,* 123–54. Frankfurt am Main: Suhrkamp, 1983.

Walser, Robert. *Aus dem Bleistiftgebiet,* vol. 1: *Mikrogramme aus den Jahren 1924–1925.* Edited by Bernhard Echte and Werner Morlang. Frankfurt am Main: Suhrkamp, 1985.

———. *Aus dem Bleistiftgebiet,* vol. 4: *Mikrogramme 1926/27.* Edited by Bernhard Echte and Werner Morlang. Frankfurt am Main: Suhrkamp, 1990.

———. *Briefe.* Edited by Jörg Schäfer. Zurich: Suhrkamp, 1979.

———. "Der Commis." In *Das Gesamtwerk,* vol. 1, edited by Jochen Greven, 49–65. Geneva: Kossodo, 1972.

———. *Der "Räuber"-Roman.* In *Das Gesamtwerk,* vol. 6, edited by Jochen Greven and Martin Jürgens, 173–350. Zurich: Suhrkamp, 1978.

———. "Ein Maler." In *Das Gesamtwerk,* vol. 1, edited by Jochen Greven, 66–90. Geneva: Kossodo, 1972.

———. *Es war einmal: Prosa aus der Berner Zeit 1927–1928.* Frankfurt am Main: Suhrkamp, 1986.

———. *Fritz Kocher's Aufsätze.* Leipzig: Insel, 1904.

———. *Fritz Kochers Aufsätze.* In *Das Gesamtwerk,* vol. 1, edited by Jochen Greven, 7–48. Geneva: Kossodo, 1972.

———. *Für die Katz: Prosa aus der Berner Zeit 1928–1933.* Frankfurt am Main: Suhrkamp, 1986.

———. *Jakob von Gunten.* In *Das Gesamtwerk,* vol. 6, edited by Jochen Greven and Martin Jürgens, 7–164. Zurich: Suhrkamp, 1978.

———. "Usually I first put on a prose piece jacket." In *Microscripts,* translated by Susan Bernofsky, 59–62. New York: New Directions, 2010.

Wander, Karl Friedrich Wilhelm, ed. *Deutsches Sprichwörter-Lexikon: Ein Hausschatz für das deutsche Volk,* vol. 3. Leipzig: Brockhaus, 1873. Reprint Darmstadt: Wissenschaftliche Buchgesellschaft, 1964.

Weber, Samuel. "Laughing in the Meanwhile." *MLN* 102, no. 4 (September 1987): 691–706.

———. *The Legend of Freud.* Stanford, Calif.: Stanford University Press, 1982.

———. *Rückkehr zu Freud: Jacques Lacans Ent-stellung der Psychoanalyse.* Vienna: Passagen-Verlag, 2000.

———. *Theatricality as Medium.* New York: Fordham University Press, 2004.

Weissberg, Liliane. *Hannah Arendt, Charlie Chaplin und die verborgene jüdische Tradition.* Graz: Leykam-Grazer Universitätsverlag, 2009.

Weitzman, Erica. "No *Fun:* Aporias of Pleasure in Adorno's Aesthetic Theory." *German Quarterly* 81, no. 2 (Spring 2008): 185–202.

Wellnitz, Philippe. "La théâtralité dans *Le Disparu* de Franz Kafka: du Grand Théâtre d'Oklahoma au *theatrum mundi?*" In *Franz Kafka, Der Verschollene: Le Disparu/L'Amérique—Écritures d'un nouveau monde?* edited by Philippe Wellnitz, 79–92. Strasbourg: Presses Universitaires de Strasbourg, 1997.

Weltsch, Felix. *Religion und Humor im Leben und Werk Franz Kafkas.* Berlin: Herbig, 1957.

Westermann, Klaus. "Nachwort." In *Werke 1. Das journalistische Werk 1915–1923,* by Joseph Roth, edited by Klaus Westermann, 1109–16. Cologne: Kiepenheuer & Witsch, 1989.

White, Hayden. *Metahistory: The Historical Imagination in Nineteenth-Century Europe.* Baltimore: Johns Hopkins University Press, 1973.

Wildenhahn, Barbara. *Feuilleton zwischen den Kriegen. Die Form der Kritik und ihre Theorie.* Munich: Fink, 2008.

Williams, Michael. "Descartes and the Metaphysics of Doubt." In *Essays on Descartes' Meditations,* edited by Amélie Oksenberg Rorty, 117–39. Berkeley: University of California Press, 1986.

Wirtz, Irmgard. *Joseph Roths Fiktionen des Faktischen. Das Feuilleton der zwanziger Jahre und "Die Geschichte von der 1002. Nacht" im historischen Kontext.* Berlin: Schmidt, 1997.

Wittgenstein, Ludwig. *Wittgenstein's Lectures: Cambridge, 1932–1935, from the Notes of Alice Ambrose and Margaret Macdonald.* Edited by Alice Ambrose. Chicago: University of Chicago Press, 1979.

Zilcosky, John. *Kafka's Travels: Exoticism, Colonialism, and the Traffic of Writing.* New York: Palgrave, 2003.

Zischler, Hanns. *Kafka geht ins Kino.* Reinbek bei Hamburg: Rowohlt, 1996.

Zmegac, Viktor. "Robert Walsers Poetik in der literarischen Konstellation der Jahrhundertwende." In *Robert Walser und die moderne Poetik,* edited by Dieter Borchmeyer, 21–36. Frankfurt am Main: Suhrkamp, 1999.

Zupančič, Alenka. *The Odd One In: On Comedy.* Cambridge, Mass.: MIT Press, 2008.

INDEX